Lillian HELLMAN

a reference guide

A
Reference
Guide
to
Literature

Ronald Gottesman
Editor

Lillian HELLMAN
Plays, Films, Memoirs

a reference guide

MARK W. ESTRIN

G.K.HALL &CO.

70 LINCOLN STREET, BOSTON, MASS.

Library of Congress Cataloging in Publication Data

Estrin, Mark W
  Lillian Hellman, plays, films, memoirs.

  (A Reference guide to literature)
  Includes index.
  1. Hellman, Lillian, 1905-   --Bibliography.
I. Title. II. Series: Reference guides to litera-
ture.
Z8395.52.E86 [PS3515.E343] 016.812'52 80-21307
ISBN 0-8161-7907-7

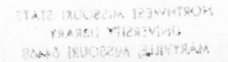

For Barbara and Robin,
who endured

Contents

Preface

   Lillian Hellman: Plays, Films, Memoirs is a bibliographical
record of writings about Hellman's life and work. Chronologically
arranged from 1934 through 1979, it reflects alternating, frequently
inconsistent critical attitudes toward her plays and films, culminat-
ing during the last decade in something amounting to adulation for
her redirected career as memoirist and heroine of her own story--and
in the critical backlash that such public admiration invariably
evokes. The chronicle begins with The Children's Hour (1934), which
brought Hellman considerable fame and success but was also surrounded
in controversy over its "daring" but finally tangential subject:
lesbianism. It essentially concludes with the controversies surrounding Scoundrel Time (1976) and Hellman's brief, tart responses to
that book's critics in Three (1979), the collected edition of her
memoirs. In between are the news accounts, interviews, and feature
articles touching upon numerous other public episodes in Hellman's
life, which acquire added, retroactive interest when read in the context of the later memoirs.

   Most of all, this volume tells the story of Hellman's career as
a major American dramatist and screenwriter whose outspokenness on
social and political issues--most dramatically exemplified by her now
famous letter of defiance to the House Un-American Activities Committee in 1952--tended from the first to entwine her literary and public
lives. By the time this volume concludes Hellman is herself the
central character of Julia, the 1977 film based on a section of her
memoir Pentimento, and is portrayed reading her letter to the Committee in Eric Bentley's play Are You Now Or Have You Ever Been, a documentary dramatization of the HUAC hearings. Such is her reputation
that, in late 1978 and early 1979, major actresses were rotating in
the brief cameo role of Hellman as a special attraction to potential
ticket-buyers for the New York production.

   In striving for comprehensiveness, I have included all works
with which Hellman has been associated, whether written by her or
adapted from her work by others. Primarily, this bibliography is intended to serve as a guide for both the student and the more advanced
scholar who may wish to study Hellman's plays and films as dramatic

or cinematic literature on the one hand and as theater or screen history on the other. Throughout, I have been also conscious of her
recently acquired role, with publication of the memoirs, as somewhat
reluctant feminist, whose lifelong independence and courage have
brought her the particular admiration of men and women who see her as
a role model for the best qualities espoused by the women's movement.
Included here are articles, reviews, publicity pieces, news reports,
interviews, books, theater surveys, M.A. theses, Ph.D. dissertations,
and the like, all of which discuss Hellman's life, work, and important productions thereof both in and out of the United States.

I have used the standard reference sources--annual bibliographies, occasional checklists, the more generalized listings in inclusive bibliographies of drama and film, bibliographies of theses
and dissertations--to a limited extent. All are cited where appropriate. Mostly I have started from scratch, having discovered early in
my research that Hellman, until recently, has been outrageously overlooked or given decidedly short bibliographical shrift and that
errors abound even in the limited attempts to catalogue the writing
about her work. Among the reliable sources that should be consulted
for future writing about Hellman are the annual bibliographies published by <u>Modern Drama</u> and the <u>MLA International Bibliography</u>, also
issued annually. <u>Educational Theatre Journal</u> notes work in progress.
Other regularly published bibliographies of twentieth-century American literature and women's studies are likely to catch up on Hellman
material, especially the memoirs, in the next several years and
should also be consulted.

I have attempted to be comprehensive through 1978; for 1979 I
have included those items available to me as of December 1979. I
have retained the exact spelling of theatre/theater used by individual writers, although I have regularized other spellings and punctua-
tion, as in the spelling of Müller (in <u>Watch on the Rhine</u>). Items I
have not seen firsthand are preceded by an asterisk, with the appropriate source cited in the annotation. I have attempted in the annotations to stress respective attitudes toward Hellman and, where
relevant, observations which seem original to the given entry. I
have generally avoided evaluative comments in the annotations,
although in extreme instances I have tried to reflect the particular
merits or flaws of certain items; I have made such judgments throughout the Introduction, however.

Older clippings in the files of the Theatre Collection at the
New York Public Library at Lincoln Center are occasionally missing
page references, which accounts for subsequent omissions in a number of entries here. Where Hellman is one of several people discussed, as in omnibus film reviews, I have given inclusive page
references on the assumption that the reader may find the entire
article useful as a context for the specific remarks about Hellman.
I have included production information in annotations referring to
the plays and films when it seems to me to be of potential special

interest to theater and film buffs. (For example, it is no small
factor in the success of the screen version of <u>The Little Foxes</u> that
Gregg Toland, cinematographer of <u>Citizen Kane</u>, served in the same
capacity for the Hellman film; in 1952, a young Richard Burton
appeared in the title role in an English production of <u>Montserrat</u>.)

My greatest difficulty has been in determining which items to
exclude, particularly problematic when a writer receives such wide
attention in the popular press. I have included numerous articles,
reviews, and features aimed primarily at a popular, not scholarly,
readership in the belief that Hellman's considerable appeal for
varied audiences especially reflects her public magnetism and versa-
tility as a writer. She has always been "good copy," a fact demonstrated anew within days of this writing, when the <u>New York Times</u>
carried a report on her feud with novelist-critic Mary McCarthy,
which has recently developed into a lawsuit by Hellman against
McCarthy. One may with some justification argue that feuds are not
the stuff of scholarship. With Hellman, however, they comprise a
vital ingredient in the story that this volume attempts to record.

February 1980

Acknowledgments

With considerably more success than Blanche DuBois, I have
depended on the kindness of family, friends, and, occasionally,
strangers. Barbara Lieben Estrin, my wife, contributed immeasurably
to the completion of this volume. She aided me in the research,
offered editorial suggestions that were invariably on target, advised
me, in fact, on virtually every aspect of the manuscript. I am in
her debt. My research assistant, Ann Rodrigues, relentlessly pursued
items that lesser mortals would have declared unlocatable and, in the
process, retrieved numerous entries that would have been otherwise
omitted. Natalie DiRissio typed the manuscript with her usual degree
of efficiency and skill; her ability to correct tactfully errors un-
detected in an original typescript continues to defy rational explanation.

The beleaguered reference staff of the Adams Library of Rhode
Island College--Louise Sherby, Barbara Cohen, Frank Notarianni--
responded to my requests with unfailingly prompt, courteous, helpful
counsel, as did Linda Catino in the Inter-Library Loan Office. I am
especially grateful, too, to Paul Myers and his staff at the Theatre
Collection of the New York Public Library at Lincoln Center and to
numerous, unknown persons at the Providence Public Library, the
Boston Public Library, and libraries at Providence College and
Boston, Brown, and Harvard Universities.

My appreciation is also extended to the Rhode Island College
Faculty Research Fund and to the College Administration, especially
Ben McClelland, English Department Chairman, James Koch, Dean of Arts
and Sciences, Eleanor McMahon, Vice President for Academic Affairs,
and David Sweet, President, for support in the research and manuscript preparation. My work on Hellman's films was supported by a
grant from the National Endowment for the Humanities.

And, finally, my thanks to Kevin Harty, Joe Plut, Leonard
Fleischer, Tess and Charles Hoffmann, Alan Pollard, Scott Duhamel,
Perry Scott, Ada Wilson, Deirdre Condon, Nancy Sullivan, Arlene
Robertson, Carolyn Scheff, Sally Wilson, Lucille Sibulkin, Charles
McNeil, Richard Olsen--and Robin Estrin, who assisted in alphabetiz-
ing and proofreading.

Acknowledgments

The author gratefully acknowledges permission to quote from the
following works by Lillian Hellman:

The Little Foxes: Copyright 1939 by Lillian Hellman; (c) renewed
1966 by Lillian Hellman. By permission of Random House and the
Harold Matson Company, Inc.

Pentimento: Copyright (c) 1969, 1973, 1976, 1979 by Lillian Hellman.
By permission of Little, Brown & Co. and Harold Matson Company, Inc.

Another Part of the Forest: Copyright 1947 by Lillian Hellman; (c)
renewed 1974 by Lillian Hellman. By permission of the Viking Press
and the Harold Matson Company, Inc.

Watch on the Rhine: Copyright 1941 by Lillian Hellman; (c) renewed
1968 by Lillian Hellman. By permission of Random House and the
Harold Matson Company, Inc.

Autumn Garden: Copyright 1951 by Lillian Hellman; (c) renewed 1978
by Lillian Hellman. By permission of Little, Brown & Co. and the
Harold Matson Company, Inc.

An Unfinished Woman: Copyright 1951 by Lillian Hellman. By
permission of Little, Brown & Co. and the Harold Matson Company, Inc.

Three: Copyright (c) by Lillian Hellman. By permission of Little,
Brown & Co. and the Harold Matson Company, Inc.

The Searching Wind: Copyright 1944 by Lillian Hellman; (c) renewed
1971 by Lillian Hellman. By permission of the Harold Matson Company,
Inc.

The Lark: Copyright (c) 1956 by Lillian Hellman. Adapted from the
French play by Jean Anouilh. By permission of Random House and the
Harold Matson Company, Inc.

Candide: Copyright (c) 1957 by Lillian Hellman. Copyright (c) 1955,
1957 by Leonard Bernstein. By permission of Random House and the
Harold Matson Company, Inc.

Introduction

This annotated bibliography records the diverse phases of
Lillian Hellman's career through 1979. The author of eight original
plays and four adaptations for Broadway between 1934 and 1963, she
also wrote original screenplays and adaptations for the screen of a
number of her own plays between 1935 and 1946, resuming briefly with
The Chase, her last film, in 1966. She directed three Broadway productions of her work (Another Part of the Forest, Montserrat, the
1952 revival of The Children's Hour), reported for newspapers and
magazines on a broad range of (often political) subjects, and, in her
plays and memoirs, provided the source material for the adaptations
by others of five films and an opera. In her mid-sixties, with the
publication of An Unfinished Woman (1969), she initiated a series of
memoirs that brought her widespread praise and reemergence as a
prominent American writer and public figure, although the third
memoir, Scoundrel Time, unleashed considerable controversy that
seemed at times to drown out the applause.

Controversy surrounded Lillian Hellman, however, long before
1976. An outspoken public figure and moral voice since the banning
of The Children's Hour in Boston and other cities in 1934, Hellman's
name--as this bibliography repeatedly demonstrates--has been linked
often with political and social issues, most significantly with her
famous and, for most reviewers, courageous letter to the House Committee on Un-American Activities in 1952. In sharp contrast to the
dark McCarthy days of blacklisting, Hellman's reputation as prose
stylist and public figure presently soars, despite the occasional
critical backlash that continues to erupt over her charges in
Scoundrel Time (1976), reprinted and defended in Three (1979),
against "the anti-Communist writers and intellectuals" of the
McCarthy period. Yet that enviable reputation seems now, unfairly,
to evolve mostly from the memoirs. Julia (1977), the film adaptation of a section of Pentimento (1973) starring Jane Fonda as
Hellman, crystallized the Hellman persona of the 1970s: the truly
liberated, independent woman. Characteristically, it is a role with
which she seems herself uncomfortable. "How is Nora [in Ibsen's A
Doll's House] going to eat that night?" she has asked.

1

Introduction

THE PLAYS

Lillian Hellman's critical reputation rests originally and primarily upon her plays. But to examine the reactions of reviewers is to discover inordinate contradictions among them, often within the reviews of identical writers. Hellman is praised for her taut dramatic construction in such plays as The Little Foxes, but is also attacked for dependency on the well-made techniques of Eugène Scribe, upon which taut dramatic construction must ordinarily rely. She is considered a staunch moralist who flays the evils of society but is frequently criticized for denoting her universe in stark extremes of good and evil. It is generally agreed that she uses the devices of melodrama to achieve her ends, a claim she gladly acknowledges in her introduction to Four Plays (1944), but that partially justified assessment is used by critics both to applaud and to attack her.

"For all its evil," writes Jacob Adler, "the story of The Little Foxes is not as grim-seeming as that of The Children's Hour. The melodramatic devices are employed masterfully, and the well-made structure is esthetically satisfying. The battles between the Hubbards are fascinating to watch and hear" (Lillian Hellman, 1969.3). Elsewhere in his monograph, Adler attempts to show that Hellman employs melodrama for legitimate ends, that she forces her audience to be interested in the highs and lows of plot in order to direct it "toward character and toward meaning," as in The Children's Hour. But those who object to the conventions which Adler and others applaud belittle Hellman as a "melodramatist rather than a dramatist" (John Simon, 1967.47). Her theatrical tricks, Charles Thomas Samuels insists in the New York Times Book Review,

> don't survive the glare of reading. That her first play, The Children's Hour (1934), reaches its crisis through an overhead conversation we can put down to beginner's expediency; but she uses this device as late as Toys in the Attic (1960). In The Autumn Garden, widely praised as a retreat from the machinations of her earlier dramas, characters regularly discover each other in uncompromising situations, recalling not so much Chekhov (as reviewers asserted) but French bedroom farce. Her plays hang skeletons in a number of closets and blow open the doors at dramatic intervals.

> (1972.32)

The Children's Hour became a cause célèbre and brought Hellman, from the first, strong praise for its tight craftsmanship and unusual theme. But generally ignored or unknown, amidst the preoccupation with Hellman's alleged reliance on well-made melodrama through the 1930s and 1940s, is the antithetical belief, expressed by Robert

Benchley and others, that her first play contains too many endings
and tends to pile up tragedy upon tragedy in the fashion of O'Neill
(New Yorker, 1934.8). Though he heartily approves of The Children's
Hour, Benchley's single caveat revolves around its perceived resem-
blance to O'Neillian tragedy, while the supposedly tragic--not melo-
dramatic--elements of the play are precisely what appeal to other
influential critics. "There have not been in the theater in years
any two characters more tragic than the two teachers whose lives are
burned down around them by the evil of the wicked child" (Literary
Digest, 1934.5); The Children's Hour is a "sound tragedy" (Percy
Hammond, 1934.12). Brooks Atkinson, combining the critical vocabu-
lary of tragedy and melodrama, considers the work "a venomously
tragic" play but complains that the third act should have concluded
before the arrival of the pistol shot and the long arm of coincidence
(New York Times, 1934.7), before, in other words, the arrival of
excessively melodramatic--not tragic--conventions.

Terminology to describe Hellman's real generic home in the drama
has proven as elusive as the terminology used to describe her preferred dramatic structure. The two plays about the rapacious Hubbard
clan, The Little Foxes (1939) and Another Part of the Forest (1946),
typically have been categorized as melodramas of social protest.
More appropriately, if much less frequently, they have been recognized as excoriating Jonsonian satires, in which the serious purpose
is tempered by the "comedy of greed" (Martin Knelman, 1977.72).
Louis Kronenberger properly compares Forest to "those sombre Elizabethan 'comedies' swarming with cheats and knaves and evildoers"
(1946.34). The unrelieved depravity mirrored in Forest's tale of
"four scoundrels, two half-wits, one insane woman, and a whore"
begins to seem "funny when exhibited for too long and completely
without foil" (Joseph Wood Krutch, 1946.35). Of course, Krutch's
comments, like those of Brooks Atkinson in his review of the same
play, fail to account for the deliberately Jacobean-Caroline grotes-
querie that permeates the Hubbard plays, particularly the sequel of
which Atkinson somewhat naively wrote that her indictment is "a
witches' brew of blackmail, insanity, cruelty, theft, torture,
insult, drunkenness, with a trace of incest thrown in for good
measure" (1946.15). John Mason Brown, incisively noting the presence
of the same ingredients as the logical source of the audience's
delight--"every possible human equivalent for the venomous toads, the
eye of newt or lizard's leg upon which Shakespeare fed his cronies"--
concludes nonetheless that the "guignol" of Forest prevents one from
taking the play seriously (1946.20). Determined to connect Hellman's
style with the social realism that launched her playwriting career,
critics like Atkinson and Brown, though often highly laudatory of her
work, remained uncomfortable with her forays into other forms.

Few critics have identified the clearly sardonic, self-deprecat-
ing dialogue spoken by Hellman's characters as early as The Little
Foxes. Oscar and Ben Hubbard, eager to convince Regina Giddens,
their sister, that a marriage between her daughter and Oscar's idiot

son would be financially advantageous to the family, engage in this
illustrative conversation:

> Ben. . . . So my money will go to Alexandra and Leo. They
> may even marry someday and--(Addie looks at Ben.)
>
> Birdie (rising). Marry--Zan and Leo--
>
> Oscar (carefully). That would make a great difference in
> my feelings. If they married.
>
> Ben. Yes, that's what I mean. Of course it would make a
> difference.
>
> Oscar (carefully). Is that what you mean, Regina?
>
> Regina. Oh, it's too far away. We'll talk about it in a
> few years.
>
> Oscar. I want to talk about it now.
>
> Ben (nods). Naturally.
>
> Regina. There's a lot of things to consider. They are
> first cousins, and--
>
> Oscar. That isn't unusual. Our grandmother and grand-
> father were first cousins.
>
> Regina (giggles). And look at us. (Ben giggles.)
>
> (The Collected Plays, pp. 150-51)

Regina and Ben, the two cleverest characters in the play, see the
joke and laugh at themselves from positions of relative strength.
Unlike the fools and whimperers of the clan, they, like their
Dickensian father, Marcus, are rarely laughed at by the audience,
although they provide considerable amusement and are frequently themselves bemused by their own capacity for skulduggery. Unlike their
brother Oscar and his son Leo, at whom we do laugh, Ben and Regina
have inherited their father's craftiness and sophisticated malice.
Each also shares with Marcus considerable self-awareness, thus
enriching the plays with that macabre comic sense which eludes
critics. Speaking of the Hubbards' relationship to her mother's
family, Hellman writes in Pentimento:

> I began to think that greed and the cheating that is its
> usual companion were comic as well as evil and I began to
> like the family dinners with the talk of who did what to
> whom. I particularly looked forward to the biannual dinner

when the sisters and brothers assembled to draw lots for
"the diamond" that had been left, almost thirty years
before, in my great-grandmother's estate. Sometimes they
would use the length of a strip of paper to designate the
winner, sometimes the flip of a coin, and once I was
allowed to choose a number up to eight and the correct
guesser was to get the diamond. But nobody, as far as I
knew, ever did get it. No sooner was the winner declared
than one or the other would sulk and, by prearrangement,
another loser would console the sulker, and a third would
start the real event of the afternoon: an open charge of
cheating. The paper, the coin, my number, all had been
fixed or tampered with. That was wild and funny. Funnier
because my mother's generation would sit white-faced, sometimes tearful, appalled at what was happening, all of them
envying the vigor of their parents, half knowing that they
were broken spirits who wished the world was nicer, but who
were still so anxious to inherit the money that they made
no protest.

(Pentimento, pp. 182-83)

Hellman intended both plays to be satirical, she says in the
same memoir. With Another Part of the Forest, "I believed that I
could now make clear that I had meant the first play as a kind of
satire. I tried to do that in Another Part of the Forest, but what I
thought funny or outrageous the critics thought straight stuff; what
I thought was bite they thought sad, touching, or plotty and melodramatic" (Pentimento, p. 197). Indeed, the comic aspects of
Hellman's plays and, later, the adaptations--especially the presence
of unrelieved villainy repeatedly and intentionally brought to
extremes--serve to heighten the strong moral implications of her
work. It is difficult now to imagine how audiences and critics
failed to see the satirical intentions implicit in the characterization of, for example, Marcus Hubbard, who in act one of Another Part
of the Forest tells Ben: "Put aside your plans for your sister's
future. Spend with profit your time today going over the store books.
(Amused) You'll find we are short of cash. Call in some cotton
loans or mortgages. (Giggles) Then go to church" (The Collected
Plays, p. 340).

Hellman's astringent superiority over her obviously foolish
characters has been more frequently and perceptibly observed than the
self-directed, comic irony of her sophisticated characters. (See,
for example, John Gassner, 1960.36; Willard Thorp, 1960.60; reviews
of My Mother, My Father and Me, passim.) There is a decided link
between the self-mockery intended to elicit laughing condemnation for
Ben, Regina, and Marcus and the sharp-tongued dialogue of such
characters as Fanny Farrelly (Watch on the Rhine, 1941) and Ned
Crossman (The Autumn Garden, 1951), whose caustic comments on the

actions of others lead to moral recognitions thematically central to
the plays in which they appear. Fanny, who has preferred to isolate
herself from the Fascist menace rising in Europe, finally gives
explicit approval to the actions of her freedom-fighting son-in-law,
Kurt Müller, who has just murdered the villain who would betray him.
Her wry, detached lines shift progressively toward a more serious,
perhaps now dated, demeanor as the play unfolds. Ostensibly describing her late husband, she tells her son:

> I was thinking that a few months before he died, we were
> sitting out there. (Points to terrace) He said, "Fanny,
> the complete American is dying." I said what do you mean,
> although I knew what he meant, I always knew. "A complete
> man," he said, "is a man who wants to know. He wants to
> know how fast a bird can fly, how thick is the crust of the
> earth, what made Iago evil, how to plow a field. He knows
> that there is no dignity to a mountain, if there is no
> dignity to man. You can't put that in a man, but when it's
> there, put your trust in him."
>
> (The Collected Plays, p. 261)

Her approval of Kurt, of whom she really speaks, signals the audience
that it, too, should accept his heroic ideals in the America of 1941.
Ned Crossman, in less sentimental fashion, concludes The Autumn
Garden by acknowledging his self-deceiving "love" for Constance
Tuckerman:

> Crossman. I've kept myself busy looking into other
>   people's hearts so I wouldn't have to look into my own.
>   (Softly) If I made you think I was still in love, I'm
>   sorry. Sorry I fooled you and sorry I fooled myself.
>   And I've never liked liars--least of all those who lie
>   to themselves.
>
> Constance. Never mind. Most of us lie to ourselves.
>   Never mind.
>
> Curtain
>
> (The Collected Plays, p. 545)

The speeches of Fanny and Crossman are much more serious than the
dialogue of the Hubbards excerpted above. But they emanate from
characters who share with the Hubbards an ironic intelligence which
can be turned inward when necessary. They lack the Hubbards'
penchant for evil because their dramatic and moral contexts demand
something else. While numerous writers have remarked, then, upon

Hellman's apparent harshness toward some of her characters, few have penetrated the subtle connection in her plays between comic irony and moral theme. It is a subject that deserves extensive study in the book on Hellman's oeuvre that has yet to be written.

Similarly, the shrewdly elliptical prose style of the memoirs has been praised as central to the success of those books, but the dialogue of Hellman's plays, containing many of the same characteristics that endow the memoirs with such controlled energy, continues to be sidestepped or dismissed as flat, functional prose. In Dialogue in American Drama, an important study of native dramatic literature, Ruby Cohn excludes Hellman's plays from analysis with the view that their language does not warrant it, although Cohn does cite The Little Foxes as one of several "atypical" twentieth-century American plays not reliant upon "genteel, anonymous English" (1971.5). General surveys of the modern drama ordinarily mention Hellman's plays, especially The Children's Hour and The Little Foxes, but tend to give them short shrift, even taking into account the space limitations of the genre. In lengthier discussions of the plays, approving and disapproving critics alike restrict severely any discussion of dialogue to devote more space to her use of "melodrama" and intricate plotting devices. Alex Szogyi, in a perceptive exploration of the plays, points to the poetic language of Toys in the Attic but calls it the only Hellman play "in which poetry pre-empts prose at every turn" (1972.38). In one of the earliest scholarly pieces on Hellman, Barrett Clark surveys the first five plays but concentrates on her morality and dramatic structure, even while acknowledging her significance as "an idealist and a philosopher." Clark properly contrasts The Searching Wind to the earlier plays, applauding Hellman for her departure from melodrama and for her newer focus on character and dialogue. But, like most critics who follow him, he pays scant attention to the function and nature of that dialogue. Nor does he explain how it differs from that of the earlier, more "melodramatic" works. (See 1944.16.) The dialogue of Hellman's plays remains to be explored in depth.

Primarily, the extensive number of reviews and the occasional critical articles on the plays revolve around the generic question-- the respective attitudes toward the melodramatic elements--and Hellman's perpetual return to moral, even angry, themes, in which basically good people (Karen and Martha in The Children's Hour; Horace, Alexandra, Birdie, and Addie in The Little Foxes; the Müller family in Watch on the Rhine; Sam Hazen in The Searching Wind; Leo Whalen in Days to Come; Julian Berniers in Toys in the Attic) perform usually futile battles against malign characters or devastating sociopolitical forces (Mary and Amelia Tilford in The Children's Hour; Ben, Regina, and Oscar in The Little Foxes; Teck de Brancovis and the Nazi menace in Watch on the Rhine; apathy and appeasement in The Searching Wind; capitalists and strike-breakers in Days to Come; Cyrus Warkins and the destructive power of love in Toys in the Attic). Critics have aptly noted that, as in the Hubbard plays,

Hellman's attention is frequently focused on her savage characters. In this respect, for all the comparisons to the well-made play, she departs significantly from the standard, poetically just, Scribean ending, with (in The Children's Hour, Days to Come, The Little Foxes, and Another Part of the Forest) "wrong in the saddle, riding hard" (Joseph Wood Krutch, 1939.29). Some critics have observed that this fact aids Hellman's moral purpose. Her portrayal of the nature of evil, writes Louis Kronenberger in a comparison of The Children's Hour and The Little Foxes, "denies us all sense of tragedy" and deliberately sends us from the theater "not purged, not released, but still aroused and indignant" (1939.27). That postproduction indignation which she desires her audience to experience is Brechtian in nature, though Hellman's usual dramatic structure is antithetical to Brechtian form. Yet Brecht continues to be ignored as one of Hellman's likely sources. More frequently, but not inappropriately, her technique and social criticism are compared to Ibsen's. (See, for example, Richard Watts, Jr., 1939.43.)

Other critics have been oddly offended by Hellman's failure to depict genuinely moral characters who are also effective against the forces of darkness. But astute observers have also pointed out what should be more obvious to such objectors: the ineffectuality of goodness in Hellman's plays, or the surface absence of goodness altogether, is essential to audience outrage; audience outrage, in turn, leads in the Brechtian sense to action, and action--assuming that any writer can incite action--leads to social change. Philip Armato enticingly proposes that The Children's Hour is really about the ways in which human relationships are often devoid of mercy and compassion. The play, he writes, is a forceful, moral study of what happens when adults behave like "children," and the ending, instead of being hard-nosed and unforgiving as critics sometimes allege, permits Karen to accept Mrs. Tilford's atonement. Hellman thereby "extends compassion--the ultimate good in the world of the play" (1973.6). Armato's view is instructive in its refutation of the persistent charge that Hellman's morality permits no forgiveness.

This critical disagreement is perhaps best illustrated by analyses of The Autumn Garden. Aside from the discussion of Hellman's apparent shift from an Ibsenite, well-made structure to a Chekhovian one (see, for example, John Mason Brown, 1951.8), reviewers typically differ on the playwright's attitude toward the people she assembles at Constance Tuckerman's home. John Lardner's review praises the play highly, especially commending Hellman for eliminating the cold fury of her earlier drama and for mellowing in her treatment of its characters (1951.27). John Chapman cites the affectionate depiction of the characters' frailties (1951.10), and Alan Downer, calling The Autumn Garden Hellman's most original work, concludes in Fifty Years of American Drama, "Humanely, it reveals the nature of our life, of our means to grace" (1951.16). John Gassner, though expressing basic approval, surveys possible reasons for the reservations of others, in which process he finds Hellman the "stern

moralist always, our hanging-judge of the American theatre." The
Autumn Garden, he continues, is infected with her despair of the
intelligentsia, while her indictment of society may be too general
and inclusive. The play's style is not Chekhov's but Hellman's
(1951.19). Harold Clurman, who directed the Broadway production of
The Autumn Garden, also reviewed it for the New Republic. It is her
most lucid, probing play but its single limitation, he suggests, lies
in Hellman's failure to consider her characters worthy of her (or
our) love. She "is a fine artist; she will be a finer one when she
melts" (1951.13). The playwright errs in her omission of even one
"redeeming character who might leave us with a glimmer of hope,"
agrees Eileen Darby in Theatre Arts. The characterizations are
among her finest but one wishes that she had shown them more compassion (1951.14).

The Autumn Garden reviews reveal once again the inability of
critics to categorize Hellman's plays generically. Intent on calling
the play a Chekhovian comedy or a tragedy or a play that might have
succeeded as tragedy had it focused on a specific figure instead of
many (see, for example, John Chapman, 1951.10; Walter Kerr, 1951.24;
George Jean Nathan, 1951.32), reviewers tend either to be lavish in
praise of Hellman's multiple character analysis ("the density of a
big novel": Clurman, 1951.12) or severely critical of precisely the
structure which seems to depart radically from that of the earlier
plays ("diffuse and somnambulistic": Nathan, 1951.32). The reflec-
tive, apolitical tone of The Autumn Garden has its structural ante-
cedents not in Chekhov, in fact, but in Hellman's own Watch on the
Rhine, The Searching Wind, and Another Part of the Forest. In these
plays, a leisurely discursiveness coexists with the tight, well-made
elements in order to create a political context for the events to
unfold.

Hellman's plays merit detailed analysis in a book-length study
that will, especially, trace their relationship to each other and
show that the critical disagreement about the nature of her moral
vision, sources, and dramatic structure reflects a complexity that
is generally evaded or denied. The ongoing association of the plays
with well-made dramaturgy has been exaggerated. In fact, only The
Little Foxes--which itself diverges from well-made structure in
several important respects--seems essentially to adhere to Scribean
principles. The Children's Hour provides controversy not only for
its sensational (in 1934) subject matter but for its highly un-
Scribean attempt to tell, in Eric Bentley's words, two different
stories. Is the enemy a "society which punishes the innocent" or a
"society which punishes Lesbians"? (See 1953.8.) Days to Come,
Hellman's one critical failure, was attacked for its non-Scribean
structure, for its desire (as Hellman acknowledges in her Introduction to Four Plays) to do too much. But the play's structure and
political themes are noticeable in later Hellman dramas which were
generally embraced by critics. Of this playwright who has so often
been identified, condescendingly, with well-made "craft," Stark Young

says: <u>Days to Come</u> is "lumpy with dramas not written. . . . It exhibits a combination of stage writing that is elliptical and stage writing that is expressionistic" (1936.74). Though critical, Young is early on pointing to Hellman's range, rarely acknowledged until the memoirs or, perhaps, <u>Toys in the Attic</u>. Brooks Atkinson, while calling <u>Watch on the Rhine</u> more "discursive" than Hellman's two great successes of the 1930s, also considers it her best play (1941.23). Kurt Müller's farewell to his children at the end of that play needs some tightening but may be compared to the "high tradition" of Sophocles, who gave "Oedipus thirty-four lines of this same farewell" (Stark Young, 1941.89).

Numerous other examples belie the easy connection that critics continue to make between Hellman's plays and the tight, pseudo-realistic form of the well-made play: the uses of flashback and the contrapuntal political and personal story lines of <u>The Searching Wind</u> (generally attacked by critics in 1944); <u>Another Part of the Forest,</u> which Louis Kronenberger and others compare to Elizabethan comedies, and which is finally "less controlled" than <u>The Little Foxes</u> but "more complex" (1946.34); the "novelistic" tendencies of <u>The Autumn Garden</u> already discussed; the Tennessee Williamsesque, psychosexual subject matter of <u>Toys in the Attic</u>, filtered through Hellman's mordant sense of money's power over people and written in her best elliptical style.

It is not necessary to be too defensive about the well-made play, whose critics Hellman herself best refutes in the Introduction to <u>Four Plays</u> by claiming her right to use "tricks" of the theater. But even in the preabsurdist American theater of the 1930s and 1940s, when neat plot lines were still the fashion, critics were loath to take seriously plays which depended so heavily upon such "tricks." An inordinate number of entries in this bibliography reflects this critical obsession: Are melodramatic devices—gunshots, safe-deposit boxes, overheard key speeches, strong curtains, and the like—incompatible with the serious social criticism of, say, <u>The Little Foxes</u> or <u>Watch on the Rhine</u>? (That needed book on the plays might well consider why O'Neill's reliance on melodramatic conventions in, for example, <u>Mourning Becomes Electra</u> and <u>Desire Under the Elms</u>, tended to escape similar controversy in their own day. O'Neill's classical models explain only part of the difference but not all of it.) Richard Watts, Jr., in his review of <u>Watch on the Rhine</u>, defends the melodramatic elements on the grounds that contemporary events depicted therein are also melodramatic (1941.80). In an incisive study, Robert Heilman argues that <u>Watch on the Rhine</u> conveys the popular emotional appeal of melodrama but alters the stereotypes of the genre to force the audience "into responses less easy than the conventional ones." Kurt's murder of Teck morally complicates our pleasure in siding with him as hero, but if the play were to dwell too long on Kurt's conflict "between moral and political imperatives," it would be veering toward tragedy. Hellman <u>chooses</u> not to treat the dilemma in tragic terms and permits the

audience to enjoy that "wholeness of a practical competence that
leads to a swift and sure action," experienced through melodrama, not
tragedy (Tragedy and Melodrama, 1968.15).

The role of money in Hellman's drama is the subject of several
provocative discussions. Robert Heilman, in another generic study,
suggests that "what is substantial [in The Little Foxes] is Miss
Hellman's sense of the intensity of monetary self-seeking, of love
of power, of how it works and what it leads to" (The Iceman, The
Arsonist and the Troubled Agent: Tragedy and Melodrama on the Modern
Stage, 1973.29). Ellen Moers believes that "the presence of money
contributes a crackling realism to her family melodramas," but lapses
into forced generalizations about money in the works of Hellman and
other women writers (Literary Women, 1976.82). More reliably, Moers
elsewhere maintains that Hellman's fictional families (especially the
Hubbards) emerge as real, despite their dramatic excesses. The plays
deal with large, public themes, but Hellman's characters display "an
arrogant assumption that the great battles of the outside world are
secondary to, but distantly dependent on, their family squabbles,"
which generally concern finances (1972.25). Some critics, including
Robert Brustein, allege that in Toys in the Attic Hellman is more at
home with the catalytic effects of money than with her "new flirta-
tion with Freudianism" (1960.23).

Money, of course, like sex, is as central a motivating factor
for human behavior in literature as it is in life. For an American
playwright in the 1930s it was an especially important subject,
likely to assume political implications, as it did for Hellman.
Amelia Tilford's wealth in The Children's Hour enables her to ruin
the two teachers and to defend successfully their libel suit against
her. Days to Come is primarily about the struggle between capital
and labor, with Hellman siding, characteristically, with labor. The
Hubbards, the rapacious foxes, will do anything for money, and those
who will not are readily devoured. Watch on the Rhine, for ideological reasons, is atypical. Teck de Brancovis, like the Hubbards,
will do anything for money but he is defeated by Kurt Müller's anti-
Fascist commitment. And Fanny Farrelly, who initially resembles
Amelia Tilford, eventually puts her money behind the ultimate political good. Writing of the Depression's influence on the American
drama, Malcolm Goldstein asserts that in The Little Foxes "Hellman
attempts to demonstrate that in the process of amassing wealth the
individual goes through the parallel process of decivilizing himself
--of losing ground as a human being and falling into the way of the
jungle." Her plays of this period, he says, side with the young
against the obstructionism of the old and thus reflect New Deal
legislation sympathetic to young people, an interesting if somewhat
forced argument that ignores the traditional generational conflict
that goes back as far as Greek and Roman drama and probably has
nothing at all to do with the New Deal (The Political Stage: American
Drama and Theater of the Great Depression, 1974.19).

Introduction

Hellman is often described as a "southern" playwright. The memoirs later clarify the influence of the South on her personality and her writing career, but her plays, while frequently set in the South, differ from those of, say, Tennessee Williams in their tendency to be more universal and political than regional in thematic purpose. The settings, especially the Hubbards' Alabama and the Berniers' New Orleans, surely convey a certain verisimilitude and the speech patterns of characters in her plays, particularly Toys in the Attic, reflect their locales. But to argue that she is essentially a southern playwright is a specious hypothesis. Several writers have made forceful statements for just this position, however. James Eatman maintains that The Little Foxes reflects turn of the century accounts of the Deep South: "Its central action is a microcosmic version of a society in transition from agrarianism to industrialization" (1973.20). Winifred Dusenbury compares the two Hubbard plays to other modern American dramas she characterizes as "southern" studies of tragic loneliness (1960.33). Typical of English reviewers of Toys in the Attic, H. A. L. Craig ridicules "the cliché of Southern heavy drama concealment: a concealed homosexuality, concealed lesbianism, concealed hatred, colour, castration, impotence" (1960.30). And a comparison of the Hubbard clan to Faulkner's Snopeses is not without foundation.

But "concealed lesbianism" is also a subject, however peripheral, of The Children's Hour, which is set in New England. The Autumn Garden, though enacted "on the Gulf of Mexico, about a hundred miles from New Orleans" (The Collected Plays, p. 464), depends more upon Chekhovian "nostalgia for a no-longer existent past and the individual's frustrating search for love and the meaning of life" than upon a specific exploration of southern mores. Its kind of drama is artistic and moral, not merely psychological (as it tends to be in Williams) or sociological (as it tends to be in Miller) (Marvin Felheim, 1960.34).

Hellman's plays deserve continued reassessment, especially in relation to the later memoirs. A short-lived Broadway revival of Watch on the Rhine early in 1980 (too late for inclusion in this bibliography) reinforces the view that the play has not aged well. The role of women in her plays has in recent years received special attention (see Conclusion, below). Professional and college companies across the country continue to perform not only the surefire Hubbard plays and The Children's Hour, but Days to Come, The Autumn Garden, and Toys in the Attic. My Mother, My Father and Me is, at this writing, being praised in a new, off-Broadway production (again too recent for inclusion here). The claim that Hellman is not in the forefront of modern American playwrights should once and for all be put to rest.

Introduction

THE ADAPTATIONS

The four plays which Lillian Hellman adapted for Broadway contain properly Hellmanesque themes: the omnipresence of evil which devours the innocent (Montserrat, The Lark, Candide); political sacrifice for a higher good (Montserrat, The Lark); the grotesque effects of money on human values (Candide, My Mother, My Father and Me). The adaptations are also illuminating for the playwright's experimentation with form, and further refute the claim that Hellman is limited by the conventions of social realism.

Generally considered static by New York reviewers, Montserrat (1949) has received occasional limited revivals, including a production on National Educational Television. Unfortunately, it opened on Broadway two evenings before the premiere of Regina, Marc Blitzstein's opera based on The Little Foxes. Critics for weekly and monthly magazines tended to combine their reviews of the two productions and, in several instances, reminded of Hellman's crackling play of ten years before, found Montserrat constrastingly turgid. John Gassner, in reverse anticipation of the reception given to My Mother, My Father and Me fourteen years later, assails Montserrat for its reluctance to depart from well-made realism, for its failure to dramatize the lives of Montserrat and the hostages through expressionistic coups de théâtre instead of tight dramaturgy (1949.43).

Hellman's libretto for Candide (1956), a collaboration by some of the most famous names in American music and letters, wavers in the judgment of critics who object to her astringent tone which seems to them too much on the side of Voltaire's pessimist, Martin. (See, for example, Richard Hayes, 1956.23, and Henry Hewes, 1956.24.) But, typically, others berate the Hellman book for Candide as insufficiently biting, devoid of Voltaire's pessimism. (See Mary McCarthy, 1956.33, and Walter Kerr, 1956.28.) Brooks Atkinson, praising the work as "a brilliant musical satire," considers Hellman's Candide a disillusioned modern hero unrelated to Voltaire's blithering idiot (1956.9).

The Lark (1955), Hellman's most successful adaptation for Broadway, evokes responses primarily for its treatment of Joan of Arc, especially as compared to Shaw's and Anouilh's heroines. (See, for example, Frank O'Connor, 1956.37; Alan Hewitt, 1956.25; and Vincent O'Flaherty, 1956.38.) Particularly applauded by reviewers for the performance of Julie Harris as Joan and for the production's theatricality, The Lark nevertheless triggers characteristically contradictory appraisals of Hellman's meaning and tone. Her adaptation has been praised as a literate, intellectually vital study of Joan, an improvement on Anouilh's original version (Theophilus Lewis, 1955.29). A woman dramatist (an appellation that recurs throughout Hellman's career), crows Walter Kerr, "has created the first really tough-minded Joan of Arc." The play's hardheaded candor "comes from the pen of the lady who carved out, and carved up, The Little Foxes" (1955.26). But the play has also been attacked as a distortion of history, as watered-down Shaw and watered-down Anouilh. Eric Bentley is disturbed by Joan's "good girl" aspects (1955.10), while Robert Hatch considers her too sentimental and spritely a figure (1955.20).

My Mother, My Father and Me (1963) is the most sardonic, anarchic work that Hellman has written. Its structure is of a piece with its content: it combines absurdist elements with the partially veiled theater of cruelty of Antonin Artaud; it takes risks, some of which fail. It relies, says Howard Taubman, upon "a series of mordant vignettes rather than a tightly made play" (1963.58). Taubman is right, but misses the point. He laments the absence of a structure that would have been entirely inappropriate for My Mother, My Father and Me, a play which depends upon outrageous exaggeration for its satiric thrusts. Marya Mannes, elsewhere astute about Hellman (see, for example, 1960.50), criticizes her for taking aim at too many targets and seeks the assumed craftsmanship of the earlier plays. Mannes admits, however, to the play's hilarity and admires its attempt to deal with large social issues, in contrast to other ambitious plays of the early 1960s (1963.47).

Lillian Hellman's adaptations, like her original plays, have prompted surprisingly inconsistent commentary from critics. Similar matters of tone, structure, and relative complexity (or lack thereof) in the characterizations arise. My Mother, My Father and Me, based on Burt Blechman's novel How Much?, attacks its own middle-class Broadway audience as Hellman had intended to attack it in The Little Foxes, but this time there ought to have been no mistaking the target. Audiences (and critics) alienated by its unwieldy structure and black humor in 1963 might justly profit from revivals today, especially by major repertory companies. The play was considerably ahead of its time. (See, for a similar view, Emory Lewis, 1969.30.) Candide continues to be praised for Leonard Bernstein's brilliant score and Richard Wilbur's lyrics. In a successful New York revival of the mid-1970s, Hellman's libretto was discarded. Her book for Candide deserves careful reconsideration, within the context of the original score and lyrics, as an expression of her social and political views. Montserrat, an especially timely play for the new decade in light of the Iranian hostage crisis, and The Lark remain interesting, if less innovative, vehicles for superlative actors.

THE FILMS

Hellman wrote seven screenplays during and following her years under contract to Samuel Goldwyn Studios: The Dark Angel (with Mordaunt Shairp, 1935); These Three (the first film version of The

Children's Hour, 1936); Dead End (1937); The Little Foxes (1941);
The North Star (1943); The Searching Wind (1946); The Chase (1966).
With Ernest Hemingway, John Dos Passos, and Archibald MacLeish, she
produced The Spanish Earth (1937), a documentary in support of the
Spanish Loyalists. Four films have been adapted from Hellman's plays
by other writers, although in some of these instances the playwright
offered advice and unspecified contributions to the scripts: Watch on
the Rhine (screenplay by Dashiell Hammett, with "additional scenes
and dialogue by Lillian Hellman," 1943); Another Part of the Forest
(1948); The Children's Hour (1962); Toys in the Attic (1963). All
twelve films are included in this bibliography, along with a thir-
teenth: Julia (1977), based on the "Julia" chapter of Hellman's
memoir, Pentimento (1973), in which Hellman herself is the leading
character.

The Spanish Earth retains its power as one of the earliest anti-
Fascist screen documents. Hellman's involvement was apparently a
financial one only, illness having delayed her scheduled arrival in
Spain for the making of the film. She considers it "a good picture,
with remarkable work by [Joris] Ivens," the director, "and a narration by Ernest Hemingway that I still like . . . because he felt
deeply enough not to care that he often sounded like a parody of
himself" (see An Unfinished Woman, chapter 6). The Spanish Earth is
an important, influential documentary, hailed from the first for the
Hemingway narration and the cinematic expression of its openly
political message. (See for representative reviews: Time, 1937.11;
Otis Ferguson, 1937.26; John T. McManus, 1937.37,38.)

Hellman's first screenplay, coauthored with Mordaunt Shairp, was
an adaptation of Guy Bolton's play The Dark Angel. Critics generally
note that the genuinely touching story, though bordering frequently
on the edge of sentimentality, escapes mawkishness (Literary Digest,
1935.18). The "understated" screenplay achieves "tragic authentici-
ty" (Canadian Magazine, 1935.20). English reviewers are more severe
(Graham Greene, 1935.39) but Grenville Vernon, who praises the film's
poignancy and dialogue of distinction (1935.53), and Andre Sennwald,
who cites the "highly literate" screenplay (1935.52), represent the
prevailing view.

These Three, contrary to all fears, managed to accommodate The
Children's Hour to the Hollywood production code, which forbade any
implication of homosexuality, and to emerge as a brilliant film
preserving Hellman's basic thematic concerns: the destructive power
of gossip, the easy acceptability of lies as truth, the cowardly
reluctance of "good" people to challenge evil directly. Mary
Tilford's lie in These Three—that she heard Karen Wright and Joe
Cardin in Karen's room all night, not Karen and Martha—seems pallid
now but, extraordinarily enough, These Three remains forceful,
moving, and considerably more subtle than the 1962 remake, which
retains the play's original title and accusation of lesbianism but
is curiously unconvincing. (See, for two interesting articles on

Introduction

issues raised by the 1962 version, an interview with Hellman by
Joseph Morgenstern, 1962.37; and Donald Labadie, 1962.30.) In marked
contrast to the mostly negative reviews of the later version, These
Three was greeted with awe. London Observer critic C. A. Lejeune,
typical of English and American commentators, praises Hellman for
writing the screenplay "in the same dark and malign mood as the
original, giving it the one little twist that would satisfy the
national conscience" (1936.53). Other major critics suggest that the
shift in the inciting plot device actually helps the film to surpass
the stage version. (See especially: Graham Greene, 1936.47; Frank
Nugent, 1936.61; Time, 1936.18; Mark Van Doren, 1936.70; Richard
Watts, Jr., 1936.72.)

The generally respectful notices for Hellman's adaptation of
Dead End, Sidney Kingsley's Depression drama, echo comments often
made about her own plays. Her resourceful screenplay, writes Howard
Barnes in the New York Herald Tribune, concentrates on the melodrama.
Her plot is more taut and unified than Kingsley's but the film suggests a piece of clever reporting rather than a dramatically distinguished work (1937.16). The reviewer for Stage applauds the "grim
and arresting photoplay" (1937.8), while Newsweek's critic commends
Dead End as a forceful, realistic film (1937.13). Hellman's skillful
adaptation "enlarges the play's design, intensifies its mood, sharpens its implications," says the critic for Time (1937.2).

"Opening up" the confined settings of a stage play for the
movies is a risky business, but usually not as risky as rigidly re-
taining the claustrophobic mise en scène of the theater. Hellman's
screenplay for The Little Foxes ("with additional dialogue by
Dorothy Parker, Arthur Kober and Alan Campbell") succeeds admirably
in periodically removing us from the Giddens home and in expanding
the action to convey a sense of how the Hubbard clan adversely
affects the town, especially its blacks. There is one sop for the
audience: the addition of a young newspaper editor, a transplanted
Yankee who challenges the Hubbards' crimes and, in the process, lends
further motivation for Alexandra's recognition scene. For the filmgoer of 1941, the most important element, no doubt, is the implied
future relationship of this man and Alexandra, who in the play will
be alone if she fulfills her vow to leave her mother. (Hellman
expected Zan to "become maybe a spinsterish social worker, disappointed, a rather angry woman." See her Paris Review interview with
John Phillips and Anne Hollander, 1965.19.)

With William Wyler's direction and a colorful cast (including
Bette Davis as Regina, Teresa Wright as Zan, and several members of
the Broadway company), Hellman's most famous play became a strong
critical and popular success on the screen. It is still a fascinating film to watch, not only for its Celluloid preservation of
Hellman's drama but for the deep focus and other camera techniques
of Wyler and cinematographer Gregg Toland (best known for his work
on Citizen Kane) and for consideration of the relationship between

theater and film. (See, for example, André Bazin, What Is Cinema?, 1967.9; and Otis Ferguson, "The Camera Way Is the Hard Way," National Board of Review Magazine, 1941.42.) With the possible exception of These Three, The Little Foxes received the widest, most consistent praise of any film with which Hellman was associated. (See, among the more intelligent assessments: Howard Barnes, 1941.26; Otis Ferguson, 1941.43; Philip T. Hartung, 1941.56; John Mosher, 1941.69.) Bosley Crowther, for many years film critic for the New York Times, deserves recognition here for his ludicrous, but typically Crowther-ian, objection to the film. He cannot accept the film's concern with "a pack of snarling jackals without a single redeeming grace"; nor can he become interested in "a dame [Regina] who is so obviously-- and theatrically--depraved" (1941.39).

The Little Foxes, on stage and on screen, does not date in the way that, for some audiences, Dead End or Watch on the Rhine does. Its social criticism is for all American times and places and does not depend intrinsically for its power on a specific period, perhaps because it takes place almost forty years before it was written. Hellman's most frequently performed play, generally agreed even by its detractors to be among the most famous and popular of modern American dramas, The Little Foxes in its screen incarnation far sur-passes most filmed plays. In fact, its release in England early in 1942 muted considerably the reception accorded to the belated London premiere of the play later that year. Potential audiences had already seen the film and, more important, key critics found the film more powerful than the London stage production (see Theatre World, 1942.33).

Most critics favored Hellman's attack on appeasement in the movie version of The Searching Wind but the film received mixed reviews overall. At times, the political attitudes of reviewers or their respective journals (or newspapers) appear to have colored their responses to the film. (See, for example, James Agee, Nation, 1946.1; Bosley Crowther, New York Times, 1946.24; John McCarten, New Yorker, 1946.39; Time, 1946.3.)

Hellman's two other original screenplays evolved into films to which she strenuously and publicly objected: The North Star and The Chase. Fears that The North Star treated the Russians too favorably, even in 1943 when Russia was an American ally, caused its bowdleriza-tion. Its critical reception also depended heavily on politics, with the controversy swirling primarily around the film's alleged propaganda in support of the Russian way of life. Some critics directly reflect their own political leanings or those of their news-papers (see Frank Antico, Daily Worker, 1943.26; Lee Mortimer, New York Daily Mirror, 1943.53; Archer Winsten, New York Post, 1943.65, 66), but the film garners strong praise from several surprising quarters (Life, 1943.12; Newsweek, 1943.23; Time, 1943.5). The most telling criticism of The North Star comes from critics who, in one way or another, reiterate the main objections of Hellman herself

Introduction

(Theodore Strauss, "The Author's Case," New York Times, 1943.59).
This view holds, legitimately, that the Russian peasants of the film
are Hollywood-pretty, that any required grittiness has been removed
in casting, performances, and camera work. (See James Agate, 1943.1;
James Agee, 1943.3; Manny Farber, 1943.42.) Yet Hellman's script,
which was also published in 1943, received considerable praise, as
did--for all the controversy--the completed film. (See Howard
Barnes, 1943.30; Philip Hartung, 1943.44; Louis Kronenberger, 1943.
47.) The excised version of The North Star is shown on television
generally under the title Armored Attack; recently the original,
full-length print has been made available. (See Andrew Sarris,
1976.92.)

The Chase, disavowed by Hellman because others "mauled about and
slicked up" her work (Irving Drutman, "Questioning Miss Hellman on
Movies," New York Times, 1966.22), received the worst set of notices
of any film on which she worked. Her screenplay and Arthur Penn's
direction are attacked as overwrought, excessively violent, prurient,
anti-southern. Pauline Kael, who later exonerates Hellman from her
initial barrage upon learning of alterations by others in Hellman's
script, expresses the majority view: the film pretends to condemn
the very attitudes in which it simultaneously revels. (See 1966.31
and 1968.21.) Several notable exceptions imply, however, that some
of Hellman's original intentions are preserved in the final cut, a
fact borne out by viewing the film. English reviewers, apparently
more willing than home critics to accept the bloody view of American
society portrayed in the film, defend the realistic, concrete depiction of "the conflict between reason and violence" (Ian Cameron,
Spectator, 1966.12). Raymond Durgnat, in Films and Filming (1966.
23), relates The Chase to other American films in which a town's
social order capsizes, while David Wilson points, in Sight and Sound,
to the John F. Kennedy and Lee Harvey Oswald murders in Dallas three
years earlier; he acknowledges the film's "Wagnerian excesses," but
proposes that its hysterical, extravagant claims pale before actual
events in American society: "Within its own exorbitant framework,
the film almost comes off" (1966.49). In a subtle analysis of The
Chase, written three years after its release, Kevin Gough-Yates
argues persuasively in favor of the film's intricate structure and
characterizations (1969.21a).

Andrew Sarris, in contrast to most American reviewers, considers
The Chase a "fascinating failure," worth seeing for the performances
of Marlon Brando, Jane Fonda, and Robert Redford but suffering from
vagueness and, especially, from director Arthur Penn's attempt "to
manipulate a junkyard into a metaphor of America" (Village Voice,
1966.40). Embittered by her experiences with The Chase, Hellman has
kept her vow not to write another film. Her "old and foolish dream"
that one could write a film the way one wrote anything else had
ended (Drutman, 1966.22).

Introduction

The movie adaptations of Another Part of the Forest and Toys in the Attic were not written by Hellman. Any role which she may have played in the final productions was limited or nonexistent. Responses to Another Part of the Forest are respectful, often considerably more than that, but the film did not duplicate the memorable success of The Little Foxes and is infrequently shown now, though it can properly boast of strong performances by Frederic March as Marcus Hubbard, and Leo Genn, Dan Duryea, and Ann Blyth as his children. The critic for Time calls the film "a nearly perfect example of how to film a play" (1948.2). Reviews of Toys in the Attic are contrastingly harsh, with occasional exceptions. Performances by Wendy Hiller and Geraldine Page as Anna and Carrie Berniers are generally praised but the casting of Dean Martin as Julian, the role originated on Broadway by Jason Robards, is properly decried as a Hollywood aberration, Martin's valiant effort notwithstanding. (See for interesting and contrasting assessments of the film: Stanley Kauffmann, 1963.38; Arthur Knight, 1963.40; Newsweek, 1963.7; Arthur Schlesinger, 1963.54; The Times [London], 1963.5.)

The screenplay for Watch on the Rhine is credited to Dashiell Hammett, with "additional scenes and dialogue" by Hellman. Their respective contributions remain unspecified but it is safe to conclude that Hellman was closely involved with the film which, abetted by its timely defense of by now active United States participation in the war, collected an impressive array of notices. Paul Lukas won an Oscar for the recreation of his role as Kurt Müller; Bette Davis played his wife. It is an interesting footnote to film history that Casablanca defeated Watch on the Rhine in the Oscar categories of best writing, direction, and overall film for 1943. Both films treat similar anti-Nazi themes, yet Casablanca does not date in the way that Watch on the Rhine does, in part because of the presence of the Bogart persona. Still, Howard Barnes expressed the representative laudatory judgment of Watch on the Rhine upon its release: Herman Shumlin (who directed the Broadway production and codirected the film with Vincent Sherman), "like Orson Welles with Citizen Kane, has demonstrated that there is no great mystery to the fabrication of films, as long as you have something to say on the screen" (1943.29).

Critical reaction to Julia, adapted by Alvin Sargent from Pentimento, was diverse, even extreme. Widely publicized, the film became a popular success, attracting considerable praise as one of several new films to champion an abiding friendship between two women (Hellman and Julia), superseding a plethora of male "buddy" pictures. (See especially: Jack Kroll and others, Newsweek, 1977.75; Harriet Lyons and Susan Braudy, Ms., 1977.84.) Comparison with the Pentimento source are intelligently drawn by Stanley Kauffmann (New Republic, 1977.67), Susan Ferris (Horizon, 1977.45), and Martin Knelman (Atlantic, 1977.72). Illuminating analyses of the film's Hellman persona appear in reviews by Philip French (Sight and Sound, 1977.46), Marc Green (Chronicle of Higher Education, 1977.54), Molly

Haskell (New York, 1977.59), and, particularly, Pauline Kael (New Yorker, 1977.66). Stephen Schiff perceives in some of the negative assessments of Julia an anti-Hellman backlash, the inevitable, thinly veiled response to the "gradual canonization of Saint Lillian" (Boston Phoenix, 1977.110). Indeed, several of the film's reviews repeat a vitriolic refrain present in certain critiques of Scoundrel Time (see discussion of the memoirs, below). Andrew Sarris notes, for example, in his review of Julia, that he has "never considered it a particular privilege to worship at the shrine of Lillian Hellman" (Village Voice, 1977.107), a sentiment he echoes in other references to her work (1978.59, 60). What Martin Knelman calls the film's completion of "the transformation of Lillian Hellman into a popular phenomenon" (1977.72) is, in fact, mirrored in many entries of this bibliography.

THE MEMOIRS

Publication of three books of memoirs, An Unfinished Woman (1969), Pentimento (1973), and Scoundrel Time (1976), introduced Hellman to new generations of readers and returned her to a prominent place on the American literary scene. The first two memoirs were critically acclaimed, won major awards, and, although Hellman has always denied that she is a feminist, appeared at a time when the feminist movement naturally saw in her independence, outspokenness, intense moralism--her refusal to conform, above all--qualities representative of the best that it espoused.

She reemerged, through the voice of An Unfinished Woman and Pentimento, as a public figure with a distinct following. She reminds us, writes Joseph Epstein in admiration of Hellman's nobili- ty, of a "female and super-literate Humphrey Bogart" (1969.17). The feisty, rebellious, tough persona of major sections in these two memoirs alternates, however, with the sensitive and--dare one say it?--feminine "I" whose admitted adoration of beautiful clothes is superseded only by her personal code of honor and friendship, most brilliantly and movingly portrayed in the chapters on Dashiell Hammett, Dorothy Parker, and Helen in An Unfinished Woman and in the "Julia" and "Turtle" sections of Pentimento. As narrator, Hellman is fully aware of her self-descriptions in these two books. She leaves the reader wanting to know more, especially about her time in the theater, which she says she never enjoyed once the plays went into production. She is reluctant to reveal too much, writes know- ingly in an elliptical style--this major dramatist earlier and mis- takenly accused of writing her plays in too explicit a style--but tells us nonetheless a great deal about herself and her relationships with others. What I have just referred to as her "femininity" is that knowing, self-conscious use of femininity referred to, for example, in her discussion of Samuel Goldwyn. Dissatisfied with the

slow progress of early conferences on The Dark Angel, Hellman fled
Hollywood for New York and Paris, until Goldwyn made her the offer
she would not refuse:

> When he found me there [in Paris] a week later he offered
> a long-term contract with fine clauses about doing nothing
> but stories I liked and doing them where and when I liked.
> I had become valuable to Mr. Goldwyn because I had left him
> for reasons he didn't understand. For many years that made
> me an unattainable woman, as desirable as such women are,
> in another context, for men who like them that way.

> (Pentimento, p. 165)

As Doris Falk (Lillian Hellman, 1978.27) and others have noted,
Hellman often speaks of herself as a "difficult" woman. (See, for
example, Pentimento, p. 164, and An Unfinished Woman, p. 186.) That
difficulty--a cantankerous unpredictability--energizes the memoirs,
provides them with a dramatic heroine even when that heroine, as in
large portions of the two books, is mostly describing other people.
She emerges, says Irving Wardle in his review of the first memoir,
as a courageous woman who gives no sign of having made peace with
herself and her environment (The Times [London], 1969.45).

While that feisty directness strikes most reviewers of the
memoirs as courageous and noble, especially with regard to Hellman's
stand before the House Un-American Activities Committee, it impresses
others as self-righteous and unforgiving. As early as An Unfinished
Woman, Robert Kotlowitz, in an otherwise heralding review, observes
that Hellman remains "perhaps too vain about her own integrity"
(1969.28). Such a view of Hellman is apparent particularly in the
imbroglio that erupted after publication of Scoundrel Time and after
Little, Brown, Hellman's publisher, refused to publish Diana
Trilling's We Must March My Darlings, which contained a response to
assertions made by Hellman in Scoundrel Time. Despite high praise
for Scoundrel Time and for Hellman's stand before the HUAC in 1952,
the book reopened old wounds among American intellectuals who
objected to charges directed by Hellman at the "anti-Communist
writers and intellectuals of those times" (Scoundrel Time, p. 154).
Also attacked was Garry Wills's Introduction to Scoundrel Time, dismissed by Walter Goodman and other anti-Hellman critics as a piece
of hurried revisionism: "By this account, the precursors of Joe
McCarthy were those liberals who turned against the Russians the
ideology and the emotions that had spurred their fight against
Fascism" (Goodman, New Leader, 1976.38).

Scoundrel Time thus became the focus for another political
controversy involving the ghost of Joe McCarthy and Hellman herself.
To understand the issues, which are often obscured by the heat of the

arguments (in contrast to Hellman's understated, measured prose in most of Scoundrel Time), it is recommended that the reader peruse the 1952 accounts of Hellman's committee appearance and letter (note, for example, the innuendoes of Time's report, 1952.4) and the 1976–1977 entries on Scoundrel Time and We Must March My Darlings. Here, as throughout the bibliography, I have attempted to encapsulate the writers' respective attitudes. Of special note in sorting out the issues are: William F. Buckley, Jr., 1977.23, 24; Nathan Glazer, 1976.37; Walter Goodman, 1976.38; Sidney Hook, 1977.63; Maureen Howard, 1976.49; Irving Howe, 1976.50; Alfred Kazin, 1977.69; Murray Kempton, 1976.56; Saul Maloff, 1976.76; William Phillips, 1976.88. See also Diana Trilling's We Must March My Darlings, 1977.123, and for contrasting reviews of the Trilling-Hellman contretemps, Thomas R. Edwards, 1977.37, and Irving Howe, 1977.64. Recommended as strongly pro-Hellman responses to Scoundrel Time are Richard A. Falk, 1977.42, and Robert Sherrill, 1976.96. The last chapter of Doris V. Falk's Lillian Hellman (1978.27) ably summarizes the controversies which followed the memoir's publication.

Three (1979) reprints the complete memoirs with Hellman's new commentaries, in which she responds to the attacks on Scoundrel Time. She does not identify her critics but alludes obviously to the Trilling flap as "a front page publicity stunt with high-tone claims about what I had never done" (p. 722). (See Robert D. McFadden, New York Times, 1976.72, and Deirdre Carmody, New York Times, 1976.22.) Hellman's hostess at a San Francisco dinner party, repeating a criticism leveled at her in print, advises Hellman to be "'more tolerant and forgiving.'" Tolerance, Hellman answers in Three, "is, to me, an arrogant conception. Who am I to forgive? To forget, not to punish, is one thing, but forgiveness is for God if you believe in him and maybe even if you don't. I wanted to tell my hostess that, couldn't, couldn't even say that it is not pleasant to correct people for what they haven't done" (p. 725). She wrote Scoundrel Time, she concludes in Three, after mistakenly convincing herself that the elapsed years enabled her to talk about the McCarthy days in a tone "that was not a jumble, not chaotic with judgments and weary storms that were meaningless to anybody but me." She had been wrong: "I am not cool about those days, I am not tolerant about them and I never wish to be." And she reaffirms, more emphatically and angrily than in Scoundrel Time, the view that initiated many of the attacks on that book:

> My mistakes and the political commitments of other more
> radical people were no excuse for the disgraceful conduct
> of intellectuals no matter how much they disagreed. . . .
> I tried to avoid, when I wrote this book [Scoundrel Time],
> what is called a moral stand. I'd like to take that stand
> now. I never want to live again to watch people turn into

liars and cowards and others into frightened, silent
collaborators. And to hell with the fancy reasons they
give for what they did.

(Three, p. 726)

The "moral stand" here taken almost as a challenge or a dare and
the denial that anybody but God can bestow forgiveness return us,
full circle, to the plays and to the Hellman persona of the earlier
memoirs. Here is Karen Wright defying, refusing to forgive Mrs.
Tilford in The Children's Hour. Here is Sam Hazen, at twenty, ring-
ing down the curtain on The Searching Wind: "How do you say you
like your country? I like this place. (With great passion) And I
don't want any more fancy fooling around with it. I don't want any
more of Father's mistakes, for any reason, good or bad, or yours,
Mother, because I think they do it harm. . . . I am ashamed of both
of you, and that's the truth. I don't want to be ashamed that way
again" (The Collected Plays, p. 324). Here, too, are Kurt Müller,
who spoke for a clearly defined cause and, more complicatedly,
Montserrat, who will not betray Bolivar even if his moral position
results in the deaths of innocent people. It is not that Hellman is
necessarily right and her targets are necessarily wrong; it is that
she argues so forcibly for her position (even when she expresses
doubts) that as one reads her, one believes it, too--as one believes
in the justness of Karen, Sam, Montserrat, and other Hellman characters. At seventy-five, Hellman is the public summation of her most
admonishingly moral, if not her most appealing creations.

INTERVIEWS AND LONGER STUDIES

There are few book-length studies devoted entirely to Hellman.
Richard Moody's Lillian Hellman, Playwright (1972.26) is instructive
for its exploration of Hellman's manuscripts and her methods of re-
writing. It contains a good deal of theater lore and biographical
information but, as some of Moody's reviewers note, he seems dependent on information supplied in much greater detail in An Unfinished
Woman and Hellman's Paris Review interview (1965; see below). His
tone is unfailingly adulatory. Most of all, as Jacob Adler writes in
his review, he disappoints "the literary critic of drama" (1973.1).
But Lillian Hellman, Playwright is well worth perusal on a number of
counts.

The manuscripts of Hellman's plays and motion picture scripts
are in the Lillian Hellman Collection at the University of Texas
(Austin), where Moody did much of his research. The play manuscripts, along with notebooks and letters from the collection, are
catalogued in detail in The Lillian Hellman Collection at the

University of Texas by Manfred Triesch (1966.46). As Triesch's
Introduction aptly notes, "the various typescript versions of each
play are arranged in chronological sequence according to internal
evidence so the reader can follow the development of each play" (p.
9). Brief checklists of Hellman criticism are also included.

Jacob H. Adler's Lillian Hellman (1969.3), a forty-four page
monograph in the Southern Writers Series, is a literate, highly
knowledgeable study of Hellman's plays that will not disappoint "the
literary critic of drama." He renders the dramatic themes, structure, and dialogue clearly and relates the plays to those of other
modern playwrights, including Ibsen and Tennessee Williams. One
needn't agree with all of Adler's judgments in order to find his
study useful and provocative. Also reliable and instructive are his
earlier study of Toys in the Attic ("Miss Hellman's Two Sisters,"
Educational Theatre Journal, 1963.1) and his comparative analysis of
Hellman and Williams ("The Rose and the Fox: Notes on the Southern
Drama," in South: Modern Southern Literature in its Cultural Setting,
ed. Louis D. Rubin and Robert D. Jacobs, 1961.2).

Lorena Ross Holmin's The Dramatic Works of Lillian Hellman
(1973.32), a Ph.D. dissertation published in Uppsala University's
English Studies series, examines the original plays (excluding Days
to Come) but relies far too heavily on plot synopsis, far too little
on original textual analysis. Most recently, Doris V. Falk's Lillian
Hellman (1978.27), part of Ungar's modern literature monograph
series, provides a good, if uneven, introduction to the playwright's
work but suffers from somewhat glib categorizations of the plays and
gallant, but forced comparisons with other American writers. Falk is
best at conveying Hellman's moral concerns and the persona which
emerges from the plays and, especially, the memoirs. The brief final
chapter is helpful in disengaging the Scoundrel Time controversies.
While finally too dependent on plot summaries of the original plays
and memoirs--the films and adaptations are virtually ignored--Falk's
book is a succinct, tentative step in the direction of the complete
study of the Hellman oeuvre. Katherine Lederer's study of Hellman in
Twayne's United States Authors Series has been recently published by
G. K. Hall (see 1979.23). A bibliography by Steven Bills has been
listed by Garland but, at this writing, has not appeared.

Among the numerous interviews and profiles, especially recommended for the light they shed on Hellman's life and work are
Margaret Case Harriman's "Miss Lily of New Orleans" (New Yorker,
1941.55) and John Phillips and Anne Hollander's "The Art of the
Theater: Lillian Hellman, An Interview" (Paris Review, 1965.19).
Christine Doudna's Rolling Stone interview is particularly interesting for Hellman's comments on the women's movement (1977.33). See
also John Hersey's delightful homage (1976.44).

Since publication of the memoirs, the number of doctoral dissertations on Hellman has dramatically increased, a trend that is likely

to continue. As noted above, several studies of Hellman are now being readied for publication. Still needed are the authorized and, perhaps, unauthorized biographies, the definitive study of the plays, films, and memoirs that will trace patterns through the various genres, and the detailed, objective portrayal of the Lillian Hellman-Dashiell Hammett relationship, idealized in the memoirs. Her possible influence on such contemporary dramatists as Sam Shepard and David Rabe also deserves investigation.

For all the renewed interest in Hellman, and for all the reviews, articles and news items contained in this bibliography, she has in her long career been overlooked or treated with condescension in certain scholarly quarters. Note, for example, the short shrift she receives in the various editions of the Literary History of the United States, both the histories and bibliographies. More mystifying--outrageous, really--are the limited, passing references which she is accorded in the new Harvard Guide to Contemporary American Writing, where, even in an essay entitled "Women's Literature," Elizabeth Janeway neither examines nor mentions Hellman's memoirs (see 1979.17). Yet the Belknap Press of Harvard University Press, in tacit recognition of potential reader interest in Hellman, prominently includes her photograph in an advertising brochure for the book.

CONCLUSION

Early in her career, Lillian Hellman first expressed her detestation for the label "woman playwright," a refrain which she was required to repeat with unfortunate frequency. (See, for example, Harriman, 1941.55.) Among the most flagrant of critics in this respect was George Jean Nathan, whose early enthusiasm for The Children's Hour turned, in his reviews of the later plays, to thinly veiled disdain for reasons that seem now to have had little to do with the plays themselves. In an article entitled "Playwrights in Petticoats" he declares: "Her latest play, Watch on the Rhine, proves two things. It proves again that Lillian Hellman is the best of our American woman playwrights and it proves that even the best of our woman playwrights falls immeasurably short of the mark of our best masculine" (American Mercury, 1941.70).

Whether in condescension or admiration, commentators have found it difficult to disregard Hellman's sex. What is explicitly said or left unstated of course varies considerably with the years. The woman whose appearance before the HUAC was treated with snide innuendo by Time (see 1952.4) was praised by that magazine for Scoundrel Time (see 1976.40), which appeared two years after Richard Nixon's resignation as president and detailed the scoundrelism that led, in Hellman's view, to his election and to Watergate. In the mid-1970s, it was far more fashionable, if belatedly appropriate, to embrace the resistance of, especially, a woman to the McCarthy pack than it was in 1952. The intertwining of the literary Hellman with the public, political woman is most dramatically evident in the last decade, when the publication of the three memoirs fortuitously coincided with increased if sometimes grudging recognition of the women's movement. Note, in this regard, the number of reviews of Julia (see 1977 and 1978, passim) that react, almost subliminally, to Hellman's reluctant role as feminist heroine. (See Hellman's criticisms of what she considers the excesses of the women's movement in her Rolling Stone interview with Christine Doudna, 1977.33.)

In this regard, too, the role of women in Hellman's plays has been reexamined in light of feminist criticism. Regina Giddens is seen, for example, as a frustrated woman, in the tradition of Hedda Gabler, whose evil ways are the direct consequences of a society that forces women to be controlled by men. (See Honor Moore, "Introduction," The New Women's Theatre: Ten Plays by Contemporary American Women, 1977.90.) Similarly, the friendship between Karen and Martha in The Children's Hour is viewed by some as anticipatory of the much-heralded friendship between Julia and Hellman in Pentimento and Julia. (See, for example, Pauline Kael, 1977.66.) Such an approach, taken especially in several doctoral dissertations of the last ten years, is likely to continue. The relationship between Carrie and Anna Berniers in Toys in the Attic would also profit from this kind of analysis.

That Lillian Hellman, as the Blackglama coat advertisement for which she posed proclaims her (see 1976.2), has become a "legend" in her own time is probably unarguable. The sharp division among those who hail those legendary qualities and those who view them with sarcasm, as a process by which she has been transformed into "a major cultural monument" (Philip French, 1977.46), is apparent throughout this volume. But the plays and memoirs, and certainly several of the films, comprise a formidable and lasting body of work. The alleged moral absolutes of, say, The Little Foxes are in fact much more complicated, in both the plays and the adaptations, than critics have allowed.

The Hellman canon, from The Children's Hour to Three, denies absolutes. One does one's best; that is the best that can be hoped for by any of us. The most laudable figures are no paragons; they do their best in a universe that is flawed, as they themselves are flawed. Hellman's Joan of Arc tells the court that man is God's greatest creation because "the same man who acts the beast will rise from a brothel bed and throw himself before a blade to save the soldier who walks beside him. Nobody knows why he does. He doesn't know. But he does it, and he dies, cleansed and shining. He has done both good and evil, and thus twice acted like a man. That makes God happy because God made him for just this contradiction. We are good and we are evil and that is what was meant" (The Lark, The

<u>Collected Plays</u>, p. 584). Human perfection is rare, and when it does appear, as in Kurt Müller, it stands as a political encomium to a nation at war or, as in Julia, it is seen from a distance of time and the author's filtered memory.

Hellman's Candide, as he tells Pangloss at play's end, has learned that harmony neither exists in the universe nor should it: "We promise only to do our best and live out our lives. Dear God, that's all we can promise in truth" (<u>Candide</u>, <u>The Collected Plays</u>, p. 678). Defending herself in <u>Three</u> against charges that she had been pro-Stalinist, Hellman writes that she was, "indeed, late to believe the political-intellectual persecutions under Stalin." She goes on to reveal her heretofore undisclosed support for Russian dissidents and other information to allay the charges. "None of this," she concludes, "disproves my critics or confirms them, either. In truth, I was nobody's girl. That is a position that for many reasons did not, does not, please or satisfy me, <u>but I did my best within the limits of myself</u>" (<u>Three</u>, p. 207, italics mine).

January 1980

Works by Lillian Hellman

The Dear Queen. With Louis Kronenberger. Unpublished/unpro-
duced. Copyright: 30 December 1932.

The Children's Hour. New York: Alfred A. Knopf, 1934; London:
Hamish Hamilton, 1937.
New York premiere: 20 November 1934.

Days to Come. New York and London: Alfred A. Knopf, 1936.
New York premiere: 15 December 1936.

The Little Foxes. New York: Random House, 1939; London:
Hamish Hamilton, 1939.
New York premiere: 15 February 1939.

Watch on the Rhine. New York: Random House, 1941.
New York premiere: 1 April 1941.

Four Plays. New York: Random House, 1942.
Modern Library edition of The Children's Hour, Days to
Come, The Little Foxes, and Watch on the Rhine, with an
introduction by Hellman.

The Searching Wind. New York: Viking Press, 1944.
New York premiere: 12 April 1944.

Another Part of the Forest. New York: Viking Press, 1947.
New York premiere: 20 November 1946.

The Autumn Garden. Boston: Little, Brown and Company, 1951.
New York premiere: 7 March 1951.

Six Plays. New York: Random House, 1960.
  Modern Library edition of The Children's Hour, Days to
  Come, The Little Foxes, Watch on the Rhine, Another Part of
  the Forest, and The Autumn Garden, with an introduction by
  Hellman.

Toys in the Attic. New York: Random House, 1960.
  New York premiere: 25 February 1960.

The Collected Plays. Boston and Toronto: Little, Brown and
  Company, 1972.
  Definitive texts of the eight original plays and four
  adaptations, with Hellman's revisions and emendations.

ADAPTATIONS

Montserrat. From the French play by Emmanuel Roblès. New
  York: Dramatists Play Service, 1950.
  New York premiere: 29 October 1949.

The Lark. From the French play by Jean Anouilh. New York:
  Random House, 1956.
  New York premiere: 17 November 1955.

Candide. A comic operetta based on Voltaire's satire. Book
  by Lillian Hellman. Score by Leonard Bernstein. Lyrics by
  Richard Wilbur. Other lyrics by John LaTouche and Dorothy
  Parker. New York: Random House, 1957.
  New York premiere: 1 December 1956.

My Mother, My Father and Me. From the novel How Much? by
  Burt Blechman. New York: Random House, 1963.
  New York premiere: 21 March 1963.

MEMOIRS

An Unfinished Woman: A Memoir. Boston and Toronto: Little,
  Brown and Company, 1969.

Pentimento: A Book of Portraits. Boston and Toronto: Little,
  Brown and Company, 1973.

Scoundrel Time. With an introduction by Garry Wills. Boston
  and Toronto: Little, Brown and Company, 1976. Published in
  England with an introduction by James Cameron and the reprinted introduction by Garry Wills. London: Macmillan,
  1976.

Works by Lillian Hellman

Three. Boston and Toronto: Little, Brown and Company, 1979.
    The collected memoirs, with new commentaries by Hellman
and an introduction by Richard Poirier.

BOOKS EDITED

The Selected Letters of Anton Chekhov. Edited and with an
    introduction by Lillian Hellman. Translated by Sidonie K.
    Lederer. New York: Farrar, Straus and Cudahy, 1955.

The Big Knockover: Selected Stories and Short Novels by
    Dashiell Hammett. Edited and with an introduction by Lillian
    Hellman. New York: Random House, 1966. Published in
    England as The Dashiell Hammett Story Omnibus. London:
    Cassell and Company, 1966.

SCREENPLAYS

The Dark Angel. Adapted, with Mordaunt Shairp, from the play
    by Guy Bolton. 1935.

These Three. The first screen adaptation of The Children's
    Hour. 1936.

Dead End. Adapted from the play by Sidney Kingsley. 1937.

The Spanish Earth. Collaboration with Ernest Hemingway, John
    Dos Passos, and Archibald MacLeish. 1937.
    Hellman's role was essentially a financial one, although
she is frequently credited with the documentary's original
story idea. The film's narration was written and spoken by
Ernest Hemingway.

The Little Foxes. With additional dialogue by Dorothy Parker,
    Arthur Kober, and Alan Campbell. 1941.

The North Star. New York: Viking Press, 1943.

The Searching Wind. 1946.

The Chase. Based on a novel and a play by Horton Foote.
    1966.

Works by Lillian Hellman

MISCELLANEOUS WRITINGS

Book reviews, New York Herald Tribune Books: (26 September 1926), pp. 21, 26; (24 October 1926), p. 22; (28 November 1926), p. 14; (23 October 1927), p. 22; (4 December 1927), p. 40; (11 December 1927), p. 16; (24 February 1929), p. 27; (2 June 1929), p. 12.
   Cited by Richard Moody, in Lillian Hellman, Playwright. New York: Pegasus/Bobbs-Merrill, 1972, p. 358. See also Moody, pp. 23-24.

"I Call Her Mama Now." American Spectator, 1 (September 1933), 2.
   Short story.

"Perberty in Los Angeles." American Spectator, 2 (January 1934), 4.
   Short story.

Review of Barchester Towers, dramatization by Thomas Job of Anthony Trollope's novel. Time, 30 (13 December 1937), 57.
   Hellman's only drama review for Time, according to Richard Moody, in Lillian Hellman, Playwright. New York: Pegasus/Bobbs-Merrill, 1972, p. 77.

"Day in Spain." New Republic, 94 (13 April 1938), 297-98.
   On the Spanish Civil War. Reprinted in Literature and Liberalism: An Anthology of Sixty Years of the New Republic. Edited by Edward Zwick. Washington, D.C.: New Republic Book Company, 1967, pp. 36-39.

"Back of Those Foxes." New York Times (26 February 1939), section 9, pp. 1-2.
   On writing The Little Foxes.

"The Little Men in Philadelphia." PM (25 June 1940), p. 6.
   In Philadelphia, during the Republican National Convention.

"They Fought for Spain." New Masses, 37 (10 December 1940), 11.
   Reprints two articles--one by Hellman and one by Lion Feuchtwanger--originally broadcast on radio, 29 November 1940.

"Preface and Postscript." New York Times (22 February 1942), section 8, pp. 1, 3.
   Excerpts most of Hellman's Introduction to Four Plays. New York: Random House, 1942.

"I Meet the Front-Line Russians." <u>Collier's</u>, 115 (31 March
     1945), 11, 68, 71.
          Account of time spent with the Soviet Army "somewhere
     on the Warsaw-Vistula front."

"Author Jabs the Critics." <u>New York Times</u> (15 December 1946),
     section 2, pp. 3-4.
          On disagreements between playwrights and critics.

"The Judas Goats." <u>Screen Writer</u>, 3 (December 1947), 7.
          Attacks Hollywood celebrities who testified before the
     House Un-American Activities Committee.

"Reports on Yugoslavia." <u>New York Star</u> (4 November 1948), p.
     13; (5 November 1948), p. 9; (7 November 1948), p. 8; (8
     November 1948), p. 9; (9 November 1948), p. 6; (10 November
     1948), p. 11.
          Articles on Hellman's trip to Prague, Belgrade, and
     Paris, including an interview with Marshall Tito.   Cited
     by Richard Moody, in <u>Lillian Hellman, Playwright</u>.   New
     York: Pegasus/Bobbs-Merrill, 1972, p. 359.

"Lillian Hellman's Credo." <u>Nation</u>, 174 (31 May 1952), 518.
          Extract of Hellman's letter to the House Un-American
     Activities Committee.

"Scotch on the Rocks." <u>New York Review of Books</u>, 1 (17
     October 1963), 6.
          Reports on the International Drama Conference, in
     Edinburgh.

"Sophronia's Grandson Goes to Washington." <u>Ladies' Home
     Journal</u>, 80 (December 1963), 78-80, 82.
          Covers the August 1963 civil rights march on Washington,
     D.C.

"Marc Blitzstein Remembered." <u>New York Times</u> (2 February
     1964), section 2, p. 3.
          Brief tribute to Blitzstein.

Statement. <u>Ladies' Home Journal</u>, 81 (March 1964), 82.
          Hellman's disassociation from the retraction by the
     <u>Ladies' Home Journal</u> of remarks in her article "Sophronia's
     Grandson Goes to Washington," <u>Ladies' Home Journal</u>, 80
     (December 1963).

"The Land that Holds the Legend of Our Lives." <u>Ladies' Home
     Journal</u>, 81 (April 1964), 56-57, 122-24.
          A trip to Israel and Jordan.

Works by Lillian Hellman

"Lillian Hellman Asks a Little Respect for Her Agony." Show,
4 (May 1964), 12-13.
  Parody, in letter form, of Arthur Miller's After the
Fall.

"Dashiell Hammett: A Memoir." New York Review of Books, 5
(25 November 1965), 16-18, 20-23.
  Hellman's Introduction to The Big Knockover: Selected
Stories and Short Novels by Dashiell Hammett. New York:
Random House, 1966. Also included as a chapter of An
Unfinished Woman. Boston and Toronto: Little, Brown and
Company, 1969.

"The Time of the Foxes." New York Times (22 October 1967),
section 2, pp. 1, 5.
  Reminiscences of the original production of The Little
Foxes, on the eve of its first New York revival at Lincoln
Center.

"Interlude in Budapest." Holiday, 42 (November 1967), 60-61.
  Travel piece.

"An Unfinished Woman." Atlantic, 223 (April 1969), 90-128.
  Lengthy excerpt from An Unfinished Woman, with editor's
note.

"Topics: The Baggage of a Political Exile." New York Times
(23 August 1969), p. 26.
  Criticizes Russian novelist Anatoly Kuznetsov.

"And Now--An Evening with Nichols and Hellman." New York
Times (9 August 1970), section 2, p. 9.
  Interview with Mike Nichols.

"Visas for the Treppers." New York Times (13 January 1972),
p. 40.
  Letter to the editor, signed by Hellman, John Hersey,
and five others, protesting Poland's refusal to grant visas
to Leopold Trepper and his wife for emigration to Israel.
Trepper's activities during World War II, the letter
states, "contributed substantially" to its shortening and
"cost the German Army the lives of 200,000 soldiers."

"Baby Cries." New York Times (21 January 1973), section 2,
p. 18.
  Brief letter to the drama editor defending actress
Barbara Harris.

Excerpts from Pentimento: "Man of Unnecessary Things."
Atlantic, 231 (June 1973), 56-62+; "Turtle." Esquire, 79
(June 1973), 146-49+; "Julia." Esquire, 80 (July 1973),

95-101+; "Theatre Pictures." Esquire, 80 (August 1973),
64-68+; "Flipping for a Diamond." New York Review of
Books, 20 (20 September 1973), 33-34; "Death Ain't What You
Think." The Times [London] (6 April 1974), 9.

Review of H. G. Wells and Rebecca West, by Gordon N. Ray. New
York Times Book Review (13 October 1974), pp. 4-5.

"A Scene from an Unfinished Play." New Republic, 171 (30
November 1974), 35-39.

"For Truth, Justice and the American Way." New York Times (4
June 1975), p. 39; "On Jumping into Life." Mademoiselle,
81 (August 1975), 166-67.
    Identical reprints of Hellman's commencement address at
Barnard College, 14 May 1975.

"Plain Speaking with Mrs. Carter." Rolling Stone, no. 226 (18
November 1976), 43-45.
    Interview with Rosalynn Carter.

Adaptations by Others
of Hellman's Works

FILMS

Watch on the Rhine. Screenplay by Dashiell Hammett, with
additional scenes and dialogue by Lillian Hellman. 1943.
In Best Film Plays of 1943-1944. Edited by John Gassner
and Dudley Nichols. New York and London: Garland
Publishing, Inc., 1977.

Another Part of the Forest. Screenplay by Vladimir Pozner.
1948.

The Children's Hour. Screenplay by John Michael Hayes. Released in England as The Loudest Whisper. The second
screen version of Hellman's play. 1962.

Toys in the Attic. Screenplay by James Poe. 1963.

Julia. Screenplay by Alvin Sargent. Based on the "Julia"
chapter of Pentimento. 1977.

OPERA

Regina. Adapted by Marc Blitzstein from The Little Foxes.
1949. New York: Schappel and Company, 1954. Recorded by
the New York City Opera, 1970: Columbia Odyssey #Y3 35236.
New York premiere: 31 October 1949.

Writings About Lillian Hellman, 1934-1979

1934

1 ANDERSON, JOHN. "How Child's Lie Brought Ruin to 2 Teachers' Lives Told in Play." New York Evening Journal (21 November).
    The Children's Hour provides "an adult, literate and interesting evening among the drama's morbid tragedies."

2 ANON. "Current Entertainment: The Children's Hour." Newsweek [sic], 4 (1 December), 22.
    Brief listing of The Children's Hour as a recommended play, in which "the maligned teachers fight against their fate."

3 ANON. Photo. Literary Digest, 118 (29 December), 22.
    Scene from The Children's Hour.

4 ANON. "The Theatre: New Plays in Manhattan." Time, 24 (3 December), 24.
    Review of The Children's Hour says Hellman has learned how to put a play together. "She is also wise to the arcane criminality of childhood, to the no less delicate subject of female homosexuality."

5 ANON. "The Thunderbolt of Broadway." Literary Digest, 118 (1 December), p. 20.
    Calls The Children's Hour a terrifying and ennobling experience. "There have not been in the theater in years any two characters more tragic than the two teachers whose lives are burned down around them by the evil of the wicked child."

6 ATKINSON, BROOKS. "Children's Hour." New York Times (2 December), section 10, p. 1.
    Sunday analysis of The Children's Hour appreciates the play as "stinging tragedy," written with economy and force. Atkinson objects to the play's ending, however, and urges

1934

Hellman to recognize that she has allowed craft to trifle
with her theme.

7 _____. "The Play." New York Times (21 November), p. 23.
Praises The Children's Hour as a "venomously tragic"
play but complains that it should conclude before the
pistol shot and long arm of coincidence arrive on stage in
the final fifteen minutes. Until that final scene, The
Children's Hour "is one of the most straightforward, driv-
ing dramas of the season, distinguished chiefly for its
characterization of little Mary."

8 BENCHLEY, ROBERT. "The Theatre: Good News." New Yorker, 10
(1 December), 34, 36, 38.
Review of The Children's Hour. Although the play has
too many endings and tends to pile up tragedy upon tragedy
in the fashion of O'Neill, it is finely and bravely written. Until the last minutes, The Children's Hour contains
"not one second when you can let your attention wander,
even if you wanted to."

9 BROWN, JOHN MASON. "The Play." New York Evening Post
(November 21).
Review of The Children's Hour. It is a frank, poignant
play that is interestingly written, but the second act is
unbelievable and the third needs drastic cutting.

10 GABRIEL, GILBERT W. Review of The Children's Hour. New York
American (21 November).
Calls it a play of "extraordinary honesty, sensitive-
ness, strength."

11 GARLAND, ROBERT. "Children's Hour a Moving Tragedy." New
York World-Telegram (21 November).
Finds The Children's Hour "an ardent and arresting study
in abnormality."

12 HAMMOND, PERCY. "The Theaters." New York Herald Tribune (21
November), p. 16.
Considers The Children's Hour a "sound tragedy," told
with "honest audacity and honest craftsmanship." Skillful
devices to elicit suspense are subordinated to sincerity.

13 _____. "The Theaters: Perils of the Advanced Drama." New
York Herald Tribune (2 December), section 2, pp. 1, 5.
Recommends reading the published edition of The
Children's Hour as further evidence that it is a "first-
class drama that illustrates, in a thoughtful and

disturbing manner, the mysterious and tragic ways of a maiden and another maiden." Few scenes in recent drama compare to that in which the two heroines confront their accusers. Still, "even the most hardened playgoer may find the theme affronting."

14 KAUF[MAN, WOLF]. Review of The Children's Hour. Variety (27 November).
    "A splendid piece of dramaturgy with the added distinction of being good theatre"; one of the strongest candidates for the Pulitzer Prize.

15 KRUTCH, JOSEPH WOOD. "Drama: The Heart of a Child." Nation, 139 (5 December), 656-57.
    Review of The Children's Hour. The first two acts are powerful and gripping in their presentation of Mary Tilford, upon whom audience attention is focused. Her disappearance from the play results in a boring, improbable third act which seems not to have been "the real conclusion of the play as previously developed." The play must have started as a "story of two girls wrongly accused of Lesbian love. In the writing, what was originally intended as merely a device to precipitate the situation developed into the principal action without the author's becoming fully aware of the fact. Hence this author never noticed that the last act was the last act of the play as originally conceived instead of being, as it should have been, the last act of the play as actually written."

16 LOCKRIDGE, RICHARD. "The New Play." New York Sun (21 November).
    The Children's Hour is "a sensitively written tragedy" of biting irony.

17 POLLOCK, ARTHUR. "The Theater." Brooklyn Daily Eagle (21 November).
    Finds The Children's Hour an arresting play--bold, honest, and superbly done.

18 RUHL, ARTHUR. "Second Nights." New York Herald Tribune (25 November), section 10, p. 1.
    The Children's Hour is completely engrossing for its first two acts.

19 WINCHELL, WALTER. "Tense Drama at Elliott a New Hit." New York Daily Mirror (21 November).
    Reviews The Children's Hour. Considers it a fine and intelligent play. "Movie possibilities: Hardly." Its

1934

author, "who has confined her craftsmanship to some
articles in the magazines and the literary review pages of
the Sunday newspapers, is a New York lass, whose talented
mind threatened long ago to demand recognition in the
theatre. This morning finds her perched high on the
pedestal because of her fine play."
Reprinted 1952.37.

20 YOUNG, STARK. Review of The Children's Hour. New Republic
81 (19 December), 169.
The first two acts command the audience's strict attention but the last act lapses into "adolescent banality."

1935

1 ANON. "American Play Banned." New York Times (12 March), p.
24.
Brief item reporting the banning of The Children's Hour
in London by the Lord Chamberlain.

2 ANON. "Boston Sued on Play Ban." New York Times (27
December), p. 15.
Item reporting lawsuit against Boston censors of The
Children's Hour.

3 ANON. "Censorship Conflict in Theater." Literary Digest, 120
(28 December), 20.
Discusses censorship controversy surrounding The
Children's Hour. Photo of Hellman.

4 ANON. "Children's Hour Ban Extended." New York Times (18
December), p. 33.
Item reporting denial of a permit to perform The
Children's Hour in Beverly, Massachusetts.

5 ANON. "Children's Hour Banned in Boston." New York Times
(15 December), p. 42.
Report of the banning of The Children's Hour by the
Boston Board of Censors.

6 ANON. "Cinema." Time, 26 (16 September), 61-62.
Review of The Dark Angel. "It is notable for the fine
acting of its three attractive principals, a superior
screen script and a climax which deserves a place on that
roll of honor and profit which includes such classics as
the life-preserver sequence in Cavalcade, the dance of the

coffee rolls in The Gold Rush, the heroine's suicide in
Anna Karenina."

7 ANON. "Continuing the Full Saga of Drama's Enterprise." New
York Times (17 November), section 9, p. 3.
Discussion of The Children's Hour's completion of one
year on Broadway. Emphasizes the relative absence of complaints by theatergoers against the play's controversial
nature.

8 ANON. "Current Plays in New York: The Children's Hour."
Stage, 12 (January), 3.
Laudatory review of The Children's Hour. Despite flaws
in the last act, the play offers "one of Broadway's most
literate and exciting evenings." It is a "haunting and
gnawing play."

9 ANON. "Dark Angel: Tears with Sound at Demand Performance."
News-week [sic], 6 (7 September), 22-23.
Reviews The Dark Angel, calling it an intelligently
directed version of the sentimental story.

10 ANON. "Excerpta from the Critics' Observations on The Recent
Plays." Stage, 12 (January), 52.
Briefly quotes from reviews of The Children's Hour in
the New Yorker, the New York Herald Tribune, and the New
York American.

11 ANON. "Fight Boston Play Ban." New York Times (16 December),
p. 22.
Quotes Hellman's response to the Boston banning of The
Children's Hour.

12 ANON. Item. Stage, 12 (March), 8.
Includes photo of Hellman.

13 ANON. Item. Stage, 12 (April), 6-7.
Illustrated excerpt from The Children's Hour.

14 ANON. Item. Theatre Arts Monthly, 19 (March), 200-201.
Illustrated excerpt from The Children's Hour.

15 ANON. Item. Vanity Fair, 43 (February), 31.
Photo of Hellman.

16 ANON. "London Success Seen for Children's Hour." New York
Times (15 March), p. 24.

1935

>   Item relating to the banning of The Children's Hour in
>   London.

17 ANON. "The New Books: The Children's Hour." Saturday Review
    of Literature, 11 (2 March), 523.
        Reviews the published text of The Children's Hour. A
    difficulty of the play, less apparent in the script than on
    the stage, is presented by the disappearance of the school-
    girls in the last act. "Miss Hellman feels the need, evi-
    dently, of showing the tragic results of the child's un-
    founded accusations, but has not been able to do this
    without slowing up and clogging action which, up until the
    end of the second act, marches straight ahead. The play is
    not for children but is decidedly a contribution to the
    adult theatre."

18 ANON. "On the Current Screen." Literary Digest, 120 (14
    September), 33.
        Review of The Dark Angel and short feature article on
    Hellman. The screenplay, on which Hellman collaborated
    with Mordaunt Shairp, is sincerely touching without being
    mawkish. The brief outline of her career notes: "A slim,
    reddish blonde, Miss Hellman wrote the role of the satanic
    adolescent, Mary Tilford, who creates the tragic havoc of
    The Children's Hour, from her knowledge of children she had
    encountered."

19 ANON. Photo. Vanity Fair, 43 (February), 44.
        Photo of actors in The Children's Hour.

20 ANON. Review of The Dark Angel. Canadian Magazine, 84
    (December), 43.
        Praises The Dark Angel as a film that avoids bathos and
    achieves "tragic authenticity."

21 ANON. Review of The Dark Angel. Daily Film Renter (26
    September).
        Considers The Dark Angel a powerful film.

*22 ANON. Review of The Dark Angel. New Statesman and Nation, 10
     (5 October), 447.
        Cited in The Dramatic Index for 1935, edited by F. W.
    Faxon. See 1936.42.

*23 ANON. Review of The Dark Angel. Saturday Review (London),
     160 (5 October), 288.
        Cited in The Dramatic Index for 1935, edited by F. W.
    Faxon. See 1936.42.

24 ANON. Review of The Dark Angel. Stage, 13 (October), 6.
   Commends the excellent adaptation of The Dark Angel by
   Hellman and Mordaunt Shairp. "They have gained the most
   from understatement, many of the scenes being dramatically
   gripping for the reason that little is said or done."

25 ANON. Review of The Dark Angel. The Times [London] (26
   September).
   Calls The Dark Angel a skillful assault on the emotions.

26 ANON. "Summer's Children." New York Times (20 January),
   section 10, p. 2.
   Feature article on the three actresses cast in the major
   roles of The Children's Hour.

27 ANON. "They Stand Out from the Crowd." Literary Digest, 119
   (4 May), 22.
   Brief profile, with photograph, of Hellman, "a leading
   contender for the coveted Pulitzer Prize" for The
   Children's Hour.

28 ANON. "Through the Keyhole: The Children's Hour." Stage, 12
   (January), 28-29.
   Review of The Children's Hour by a high-school junior,
   who compares events in the play to occurrences in her own
   school. Photos of the leading actresses in their roles.

29 BULLARD, F. LAURISON. "Censor Still Rules Boston Theatres."
   New York Times (22 December), section 4, p. 11.
   Discussion of Boston theater censorship, prompted by the
   banning of The Children's Hour.

30 CARROL, SYDNEY W. "Film Notes." Sunday Times [London] (29
   September).
   Rates The Dark Angel a "sure-fire sob story."

31 COOKE, ALISTAIR. "Films of the Quarter." Sight and Sound, 4
   (Autumn), 120-22.
   Includes critical remarks on The Dark Angel. "Beware of
   its 'literate' script. This is just a tribute to the
   general toniness of dialogue, which is meant to deceive you
   into thinking you are seeing a passable film concerned with
   refined issues. A pity that Lillian Hellman should have
   been wasted so. . . ."

32 CRAVEN, THOMAS. "These American Plays: Are They American?"
   Stage, 12 (January), 14-15.

1935

> Praises aspects of The Children's Hour but objects
> strongly to the last act. "Having proved to the satis-
> faction of everyone the innocence of the accused women--the
> excuse for the play's existence--she ends by trying to con-
> vict them, or one of them, of the charges which, in lying
> mouths, caused all the trouble."

33 DIXON, CAMPBELL. Review of The Dark Angel. London Daily
      Telegraph (26 September).
      Evaluates The Dark Angel as a notable film.

34 ELSTON, LAURA. Review of The Dark Angel. Canadian Magazine,
      84 (October), 41-42.
      Calls The Dark Angel a film of great distinction and
      pathos.

35 FAIRWEATHER, D. Review. Theatre World, 24 (November), 236,
      238.
      Reviews The Children's Hour.

36 FAXON, FREDERICK WINTHROP, ed. The Dramatic Index for 1934.
      Boston: F. W. Faxon Company, pp. 51, 121; appendix, p. 30.
      Lists four magazine reviews of The Children's Hour and
      cites a photo from the production in The Literary Digest.

37 GARLAND, ROBERT. "Shumlin's Production Completes First Twelve
      Months of its Notable Run." New York World-Telegram (21
      November).
      Commemorates the first anniversary of The Children's
      Hour.

38 GREEN, E. M. Review. Theatre World, 24 (August), 77.
      An illustrated appreciation of The Children's Hour.

39 GREENE, GRAHAM. Review of The Dark Angel. Spectator, 155 (4
      October), 506.
      The Dark Angel "must be one of the worst films of the
      year." It has been ridiculously praised by other critics
      as "classic tragedy," with "great" acting by Merle Oberon,
      when in fact "ballyhoo has done it."
      Reprinted 1972.16.

40 GRUBER, IDE. "The Playbill." Golden Book Magazine, 21
      (February), 28a.
      Reviews The Children's Hour. The play is so skillfully
      written and acted that "not even the baying censors, unless
      completely demoralized, will find the slightest suggestion
      of bad taste."

41 ISAACS, EDITH. "Without Benefit of Ingenue." Theatre Arts
    Monthly, 19 (January), 9-20.
        Reviews The Children's Hour as one of several new plays.
    Suggests that the first two acts are strong and effective,
    but that Hellman loses control of the inevitable action of
    the play in the third act.

42 KRUTCH, JOSEPH WOOD. "Drama: 'Best Play.'" Nation, 140 (22
    May), 610.
        Argues that The Children's Hour or Clifford Odets's
    Awake and Sing should have won the Pulitzer Prize for
    drama, not The Old Maid, by Zoë Akins. For sheer power and
    originality, Hellman's play is the best of many years. Its
    flaws occur as a result of the child's disappearance in the
    last act and in the playwright's attempt to make us believe
    that we are more interested in the two teachers. "Whatever
    the original intention of the author may have been, it is
    plain enough that the play as it stands is a play about a
    Machiavellian child, not a play about two women falsely
    accused of a Lesbian attachment. But the mistake was made,
    partly at least, because the author could not imagine a
    satisfactory end to the real story and so gave us instead
    the end of a different one."

43 LEJEUNE, C. A. "At the Films." London Observer (29
    September), p. 16.
        Says of The Dark Angel that "this war story of Mr.
    Goldwyn's is so commendably earnest in its intentions and
    so anxious to do right by the players, the moral and the
    English atmosphere that it is impossible not to respect it
    a little."

44 LUCAS, E. V. "At the Pictures." Punch, 189 (9 October), 400.
        Calls The Dark Angel "a skillful compound of sentiment."

45 MANEY, RICHARD. "Even the Keyhole was Absent in the Real
    Children's Hour." New York Herald Tribune (4 August).
        Account of Hellman's source for The Children's Hour,
    William Roughead's Bad Companions.

46 MANTLE, BURNS. "Play Censors Active; Bar Children's Hour in
    London on Radio." New York Daily News (15 March).
        Report on the continuing censorship of The Children's
    Hour.

47 _____, ed. The Best Plays of 1934-35. New York: Dodd, Mead
    and Company, pp. 11, 33-65, 354, 412.

1935

Synopsizes The Children's Hour; also gives cast and
production data and a brief review of Hellman's career.

48 NATHAN, GEORGE JEAN. Review of The Children's Hour. Vanity
    Fair, 43 (February), 37.
        Praises The Children's Hour highly but concludes that
    the suicide of Martha constitutes dubious theater. The
    reappearance of Mrs. Tilford is necessary to the integrity
    of Hellman's theme.

49 NORDEN, HELEN B. "The New Oberon." Vanity Fair, 45
    (October), 47.
        Considers The Dark Angel an effective and moving film.

50 ORME, MICHAEL. "The World of the Kinema." Illustrated London
    News, 187 (5 October), 550.
        Maintains that The Dark Angel is "handsomely staged
    against a variety of backgrounds. . . . It is a polished
    picture, achieving dignity rather than greatness."

51 REED, EDWARD. "New Faces: 1935." Theatre Arts Monthly, 19
    (April), 268-77.
        Includes comments on Hellman and Florence McGee, who
    appears as Mary Tilford in The Children's Hour. Describes
    the careers of both.

52 SENNWALD, ANDRE. "The Screen." New York Times (6 September),
    p. 12.
        Praises the "highly literate" screenplay of The Dark
    Angel by Hellman and Mordaunt Shairp.

53 VERNON, GRENVILLE. Review of The Dark Angel. Commonweal, 22
    (20 September), 499.
        Although the film is uneven, depending as it does on in-
    sufficient motivation and trite story line, The Dark Angel
    contains many poignant episodes and dialogue of distinction
    by Hellman and Mordaunt Shairp, who adapted the play for
    the screen.

54 WALBRIDGE, EARLE. "'Closed Doors.'" Saturday Review of
    Literature, 11 (16 March), 548.
        Maintains, in a letter to the editor, that Hellman is
    indebted to William Roughead's account of an Edinburgh
    scandal (which he reported in Bad Companions) as her source
    for The Children's Hour. Walbridge protests the failure to
    give Roughead credit either in the theater program or the
    printed text of the play.
        See also 1958.17.

55 WATTS, RICHARD, JR. Review of The Dark Angel. New York
Herald Tribune (6 September), p. 10.
The Dark Angel is the "most honest and effective senti-
mental [screen] drama of the season."

56 WYATT, EUPHEMIA VAN RENSSELAER. Review of The Children's
Hour. Catholic World, 140 (January), 466-67.
The suffering caused by hasty judgment—and not the
taboo subject the play touches upon—"is the important content of the tragedy." The final act, though missing the
"terse intensity of the first two," does convey the devastating consequences. At the play's end, Mrs. Tilford
"creeps out, a broken woman, where many an unguarded tongue
might lead us all."

<u>1936</u>

1 ANDERSON, JOHN. "Labor and Family Give Theme to New Play by
Lillian Hellman." New York Evening Journal (16 December).
In Days to Come, Hellman "seems to have a lot on her
mind and practically nothing at all on the stage."

2 ANON. "Children's Hour Ban Brings Slander Suit." New York
Times (4 January).
News report on petition to restrain Boston from banning
The Children's Hour.

3 ANON. "The Children's Hour Is Hailed in London." New York
Times (13 November), p. 27.
Report on successful London opening of the uncensored
production of The Children's Hour at the Gate Theatre
Studio.

4 ANON. "The Children's Hour Is Weighed in Chicago." New York
Times (10 January), p. 17.
Reports on censorship problems with Chicago performances
of The Children's Hour.

5 ANON. "Court Refuses to Halt Ban on Children's Hour." New
York Herald Tribune (30 July).
Brief report on rejection of petition of the play's pro-
ducers for an injunction restraining the Boston banning of
The Children's Hour.

6 ANON. "Disapproved of 'Hour' before He Read or Saw It."
Variety (5 February), p. 54.

1936

Report on hearing in Boston concerning The Children's Hour ban.

7   ANON. "Entertainment." The Times [London] (27 April), p. 12.
Praises the "naturalness" and "spontaneity" of These Three. The leading actors "give the impression of having allowed the camera to spy on their own private feelings."

8   ANON. "Gate Theatre: The Children's Hour." The Times [London] (13 November), p. 14b.
Reviews English production of The Children's Hour. Considers the play serious and skillful in treatment, an absorbing narrative of genuine distinction. Review of The Children's Hour also appears in The Times [London] (14 November), p. 10e, 4th and 5th editions only.

9   ANON. "Gossip of the Rialto." New York Times (29 November), pp. 1-2.
Mentions Days to Come as one of several forthcoming plays about the relationship between capital and labor.

10 ANON. Item. Stage, 13 (September), 59.
Portrait of Hellman.

11 ANON. "Miss Hellman Again." New York Times (13 December), section 11, p. 4.
Feature article on Hellman, several days before the opening of Days to Come.

12 ANON. "On the Current Screen." Literary Digest, 121 (14 March), 22.
Calls These Three a "stunningly told motion-picture." Hellman's changes in The Children's Hour in no way detract from the play's original shape or meaning. Still.

13 ANON. Review of The Children's Hour. New Statesman and Nation, 12 (21 November), 810.
Scorns the Lord Chamberlain's refusal to grant The Children's Hour a license for performance in England and applauds the Gate Theatre's decision to produce the play anyway. The first two acts of The Children's Hour are "entirely, hideously, convincing," but the last act lacks credibility. The play is, finally, "merely painful, because it lacks poetic imagination: we are harrowed but unpurged."

14 ANON. Review of The Children's Hour. Saturday Review
    (London), 162 (21 November), 671.
        Reviews London production of The Children's Hour.

15 ANON. Review of The Children's Hour. Stage, no. 2903 (19
    November), p. 5.
        Reviews London production of The Children's Hour at the
    Gate Theatre. This is a fine production of a well-con-
    structed and neatly written play. However, Mary is clearly
    mentally ill and the two teachers should have recognized
    this fact.

16 ANON. Review of These Three. New Statesman and Nation, 11
    (2 May), 668.
        Regards These Three as a "sultry and admirable film."

17 ANON. Review of These Three. News-week [sic], 7 (21 March),
    24.
        Despite some sugar-coating, the screen adaptation of
    The Children's Hour, These Three, is, "in its own way, as
    adult, moving and relentlessly dramatic as the play that
    fostered it."

18 ANON. Review of These Three. Time, 27 (30 March), 33.
        Praises the screen adaptation of The Children's Hour
    highly. The "trivial change" in These Three to a hetero-
    sexual triangle actually strengthens the story.

19 ANON. Review. Revue Politique et Littéraire (Revue Bleue)
    [Paris], 74 (3 October), 675-77.
        Critical references to The Children's Hour, adapted in
    Paris as Les Innocentes, by André Bernheim.

20 ANON. "Stage and Screen: Strike Breakers." Literary Digest,
    122 (26 December), 22-23.
        Agrees with generally negative critical reaction to
    Days to Come. Says Hellman is unable to decide whether her
    sympathies lie with Andrew Rodman or his workmen. The
    central theme is lost because excessive attention is paid
    to the bored Mrs. Rodman.

21 ANON. "These Three." Canadian Magazine, 85 (April), 58.
        Reports on cast and plot of These Three.

22 ANON. "Whisper Opposed in Play." New York Times (30
    January), p. 14.
        Item on Boston banning of The Children's Hour and legal
    action taken in response.

1936

23 ATKINSON, BROOKS. "The Play." New York Times (16 December),
   p. 35.
      Review of Days to Come. The play is laboriously writ-
   ten, with confusing plots and counterplots. The tone is
   bitter and Hellman never comes sufficiently to grips with
   any of the subjects she raises.

24 BEEBE, LUCIUS. "An Adult's Hour Is Miss Hellman's Next
   Effort." New York Herald Tribune (12 December), Drama
   Section, p. 1.
      Interview with Hellman just before the opening of Days
   to Come. She compares writing for theater and film and
   discusses the new play: "It's the family I'm interested
   in principally; the strike and social manifestations are
   just backgrounds. It's a story of innocent people on both
   sides who are drawn into conflict and events far beyond
   their comprehension. It's the saga of a man who started
   something he cannot stop, a parallel among adults to what
   I did with children in The Children's Hour."

25 BERNHEIM, ANDRÉ. "Une Pièce en Trois Actes: Les Innocentes,
   par Lillian Hellman; adaptée de l'anglais par André
   Bernheim." L'Illustration (Paris), no. 4879 (5 September).
      Supplement to this issue contains complete text of
   Bernheim's French adaptation of The Children's Hour, Les
   Innocentes.

26 BOEHMEL, WILLIAM. Review of These Three. New York World-
   Telegram (19 March).
      Positive review.

27 BROWN, JOHN MASON. "Days to Come Produced at the Vanderbilt
   Theatre." New York Post (16 December), p. 18.
      Days to Come is a "dull, incredible, muddled drama."

28 C.[HURCHILL], D.[OUGLAS] W. "Potpourri from the Wonder City."
   New York Times (1 March), section 9, p. 4.
      Says Hellman has transferred the tragedy of The
   Children's Hour to the screen in These Three, "without
   losing a particle of its strength." Notes the acclaim the
   film has received in Hollywood.

29 CAMERON, KATE. Review of These Three. New York Daily News
   (19 March).
      Calls These Three a superb film.

30 CARR, PHILIP. "When the Spring Comes to Paris." New York
   Times (7 June), section 9, p. 1.

Reference to the Paris production of Children's Hour, well received by audiences but considered an ordinary melodrama by critics.

31 COLEMAN, ROBERT. Review of Days to Come. New York Daily Mirror (16 December).
    Finds Days to Come inept. The "dialogue is staccato and stuffy."

32 COOKE, ALISTAIR. "Films of the Quarter." Sight and Sound, 5 (Summer), 22-25.
    Laudatory comments on These Three. Objects to the elimination of the lesbianism charge but otherwise praises the film. "William Wyler's direction used the distance between us and the characters for the most effective and bloodless Aristotelian purposes, tracking the camera relentlessly up to their faces when we would rather have escaped from the problem."

33 CREELMAN, ELLEN. Review of These Three. New York Sun (19 March).
    Considers These Three a magnificent film of a magnificent play.

34 CREWE, REGINA. Review of These Three. New York American (19 March).
    Says the film version of The Children's Hour surpasses the play.

35 CUNNINGHAM, JAMES. "The Play and Screen: These Three." Commonweal, 23 (3 April), 636.
    Calls These Three "an unusually fine and superbly balanced motion picture." Hellman's shift of plot to accommodate Hollywood censorship actually makes the film's premise more credible.

36 DARLINGTON, W. A. "A Good Banned Play." London Daily Telegraph (13 November).
    Reviews London production of The Children's Hour at the Gate Theatre. Considers it "a very good play." Only the end of the second act is weak.

37 DELEHANTY, THORNTON. Review of These Three. New York Evening Post (19 March).
    Praises the film highly: "a glowingly honest picture."

38 DEXTER, CHARLES. "Strikes and Strikebreakers Viewed by Lillian Hellman." Daily Worker (18 December), p. 7.

1936

Reviews <u>Days to Come</u>. Hellman's good intentions and occasionally incisive dialogue are not enough to enable her "to get under the skin of her characters." She sympathizes with the problems of the worker but is unable to present the plight through his eyes. "Instead Miss Hellman chose to present the problem from the point of view of the slowly rotting capitalist."

39 DIXON, CAMPBELL. "A Child Prodigy." London <u>Daily Telegraph</u> (27 April).
Rave review of <u>These Three</u>.

40 ELSTON, LAURA. "Hot Weather Entertainment." <u>Canadian Magazine</u>, 86 (July), 30.
Includes brief review of <u>These Three</u>, a "remarkable" film.

41 F.[AIRWEATHER], D. C. Review of <u>The Children's Hour</u>. <u>Theatre World</u>, 26 (December), 263-64.
Reviews production of <u>The Children's Hour</u> at the Gate Theatre, London. Attacks the censorship of the play. Says it is "admirably constructed and astonishingly well acted."

42 FAXON, FREDERICK WINTHROP, ed. <u>The Dramatic Index for 1935</u>. Boston: F. W. Faxon Company, pp. 59, 77-78, 139.
Lists articles and profiles on Hellman, <u>The Children's Hour</u> and <u>The Dark Angel</u>.

43 FERGUSON, OTIS. "Films: Yes and No." <u>New Republic</u>, 86 (1 April), 222.
Reviews <u>These Three</u>, "Lillian Hellman's very clever rewrite of her <u>Children's Hour</u>. It makes quite a fair film --nothing extra, but the play itself was no world-beater anyway. While the picture gains in production values, it loses in point, movie morals not being the morals of the legitimate stage by quite a margin."

44 GABRIEL, GILBERT W. Review of <u>Days to Come</u>. <u>New York American</u> (16 December).
The production of <u>Days to Come</u> "gives the generally good texture of Miss Hellman's writing no sheen, no excitement at all."

45 GILBERT, DOUGLAS. "<u>Days to Come</u> Opens at Vanderbilt Theater." <u>New York World-Telegram</u> (16 December).
In <u>Days to Come</u>, Hellman can't decide whether to be Odets or O'Neill. This is more a script than a play.

46 [GREEN,] ABEL. Review of These Three. Variety (25 March).
    These Three is a "thoroughly fine cinematic transmuta-
    tion" of The Children's Hour.

47 GREENE, GRAHAM. Review of These Three. Spectator, 156 (1
    May), p. 791.
        Glowing review of These Three: "I have seldom been so
    moved by a fictional film as by These Three. After ten
    minutes or so of the usual screen sentiment, quaintess and
    exaggeration, one began to watch with incredulous pleasure
    nothing less than life."
        Reprinted 1972.16.

48 HAMMOND, PERCY. "The Theaters." New York Herald Tribune (29
    March).
        Calls These Three an exciting film that doesn't suffer
    from the changes made to bring The Children's Hour to the
    screen.

49 H.[OBSON], H.[AROLD]. "The Week's Theatre." London Observer
    (15 November), p. 17.
        Claims, in a review of the London staging of The
    Children's Hour, that Hellman "commands her material. She
    not merely presents but substantiates her characters. She
    creates tension by fulfilling anticipation and only stam-
    mers when havoc has left its victims to express anguish in
    words."

50 IBEE [PULASKI, JACK]. Review of Days to Come. Variety (23
    December).
        Considers Days to Come a "grim, curiously written" play
    with "little appeal to the average playgoer."

51 KRUTCH, JOSEPH WOOD. "Drama: Plays Pleasant and Unpleasant."
    Nation, 143 (26 December), 769-70.
        Reviews Days to Come. Finds it almost as powerful and
    disturbing as The Children's Hour. While the earlier play
    was "a study of a purely individual problem in abnormal
    psychology," Days to Come appears to have a "definite
    Marxian moral--namely, that men are sundered from one
    another by a difference in class interests between which
    no personal good-will can adjudicate." Both plays are
    clearly by the same author: "Miss Hellman is a specialist
    in hate and frustration, a student of helpless rage, an
    articulator of inarticulate loathings. Ibsen and also
    Chekhov have been mentioned in connection with her plays.
    Strindberg would be nearer, though perhaps still far
    enough from the mark."

1936

52 LAWSON, JOHN HOWARD. <u>Theory and Technique of Playwriting</u>.
New York: G. P. Putnam's Sons, 315 pp.
Contains chapter, "The Obligatory Scene," which analyzes
the rising action, climax, and obligatory scene of <u>The
Children's Hour</u>. "In the relationship between Karen and
Martha, the author strains to find some meaning, some
growth in the story of the two women. She wants something
to <u>happen</u> to her people; she wants them to learn and
change. She fails; her failure is pitilessly exposed in
the climax. But in this failure lies Miss Hellman's great
promise as a playwright."
Reprinted 1949 by G. P. Putnam's Sons.
Reprinted 1960, 1961, 1964, 1965, 1967, 1968, 1969 by
Hill and Wang (Dramabook edition). <u>See</u> 1949.52 and
1960.47.

53 LEJEUNE, C. A. "Films of the Week." London <u>Observer</u> (26
April), p. 18.
Praises <u>These Three</u>. Congratulates Sam Goldwyn for
hiring Hellman to prepare the adaptation of her own play.
She wrote the screenplay "in the same dark and malign mood
as the original, giving it the one little twist that would
satisfy the national conscience."

54 LOCKRIDGE, RICHARD. "The New Play." <u>New York Sun</u> (16
December).
Finds <u>Days to Come</u> "a bad tangle of playwriting."

55 LUCAS, E. V. "At the Pictures." <u>Punch</u>, 190 (13 May), 542-43.
Calls <u>These Three</u> "a concoction as American as <u>Tudor
Rose</u> is English; but not a good sample of the American
brand."

56 MANTLE, BURNS. "Story of a Strike That Shook a Town and
Shattered a Few Souls." New York <u>Daily News</u> (16 December).
<u>Days to Come</u> contains honest purpose and conviction in
the writing but lacks theatrical credibility.

57 MOK, MICHAEL. "The Reporter at the Play." <u>New York Evening
Post</u> (16 December).
Report of celebrities at the opening of <u>Days to Come</u>
and their comments about the play.

58 MORGAN, CHARLES. "American Week in London." <u>New York Times</u>
(29 November), section 12, p. 2.
Brief comments on London opening of <u>The Children's
Hour</u>. Doubts that the play will have wide popularity
because of its "burden of gloom."

59 NATHAN, GEORGE JEAN. The Theatre of the Moment. New York:
   Alfred A. Knopf, pp. 16, 248-50.
   Discusses The Children's Hour. Except for the dubiously
   theatrical suicide, critical arguments against the play are
   unjustified. Hellman's reintroduction "of the apologetic
   grandmother and the explanation of the brat's malfeasance"
   are essential to the integrity of her theme. "What she has
   written is necessary."

60 NICOLL, ALLARDYCE. Film and Theatre. London: George C.
   Harrap and Company, 255 pp.
   Chapter five contains a brief but interesting reference
   to The Children's Hour. "Thousands have gone to The
   Children's Hour and come away fondly believing that what
   they have seen is life; they have not realised that here
   too the familiar stock figures, the type characterisations,
   of the theatre have been presented before them in modified
   forms. From this the drama cannot escape; little possi-
   bility is there of its delving deeply into the recesses of
   the individual spirit."
   Reprinted 1972.28 and 1974.33.

61 NUGENT, FRANK. "The Screen." New York Times (19 March), p.
   22.
   These Three, Hellman's screen adaptation of The
   Children's Hour, lacks the bitter tone of tragedy present
   in the original, but Hellman has brilliantly overcome the
   censorship problems in her screenplay. In spite of the
   omission of Martha's unnatural affection for Karen, the
   heart of the original has been retained, resulting in a
   "capital" film.

62 _____. "These Three, Those Five." New York Times (22 March),
   section 11, p. 3.
   Sunday review of These Three. Rates the film as "one
   of the finest screen dramas in years."

63 ORME, MICHAEL. "The World of the Kinema." Illustrated London
   News, 188 (2 May), 778.
   Considers These Three "somewhat sentimental" but praises
   the production.

64 PELSWICK, ROSE. Review of These Three. New York Evening
   Journal (19 March).
   Praises These Three as a superior film.

1936

65 POLLOCK, ARTHUR. "The Theater." Brooklyn Daily Eagle (16
    December).
        Reviews Days to Come. Hellman's attempts at something
    intellectual have resulted in "a ponderous drama hardly
    worth its weight in ideas."

66 PURDOM, C. B. "Plays of the Month." Drama, 15, no. 3
    (December), 33-34.
        Discusses Gate Theatre Studio (London) production of
    The Children's Hour. The play should be seen for its
    "exposure of the cruelty of human beings to each other."

67 QUINN, ARTHUR HOBSON. A History of the American Drama from
    the Civil War to the Present Day. New York: Appleton-
    Century-Crofts, pp. 300-301, 359.
        Briefly discusses The Children's Hour. Calls Hellman "a
    much more talented playwright" than Clifford Odets. Quinn
    admires her mastery of exposition but criticizes the play's
    unbelievability.

68 TANNER, JUANITA. "They Know Their Heroines." Independent
    Woman, 15 (March), 74-75.
        General discussion of portrayals of women on stage.
    Includes photo of Hellman. Magazine later renamed National
    Businesswoman.

69 TAYLOR, ALEXANDER. "Sights and Sounds." New Masses, 22 (29
    December), 27.
        Review of Days to Come. Hellman's attempt to dramatize
    "those twin phenomena of capitalist society, the outbreak
    of class strife and the decay of human relations in the
    bourgeois stratum," is a much better play than its five-day
    run would seem to indicate. The play lacks dramatic unity
    but "taken as a portent, it suggests very interesting
    things from her in the future."

70 VAN DOREN, MARK. "Films." Nation, 142 (15 April), 492.
        Considers These Three a rather successful adaptation of
    The Children's Hour. It does not matter much that the
    "supposed sin is modified to mere adultery."

71 VERSCHOYLE, DEREK. Review of The Children's Hour. Spectator,
    157 (20 November), 905.
        Calls the production of The Children's Hour, at the Gate
    Theatre, London, after denial of a license, admirable. The
    play's censorship problems are absurd as the emphasis is
    not on Martha's love for Karen but on the "criminality of
    inventing gossip about innocent people."

72 WATTS, RICHARD, JR. Review of These Three. New York Herald
   Tribune (19 March), p. 16.
       "Miss Lillian Hellman has wrought a stirring, mature and
   powerful motion picture that is in every way worthy of its
   celebrated original, and perhaps, in one or two ways, sur-
   passes it." Changes made in the plot of The Children's
   Hour do not weaken These Three as a film. Rather, they
   give the film "a creative vitality of its own which keeps
   it from ever seeming a mere photographic carbon copy of
   the drama upon which it was based."

73 _____. "The Theaters." New York Herald Tribune (16
   December), p. 22.
       Reviews Days to Come. Hellman is saying that class war
   is inevitable in a capitalistic society but its victims are
   of both classes. Her literary, economical style, provocative theme, and occasionally dramatic sequences do not
   compensate for a preponderance of confused, ineffective
   scenes and novelistic dialogue.

74 YOUNG, STARK. Review of Days to Come. New Republic, 89 (30
   December), 274.
       Days to Come, "lumpy with dramas not written," fails to
   overcome its stylistic hurdles. "It exhibits a combination
   of stage writing that is elliptical and stage writing that
   is expressionistic."

1937

1 ANON. "All Over the Lot." Stage, 14 (September), 41.
   Photos from Dead End.

2 ANON. "Cinema: Dead End." Time, 30 (6 September), 61-62.
   Hellman's adaptation of Dead End for the screen "enlarges the play's design, intensifies its mood, sharpens
   its implications." Still.

3 ANON. Item. Vogue, 89 (1 January), 54.
   Portrait of Hellman.

4 ANON. "Just Like the Movies." Literary Digest, 124 (11
   December), 4.
       Cites the dangerous influence of Dead End on children
   in a New York neighborhood, who imitated events in the
   film. Argues that all films should not be open to viewers
   of all ages.

1937

This issue of Literary Digest may be cited as Digest, 1
(11 December).

5 ANON. "MacLeish on Spain." Cinema Arts, 1 (September).
    Interview with Archibald MacLeish concerning The
    Spanish Earth.

6 ANON. "Movie of the Week: Dead End." Life, 3 (30 August),
    62-64.
    Photos and laudatory comments. Dead End has "all the
    punch of the play, plus a realism and intimacy which only
    the screen can give."

7 ANON. Review of Dead End. Scholastic [High School Teacher
    Edition], 31 (25 September), 36.
    Says the film version of Dead End will move audiences
    to "fight for slum clearance and better housing condi-
    tions." Becomes Senior Scholastic with edition of 6 March
    1943.

8 ANON. Review of Dead End. Stage, 14 (September), 6.
    Brief review of Dead End, with a listing of screen
    credits. Praises the "grim and arresting photoplay."

9 ANON. Review of Dead End. The Times [London] (22 November).
    Calls screen adaptation of Dead End a powerful attack
    on social evils.

10 ANON. Review of The Spanish Earth. The Sunday Times [London]
    (9 November), p. 14.
    Reviews The Spanish Earth.

11 ANON. Review of The Spanish Earth. Time, 30 (23 August),
    48-49.
    Praises the film's documentary artistry, its concern to
    tell the story of the Spanish revolution in terms of people
    rather than in terms of action. "Not since the silent
    French film, The Passion of Joan of Arc, has such dramatic
    use been made of the human face."

12 ANON. Review of The Spanish Earth. The Times [London] (5
    November), p. 12.
    Comments mainly on Hemingway's romantic narration for
    the film. Finds it at odds with the nature of the tragedy
    depicted.

13 ANON. "Screen: New York Tenements Provide Melodrama and
    Moral." News-week [sic], 10 (28 August), 24.

Hellman's screenplay and Wyler's direction have resulted in "an almost literal transcription" of Dead End. The film is forceful and realistic. Photo.

14 ANON. "The Youngsters of Dead End." Vogue, 90 (1 November), 91.
    Item, with photo, on the film version of Dead End.

15 BAIRD, THOMAS. Review of The Spanish Earth. Sight and Sound, 6 (Autumn), 145-46.
    Praises The Spanish Earth as "an intelligent realisation of the power of documentary."

16 BARNES, HOWARD. Review of Dead End. New York Herald Tribune (25 August), p. 10.
    Hellman's resourceful screen adaptation of Dead End concentrates on the melodrama. The plot has been made more taut and unified, but Dead End continues to be a piece of clever reporting rather than a dramatically distinguished work.

17 _____. Review of The Spanish Earth. New York Herald Tribune (21 August), p. 4.
    The Spanish Earth is "the most powerful and moving documentary ever screened."

18 BATES, MARY E., ed. The Dramatic Index for 1936. Boston: F. W. Faxon Company, pp. 55, 74, 137, 297; appendix, p. 39.
    Lists reviews of The Children's Hour, Days to Come, and These Three.

19 CAMERON, KATE. Review of Dead End. New York Daily News (25 August).
    Positive review.

20 CREELMAN, ELLEN. "The New Talkie." New York Sun (25 August).
    Reviews Dead End. Calls the film distinguished, better than the play.

21 CHURCHILL, DOUGLAS W. "Leg Art: Hollywood's New Crisis." New York Times (30 May), section 10, p. 3.
    Discusses the sets and sound effects used in Dead End.

22 CUNNINGHAM, JAMES P. "The Screen." Commonweal, 26 (20 August), 406.
    Praises the screen adaptation of Dead End as a masterful blend of story, acting, direction, and production.

1937

23 ELLIS, PETER. "Sights and Sounds: Joris Ivens's The Spanish
   Earth and Hollywood's Dead End." New Masses, 24 (24
   August), 28.
      Combined review of The Spanish Earth and Dead End.
   Mentions Hellman as one of the scenarists for the documentary, which has been made by Ivens into "a brilliant
   motion picture." Hellman, "who has written a swell script
   [for Dead End], preserves the minor motif of police brutality in a strike situation which was in playwright [Sidney]
   Kingsley's original."

24 FERGUSON, DONITA. "Movie of the Week: Dead End." Literary
   Digest, 124 (4 September), 30.
      Hellman's screenplay and William Wyler's direction
   necessarily tone down Dead End for the screen. Certain key
   scenes shine through, however.
      This issue of Literary Digest may be cited as Digest, 1
   (4 September).

25 _____. "Movie of the Week: The Spanish Earth." Literary
   Digest, 124 (11 September), 33.
      The Spanish Earth "is a valiant failure," worth seeing
   for its picture of peasant life and for its artistic
   merits, but not tough enough as a Loyalist plea. "Hollywood war pictures have laid the gore on so thickly that it
   now takes an overdose of dynamite to stir our emotional
   stumps." Photos.
      This issue of Literary Digest may be cited as Digest, 1
   (11 September).

26 FERGUSON, OTIS. "'And There Were Giants on the Earth.'" New
   Republic, 92 (1 September), 103-104.
      Reviews The Spanish Earth and Dead End. Praises The
   Spanish Earth as a testimonial to the way people can
   transcend their limitations in response to the demands of
   their time. Dead End on the screen is a vivid, truthful
   film.
      Reprinted 1971.9.

27 FLIN [JOHN]. Review of Dead End. Variety (4 August).
      Calls the film version of Dead End a nearly literal
   translation. Hellman has changed the play only in "heroiz-
   ing" the character of Dave.

28 GALWAY, PETER. "The Movies." New Statesman and Nation, 14
   (13 November), 795.

Reviews The Spanish Earth. Considers it a "sensational" film that chronicles events which "are themselves sensational."

29 _____. "The Movies." New Statesman and Nation, 14 (20 November), 836.
Reviews Dead End. William Wyler's direction, Gregg Toland's photography, and Lillian Hellman's dialogue "are alike swift, cunning and aware of beauty in the heart of ugliness."

30 GREENE, GRAHAM. Review of Dead End. Night and Day (25 November).
Despite some flaws, Dead End is "one of the best pictures of the year."
Reprinted 1972.16. (Seen in reprinted form only.)

31 LAWSON, JOHN HOWARD. "A Comparative Study of The Children's Hour and Days to Come." New Theatre, 4 (March), 15-16, 60-61.
Argues that Days to Come is almost identical to The Children's Hour in its dual structural pattern and that the failure of Days stems from Hellman's struggle "with psychological and technical problems which go beyond the present scope of her social thinking." Both plays suffer from an Ibsenite view of society which suggests that the recognition of moral decay is in itself "an ethical act." Photo of Hellman.

32 LOCKRIDGE, RICHARD. "The Stage in Review." New York Sun (11 September).
Compares stage and screen versions of Dead End. Faults the film.

33 LUCAS, E. V. "At the Pictures." Punch, 193 (1 December), 596.
Gives a mostly negative review to Dead End, but argues that "the real persons" of the film "are the hooligans. . . . It is they who 'put' this squalid drama 'over.'"

34 McCALEB, KENNETH. Review of Dead End. New York Daily Mirror (22 August).
Calls Dead End a fine film.

35 McMANUS, JOHN T. "Down to Earth in Spain." New York Times (25 July), section 10, p. 4.
Feature article on The Spanish Earth and its director, Joris Ivens.

1937

36 _____. "East River Chiaroscuro." New York Times (29 August),
section 10, p. 3.
   Sunday analysis of Dead End. Applauds the film, including Hellman's screenplay, as an "important addition to
the roster of fine motion pictures."

37 _____. "Realism Invades Gotham." New York Times (22 August),
section 10, p. 3.
   Analyzes The Spanish Earth, "a great propaganda picture,
bitter and hard and unrelenting in its hatred of Spain's
enemies."

38 _____. "The Screen." New York Times (21 August), p. 7.
   Reviews The Spanish Earth. Calls the film a compelling
appeal for Spanish democracy.

39 _____. "The Screen." New York Times (25 August), p. 25.
   Reviews Dead End. Hellman's screenplay simplifies the
character of Dave for the film audience and the salty language of the play has been necessarily cleaned up, but
curtain calls are in order for all concerned. Dead End is
a forceful film brought smoothly to the screen.

40 MANTLE, BURNS. Review of Dead End. New York Daily News (5
September).
   Compares stage and screen versions of Dead End.

41 _____, ed. The Best Plays of 1936-37. New York: Dodd, Mead
and Company, pp. 9, 441, 513.
   Gives cast and synopsis of Days to Come (an "important
failure"; "a thoughtful and provocative study of the labor
versus capital problem").

42 NATHAN, GEORGE JEAN. "Theater." Scribner's Magazine, 102
(November), 66, 68.
   Acerbic discussion of dramatists who desert the stage
for Hollywood and give lip service to the superiority of
film over theater. Exempts American playwrights of true
merit, including Hellman, from this group, suggesting that
it is possible to write for both media without falling
prey to the phony elevation of film over drama. Also a
brief mention of Dead End.

43 NUGENT, FRANK S. "Home Is the Sailor." New York Times (12
September), section 11, p. 3.
   Briefly assesses the film version of Dead End.

44 ORME, MICHAEL. "The World of the Kinema." Illustrated London
    News, 191 (27 November), 955.
        Praises the screen adaptation of Dead End as "a Zola-
    esque slice of life, vibrant, violent and wholly concerned
    with the bitter truth. Its relentless realism is balanced
    by the film's significance and its undeviating develop-
    ment."

45 PLATT, DAVID. "Dead End Scores Slum Conditions." Daily
    Worker (27 August), p. 7.
        Calls Dead End an accurate, penetrating, powerful study
    of slum life.

46 PRYOR, THOMAS M. "Local Boys Make Good in Films." New York
    Times (22 August), section 10, p. 3.
        Feature article on the New York boys cast as the "kids"
    in Dead End.

47 SELDES, GILBERT. Review of Dead End. Scribner's Magazine,
    102 (November), 63-64.
        Criticizes the screen adaptation of Dead End for failing
    to translate the play into cinematic terms.
        Reprinted with minor excisions, 1972.34.

48 SHUMLIN, HERMAN. "On Billing." New York Times (3 January),
    section 10, p. 3.
        Letter to the drama editor about contractual agreements
    between Hellman and Shumlin for Days to Come.

49 VERNON, GRENVILLE. "The Play and Screen: Days to Come."
    Commonweal, 25 (1 January), 276.
        Days to Come suffers from Hellman's confusion between
    fiction and drama. "Had she contented herself with making
    her play merely a melodrama with a purpose, it is alto-
    gether possible that she would have turned out a very
    workmanlike job. Unfortunately, she wanted to make it
    more than this: the studies also of a woman seeking for an
    ideal, of an idealistic labor leader, of a well-meaning
    employer deceived by his wife, and of an acidulous old
    maid."

50 WINSTEN, ARCHER. Review of Dead End. New York Post (25
    August).
        Says the film version of Dead End is similar to the
    play. Reviews it positively.

51 WRIGHT, BASIL. Review. Spectator, 159 (12 November), 844.
        Reviews The Spanish Earth.

1937

52 _____. Review. Spectator, 159 (3 December), 992.
Reviews Dead End.

53 _____. Review of The Spanish Earth. World Film News
[London] (December).
Considers The Spanish Earth a great film.
Reprinted 1979.19.

1938

1 BATES, MARY E., ed. The Dramatic Index for 1937. Boston: F. W.
Faxon Company, pp. 69, 124, 246.
Lists reviews of Dead End and The Spanish Earth.

2 FARR, WILLIAM. "Documentaries." Sight and Sound, 6 (Winter
1937-38), 201.
Considers The Spanish Earth a noble tribute to the
Spanish people and a notable contribution to filmmaking.

3 FLEXNER, ELEANOR. American Playwrights: 1918-1938. New
York: Simon and Schuster, pp. 7, 18, 22, 89.
Brief references to Hellman as an emerging dramatist
and film writer.

4 GREENE, GRAHAM. "Movie Parade, 1937." Sight and Sound, 6
(Winter 1937-38), 206.
Refers briefly to Dead End as a "magnificent picture."

5 HOLMES, WINIFRED. "Forty Years." Sight and Sound, 7
(Summer), 57-59.
Briefly discusses, in an analysis of filmmaking in
Holland, the career of Joris Ivens, director of The
Spanish Earth.

6 MANTLE, BURNS. Contemporary American Playwrights. New York:
Dodd, Mead and Company, pp. 180-81.
Comments on The Children's Hour (a "vividly tragic
drama") and briefly describes Hellman's earlier career.

7 PAGE, ALAN. "Memorable and Not So Memorable." Sight and
Sound, 6 (Winter 1937-38), 186-87.
Praises the atmosphere and acting of Dead End, but says
too many problems are happily resolved in one day, "a
legacy from the stage version of the film."

1939

1   ANDERSON, JOHN. "The Little Foxes Opens at National Theatre."
    New York Journal-American (16 February).
       Finds The Little Foxes better than The Children's Hour,
    deeply absorbing, thoughtful, exciting.

2   ANON. "Footnotes on Headliners." New York Times (23 April),
    section 4, p. 2.
       Item noting the failure of the New York Drama Critics'
    Circle to agree on a favorite play of the season, although
    The Little Foxes received six votes. Mentions the critical
    reception of Hellman's earlier plays. Photo.

3   ANON. "Lillian Hellman." Wilson Library Bulletin, 12 (May),
    632.
       Biographical sketch, with photo. Includes brief com-
    ments on the plays.

4   ANON. "Lillian Hellman Buys Estate of 130 Acres." New York
    Times (7 June), p. 43.
       Reports Hellman's purchase of estate at Mount Pleasant,
    New York.

5   ANON. "The Little Foxes." Life, 6 (6 March), front cover,
    70-73.
       Cover photo and photo-essay on Tallulah Bankhead (as
    Regina Giddens) and The Little Foxes. "Against the cold,
    steely force of the year's strongest play, the glitter of
    her acting lights up a whole era of U.S. history."

6   ANON. "Name in Lights." Stage, 16 (15 March), 46.
       Comments on The Little Foxes, calling Hellman "American
    Woman Playwright Number One." The play, in the Ibsen
    tradition, has a "social conscience, universality and a
    timeless theme." Says Hellman first considered "something
    like" Preface or Prelude for a title because The Little
    Foxes "does not end, but begins, at final curtain." Photo.

7   ANON. "New York Stage." The Times [London] (29 March).
       Calls The Little Foxes (New York production) an acid,
    unrelenting portrayal.

8   ANON. "The Theatre: New Play in Manhattan." Time, 33 (27
    February), 38, 40.
       Review of The Little Foxes. "Both the Hubbards and
    their playwright-inquisitor work at a pitch too relentless
    for real life. But it is the special nature of the theatre

to raise emotions to higher power, somewhat simplifying,
somewhat exaggerating, but tremendously intensifying.
Playwright Hellman makes her plot crouch, coil, dart like
a snake, lets her big scenes turn boldly on melodrama.
Melodrama has become a word to frighten nice-nelly playwrights with; but, beyond its own power to excite, it can
stir up genuine drama of character and will. Like the
dramatists of a hardier day, Lillian Hellman knows this,
capitalizes on it, brilliantly succeeds at it." Concludes
with a discussion of Hellman and her plays, praising her as
"a moralist, not a misanthrope." Photos.

9 ATKINSON, BROOKS. "Miss Bankhead Has a Play." New York Times
    (26 February), section 9, p. 1.
        Sunday review of The Little Foxes. Praises the play as
    an excoriating and intense study but criticizes the exces-
    sive contrivance on Hellman's part. If Hellman means "to
    indict rugged individualism as one of the social evils,"
    her own craftsmanship overwhelms her philosophy.
        Reprinted 1947.2.

10 _____. "The Play." New York Times (16 February), p. 16.
        Review of The Little Foxes. The play suffers in com-
    parison to The Children's Hour. A melodramatic exercise
    in malice, it never approaches tragic proportions; its
    contrivances are apparent as is its "Pinero frown of
    fustian morality." Still, The Little Foxes is a "vibrant
    play that works," in large part because it offers splendid
    acting opportunities. "Out of rapacity, Miss Hellman has
    made an adult horror-play."

11 BENCHLEY, ROBERT. "The Theatre: The Little Foxes." New
    Yorker, 15 (25 February), 25.
        The Little Foxes is a "tightly woven, well-conceived,
    and probably very significant contribution to the theatre.
    The fact that it panders in no way to what the public
    might possibly want makes it even better."

12 BLOCK, ANITA. The Changing World in Plays and Theatre.
    Boston: Little, Brown and Company, pp. 22, 120-26, 137,
    139-40, 431.
        Discusses The Children's Hour as a striking, vital play
    that breaks the taboo on stories of homosexuality. "It is
    to Miss Hellman's credit that she makes the crux of her
    play not the question of homosexuality itself, but
    society's savage treatment of the homosexual, arising out
    of cruelly persisting ignorance." Briefly compares
    Hellman's method to O'Neill's.

13 BROWN, JOHN MASON. Review of The Little Foxes. New York
   Post (11 March).
   See 1940.8.

14 BURM. Review of The Little Foxes. Variety (8 February).
   The writing in The Little Foxes is "dynamic and expert"
   but the play finally falls short.

15 CAMBRIDGE, JOHN. "The Little Foxes a Story of Southern
   Aristocrats." Daily Worker (17 February), p. 7.
   Reviews The Little Foxes. The play, with deceptive
   simplicity, conveys universal truths about the rise of
   capitalism. Hellman's best play, The Little Foxes is
   written with a sense of irony although it contains elements of melodrama. It is a drama of "controller power."

16 COLEMAN, ROBERT. "In The Little Foxes Is Good Acting, of
   Grim Play." New York Daily Mirror (16 February).
   The Little Foxes has electric moments but the bitter
   and grim script is on the thin side.

17 FERGUSON, OTIS. "A Play, a Picture." New Republic, 98 (12
   April), 279.
   Review of The Little Foxes. The play is generally
   satisfying but melodramatic and inconclusive. Much of the
   acting is bombastic. Even in a role which allows her to
   dominate a play, Tallulah Bankhead "should not try to be
   Maurice Evans."

18 GASSNER, JOHN. Review of The Little Foxes. One Act Play
   Magazine, 2 (February), 748-49.
   Despite its shortcomings, The Little Foxes is a powerful
   and provocative work.

19 _____. "Stage." Direction, 2 (May-June), 35.
   Brief allusion to The Little Foxes as a "powerful exposé
   of the predatory spirit of our laisser-faire society."

20 _____, ed. Twenty Best Plays of the Modern American Theatre.
   New York: Crown, 874 pp.
   Includes text of The Children's Hour, with commentary.

21 GILDER, ROSAMOND. "The Sweet Creatures of Bombast." Theatre
   Arts, 23 (April), 240-51.
   Includes favorable review of The Little Foxes: "an exciting melodrama" which conveys the belief that "it is not
   so much the vicious capitalistic system which is to blame
   for the evils of this world, as the fact that man is still
   largely unregenerated, still at heart a beast of prey."

1939

22 GREEN, E. M. Review. Theatre World, 32 (July), 35.
    Reviews The Little Foxes.

23 HEALEY, JAMES. Review of The Little Foxes. New York Teacher
    (March).
    Praises the play.

24 HURRIE, WILLIAM G. "The Argentine Republic and Its Film
    Industry." Sight and Sound, 8 (Autumn), 93-96.
    Cites the unpopularity of The Spanish Earth in
    Argentina.

25 IBEE [PULASKI, JACK]. Review of The Little Foxes. Variety
    (22 February).
    The play tells a bitter story which excels in crafts-
    manship.

26 JACOBS, LEWIS. The Rise of the American Film. New York:
    Harcourt, Brace and Company, pp. 449, 490, 514, 529.
    Brief references to three Hellman films: Dead End,
    These Three, The Spanish Earth. Revised editions, 1948,
    1967, 1968.

27 KRONENBERGER, LOUIS. "Greed." Stage, 16 (1 April), 36-37,
    55.
    Compares the nature of evil in The Children's Hour and
    The Little Foxes, praising both plays highly. "The Little
    Foxes denies us all sense of tragedy, offers us nothing--
    as The Children's Hour did--of the tragic sense of life.
    For just that reason The Little Foxes comes through as the
    most effective kind of protest; it sends us out of the
    theatre, not purged, not released, but still aroused and
    indignant."

28 KRUTCH, JOSEPH WOOD. American Drama Since 1918. New York:
    Random House, pp. 130-33.
    Denies that The Children's Hour or The Little Foxes can
    be called "genuine tragedy," as the emotional tensions are
    not resolved in either play. Both works are "striking"
    melodramas which conclude with the triumph of villainy.
    While Hellman's rage is genuine, the plays--skillful as
    they are--offer "fables that are not really suitable
    vehicles for the emotion which they are intended to carry."
    Revised edition, 1957.12.

29 _____. "Unpleasant Play." Nation, 148 (25 February), 244-45.
    The Little Foxes, like Hellman's two earlier plays, is
    an exploration of hateful people in which the curtain falls

with "wrong in the saddle, riding hard." Her technique
resembles that of Ibsen. The Little Foxes is less perfect
than The Children's Hour because "it is less inevitable in
its development and occasionally more melodramatic than it
should be." Yet Hellman "possesses the Ancient Mariner's
gift--one stays in one's seat because one cannot choose
but hear."

30 LOCKRIDGE, RICHARD. "Lillian Hellman's The Little Foxes
    Opens at the National Theater." New York Sun (16
    February).
        Considers The Little Foxes an absorbing and convincing
    play, despite some static passages and a somewhat falter-
    ing last act.

31 McKENNEY, RUTH. Review of The Little Foxes. New Masses, 30
    (28 February), 29-30.
        Considers Little Foxes "one of the great events of this
    or any Broadway season," in which Hellman suggests that the
    American road to riches is paved with thievery, race
    hatred, and government corruption. The story of the
    Hubbards is also "a story of America"; though the play is
    savage, it is not cynical, as "it ends with hope."

32 MANTLE, BURNS. The Best Plays of 1938-39. New York: Dodd,
    Mead and Company, pp. 10, 75-109, 398, 460, 497, 507.
        Praises The Little Foxes highly and gives condensed
    version of the play and production data.

33 _____. "The Little Foxes Taut Drama of a Ruthless Southern
    Family." New York Daily News (16 February).
        Objects, in a review of The Little Foxes, to Hellman's
    inconclusive ending but approves of her uncompromising
    playwriting standards and taut story line. A feeling of
    "impending tragedy" overshadows the action.

34 MOORE, BEATRIX. "Censor the Censor!" Sight and Sound, 7
    (Winter 1938-39), 149.
        Interview with film director G. W. Pabst, who mentions
    Dead End as an example of an American film concerning
    social conditions.

35 NATHAN, GEORGE JEAN. "Theater Week: Dour Octopus."
    Newsweek, 13 (27 February), 26.
        Highly favorable review of The Little Foxes. Hellman
    "indicates a dramatic mind, an eye to character, a funda-
    mental strength, and a complete and unremitting integrity
    that are rare among her native playwriting sex."

1939

Strindberg's influence seems apparent in Hellman's handling
of character, while Ibsen's ghost peers over her shoulder
in the treatment of theme. The play "betrays not an inch
of compromise, not a sliver of a sop to the comfortable
acquiescence of Broadway or Piccadilly." It relies periodically on melodramatics and fails "to invest its explo-
sion with that complete sense of tragic purge," but is
finally "a credit to its author and to American dramatic
writing."
    Reprinted in Nathan's Encyclopaedia of the Theatre,
1940.12.

36 O'HARA, FRANK HURBERT. Today in American Drama. Chicago:
    University of Chicago Press, pp. 83-101.
        Detailed analysis of The Little Foxes, heavily reliant
    on plot synopsis but occasionally penetrating. "The play,
    within the conventional restrictions of a theater-piece
    though it is, seems somehow to have the dimensions of a
    novel--characters fully drawn, circumstances in perspec-
    tive. . . . Behind this play about the Hubbards there
    seems to be another play on a grander scale, depicting the
    rise of industrialism sowing its own seeds of future con-
    fusions . . . and a play about the inefficacy of all those
    who, like Birdie, do not understand the forces which
    threaten their extinction . . . and a play about the dawn
    of some new day when youth will begin life again 'some
    place where people don't just stand around and watch.'"

37 POLLOCK, ARTHUR. "The Theaters." Brooklyn Daily Eagle (16
    February).
        Reviews The Little Foxes, the best of Hellman's plays.
    "She writes like deMaupassant." A rare job all around.

38 ROSS, GEORGE. "Decay of the South Hellman Play Theme." New
    York World-Telegram (16 February).
        Considers The Little Foxes an electrifying play. Com-
    pares its tense narrative to Daphne Du Maurier's Rebecca
    and its melodramatic tricks to those used by Agatha
    Christie to heighten suspense.

39 SILLEN, SAMUEL. "American Writers: 1935 to 1939." New
    Masses, 31 (20 June), 22-24.
        Mentions Hellman as a participant in the Third American
    Writers Congress.

40 VERNON, GRENVILLE. "The Stage and Screen: The Little Foxes."
    Commonweal, 29 (3 March), 525.

Calls The Little Foxes an admirably written and constructed play, not a pleasant one but one that is "about
real people." Tallulah Bankhead gives a "remarkable"
performance: "Her Regina is a figure who might have
stepped out of the pages of Balzac."

41 WALDORF, WILELLA. "The Little Foxes Opens at the National
Theatre." New York Post (16 February).
Negative review of The Little Foxes. The Hubbards "put
on an act that needs only the addition of curled mustachios
and a few hisses from the audience to qualify as something
out of Boucicault."

42 WATTS, RICHARD, JR. "The Theater: Miss Hellman's Play." New
York Herald Tribune (26 February), section 6, pp. 1, 2.
The Little Foxes assaults "the forces in Southern life
that tend toward Fascism when their plunder is endangered.
In addition it is a distinguished drama that makes Miss
Hellman a playwright of distinction." It is, moreover,
the proper antidote to "the plague of Gone With the Wind
romanticism" now sweeping the country.

43 _____. The Theaters." New York Herald Tribune (16 February),
p. 14.
The Little Foxes, a grim, bitter, merciless study, sur-
passes The Children's Hour. Hellman is sympathetic with
Birdie's gentleness but "realizes that there is no intelligence or sense of realism in her" or the class which she
represents. "The one hope she finds is in a newer generation that might combine a trace of the old romanticism with
a great deal of the new hardness." The Little Foxes, with
"Ibsenesque directness," contemplates "the relentless
emergence of a new industrialism from the ashes of a sentimental past, the coming to power of a social order that
lifted itself from the ranks of the one-time poor whites
and used the emotional code of the old South only as a
mask for its ascent." See 1959.8.

44 WEINBERG, HERMAN G. "American Letter." Sight and Sound, 8
(Spring), 6.
Refers to The Spanish Earth.

45 _____. "Herman G. Weinberg Reviews Alexander Nevsky and Two
Other Films." Sight and Sound, 8 (Spring), 6-7.
Mentions The Spanish Earth.

1939

46 WINGE, JOHN W. "The Laughter of the Gods." Sight and Sound,
 7 (Winter 1938-39), 146-48.
  Briefly mentions These Three.

47 WINTER, ELLA. "Screen Writers Close Ranks." New Masses, 33
 (3 October), 27-29.
  Account of attempts by the Screen Writers' Guild to be
  declared bargaining agent for Hollywood writers. Notes
  that Hellman was a member of the SWG bargaining committee.

48 WYATT, EUPHEMIA VAN RENSSELAER. Review of The Little Foxes.
 Catholic World, 149 (April), 87-88.
  The Little Foxes is technically superior to The
  Children's Hour. "It offers keen interest but not much
  pleasure." Tallulah Bankhead's depiction of Regina reminds
  us of Ibsen's Hedda and Rebecca.

1940

1 ANON. "Actors Widen Split on Finn Benefits." New York Times
 (20 January), p. 17.
  Reports the continuing Broadway controversy over benefit
  performances for the Finnish Relief Fund, involving, among
  many others, Hellman and Tallulah Bankhead.

2 ANON. "Benefits for Finns Stir Theatre Row." New York Times
 (19 January), p. 21.
  Reports on the mushrooming controversy over performances
  of Broadway shows for the benefit of the Finnish Relief
  Fund. Cites Herman Shumlin's objections to participation
  by The Little Foxes company and Tallulah Bankhead's contrasting support for Finnish relief.

3 ANON. "Ink-Stained Wretches All." Mademoiselle, 11 (May),
 123.
  Biographical sketches of a number of successful contemporary women, each representing a specific field of
  endeavor (including Hellman, Willa Cather, and Dorothy
  Thompson). Each woman offers advice to aspirants in her
  particular field. Among Hellman's remarks: "Playwrights
  often have collaborators, but they are rarely husbands."
  Photo.

4 ANON. "Lin Yutang Holds 'Gods' Favor China." New York Times
 (10 January), p. 19.

Report on talks given by Hellman and others at Book and Author luncheon, sponsored by American Booksellers' Association and the New York Herald Tribune.

5   ANON. "Miss Hellman and Miss Ferber Discuss Jewish Author's Plight." New York Herald Tribune (10 January).
Reports on Hellman's comments at a luncheon sponsored by the American Booksellers' Association and the New York Herald Tribune. Discussion focused on being a writer and a Jew "in a world where censorship and bigotry appear to be on the increase."

6   ANON. "Sees Finnish Aid Imperiling Peace." New York Times (21 January), p. 27.
News report of Hellman's opposition to benefit per-formances of Broadway plays for Finnish war relief.

7   BATES, MARY E., ed. The Dramatic Index for 1939. Boston: F. W. Faxon Company, pp. 134, 171-72; appendix, p. 50.
Lists profiles of Hellman and reviews of The Little Foxes. Also cites editions of Hellman plays published in 1940, including anthologies.

8   BROWN, JOHN MASON. "Miss Bankhead and The Little Foxes," in his edition of Broadway in Review. New York: Norton and Company, pp. 116-20.
Reprints review of The Little Foxes which appeared in the New York Post (11 March, 1939), 1939.13. Says the play is thoroughly engrossing, brilliantly acted, espe-cially by Tallulah Bankhead as Regina, and superlatively "good theatre." But "it suffers from being far too well contrived for its own enduring health." The audience is seduced into "believing that at almost any minute all of Ibsen's and Strindberg's most unattractive heroes and heroines, having crossed the Atlantic without a sea change, will suddenly bob up on the stage as Sons and Daughters of the Confederacy, in convention met near Atlanta." The play is so expert, so "well-made," that it deludes us into believing that it has "sociological significance and abiding literary importance." Hellman is a genius at the slightly old-fashioned art of plotting. The period set-ting and some commendably valid observations help the storytelling, as does "the way in which she seems to look into the hearts of evil characters and goad these people into action."
Reprinted 1969.14.

1940

9 BUCK, PHILO, JOHN GASSNER, and H. S. ALBERSON. A Treasury of
   the Theatre: An Anthology of Great Plays from Ibsen to
   Odets. 2 Vols. New York: Simon and Schuster, pp. 40,
   894, 1200.
        Brief references to The Children's Hour and The Little
   Foxes.

10 CRITICS' THEATRE REVIEWS, 1940. Volume 1. New York: Critics'
   Theatre Reviews, pp. 490-492.
        Reprints reviews of The Little Foxes from New York
   daily newspapers for 16 February 1939: Daily News, New York
   Times, New York Herald Tribune, New York World-Telegram,
   New York Sun, New York Post.

11 CROWTHER, BOSLEY. "Realistic Stepchild of the Movies." New
   York Times Magazine (25 August), pp. 12-13.
        Discusses developments in documentary filmmaking; in-
   cludes comments on Spanish Earth, with photo.

12 NATHAN, GEORGE JEAN. Encyclopaedia of the Theatre. New
   York: Alfred A. Knopf, pp. 170-72, 427.
        Reprints 1939.35 (pp. 170-72). Additional reference
   (p. 427).

13 NORTON, ELLIOT. Review of The Little Foxes. Boston Post (3
   March).
        Compares The Little Foxes to The Children's Hour.

                              1941

1 [AGEE, JAMES]. Review of The Little Foxes [film]. Time, 38
   (1 September), 86-87.
        Although somewhat static for the screen, The Little
   Foxes is "a memorable portrait of greed." Photo.

2 ALLEN, KELCEY. Review of Watch on the Rhine. Women's Wear
   Daily (2 April).
        Positive reaction.

3 ANDERSON, JOHN. "Watch on the Rhine at the Martin Beck."
   New York Journal and American (2 April).
        Finds Watch on the Rhine "a play which is passionately
   anti-Fascist and often deeply moving, yet which falters
   badly in its craftsmanship and loses its most vivid and
   vigorous points in overwriting."

4 ANON. "Critics' Prize Goes to Watch on Rhine." New York
   Times (23 April), p. 24.
       Names Watch on the Rhine winner of the annual New York
   Drama Critics' Circle Award as best American play.

5 ANON. "Drama Award Presented." New York Times (28 April),
   p. 10.
       Item reporting the formal presentation of the New York
   Drama Critics' Circle Award to Hellman for Watch on the
   Rhine and the ensuing radio broadcast of scenes from the
   play.

6 ANON. "Footnotes on Headliners: Producer." New York Times
   (27 April), section 4, p. 2.
       Names Watch on the Rhine as winner of the Drama Critics'
   Award for best American play. Briefly reviews the career
   of its producer-director, Herman Shumlin, who also produced and directed The Children's Hour and The Little
   Foxes.

7 ANON. "Governor to Shun 'Communist' Forum." New York Times
   (4 October), p. 34.
       Report of controversy between New York Governor Lehman
   and Hellman, cochairman with Ernest Hemingway of a dinner
   forum on Europe Today. Hellman "insisted that the dinner
   was solely to raise funds to evacuate from French concentration camps fifty anti-Fascists threatened with death,"
   in response to Lehman's claim that persons connected with
   the function "have long been connected with Communist
   activities."

8 ANON. Item. Newsweek, 17 (28 April), 64.
       Portrait of Hellman.

9 ANON. "Laughter against Hitler." New York Times (24 April),
   p. 20.
       Alludes to Watch on the Rhine and the relevance of
   American theater to the Hitler menace. See also "Critics
   Are Serious," which appears on the same page.

10 ANON. "Lillian Hellman," in Current Biography. New York:
   Wilson Company, pp. 375-76.
       Biographical sketch to Watch on the Rhine. Lists
   twelve bibliographical references. Photo.

11 ANON. "The Little Foxes, Styled for Bette Davis." PM's
   Weekly [New York] (17 August), pp. 62-63.

1941

> Photos and explanatory captions from the film version of The Little Foxes.

12 ANON. "The Little Foxes." Theatre Arts, 25 (October), 730.
Brief review, with photo, of the film version of The Little Foxes. Praises the adaptation highly.

13 ANON. "Movie of the Week: The Little Foxes." Life, 11 (1 September), 47-50.
Photo-essay on the movie version of The Little Foxes. A rather static play has been turned into a superior motion picture.

14 ANON. "Movies: Hate in a House Divided." Newsweek, 18 (25 August), 53-54.
Calls the film version of The Little Foxes one of the best Hollywood films in years. The role of Alexandra has been expanded and her new romance with the young newspaper editor provides a "welcome leaven of warmth and humanity," without compromising the text of the play. "This incidence of adult theme and realistic characters is all too rare on the screen." Photos from the film.

15 ANON. "New Play in Manhattan." Time, 37 (14 April), 64.
Review of Watch on the Rhine praises the third act and the performance of Paul Lukas as Kurt Müller ("one of the great performances of recent years"), but criticizes the first two acts as excessively talky and inactive. Says, however, that the play is "by far the best on the subject" of Nazism to date.

16 ANON. "Opera and Drama Given in Baltimore." New York Times (25 March), p. 26.
Item reporting the world premiere of Watch on the Rhine in Baltimore.

17 ANON. "Radio: The U.S. Short Wave." Time, 38 (3 November), 56.
Mentions a short-wave radio broadcast to Europe of a condensed German version of Watch on the Rhine.

18 ANON. "Scores Attack on Fund." New York Times (10 October), p. 9.
Item describing Hellman's speech at a fundraising dinner for the evacuation of anti-Fascists from French concentration camps. Her remarks criticized the "cowardly and malicious" attacks on sponsors of the dinner.

19 ANON. "Theater." Life, 10 (14 April), 81-82, 84.
     Review, with photos, of Watch on the Rhine. Hellman
shows less of her usual sting and craftsmanship but the
play is a "superior" one because it presents the current
world crisis "in simple, human terms" and offers in Kurt
Müller a "truly heroic" figure.

20 ANON. "Theater." Newsweek, 17 (14 April), 70.
     Review of Watch on the Rhine cites the play for its
propaganda, calling it an eloquent indictment of totali-
tarianism. The critic finds the play disappointing as
drama, however, and suggests that stronger craftsmanship
and character delineation should have been expected from
the author of Little Foxes and Children's Hour. The
warmth and power of the third act overshadow the melodramatic climax. The acting, especially by Paul Lukas, is
highly praised.

21 ANON. "What Is Life Worth?" New York Times (6 April),
     section 4, p. 8.
     Editorial on risks necessary in the defense of liberty
should the United States enter the war against fascism.
Cites Watch on the Rhine and its theme, as defined by
Times drama critic Brooks Atkinson. See 1941.24.

22 ATKINSON, BROOKS. "Critics' Prize Plays." New York Times
     (27 April), section 9, p. 1.
     Reveals the arduous process of balloting which resulted
in the selection of Watch on the Rhine as winner of the New
York Drama Critics' Circle Award for best American play of
the season.

23 _____. "Hellman's Watch on the Rhine." New York Times (13
     April), section 9, p. 1.
     Sunday review of Watch on the Rhine compares it to
Hellman's earlier successes (skillful but "unpleasant"
plays) and to other plays about fascism. While more discursive than The Little Foxes or The Children's Hour,
Watch on the Rhine is more humane and spontaneous and is,
therefore, Hellman's best drama. Its greatest virtue is
that its characters are not finally political spokesmen but
rounded human beings.
     Reprinted 1947.2.

24 _____. "The Play." New York Times (2 April), p. 26.
     Review of Watch on the Rhine. The play, her finest,
"says that the death of fascism is more desirable than the
lives and well-being of the people who hate it."

1941

25 _____. "Watch on the Rhine." New York Times (24 August),
section 9, p. 1.
Reassessment of Watch on the Rhine, after five months
on Broadway, finds the play "as good as it ever was." It
"ought to be full of meaning a quarter century from now
when people are beginning to wonder what life was like in
America when the Nazi evil began to creep across the sea."
Hellman's contrast of guileless, good-humored life in
America with the bitter corruption of life in Europe is
especially perceptive.

26 BARNES, HOWARD. Review of The Little Foxes [film]. New York
Herald Tribune (22 August), p. 8.
Rarely has screen language proved "more eloquent,
moving and dramatic" than in The Little Foxes. "It is
not often that the screen outdoes the stage in a tough and
compelling approach to material. With The Little Foxes it
has done so triumphantly."

27 BEAUFORT, JOHN. Review of The Little Foxes [film]. Christian
Science Monitor (22 August).
Although the performance of Bette Davis as Regina is
inadequate, The Little Foxes is "an overwhelming film."

28 _____. Review of Watch on the Rhine. Christian Science
Monitor (2 April).
Laudatory review.

29 BEEBE, LUCIUS. "Stage Asides: Miss Hellman Speaks Up." New
York Herald Tribune (18 May).
Item.

30 BERKOWITZ, ROZIA. "No Rumanian Count." New York Times (13
April), section 9, p. 3.
Letter to the drama editor raising point of information
about Watch on the Rhine.

31 BESSIE, ALVAH. Review of Watch on the Rhine. New Masses, 39
(15 April), 26-28.
Admires Hellman's sincerity of purpose and her ability
to involve the audience emotionally in the plight of Kurt
Müller. Bessie criticizes Watch on the Rhine on political
grounds, however, claiming that Hellman never defines the
nature of Kurt's struggle against fascism, for just as
Kurt "never enlarges upon the origins of the 'fascism' he
is fighting (in common with Roosevelt, Wilkie, and all the
other crusaders), so he never states the cure for this
pestilence of our time--world-wide organization by the

working people against their separate home-grown brands of fascism." Bessie also attacks the play because it "can be and has already been misused by those who would like to whip us or cajole us into imperialist war under the banner of fighting fascism in Germany." While Hellman "gives evidence that she would like to prevent this," she fails to clarify "the issues of anti-Nazism versus true international anti-fascism." She thereby opens Watch on the Rhine to distortion "by the enemies of the people, those fascists who are currently disguised as anti-fascists." See 1943.56 and 1946.42.

32 BOEHMEL, WILLIAM. Review of The Little Foxes [film]. New York World-Telegram (22 August), p. 8.
    Considers The Little Foxes one of the great films of the year.

33 BROWN, JOHN MASON. "Lillian Hellman's Watch on the Rhine Presented." New York Post (2 April).
    Reviews Watch on the Rhine. Misses Hellman's usually tight construction and finds it occasionally talky and awkward, but still considers it one of the most rewarding plays of the season. "A keen mind and a warm heart lie behind its writing. Its dialogue can crackle with wit or rise to eloquence."

34 _____. Review of The Little Foxes [film]. New York World-Telegram (13 September).
    Compares the stage and screen versions of The Little Foxes. Brown finds the film missing "the horrendous concentration of Miss Hellman's melodramatics."

35 _____. "Watch on the Rhine Seen a Second Time." New York Post (17 April).
    Follow-up review.

36 CAMERON, KATE. "The Little Foxes in World Premiere." New York Daily News (22 August).
    Rave review of the film version of The Little Foxes.

37 CERF, BENNETT, and VAN H. CARTMELL, eds. Sixteen Famous American Plays. New York: Garden City Publishing Company.
    Includes text of The Little Foxes.
    Reprinted as a Modern Library edition, 1942.

38 CRITICS' THEATRE REVIEWS, 1941. Vol. 2. New York: Critics' Theatre Reviews, pp. 341-44.

1941

Reprints reviews of Watch on the Rhine from New York
daily newspapers for 2 April 1941: New York Times, New
York Post, New York Journal and American, New York Herald
Tribune, PM, New York World-Telegram, Daily News, New York
Sun.

39 CROWTHER, BOSLEY. "Mildly Unpleasant." New York Times (24
    August), section 9, p. 3.
        Odd Sunday review of The Little Foxes which praises the
    excellence of the film but objects to its concern with "a
    pack of snarling jackals without a single redeeming grace.
    . . . We simply can't get interested in a dame who is so
    obviously--and theatrically--depraved."

40 _____. "The Screen in Review." New York Times (22 August),
    p. 19.
        Praises the film version of The Little Foxes highly.
    The play's original viciousness has been preserved, abetted
    by the "relentless" camera of William Wyler and the acting
    of Bette Davis as Regina. The Little Foxes is "one of the
    most cruelly realistic character studies yet shown on the
    screen."

*41 EVANS, ALICE. "Bits of Broadway." New Theatre News (May),
    unpaged.
        Cited by Malcolm Goldstein, The Political Stage (1974.
    19), pp. 216, 440. Attacks Watch on the Rhine as a play
    that can contribute little to "genuine anti-fascism," but
    one that "can be easily used by the demagogic 'anti-Nazi'
    warmongers who represent the people's main enemy today."

42 FERGUSON, OTIS. "The Camera Way Is the Hard Way." National
    Board of Review Magazine (October).
        Observes filming of The Little Foxes, paying particular
    attention to positions of the camera. Diagram.
        Reprinted 1971.9. (Article seen in reprinted form
    only.)

43 _____. "The Man in the Movies." New Republic, 105 (1
    September), 278.
        Praises all aspects of the screen adaptation of The
    Little Foxes highly, especially William Wyler's direction.
    This film "is one of the really beautiful jobs in the
    whole range of movie-making, and that includes any time or
    place or name."
        Reprinted 1971.9.

44 FIELD, ROWLAND. Review of Watch on the Rhine. Newark Evening
      News (2 April).
        "A major accomplishment."

45 FREEDLEY, GEORGE. "The Stage Today." New York Morning
      Telegraph (3 April).
        Reviews Watch on the Rhine. Says unnecessary complica-
      tions mar what might have been Hellman's best play.

46 _____, and JOHN A. REEVES. A History of the Theatre. New
      York: Crown Publishers, p. 598.
        Brief survey of Hellman's career through The Little
      Foxes. Praises The Children's Hour as "a brilliant study"
      which suffers from some psychological weaknesses. The
      secondary plot of Days to Come "paved the way" for The
      Little Foxes, "one of the most satisfactory dramas seen on
      the New York stage in recent years."
        Reprinted with supplement, 1968.10.

47 GASSNER, JOHN. "Stage." Direction, 4 (Summer Fiction
      Number), 42-43.
        Defends Hellman against the criticism that she is too
      dependent upon Scribean form and analyzes her latest suc-
      cess, Watch on the Rhine. No one in today's theater is so
      able to turn drama of situation into drama of character.
      Never has Hellman cared to create "those nebulous nuances
      of characterization that often pass for art simply because
      they are elusive. Nor has she ever created situations that
      lacked a larger point of reference, that failed to illumine
      some phase of social reality." Watch on the Rhine is "in-
      finitely rich in feeling and suggestiveness." Kurt Müller
      is a modern hero. Photo from the play. Hellman is also
      briefly mentioned in an anonymous editorial, p. 2.

48 GIBBS, WOLCOTT. "The Theatre." New Yorker, 17 (12 April),
      32.
        Reviews Watch on the Rhine, which Gibbs considers the
      best play of several seasons. For the first time, "the
      fundamental issue of our time has been treated with the
      dignity, insight and sound theatrical intelligence that it
      demands." One's complaints about the play amount to very
      little when compared to the many unforgettable moments.

49 GILDER, ROSAMOND. "The Kingdom of War." Theatre Arts, 25
      (November), 787-92.
        Discusses Watch on the Rhine in comparison to There
      Shall Be No Night. Hellman has the courage to say "quite
      ruthlessly and logically that it is sometimes necessary to

1941

kill, even when the killing is the personal, individualis-
tic kind called murder and not the abstract, mass type
called war." Reprinted in Theatre Arts Anthology. See
1950.9.

50 _____. "Prizes That Bloom in the Spring." Theatre Arts, 25
(June), 409–411.
Discusses Watch on the Rhine. Finds the play too
leisurely in its structure and excessively sentimental.
But it so successfully presents "a fundamental human ideal
that all its shortcomings are forgotten." Kurt Müller "in
Paul Lukas' hands becomes the prototype of all those who,
like Hamlet, revolt against the 'cursed spite' that calls
upon them to set right by violence a world gone out of
joint."

51 GOULD, JACK. "Paul Lukas, Late of Hollywood." New York
Times (6 April), section 9, pp. 1–2.
Feature article on Paul Lukas, who comments on preparing
for the role of Kurt Müller in Watch on the Rhine.

52 [GREEN,] ABEL. Review of Watch on the Rhine. Variety (9
April).
Favorable review.

53 GREEN, E. M. Review. Theatre World, 34 (June), 133–34.
Reviews Watch on the Rhine.

54 _____. Review. Theatre World, 36 (October), 30.
Reviews the film version of The Little Foxes.

55 HARRIMAN, MARGARET CASE. "Profiles: Miss Lily of New
Orleans." New Yorker, 17 (8 November), 22–26, 28–29, 32,
34–35.
Important, frequently cited profile of Hellman. Numerous items alluded to here reappear in further detail in
Hellman's later memoirs. Harriman's witty essay ranges
over a variety of areas, including Hellman's background,
writing habits, politics, friendships, hatred of being
called a "woman playwright," her "curiously split social
attitude, which combines a sensible fondness for money with
a violent dislike for people who wallow in it."
Reprinted in Harriman's Take Them Up Tenderly. See
1944.29.

56 HARTUNG, PHILIP T. "The Screen: The Evil That Men Do."
Commonweal, 34 (5 September), 473–74.

Considers the film version of The Little Foxes even
more stirring and uncompromising than the play. The added
emphasis on Alexandra and the creation of the character of
the young reporter "add to the realism of the whole by
giving a life-force to carry on after the Hubbards have
burned each other out." Gregg Toland's photography
deserves special commendation. "Action is injected as
often as possible by his moving camera; and his closeups
and interesting angle shots of streets, rooms, staircases
and particularly of faces add to the understanding of what
goes on in the homes and minds of this breed of little
foxes."

57 HEROLD, DON. "Seat at the Cinema." Scribner's Commentator,
    11 (November), 105-106.
        Reviews The Little Foxes (film). Praises the acting and
    the Hubbard skulduggery as cinematic "fun" but finds that
    the "screen technique has diffused the dramatic ferocity
    of the story."

58 HUGHES, CHARLOTTE. "Women Playmakers." New York Times
    Magazine (4 May), pp. 10-11, 27.
        Feature article comparing writing methods, work habits,
    and backgrounds of successful women writers--Hellman, Rose
    Franken, Zoë Akins, and Rachel Crothers. Photos.

59 KRONENBERGER, LOUIS. "Watch on the Rhine--The Best Play of
    the Season." PM (2 April).
        Reviews Watch on the Rhine. "It is an anti-Nazi play
    which differs from all the others as completely as it
    transcends them. It is a play about human beings, not
    their ideological ghosts; a play dedicated to the deeds
    they are called upon to perform, not the words they are
    moved to utter."

60 _____. "Watch on the Rhine Is Called One of Our Few Great
    Plays." PM (13 April).
        Sunday follow-up analysis of Watch on the Rhine.

61 KRUTCH, JOSEPH WOOD. "Drama: No Such Animal." Nation, 152
    (12 April), 453.
        Review of Watch on the Rhine, in which Hellman once
    again demonstrates her playwriting skill. Although
    superior drama, the play is most effective when it pre-
    sents material not directly concerned with Hellman's anti-
    Nazi theme. The central action suffers from old-fashioned
    melodramatics. It may not be her fault that this is a

1941

melodramatic world, that life is presently imitating art.
"It is, nevertheless, her misfortune."

62 LOCKRIDGE, RICHARD. "Lillian Hellman's Watch on the Rhine
Opens at the Martin Beck." New York Sun (2 April).
Reviews Watch on the Rhine. Calls the first part of the
play uncertain and digressive but says the final scenes are
magnificent. "You will have to wait a good while for the
point of Watch on the Rhine. It is worth waiting for."

63 MANTLE, BURNS. "Lillian Hellman's Watch on the Rhine Enters
Season's Best Play Contest." New York Sunday News (13
April).
Laudatory analysis of Watch on the Rhine.

64 _____. "Watch on the Rhine Stirring Drama of a Family of
Refugees." New York Daily News (2 April).
Generally favorable review of Watch on the Rhine.
"There is a good deal of that superb sense of drama that
Lillian Hellman expressed with such stunning effect in The
Children's Hour and The Little Foxes in the newest Hellman
drama."

65 _____, ed. The Best Plays of 1940-41. New York: Dodd, Mead
and Company, pp. 12, 64-93, 369, 422, 436, 446, 448.
Condenses Watch on the Rhine. Calls it the "most
soberly reasoned and the most convincingly written" of
plays about the war. Production information.

66 MERSAND, JOSEPH. The American Drama, 1930-1940. New York:
The Modern Chapbooks.
Includes Hellman.

67 MISHKIN, LEO. Review of The Little Foxes [film]. New York
Morning Telegraph (22 August).
Says The Little Foxes is brilliantly realized on screen.

68 MORTIMER, LEE. Review of The Little Foxes [film]. New York
Daily Mirror (22 August).
Favorable review.

69 MOSHER, JOHN. "The Current Cinema." New Yorker, 17 (23
August), 63.
Praises the film adaptation of The Little Foxes as a
murder story for adults, "one that belongs, perhaps,"
thanks to Hellman and to Bette Davis (as Regina), "in the
category of tragedy on a grand scale."

70 NATHAN, GEORGE JEAN. "Playwrights in Petticoats." American
Mercury, 52 (June), 750-55.
Watch on the Rhine proves two things: Hellman is "the
best of our American women playwrights and . . . even the
best of our women playwrights falls immeasurably short of
the mark of our best masculine [sic]."
Reprinted as "The Status of the Female Playwrights," in
Nathan's The Entertainment of a Nation. See 1942.29.

71 R., G. "The New Movie." New York Sun (22 August).
Reviews film version of The Little Foxes. Considers it
"an event."

72 RUSSELL, N. Condensation of The Little Foxes. Photoplay, 19
(September), 44-45, 80-82.
Condensed "fictionalization" of the film version of The
Little Foxes, with photos.

73 SCHO[ENFELD, JOSEPH]. Review of The Little Foxes [film].
Variety (13 August).
Rave review.

74 SYLVESTER, ROBERT. "Lillian Hellman Talks of Plays; An Agent
Finds New Field for Musicals." New York Daily News (28
April).
Discussion with Hellman of changes she would still like
to make in Watch on the Rhine and Days to Come. Mentions
that the cast of Watch on the Rhine is urging her to stage
a special matinee of Days to Come which would include those
changes.

75 VAN GELDER, ROBERT. "Of Lillian Hellman." New York Times
(20 April), section 9, pp. 1, 3.
Conversation with Hellman in which she comments on
choosing titles for her plays, the evolution of Watch on
the Rhine, and related matters.

76 VERNON, GRENVILLE. "The Stage and Screen: Watch on the
Rhine." Commonweal, 34 (25 April), 15-16.
Criticizes Watch on the Rhine for its poor construction,
its strained and artificial dialogue and characters. Also
objects to Hellman's substitution of the term "fascist"
for "nazi." "An anti-nazi play with occasional obeisances
to Moscow is a contradiction in terms." Remarks made by
Bodo "are decidedly of a Communist tinge."

77 WARNER, RALPH. "Watch on the Rhine Poignant Drama of Anti-
Fascist Struggle." Daily Worker (4 April), p. 7.

1941

Watch on the Rhine is "a first-rate theatre piece" but
must be examined more closely than most plays because "it
is the first even partially successful attempt to project
the realities of anti-fascist struggle for the overthrow
of Hitler by the only certain means--a German people's
revolution." Hellman skirts a number of questions, including whether or not Kurt "is a member of a Communist
group fighting for German freedom."

78 WATTS, RICHARD, JR. "The Theater: A New Heroic Drama." New
York Herald Tribune (13 April), section 6, p. 1.
Analyzes the strengths and occasional flaws of Watch on
the Rhine. The play's particular asset is its focus on
the "democratic hero." The melodramatic events of the
drama's concluding minutes "seem melodramatic because that
is the spirit of the times, not because they are highly
colored fabrications."

79 _____. "The Theater: Who's to Write Next Season's Dramas?"
New York Herald Tribune (18 May).
Discusses Hellman and other major American playwrights.

80 _____. "The Theaters." New York Herald Tribune (2 April),
p. 20.
Considers Watch on the Rhine an eloquent, heroic play.
It is melodramatic only insofar as contemporary events are
melodramatic. Hellman, usually among the most economical
of playwrights, grows a bit garrulous here, but Watch on
the Rhine "is essentially a quiet and orderly work, which
rarely raises its voice."

81 _____. "A Tribute to Miss Hellman's Departed Play." New
York Herald Tribune (1 March).
On The Little Foxes.

82 _____. "Watch on the Rhine as the Outstanding New Play."
New York Herald Tribune (27 April).
Report on selection of Watch on the Rhine as New York
Drama Critics' Circle winner.

83 WEINBERG, HERMAN G. "Herman G. Weinberg Writes from New
York." Sight and Sound, 10 (Summer), 25-26.
Notes the impending filming of Watch on the Rhine.

84 _____. "News from New York." Sight and Sound, 10 (Autumn),
51-53.
Reviews The Little Foxes and other films, recently
opened in New York. Compares The Little Foxes to Greed.

Praises the film highly, calling it "a cold study in human greed, with shocking moments when they should be shocking. It compromises less with the truth than almost everything we have seen in Hollywood in many moons of assorted screen junk."

85   WHIPPLE, SIDNEY B. "Revisions Strengthen Watch on the Rhine." New York World-Telegram (12 May).
      Discusses improvements in the production of Watch on the Rhine.

86   ____. "Watch on the Rhine Avoids the Soap-Box." New York World-Telegram (2 April).
      Considers Watch on the Rhine a compassionate and idealistic discussion of the conflict between totalitarian and democratic principles. The play is a "hymn of praise for the courage and nobility of Fascism's opponents rather than an indictment of European political gangsterism."

87   WINSTEN, ARCHER. "The Little Foxes Opens at Radio City Music Hall." New York Post (22 August).
      Praises the film version of The Little Foxes as powerful entertainment and a memorable tragedy.

88   WYATT, EUPHEMIA VAN RENSSELAER. "The Drama: Watch on the Rhine." Catholic World, 153 (May), 215-16.
      Highly favorable review of Watch on the Rhine. Compares the play to Sherwood's There Shall Be No Night, especially in the portrayals of the respective heroes, Kurt Müller and Dr. Valkonen.

89   YOUNG, STARK. Review of Watch on the Rhine. New Republic, 104 (14 April), 498-99.
      Praises the play, especially Hellman's "remarkable gift for character," but wishes the mutual confrontation between Europe and America had been more fully explored. Artificial contrivance is more in evidence in Watch on the Rhine than in The Children's Hour. Kurt's farewell to his children is appropriate though in need of tightening; it is within the "high tradition--Sophocles, for example, where at the very end of the play almost, Oedipus is given thirty-four full lines of this same farewell."

1942

1942

1 ANDERSON, JOHN. "Lillian Hellman." New York Journal American (25 March).
   On Hellman and her plays.

2 ANON. "'Command' Performance for Watch on the Rhine." New York Times (6 January), p. 26.
   Item reporting the selection of Watch on the Rhine for a command performance, in honor of the president's birthday, in Washington, D.C.

3 ANON. "Entertainments." The Times [London] (19 January), p. 8.
   Considers the film version of The Little Foxes "a delicately perceptive study of avarice in a small town of the Southern states [that] has been transferred from stage to screen without any apparent loss."

4 ANON. "Entertainments." The Times [London] (23 April), p. 6.
   The London production of Watch on the Rhine demonstrates that "the international situation explored by Henry James in terms of European aristocrats and American heiresses . . . appears still to be in essence much what it was. Titles and dollars are given a new emphasis, violence has broken in, but it is still seamy old Europe confounding good Americans by its complicated codes of conduct."

5 ANON. "Entertainments." The Times [London] (22 October), p. 6.
   Reviews the London production of The Little Foxes. Hellman almost has "Balzac's sense of the passion for money." It is not "strong enough to produce a fine play, but it serves to spin an effective melodrama."

6 ANON. "Footnotes on Headliners." New York Times (11 January), section 4, p. 2.
   Item noting the selection of Watch on the Rhine for a "command" performance in Washington, D.C., as part of the president's birthday celebration. Photo.

7 ANON. "Hellman Play in London." New York Times (24 April), p. 20.
   Brief report on the London opening of Watch on the Rhine, citing the rave review of the Daily Telegraph and the somewhat less positive notice of The Times (London).

8   ANON. Review of The Little Foxes. New Statesman and Nation,
      24 (7 November), 304.
          Calls the London production of The Little Foxes disap-
      pointing, especially after the release of the film version.
      "The merit of the play is that the implicit sermon against
      big business is left unspoken."

9   ANON. Review of The Little Foxes. Stage, no. 3213 (29
      October), p. 5.
          Gives muted approval to the London production of The
      Little Foxes.

10 ANON. Review of Watch on the Rhine. Stage, no. 3187 (30
      April), p. 5.
          Generally positive review, with some reservations, of
      the London production of Watch on the Rhine.

11 ANON. "Special Edition of Hellman Play for Benefit of
      Refugees." Publishers Weekly, 142 (18 July), 170.
          Announces forthcoming publication of limited, numbered
      edition of Watch on the Rhine, with illustrations by eleven
      well-known artists and a foreword by Dorothy Parker, for
      the benefit of the Joint Anti-Fascist Refugee Committee.

12 ANON. "To Show Hellman Manuscript." New York Times (25
      January), p. 37.
          Notice of exhibit of original manuscript of Watch on
      the Rhine.

13 ANON. "Watch on Rhine Seen by President." New York Times
      (26 January), p. 18.
          Report on command performance of Watch on the Rhine, in
      Washington, D.C., attended by President Roosevelt in his
      "first public appearance away from the White House since
      the war began, except to address Congress and attend
      church."

14 ANSTEY, E. Review. Spectator, 168 (23 January), 82.
          Reviews film version of The Little Foxes.

15 BATES, MARY E., and ANNE C. SUTHERLAND, eds. The Dramatic
      Index for 1941. Boston: F. W. Faxon Company, pp. 112, 143,
      255; appendix, p. 36.
          Cites biographical sketch of Hellman and reviews of The
      Little Foxes (film version) and Watch on the Rhine. Also
      notes editions of Hellman plays published in 1941.

1942

16 BESSIE, ALVAH. "Life as It Is." New Masses, 44 (4 August),
    30-31.
        Review of film adaptation of Ellen Glasgow's In This
    Our Life compares its treatment of Negroes to that of The
    Little Foxes, the first movie to portray a Negro character
    "in his true perspective in American life." Bessie also
    claims that events in this film start "where The Little
    Foxes left off" and carry "the portraiture an epochal step
    forward."

17 BROWN, IVOR. Review. London Observer (26 April), p. 7.
        Reviews the London production of Watch on the Rhine. It
    is "a play of its time, harsh and terrible, a play of
    mental challenge, and yet a play of the theatre in which
    the artistry of acting is never subdued by too forceful an
    impress of the author's own ideas."

18 _____. "At the Play." Punch, 202 (3 June), 466.
        Gives a mostly favorable review to the London production
    of Watch on the Rhine, noting that the "play rises, rather
    slowly at times, to a climax of strength and quiet pathos."

19 _____. "Theatre and Life." London Observer (25 October), p.
    2.
        Stresses, in a mostly negative review of the London
    production of The Little Foxes, that "people who have ad-
    mired Watch on the Rhine may think Miss Hellman to be an
    author who drives realistically into the trials and terrors
    of our Nazi-ridden time. But evidently she can serve a
    dish of gammon and spinach. The characters in this play
    come not from life but from the cupboard of those who
    specialize in theatrical fat-stock."

*20 BURNETT, WHITTIER. This Is My Best. New York: Dial, p. 1140.
        Cited by Norma Olin Ireland, Index to Women of the
    World, 1970.19, p. 236.

21 DARLINGTON, W. A. "Americans in London." New York Times (1
    November), section 8, p. 2.
        Review of the belated London premiere of The Little
    Foxes finds the production inadequate, particularly in Fay
    Compton's performance as Regina.

22 _____. "Watch on the Rhine: Miss Hellman's Play Provides
    London with Another Smash Hit." New York Times (3 May),
    section 10, p. 1.
        Report on acclaimed London production, directed by
    Emlyn Williams.

23 DENT, ALAN. "A Critic Criticizes." Sight and Sound, 11
    (Autumn), 34-35.
        Dent criticizes fellow reviewers for failing to recog-
    nize theater's "parentage" of film. They appreciate The
    Little Foxes "in spite of the fact that it must have re-
    minded them of a play, whereas I like it because it was
    highly theatrical in the true sense of that abused word."

24 ____. "At the Play." Punch, 203 (28 October), 366.
        Observes that The Little Foxes, in its London produc-
    tion, "obeys 'unity of place' and is almost as taut and
    telling as Ibsen himself could make it."

25 GILDER, ROSAMOND. Review. Theatre Arts, 26 (May), 346.
        Reviews Hellman's Four Plays (New York: Random House,
    1942).

26 KUNITZ, STANLEY, and HOWARD HAYCRAFT, eds. Twentieth-Century
    Authors. New York: Wilson, p. 634.
        Autobiographical sketch of Hellman, with additional
    notes on her career and short lists of her works and items
    about her. Photo. Updated 1955.28.

27 MALLET, RICHARD. "At the Pictures." Punch, 202 (4 February),
    88.
        Finds The Little Foxes a "most satisfying piece of work"
    on screen. The advertisements "rather eccentrically pro-
    claim that it shows [Bette] Davis 'as you love her best.'
    I should doubt whether love is exactly what you feel for
    the money grubbing murderess she portrays here, but the
    affections of an audience are notoriously unpredictable."

28 MARTIN, KINGSLEY. "A Fine Play." New Statesman and Nation,
    23 (2 May), 288.
        Review of the London production of Watch on the Rhine.
    Hellman "has painted an honest picture of a brutal struggle
    about supreme issues cutting into comfortable homes, com-
    pelling those who love to recognize that society may have
    to come first before their love, since their love is
    founded on the recognition of qualities that forbid escape
    from danger and reality. Watch on the Rhine is a harrow-
    ing, truthful and satisfying play."

29 NATHAN, GEORGE JEAN. The Entertainment of a Nation. New
    York: Alfred A. Knopf, pp. 34-41, 66, 127, 181-82, 190.
        Reprints 1941.70 (pp. 34-41). Other brief references
    to Hellman.

1942

30 PARKER, DOROTHY. Foreword to Limited Edition of Watch on the
    Rhine. New York: Privately Published.
        Comments on Hellman and Watch on the Rhine for an illus-
    trated, special edition of the play, numbered and limited
    to 349 copies, for the benefit of the Joint Anti-Fascist
    Refugee Committee. "The woman who wrote this play and the
    men who made these drawings give this, their book, to
    those who earliest fought Fascism. . . . They are brave
    men who lay down their lives and their liberty that men to
    come may live and be free. This play, these pictures, more
    shining than marble, more enduring than brass, stand here
    to the glory of their courage."

31 REDFERN, JAMES. "The Theatre." Spectator, 169 (30 October),
    407.
        Briefly reviews London production of The Little Foxes,
    with Fay Compton as Regina. Praises the play as a "vivid
    piece of present-day realism" with characters "drawn from
    life."

32 ROBINSON, CLARKE. "Silhouettes of Celebrities." World
    Digest, 15 (January), 78-83.
        Profile of Hellman's life and work, emphasizing her ex-
    tensive research for The Little Foxes. Robinson quotes
    Hellman on the writing of Foxes and Watch on the Rhine,
    and on her definition of "melodrama": "'If you are sup-
    posed to believe, as the Greeks did, that man is at the
    mercy of gods he might offend and who will punish him for
    the offense, then you would write what was tabbed tragedy.
    The end is inevitable from the beginning. But if you
    believe that man is intelligent enough to solve his own
    problems and is at nobody's mercy, then you probably write
    what is called melodrama.'"

33 S., F. Review of The Little Foxes. Theatre World, 37
    (November), 6.
        Reviews London production of The Little Foxes. Finds
    the play a trifle disappointing, especially after the bril-
    liant film version, the play's reputation, and the London
    production of Watch on the Rhine, earlier in the year.

34 _____. Review of Watch on the Rhine. Theatre World, 37
    (June), front cover, 5.
        Reviews London production of Watch on the Rhine. Con-
    siders it "a play in a thousand and one that enhances one's
    faith in the English-speaking theatre a hundred-fold." The
    play's great achievement is in the characterization of Kurt
    Müller. Cover photo from the production.

35 WATTS, RICHARD, JR. "The Theater: A Tribute to Miss Hellman's
    Departed Play." New York Herald Tribune (1 March).
        Praises Watch on the Rhine as the only recent play to
    offer a representative hero for the times.

36 WEINBERG, HERMAN G. "American Letter." Sight and Sound, 11
    (Autumn), 38-41.
        Notes the planned filming of Watch on the Rhine.

37 WHITEBAIT, WILLIAM. "The Movies." New Statesman and Nation,
    23 (24 January), 57.
        Favorably reviews the screen adaptation of The Little
    Foxes.

38 WRIGHT, BASIL. Review of Watch on the Rhine. Spectator, 168
    (1 May), 419.
        Reviews the London production of Watch on the Rhine.
    Hellman's tale could have been treated as a thriller or a
    political tract but she has chosen it "as the framework
    for the expression of the European tragedy and of the hid-
    den sense of guilt which those who were too much outside
    it will never lose; and because she is a dramatist of the
    first order she has made of it the richest and most moving
    play we have seen since Thunder Rock." Hellman's message
    to us is that "we are all guilty and that if it is now too
    late to undo what has been done, it is by no means too late
    to re-make, to create again a world in which decent humani-
    ty may live, unpursued and undevoured."

1943

1 AGATE, JAMES. Review of The North Star. Tatler and
   Bystander (15 December), p. 324.
        Attacks the film. Says the characters are American
   actors, not Russian peasants.

2 AGEE, JAMES. "Films." Nation, 157 (25 September), 360-61.
        Comments briefly on the film version of Watch on the
   Rhine. It seems much better on screen than on stage—
   "though I still wished Henry James might have written it."
        Reprinted in Agee on Film: Reviews and Comments. See
   1958.1, 1964.1, 1966.1.

3 _____. "Films: So Proudly We Fail." Nation, 157 (30
   October), 509-10.
        Reviews The North Star. Good intentions go awry be-
   cause Hollywood fails to trust its audience. "In its

1943

basic design Lillian Hellman's script could have become a
fine picture: but the characters are stock, their lines
are tinny-literary, their appearance and that of their
village is scrubbed behind the ears and 'beautified'; the
camera work is nearly all glossy and overcomposed."
Reprinted in Agee on Film: Reviews and Comments. See
1958.1, 1964.1, 1966.1.

4 _____. "Prize Day." Nation, 157 (25 December), 768-69.
Brief, disparaging reference to film version of Watch
on the Rhine.
Reprinted in Agee on Film: Reviews and Comments. See
1958.1, 1964.1, 1966.1.

5 ANON. "Cinema: The North Star." Time, 42 (8 November), 54.
Says that no other Hollywood film has brought the experience of modern war to American moviegoers as effectively as The North Star. Photo.

6 ANON. "Cinema: Watch on the Rhine." Time, 42 (6 September),
94, 96.
Review of Watch on the Rhine. Says the play has been
transferred to the screen virtually intact; especially
praises Paul Lukas's performance as Kurt. Still.

7 ANON. "Entertainments." The Times [London] (9 December), p.
6.
States that "all the bits and pieces of laborious good
intention do not make [The North Star] a satisfying whole."

8 ANON. "Following the Films." Senior Scholastic [High School
Teacher Edition], 43 (27 September), 28.
Reviews film version of Watch on the Rhine. Praises it
highly.

9 ANON. "Following the Films." Senior Scholastic [High School
Teacher Edition], 43 (29 November), 26.
Reviews The North Star. Considers it a superior film,
"a tribute to the Russian people—and to all people every-
where who put up their lives as security against fascism."

10 ANON. "Movies: Lukas Triumph." Newsweek, 22 (6 September),
96.
Praises the film version of Watch on the Rhine, particularly the performance by Paul Lukas as Kurt. Hellman's
story is as topical as it was when her play was first written. Dashiell Hammett's screen adaptation, "without sacrificing a line of the drama's brilliant dialogue," expands

the action only when necessary and gathers together "the few loose strings." Photo from the film.

11 ANON. "Movie of the Week: Watch on the Rhine." Life, 15 (13 September), 73-74, 76.
    Review, with photos, of Watch on the Rhine: "a distinguished and provocative film."

12 ANON. "Movie of the Year: North Star." Life, 15 (1 November), 118-22, 125.
    Short review, with twelve photos; calls The North Star an eloquent film of epic dimensions. "Unlike many thin-skinned Hollywood products it is a tone poem in motion pictures that moves slowly and deeply and says things worth saying."

13 ANON. "N.B." Direction, 6 (November), 3.
    Brief reference to Watch on the Rhine and The North Star as two of the best films of the year.

14 ANON. "New Films in London." The Times [London] (6 September), p. 8.
    Says that the film version of Watch on the Rhine "is a faithful transcription of the play which means that it is unfailingly interesting to watch. Miss Hellman's business is not with the physical side of the Nazi regime but with its effect on the mind."

15 ANON. "The North Star." Theatre Arts, 27 (December), 716.
    Praises Hellman for her authoritative screenplay for The North Star. Photo from the film.

16 ANON. "Peasant Epic of Russia." New York Times Magazine (10 October), p. 16.
    Photos from The North Star with captions.

17 ANON. Photos. Theatre Arts, 27 (November), 656.
    Scenes from the London production of Watch on the Rhine.

18 ANON. Photos. Theatre World, 38 (March), 31.
    Scenes from the London production of Watch on the Rhine.

19 ANON. Plot Synopsis. Photoplay, 23 (November), 23.
    Summary of film version of Watch on the Rhine.

20 ANON. Review. Spectator, 171 (17 December), 575.
    Reviews The North Star.

1943

21 ANON. Review of The North Star. New Statesman and Nation, 26
       (18 December), 400.
         Critical review of The North Star: "sentimental and
       dated."

22 ANON. "Three Good Bets." Cosmopolitan, 114 (April), 76.
         Brief, strongly positive review of the film version of
       Watch on the Rhine. Illustrated.

23 ANON. "Valentine Russe." Newsweek, 22 (8 November), 86.
         Review of The North Star. Hellman's screenplay estab-
       lishes the Russian villagers as people rather than stock
       symbols of ordinary anti-Nazi films. They are "readily
       identifiable with their American counterparts in any farm-
       ing community." The film provides timely, exciting enter-
       tainment. Film stills.

24 ANON. "Watch on the Rhine." Theatre Arts, 27 (October), 597.
         Brief remarks, with two photos from the film, on the
       screen adaptation of Watch on the Rhine.

25 ANON. "Watch on the Rhine Voted Best Film." New York Times
       (29 December), p. 19.
         Report on the naming of Watch on the Rhine as best film
       of 1943 by the New York Film Critics.

26 ANTICO, FRANK. Review of The North Star. Daily Worker (5
       November), p. 5.
         Praises The North Star in superlative terms. The film
       "binds two great peoples even closer together in their
       united struggle against fascism." It serves the cause of
       the United Nations and portrays the people of the Soviet
       Union with power and truth. Hellman's script offers the
       actors every opportunity to be effective, although she
       might have added scenes showing "the presence of Marshal
       Stalin and the philosophy of his party in the life of the
       villagers" and the collective planning on which the leader-
       ship principles are based. Such scenes "might have pro-
       vided a more complete picture of Soviet life."

27 BARNES, HOWARD. Review of The North Star. New York Herald
       Tribune (5 November), p. 10.
         Calls The North Star a striking, sometimes brilliant
       film. Hellman's script is passionate and eloquent.

28 _____. Review of Watch on the Rhine [film]. New York Herald
       Tribune (28 August), p. 6.

Hellman's impassioned and moving play fares brilliantly
on the screen. The film adaptation of Watch on the Rhine
"has even greater depth of character and meaning."

29 _____. Review of Watch on the Rhine [film]. New York Herald
Tribune (5 September), sections 5-6, p. 1.
Watch on the Rhine has been expertly adapted for the
screen and actually improves upon the integration of the
play's dramatic threads. "To a remarkable degree Miss
Hellman hit the bull's eye in her prelude to our particular
participation in the war. With Dashiell Hammett's aid, as
scenarist, her play has as much meaning and emotional power
as ever." Herman Shumlin, "like Orson Welles with Citizen
Kane, has demonstrated that there is no great mystery to
the fabrication of films, as long as you have something to
say on the screen. His direction has a slight tendency to
be static, which is quite understandable in a piece where
the essential drama is implicit. It never fails to be
outspoken and moving."

30 _____. "With a Bow to the Screen." New York Herald Tribune
(14 November), section 4, pp. 1, 3.
Reviews The North Star. The film suffers from certain
Hollywood touches contrived to entertain the masses, but
as a whole it is sincere and stirring, "a splendid show and
a telling tribute to the unconquerable spirit of our
Russian ally." Hellman's script, as the published version
shows, "is more sternly integrated than the sequences which
emerge on the screen."

31 BATES, MARY E., and ANNE C. SUTHERLAND, eds. The Dramatic
Index for 1942. Boston: F. W. Faxon Company, pp. 63, 125;
appendix, p. 30.
Lists reviews of The Little Foxes (London production and
the film version) and Watch on the Rhine (London production).

32 BLACKFORD, G. E. Review of The North Star. New York Journal
American (5 November), p. 14.
Condemns The North Star as "insidious propaganda."

33 BOWLES, PAUL. "Film Scores by Copland and Tansman." New
York Herald Tribune (21 November).
Analyzes Aaron Copland's music for The North Star.

34 CAMERON, KATE. Review of The North Star. New York Daily News
(5 November).

1943

> Calls the film more communistic than the Russians them-
> selves.

35 COOK, ALTON. Review of The North Star. New York World-
Telegram (5 November), p. 18.
> Says The North Star is a "powerful" film.

36 _____. Review of The North Star. New York World-Telegram
(13 November).
> Calls The North Star "just short of great."

37 CREELMAN, ELLEN. Review of Watch on the Rhine [film]. New
York Sun (28 August).
> Comments that the film version of Watch on the Rhine
> surpasses the play "in violence but not in forcefulness."

38 CROWTHER, BOSLEY. "Fiction or Fact?" New York Times (7
November), section 2, p. 3.
> Sunday review of The North Star. Finds the film "too
> pretty" in certain respects, but states that "there is
> also a great deal of honest dignity displayed--and a great
> deal of tense, exciting action."

39 _____. Review of Watch on the Rhine [film]. New York Times
(5 September), section 2, p. 3.
> Sunday analysis of screen version of Watch on the Rhine.
> It is "the finest--if not the most lurid--war film that
> Hollywood has yet made." It is also the first Hollywood
> film to consider deeply the "fundamental nature of
> fascism."

40 _____. "The Screen." New York Times (28 August), p. 15.
> Strongly favorable review of the film version of Watch
> on the Rhine. Although Hammett's "almost literal adapta-
> tion" of the play tends to be static in the early scenes,
> Hellman's sure characterizations, lucid prose and forceful,
> apt theme combine to make a powerful film. The last scene,
> added to show Sara permitting her older son to join the
> resistance, is "dramatically superfluous" but consistent
> with the film's heroic spirit.

41 _____. "The Screen in Review." New York Times (5 November),
p. 23.
> Review of The North Star praises the film highly, but
> objects to the tone of operetta present in the early sec-
> tion, which purports to show the peasants' lives before
> the Nazi invasion.

42 FARBER, MANNY. "The Cardboard Star." New Republic, 109 (8
    November), 653.
        Reviews The North Star as a well-intentioned but sim-
    plistic film. People and events of the movie are too care-
    fully and clearly presented and explained; all action seems
    posed, not spontaneous.

43 _____. "Parting Is Such Sweet Sorrow." New Republic, 109
    (13 September), 364.
        Praises the film version of Watch on the Rhine as gen-
    erally satisfactory and moving. However, Herman Shumlin's
    direction and Dashiell Hammett's adaptation are too
    reverential. "One of Miss Hellman's greatest virtues is
    an ability to spread a rich, human group of characters
    over her plays, but where her lines may have developed the
    character sufficiently on the stage they are, as movie
    lines, so overpacked that they exist as a thing apart from
    the characters."

44 HARTUNG, PHILIP T. "All That I Know of a Certain Star."
    Commonweal, 39 (19 November), 117-18.
        Review of The North Star. "In spite of much of the
    film's phoniness, Lillian Hellman's story comes through."
    The film is stirring cinematically, but the village and
    its peasants are "too clean, too noble, too handsome."

45 _____. "Watch!" Commonweal, 38 (24 September), 563-64.
        Calls Watch on the Rhine one of the most provocative
    war films ever made. Its theme may have dated slightly
    since "American standoffishness has melted a great deal
    since 1940," but the film, especially in its depiction of
    its noble hero, "clarifies what we are fighting for."

46 JOSEPH, ROBERT. "Hollywood Discovers Russia." California
    Arts and Architecture, 60 (February), 24-25, 42.
        Article on the making of The North Star, stressing the
    film's attempt to capture realistic details of Russian
    life.

47 KRONENBERGER, LOUIS. "Introduction." The North Star. New
    York: Viking, pp. 5-10.
        Commends Hellman's screenplay for The North Star as
    "human and heroic," written with a cinematic eye and an
    absence of rhetoric. The economy of the script and the
    deliberate introduction of the characters' peacetime
    existence before they are plunged into war contribute to
    the successful presentation of Hellman's "large" theme.

1943

The sharp dialogue and command over detail evident in her plays are also present here.

48 LARDNER, DAVID. "The Current Cinema." New Yorker, 19 (28 August), 50.
Calls the film version of Watch on the Rhine a faithful rendition of the play. Only the final scene, added by Dashiell Hammett, seems unnecessary. "The scene is prewar America, but the picture has as much timeliness as some of the harum-scarum, up-to-the-minute ones and more sense than most of them."

49 MALLET, RICHARD. "At the Pictures." Punch, 205 (15 September), 233.
Finds the film version of Watch on the Rhine "little more than a photographed play . . . that was and is an adult play, and with only slight alteration makes a film worth seeing."

50 ____. "At the Pictures." Punch, 205 (22 December), 522.
Calls The North Star "a remarkable waste of talent."

51 MISHKIN, LEO. Review of Watch on the Rhine [film]. New York Morning Telegraph (28 August), p. 2.
Says Watch on the Rhine retains all its power as a film.

52 [MORRISON,] HOBE. Review of Watch on the Rhine [film]. Variety (28 July).
Praises Watch on the Rhine as a distinguished film.

53 MORTIMER, LEE. Review of The North Star. New York Daily Mirror (5 November), p. 24.
Attacks The North Star as "red propaganda." Says it preposterously idealizes Russia.

54 PELSWICK, ROSE. Review of Watch on the Rhine [film]. New York Journal American (28 August).
Calls the film a successful adaptation.

55 PLATT, DAVID. Review of Watch on the Rhine [film]. Daily Worker (30 August), p. 7.
Considers Watch on the Rhine a stirring and honest motion picture, overwhelming in its treatment of the most important theme in a time of war. Particularly effective are the bits of dialogue written by Hellman and Dashiell Hammett on the Spanish war. "They are the best introduction to the kind of work Kurt is doing, [and] make his whole character clear to everyone."

56 PRENTISS, DANIEL. Review of Watch on the Rhine [film]. New
    Masses, 47 (14 September), 30-31.
        Rates the film adaptation of Watch on the Rhine an un-
    qualified success, especially for political reasons.
    Hellman gives "artistic expression to the ideals and
    aspirations of the best people of our time--the fighters
    in the ranks of anti-fascism." It is also one of the
    film's merits that "it makes payment on humanity's long-
    standing debt to the heroes of the Spanish republic."
    Those who underestimate the film's propagandistic value
    "simply do not reckon with the terrific persuasiveness of
    Hellman's work." The Müllers are hunted people who are
    mightier than the hunters, characters in a "great opti-
    mistic tragedy." See 1941.31 and 1946.42.

57 RUSSELL, EVELYN. "Films of 1942." Sight and Sound, 11
    (Spring), 99-101.
        Mentions the fine performances of Teresa Wright and
    Bette Davis in the film version of The Little Foxes.

58 SIMON, HENRY. Review of Watch on the Rhine [film]. PM (28
    August), p. 22.
        Strongly favorable review.

59 STRAUSS, THEODORE. "The Author's Case." New York Times (19
    December), section 2, p. 5.
        Account of Hellman's objections to changes made in her
    shooting script of The North Star. "Miss Hellman still
    holds that, despite her criticisms, The North Star is a
    worthy and important film. She is simply criticizing it
    on the basis of what she believes it might have been, had
    it remained truer to the author's intentions."

60 _____. "Of Lillian Hellman, A Lady of Principle." New York
    Times (29 August), section 2, p. 3.
        Discusses Hellman's dedication to her principles in her
    screenwriting jobs.

61 T., E. R. "The Films." London Observer (12 December).
        Criticizes The North Star as "a well-meaning compound
    of musical comedy, horror, and cowboys and Indians dressed
    up as Soviet gorillas and German soldiers." The film
    offers elaborate proof "of Hollywood's sympathetic isola-
    tion from the realities of war."

62 WEINBERG, HERMAN G. "American Letter." Sight and Sound, 11
    (Spring), 95-97.
        Brief mention of The North Star.

1943

63 _____. "Letter from New York." Sight and Sound, 12 (Summer), 5-7.
   Brief mention of The North Star.

64 WHITEBAIT, WILLIAM. Review of Watch on the Rhine [film].
   New Statesman and Nation, 26 (4 September), 152.
   Watch on the Rhine is a less effective play than The
   Little Foxes. The film version also falls short of the
   film adaptation of The Little Foxes.

65 WINSTEN, ARCHER. "Joining the Controversy on North Star."
   New York Post (8 November).
   Says The North Star is not a propaganda film.

66 _____. Review of The North Star. New York Post (5 November).
   Judges The North Star favorably.

67 _____. Review of Watch on the Rhine [film]. New York Post
   (28 August).
   Praises Dashiell Hammett's adaptation of Watch on the
   Rhine for the screen.

1944

1 ALLEN, KELCEY. Review of The Searching Wind. Women's Wear
   Daily (13 April).
   Says Hellman and Herman Shumlin "have again hit the
   bull's eye."

2 ANON. "How War Came." New York Times Magazine (23 April),
   p. 19.
   Photo-essay on The Searching Wind.

3 ANON. Item. Theatre World, 40 (August), 32.
   Notes on the production of Watch on the Rhine at the
   Intimate Theatre, London.

4 ANON. Item. Vogue, 103 (15 April), 98.
   Biographical sketch with photo.

5 ANON. Item. Vogue, 103 (1 June), 110.
   Portrait of Hellman.

6 ANON. "Lillian Hellman in Moscow." New York Times (16
   November), p. 18.
   Brief item reporting Hellman's arrival in Moscow, where
   Watch on the Rhine is in rehearsal.

7 ANON. Plot Synopsis. Photoplay, 24 (January), 6.
Summary of The North Star, with photos.

8 ANON. "Scene Shifting Queried." New York Times (12 July), p. 21.
Item reporting lawsuit involving The Searching Wind.

9 ANON. "Theater: Hellman's Blue Ribbon." Newsweek, 23 (24 April), 86-88.
The Searching Wind at its best is a brilliant dissection of "postwar appeasers, fuzzy thinkers, and the summer soldiers in the liberal ranks. At its weakest—and may the theater always be as literate and potent—The Searching Wind is a blurry triangle projected in a political vacuum." Photo.

10 ANON. "Theater: The Searching Wind." Life, 16 (1 May), 43-44, 46, 48.
The play is among Hellman's most important works because it states "profound and disturbing truths." But The Searching Wind fails to unify two story lines, thus bewildering the audience. A series of photos from the play, with captions, "undertakes to clarify The Searching Wind by presenting a chronological arrangement of its main scenes."

11 ANON. "The Theater." Time, 43 (24 April), 72.
Review of The Searching Wind. The play has genuine bite, challenging ideas and adult talk, but it attempts to do too much. The theme tends to hamper the plot while the love story "lacks fullness." Photo.

12 BARNES, HOWARD. "The Theater: Eloquence, Art in The Searching Wind." New York Herald Tribune (23 April), section 4, p. 1.
Sunday review calls The Searching Wind the finest "dramatic reflection of the war" to have reached either stage or screen.

13 _____. "The Theaters." New York Herald Tribune (13 April), p. 16.
"In The Searching Wind Lillian Hellman has brought back a full measure of dignity, perception and beauty to the theater." While the characters' romantic misadventures are necessarily dwarfed by the international backdrop against which their story is told, the play manages to avoid bombastic propaganda and, as in the final scene, to flood "the stage with meaning and high poetry."

1944

14 BATES, MARY E., and ANNE C. SUTHERLAND, eds. The Dramatic
Index for 1943. Boston: F. W. Faxon Company, pp. 32-33,
103, 163; appendix, p. 32.
Lists reviews of The North Star and Watch on the Rhine
(London production and film version). Also cites editions
of Hellman works published in 1943.

15 CHAPMAN, JOHN. "The Searching Wind a Forceful Drama About
World Appeasers." New York Daily News (13 April).
Finds The Searching Wind a grimly and forcefully written
drama. The characters in the romantic triangle become
boring eventually, but the play is absorbing and intelligent. It is not "stirring," however.

16 CLARK, BARRETT. "Lillian Hellman." College English, 6
(December), 127-33.
Analyzes Hellman's five plays to The Searching Wind.
Her plays contain propaganda but she is also "an idealist
and a philosopher," an inescapably moral artist. Hellman's
"particularized hatred of this or that individual or idea,
as exemplified in The Children's Hour or Days to Come, is
in the last three plays, with one or two minor exceptions,
attenuated, merged into what closely resembles pity or a
remote kind of contempt." For example, Teck, in Watch on
the Rhine, is a completely rounded character who is "pursued by an idea and a philosophy which cannot be so con-
veniently disposed of." The Little Foxes is Hellman's
most mature and satisfactory play. In The Searching Wind,
Hellman eschews the melodrama of the earlier plays and
focuses on character and dialogue, not on plot. "She is
no longer the special pleader for this or that type of
reform." Already a master of her craft in just a decade,
she is advised to forget the immediate good to be won by a
specific reform and to defend the downtrodden instead by
"illuminating the world she knows as she sees it" in her
future work.

*17 DAWSON, MARY E. "The Idea of Tragedy in the Contemporary
American Theatre." Ph.D. dissertation, English, University
of Iowa.
Includes Hellman. Cited in Emerson and Michael,
Southern Literary Culture: A Bibliography of Masters' and
Doctors' Theses, 1979.10.

18 DRUTMAN, IRVING. "Herman Shumlin's Favorite Dramatist." New
York Herald Tribune (7 May).
Profile of Hellman's association with Shumlin through
The Searching Wind. Caricature of Hellman and Shumlin.

19 FARBER, MANNY. "Movies in Wartime." New Republic, 110 (3
    January), 18.
        Refers to the ludicrous situation involving The North
    Star, "in which the producer censored his writer's script
    for mention of communism, the Hearst press excoriated the
    producer for mentioning communism, and the film's most
    ardent upholders praised it for not having any communism
    whatsoever."

20 _____. "Mrs. Parsons, etc." New Republic, 110 (10 January),
    53.
        Mentions publication of the script of The North Star.
    The script shows that the film did not do it justice,
    although the printed text remains too obviously "a pat on
    the back for the Russians, without being at the same time
    even close to an important experience of them."

21 FIELD, ROWLAND. "Broadway." Newark Evening News (13 April).
        Reviews The Searching Wind. Considers it a drama of
    "brilliant distinction."

22 FREEDLEY, GEORGE. "The Stage Today." New York Morning
    Telegraph (14 April).
        Considers The Searching Wind "the most provocative and,
    perhaps, the best serious drama of the new season."

23 GARLAND, ROBERT. "The Searching Wind on the Fulton Stage."
    New York Journal American (13 April).
        Calls The Searching Wind a vivid play of the first
    importance.

24 GASSNER, JOHN. "Stage: Reflections on the Season 1943-44."
    Direction, 7, Summer Fiction Number (July), 27, 31.
        It is fortunate that The Searching Wind has proved suc-
    cessful. Its theme was badly needed at this time and it
    avoids political diatribe and easy villains. There is a
    Chekhovian strain as well. But the play's two themes are
    not blended and Hellman misses the opportunity to relate
    her characters' flaws to environmental factors.

25 GIBBS, WOLCOTT. "The Theatre: Miss Hellman Nods." New
    Yorker, 20 (22 April), 42-44.
        Review of The Searching Wind. It is a play that mixes
    up love and politics, saying nothing original about either
    one.

26 GILDER, ROSAMOND. Review of The Searching Wind. Theatre
    Arts, 28 (June), 331-32.

1944

Calls The Searching Wind discursive and generally disappointing, although the play closes movingly. "Miss Hellman
can put passionate conviction into words as well as anyone
now writing when she wishes to do so."

27 GRANT, ELSPETH. "Those Critics." Sight and Sound, 12 (May),
    12-13.
    Mentions the "superb portrayal" by Paul Lukas in Watch
    on the Rhine and his citation by New York film critics for
    that role.

28 GREEN, E. M. Review. Theatre World, 40 (September), 24.
    Reviews The Searching Wind.

29 HARRIMAN, MARGARET CASE. "Miss Lily of New Orleans: Lillian
    Hellman," in Take Them Up Tenderly. New York: Alfred A.
    Knopf, pp. 94-109.
    Reprints 1941.55 in a collection of New Yorker profiles
    by Harriman.

30 IBEE [PULASKI, JACK]. Review of The Searching Wind. Variety
    (19 April).
    Calls The Searching Wind expert theater.

31 ISAACS, EDITH. "Lillian Hellman, a Playwright on the March."
    Theatre Arts, 28 (January), 19-24.
    Analyzes Hellman's work for stage and screen. The
    stories she writes are about different people in different
    times and places but her themes are always the same: "the
    struggle between good and active evil, between evil and
    good that are sometimes ignorant of themselves, sometimes
    in full knowledge of what they are." The core of Hellman's
    social anger is expressed powerfully and persuasively in
    Addie's speech in The Little Foxes ("There are people who
    eat the earth . . .") and in Dr. Kurin's speech to Dr. Von
    Harden in The North Star ("I have heard about men like
    you . . ."). "It is the plea for an active, fighting,
    total goodness (toward which words and ideas count little
    and only brave deeds make a real contribution)."
    Reprinted in Discussions of Modern American Drama, ed.
    Walter Meserve. See 1965.17.

32 KRONENBERGER, LOUIS. "A Drama with Teeth to It." PM (13
    April).
    Reviews The Searching Wind as a striking, challenging
    play that contains several flaws. There is a cleavage be-
    tween the personal and political plot lines. The final
    scene, though moving, is excessively didactic.

33 MANEY, RICHARD S. "From Hellman to Shumlin to Broadway."
    New York Times (9 April), section 2, p. 1.
        Discusses Hellman's collaborations with Herman Shumlin,
    who produced and staged The Children's Hour, Days to Come,
    The Little Foxes, Watch on the Rhine--and The Searching
    Wind, about to open on Broadway. "They are as one in
    thinking that in time of crisis the theatre has a function
    that goes beyond coddling amatory neuroses."

34 MANTLE, BURNS. "It's a Good Trick If You Can Work It," in
    New York Theatre Critics' Reviews. Vol. 5. New York:
    Critics' Theatre Reviews, p. 226.
        Discusses The Searching Wind; refers to Hellman as
    "thoughtful and passionately earnest."

35 _____, ed. The Best Plays of 1943-44. New York: Dodd, Mead
    and Company, pp. 3, 14, 69-103, 394, 467, 494-96, 507, 509,
    510.
        Condenses The Searching Wind ("one of the few thoughtful
    dramas of the season"). Production information.

36 MARSHALL, MARGARET. "Drama." Nation, 158 (22 April), 494-95.
        Review of The Searching Wind. There is some deft writ-
    ing but the play lacks clarity of thought and feeling.
    There ought to have been a fourth flashback referring to
    the Soviet-German pact, "but it is clear from the context
    that Miss Hellman is one of those people who assume that
    there is a moral difference, though they never explain why,
    between Chamberlain's attempt to turn Hitler east and
    Stalin's attempt to turn him west."

37 MOREHOUSE, WARD. "Lillian Hellman's Play, The Searching Wind,
    Eloquent and Powerful." New York Sun (13 April).
        While not Hellman's best play, The Searching Wind is "a
    drama of sincerity and stature."

38 NATHAN, GEORGE JEAN. The Theatre Book of the Year, 1943-44.
    New York: Alfred A. Knopf, pp. 295-99.
        Analyzes The Searching Wind. Hellman is turning herself
    into a crusader on stage and screen, and off. Her public-
    spiritedness seems to have taken its toll on her as a
    dramatist, for "hot wrath is the province of cheap melo-
    drama." The Searching Wind at times resembles Strindberg's
    The Stronger. Neither the political nor love interests are
    ever clear. "The play throughout has the air of being
    about to say something of enormous weight and consequence
    and never saying it."

1944

39 NEW YORK THEATRE CRITICS' REVIEWS, 1944. Vol. 5. New York:
   Critics' Theatre Reviews, pp. 217-20.
       Reprints reviews of The Searching Wind from New York
   daily newspapers for 13 April 1944 (New York Sun, New York
   Journal American, New York Post, New York World-Telegram,
   PM, New York Herald Tribune, Daily News, New York Times).

40 NICHOLS, LEWIS. Review of The Searching Wind. New York Times
   (13 April), p. 25.
       Rates the play as "timely" and "a credit to the
   theatre," but criticizes Hellman's treatment of the love
   triangle. Photo from the play.

41 _____. Review of The Searching Wind. New York Times (23
   April), section 2, p. 1.
       A "good" play, though not Hellman's best, The Searching
   Wind contains two separate plots which tend to interrupt
   each other. Hellman is best in the political story of the
   play; the love story suffers from unclear characterizations
   of Emily and Catherine.

42 ORMSBEE, HELEN. "Miss Hellman All But Dares Her Next Play to
   Succeed!" New York Herald Tribune (9 April), section 4,
   pp. 1-2.
       Discussion with Hellman prior to the Broadway opening
   of The Searching Wind. Drawing.

43 PHELAN, KAPPO. Review of The Searching Wind. Commonweal, 40
   (28 April), 40.
       Says The Searching Wind fails to define the nature of
   the appeasement it attacks. The role of the "other woman"
   is virtually unactable.

44 POLLOCK, ARTHUR. "Playthings." Brooklyn Daily Eagle (16
   April).
       Reviews The Searching Wind. "The dramatist most alive
   in the theatre today and the best equipped for living,
   Miss Hellman stands out as a symbol of what the theatre
   can do and few of its playwrights attempt."

45 _____. "Theater." Brooklyn Daily Eagle (13 April).
       Reviews The Searching Wind. "This is the big play of
   the year, the richest, the fruitiest."

46 RANDOLPH, ALAN F., and MARGARET MOWER. "Dissent in the Drama
   Mailbag." New York Times (16 July), section 2, p. 1.
       Two letters to the Drama Editor on The Searching Wind.

Randolph suggests that the play be called The Long Wind; Mower defends the play's romantic subplot.

47 RASCOE, BURTON. "Has Miss Hellman Disappointed 'The Party'?" New York World-Telegram (22 April).
Follow-up piece on The Searching Wind.

48 _____. "The Searching Wind Miss Hellman's Finest." New York World-Telegram (13 April).
Considers The Searching Wind Hellman's best play and one of the finest Broadway plays of many seasons.

49 SHERBURNE, E. C. Review of The Searching Wind. Christian Science Monitor (13 April).
The Searching Wind is a stimulating, well-crafted play with realistic dialogue and individualized characters.

50 SILLEN, SAMUEL. Review of The Searching Wind. New Masses, 51 (2 May), 26-27.
Criticizes The Searching Wind for failing to unite its personal and political themes. The play blurs the distinction between "appeasement America and anti-appeasement America" by pretending that the "great popular movement against fascism which embraced millions" between the two world wars never took place.

51 WALDORF, WILELLA. "The Searching Wind a Mild Blast at Compromise and Appeasers." New York Post (13 April).
Calls The Searching Wind a pretentious, well-meaning play that is more windy than searching.

52 WARNER, RALPH. "The New Lillian Hellman Play." Daily Worker (17 April), p. 5.
Calls The Searching Wind an eloquent drama "about Americans who saw fascism's face but did not recognize it for the monster it is." But Hellman does not go far enough, even in Sam's final plea; she fails to "link the appeasers of yesterday with the defeatists, the 'nationalists' and 'isolationists' of today."

53 WEINBERG, HERMAN G. "American Letter." Sight and Sound, 12 (January), 88-89.
Strongly negative review of The North Star. Deplores the film's failure to convince and the fact that all scenes of "Nazi bestiality" have rational explanations.

54 WINCHELL, WALTER. "The Searching Wind Is New Hellman Hit." New York Daily Mirror (13 April).

1944

> Highly recommends The Searching Wind as a "spellbinder."
> Hellman here "is deft at depicting people as they really
> are, particularly civilized adults. She has always drawn
> them as cruel, selfish and animal-like."

55 WYATT, EUPHEMIA VAN RENSSELAER. Review of The Searching Wind.
   Catholic World, 159 (May), 170-71.
   > Her new play places Hellman among the foremost American
   > dramatists. The Searching Wind is telling us that "the
   > world's tragedy is the sum total of all of our personal
   > weakness." It is to Hellman's credit that she draws no
   > easy conclusions.

56 YOUNG, STARK. "Behind the Beyond." New Republic, 110 (1
   May), 604.
   > Review of The Searching Wind. The historical scenes
   > are written with competence and the play's topicality holds
   > one's interest. But the love story is totally unconvincing
   > and The Searching Wind ends up being "by far more windy
   > than searching."

1945

1 ANON. "Hellman Play Opens in Moscow." New York Times (26
   February), p. 10.
   > Notes the Moscow premiere of Watch on the Rhine.

2 ANON. "Russia Acclaimed by Miss Hellman." New York Times
   (2 March), p. 5.
   > Reports on Hellman's five-month stay in Russia, where
   > she became "the first civilian foreigner to visit the Red
   > Army front."

3 ANON. "The Week's Work." Collier's, 115 (31 March), 77.
   > Brief profile of Hellman, with photo, as introduction
   > to her article in this issue of Collier's, "I Meet the Front
   > Line Russians."

4 CLURMAN, HAROLD. The Fervent Years: The Story of the Group
   Theatre and the Thirties. New York: Alfred A. Knopf, pp.
   254, 279.
   > Brief mention of Hellman's contribution to the theatri-
   > cal movement of the 1930s.
   > Reprinted, with an epilogue, 1957.5.

5 FLEISCHMAN, EARL E. (EUGENE EARL). "The Searching Wind in the
   Making." Quarterly Journal of Speech, 31 (February), 22-28.

112

An analysis of the New York production of The Searching Wind by an actor who played the small role of the confidential secretary to the American ambassador in Paris. Discusses flaws and merits of the acting, sets, the direction of Herman Shumlin and the writing of Hellman. Suggests that Hellman failed to clarify the relationship between the action and the theme of the play both for her audience and members of the company. It is, however, her "most ambitious play, if not one of the most ambitious plays yet undertaken by an American playwright."

6 GASSNER, JOHN, and DUDLEY NICHOLS, eds. Best Film Plays of 1943-44. New York: Crown Publishers, pp. ix-xx, 299-356.
   Contains the complete screenplay of Watch on the Rhine (pp. 299-356), with four stills. Credits the screenplay to Dashiell Hammett, with "additional scenes and dialogue by Lillian Hellman." Gassner's introductory essay, "A Film Play Annual" (pp. ix-xx), asserts that Watch on the Rhine on screen "remained a worthy stage play somewhat literally transferred to another medium, [but] its earnestness and general solidity of characterization gave the screen a telling, concentrated human drama." This edition contains two other essays relevant for Watch on the Rhine, though neither specifically mentions it: Dudley Nichols, "Writer, Director and Film" (pp. xxi-xxx); Walter Wanger, "The Motion Picture Industry and the War Effort" (pp. xxxi-xxxiv).
   Reprinted 1977.49.

*7 KRUTI, I. "Sem'ia Ferelli obretaet muzhestvo (Sem'ia Ferelli teriaet pokoi)" [The Farrelly family gains courage (The Farrelly family loses its quiet)]. Soveskoe iskusstvo (8 March).
   Discusses the Russian production of Watch on the Rhine (retitled The Farrelly family loses its quiet). Cited in Valentina Libman, Russian Studies of American Literature, 1969.31.

*8 KULAKOVSKAIA, T. Review of Sem'ia Ferelli teriaet pokoi. Ogonek (no. 12-13), p. 12.
   On the Russian production of Watch on the Rhine (retitled The Farrelly family loses its quiet). Cited in Valentina Libman, Russian Studies of American Literature, 1969.31.

*9 MENDEL'SON, M. "Khellman i Pristli na moskovskoi stsene" [Hellman and Priestley on the Moscow stage]. Teatre (no. 2), pp. 14-19.

1945

Cited in Valentina Libman, Russian Studies of American
Literature, 1969.31.

10 NATHAN, GEORGE JEAN. "Introduction." The Critics' Prize
     Plays. Cleveland and New York: World Publishing Company,
     pp. 7, 10, 11, 13.
          Comments on Watch on the Rhine, the complete text of
     which is printed on pp. 272-322.

11 STANLEY, FRED. "Escape in Hollywood." New York Times (1
     July), section 2, pp. 1, 3.
          Discusses plans to film The Searching Wind.

12 SUTHERLAND, ANNE C., ed. The Dramatic Index for 1944.
     Boston: F. W. Faxon Company, pp. 102-103, 164, 198, 240;
     appendix, p. 30.
          Lists articles and reviews on Hellman, The North Star,
     The Searching Wind, and Watch on the Rhine.

*13 TRIPLETT, EVA B. "A Study of War Drama from 1915 to 1941."
     Master's thesis, English, University of Pittsburgh.
          Includes Hellman. Cited in Emerson and Michael,
     Southern Literary Culture: A Bibliography of Masters' and
     Doctors' Theses, 1979.10.

1946

1 AGEE, JAMES. Review of The Searching Wind [film]. Nation,
    163 (6 July), 25.
          Personal and political aspects of The Searching Wind
    get in each other's way but the film is a "careful, angry,
    honest" piece of work.
          Reprinted in Agee on Film: Reviews and Comments. See
    1958.1, 1964.1, 1966.1.

2 ANON. "Applause in December." Harper's Bazaar, 80
    (December), 220-21.
          Brief survey of plays on Broadway (and one film) that
    promise considerably more than escapist entertainment in-
    cludes Another Part of the Forest in that category. Photo
    of Patricia Neal as Regina Hubbard.

3 ANON. "Cinema: The Searching Wind." Time, 48 (1 July), 94.
          Hellman's screen adaptation of The Searching Wind is
    intelligent and frequently moving. Her propaganda gets in
    the way of her plot, however. Still.

4 ANON. "Entertainments." The Times [London] (16 August), p.
   8.
        Reviews the film version of The Searching Wind. Hellman
   "has a mind of quality and her craftsmanship shows itself
   in her ability to conduct a dramatic case without doing
   violence to the laws of evidence."

5 ANON. Item. Life, 21 (7 October), 50.
        Photo.

6 ANON. Item. Theatre World, 42 (February), 20.
        Notes the Moscow production of The Little Foxes.

7 ANON. "The Little Foxes as Cubs." New York Times Magazine
   (17 November), p. 68.
        Photos and brief comments on the impending return of
   the Hubbards to Broadway, in Another Part of the Forest.

8 ANON. "Movies: Return of the Wind." Newsweek, 28 (15 July),
   97.
        Although Hellman's screen adaptation of The Searching
   Wind "retains the basic faults of her original play, her
   message comes through as forcefully as on the stage and,
   considering the uneasy peace, with even better timing."
   Photo from the film.

9 ANON. Photos. Vogue, 108 (1 December), 206.
        Scenes from Another Part of the Forest.

10 ANON. "Theater: Foxes in the Forest." Newsweek, 28 (2
   December), 94.
        Reviews Another Part of the Forest. The play stands on
   its own as one of the finest dramas by an American author
   in years. Claims the title is taken from a stage direction in As You Like It.

11 ANON. "Theater." Life, 21 (9 December), 71-72, 74.
        Brief review of Another Part of the Forest, with a
   series of photos from the play. Finds the sequel to The
   Little Foxes occasionally melodramatic "but always convincing and entertaining."

12 ANON. "The Theater." Time, 48 (2 December), 54, 56.
        Review of Another Part of the Forest. Vivid characters
   and a sharp, biting tone make the play compelling. Yet
   melodrama "is catapulted from without," thus preventing
   the play from becoming "large-sized drama."

1946

13 ANON. "The Week's Openings." New York Times (17 November),
     section 2, p. 1.
       Announcement of the opening of Another Part of the
     Forest. Photo of Patricia Neal and Percy Waram as Regina
     and Marcus Hubbard.

14 ATKINSON, BROOKS. "Eating the Earth." New York Times (1
     December), section 2, p. 1.
       Another Part of the Forest "is not so much a drama of
     people and ideas as a contrived theatre piece put together
     by sheer will power. The Hubbards work so hard to illus-
     trate Miss Hellman's point that they defeat it."
     Reprinted 1947.2.

15 _____. "The Play in Review." New York Times (21 November),
     p. 42.
       Reviews Another Part of the Forest. Hellman's hatred
     of the Hubbards drives the play "over the line into old-
     fashioned melodrama." Her indictment is "a witches' brew
     of blackmail, insanity, cruelty, theft, torture, insult,
     drunkenness, with a trace of incest thrown in for good
     measure and some chamber music in the background."
     Hellman's writing and direction and the splendid cast make
     "the horrible Hubbards people you cannot ignore."

16 BARNES, HOWARD. "The Predatory Hubbards of Miss Hellman's
     Play." New York Herald Tribune (1 December), section 5,
     pp. 1, 3.
       Sunday review of Another Part of the Forest. The play
     is a fascinating study of evil but occasionally lacks con-
     vincing motivation. Marcus is "far too vital a villain to
     be done in so speciously by the sleazy son." Hellman's
     direction of her play rivets audience attention on the
     action of the stage. As playwright, she succeeds best "in
     the small incidents of the tragedy," such as the musicale
     sequence.

17 _____. Review of The Searching Wind [film]. New York Herald
     Tribune (27 June), p. 22.
       The material of The Searching Wind is more at home on
     stage than on screen. The dreary romantic plot gets en-
     tangled with world politics and interferes with what
     Hellman has to say.

18 _____. The Theaters." New York Herald Tribune (21 November),
     p. 25.
       Finds Another Part of the Forest compelling, but disap-
     pointing. "Miss Hellman has had much to add to her

indictment of the little foxes in our past. She fails to
make it more revealing than it was in the first place.
The moments of solid impact in her drama are few and far
between."

19 BENTLEY, ERIC. The Playwright as Thinker. New York:
    Harcourt, Brace and Company.
        Quotes and contradicts statements made by Allardyce
    Nicoll about the nature of drama. Nicoll's remarks use
    The Children's Hour as an example of a play that demon-
    strates the innate limitations of the genre. See also
    Allardyce Nicoll, Film and Theatre, 1936.60.
        Bentley's book is reprinted, 1955.9.

20 BROWN, JOHN MASON. "Seeing Things: And Cauldron Bubble."
    Saturday Review, 29 (14 December), 20-23.
        Review of Another Part of the Forest focuses upon its
    Elizabethan excesses. A witches' broth with which Hellman
    is delighting her audiences, the play contains "every pos-
    sible human equivalent for the venomous toads, the eye of
    newt, or lizard's leg upon which Shakespeare fed his
    crones." Ibsen and the Duchess of Malfi are Hellman's
    spiritual parents. The play is "guignol" rather than a
    drama, easy to enjoy but difficult to take seriously.

21 CHAPMAN, JOHN. "Another Part of the Forest Makes The Little
    Foxes a Mere Warmup." New York Daily News (21 November).
        In the hands of a less skillful playwright, Another
    Part of the Forest might seem overwrought. As written by
    Lillian Hellman, it is an exciting study of malevolence.
    "As Regina, Patricia Neal is the handsomest and toughest
    snake-woman I ever saw, making Tallulah Bankhead look like
    Themesong."

22 COLEMAN, ROBERT. "New Hellman Play Magnetic Hit." New York
    Daily Mirror (21 November).
        Calls Another Part of the Forest "magnetic and lusty
    theatre."

23 CROWTHER, BOSLEY. "Ladies Know Best." New York Times (30
    June), section 2, p. 1.
        Critical review of the film version of The Searching
    Wind.

24 _____. "The Screen in Review." New York Times (27 June), p.
    29.
        Reviews the film version of The Searching Wind. Says
    the rifts between the characters are vague and inconclusive,

1946

devoid of the sharp conflicts employed in Watch on the
Rhine. The villains of the piece are portrayed too
sympathetically and the film's general structure is weak,
as static as it "apparently was on the stage."

25 FARBER, MANNY. "Hellman's Movietone News." New Republic,
    115 (5 August), 142.
        Criticizes the screen version of The Searching Wind as
    a "vacuous, journalistic, middle-aged film." As adapted
    by Hellman from her own play, "it is a sort of March of
    Time résumé of what seems like the last six hundred and
    fifty thousand years of international politics."

26 FREEDLEY, GEORGE. "The Stage Today." New York Morning
    Telegraph (22 November).
        Highly positive review of Another Part of the Forest.

27 FUNKE, LEWIS B. "News and Gossip of the Rialto." New York
    Times (10 March), section 2, p. 1.
        Hellman comments on her untitled play in progress
    (Another Part of the Forest) and her intention of complet-
    ing a Hubbard trilogy.

28 GARLAND, ROBERT. "At Fulton--Another Part of the Forest."
    New York Journal American (21 November).
        Calls Another Part of the Forest a "well-nigh perfect"
    play and production.

29 GASSNER, JOHN. "The Theatre Arts." Forum, 106 (August),
    175-79.
        Includes discussion of the film version of The Searching
    Wind. The film intertwines the personal and political
    threads more successfully than the play. Hellman's screen
    treatment is faithful in other respects, though her politi-
    cal protest depends somewhat upon "circumstantial" proof.
    The Searching Wind is not sufficiently cinematic.

30 GIBBS, WOLCOTT. "Theatre: Ladies' Day." New Yorker, 22 (30
    November), 58-60.
        Reviews Another Part of the Forest as "merely an untidy
    sequel to an infinitely superior play."

31 HARTUNG, PHILIP T. "The Screen: A Time to Remember."
    Commonweal, 44 (12 July), 308-309.
        The Searching Wind, Hellman's "preachy indictment of
    fascism and appeasers," remains an "illustrated sermon" in
    its screen adaptation.

32 HAWKINS, WILLIAM. "The Forest a Modern Theater Classic."
    New York World-Telegram (21 November).
        Reviews Another Part of the Forest. Commends it as "one
    more classic of the modern theater."

33 IBEE [PULASKI, JACK]. "Plays on Broadway: Another Part of the
    Forest." Variety (27 November).
        Another Part of the Forest is a dour drama splendidly
    acted and produced. It "figures to repeat the click of The
    Little Foxes."

34 KRONENBERGER, LOUIS. "Lillian Hellman Writes Another Compel-
    ling Drama." PM (22 November).
        Reviews Another Part of the Forest. Compares the play
    to "those sombre Elizabethan 'comedies' swarming with
    cheats and knaves and evildoers." The play is less effec-
    tive but more interesting than The Little Foxes. It is
    also "less controlled but more complex."

35 KRUTCH, JOSEPH WOOD. "Drama." Nation, 163 (7 December), 671-
    72.
        Review of Another Part of the Forest, "the story of four
    scoundrels, two half-wits, one insane woman, and a whore."
    The play displays theatrical virtuosity and makes The
    Little Foxes appear to be an idyl by comparison. The play
    is more expertly written than any of Hellman's earlier
    works but unrelieved depravity "has a way of beginning to
    seem funny when exhibited for too long and completely
    without foil."

36 LEJEUNE, C. A. "At the Films." London Observer (6 October),
    p. 2.
        Criticizes the film version of The Searching Wind,
    Hellman's "angry sermon against a policy of appeasement in
    Europe with all the major events of the past twenty-five
    years recapitulated." The film is honest in intention and
    technically competent, but boring.

37 LEONARD, HAROLD. "Present and Accounted For." Sight and
    Sound, 15 (Autumn), 86-88.
        Briefly mentions the "touchstone" photography of Gregg
    Toland for such films as Citizen Kane and The Little Foxes.
    Updates the war and postwar activities of Toland, William
    Wyler, and Joris Ivens.

38 LORRAINE, PHILIP. "A Theatre Conference." Drama, New Series,
    no. 2 (Autumn), 16-22.

1946

> Includes comments on The Little Foxes. Photo from pro-
> duction of The Little Foxes at Highbury Little Theatre,
> Sutton Coldfield, England.

39 McCARTEN, JOHN. "The Current Cinema." New Yorker, 22 (29
>   June), 64, 66.
>   "In adapting her play The Searching Wind for the screen,
>   Lillian Hellman has regrettably failed to remove any of the
>   faults it had on the stage." The film contains too much
>   propaganda and not enough drama, and Hellman is "still too
>   belligerently intolerant" of human mistakes in judgment.

40 McCARTHY, MARY. "Theater Chronicle: Dry Ice." Partisan
>   Review, 13 (November-December), 577-79.
>   Brief, derogatory reference to the "oily virtuosity" of
>   Hellman, Odets, and others (p. 577).
>   Reprinted 1956.32 and 1963.45.

41 MALLET, RICHARD. "At the Pictures." Punch, 211 (28 August),
>   166.
>   Thinks the story of The Searching Wind (film) is a
>   cliché about understanding, and failing to understand,
>   evil. But the film is well acted and worth seeing.

42 MALTZ, ALBERT. "What Shall We Ask of Writers?" New Masses,
>   58 (12 February), 19-22.
>   Argues that creative works should not be judged pri-
>   marily by their ideological positions, citing the conflict-
>   ing reviews given to the stage and screen versions of Watch
>   on the Rhine by New Masses: "When Lillian Hellman's mag-
>   nificent play . . . was produced in 1940 [sic], the New
>   Masses' critic attacked it. When it appeared, unaltered,
>   as a film in 1942, the New Masses' critic hailed it. The
>   changed attitude came not from the fact that two different
>   critics were involved, but from the fact that events had
>   transpired in the two years calling for a different politi-
>   cal program. This work of art was not viewed on either
>   occasion as to its real quality--its deep revelation of
>   life, character and the social scene--but primarily as to
>   whether or not it was the proper 'leaflet' for the moment."
>   (Maltz is alluding to reviews which appeared in New Masses
>   in 1941 and 1943, not 1940 and 1942. See 1941.31 and
>   1943.56.)

43 MANVELL, ROGER. "Films of the Quarter." Sight and Sound, 15
>   (Spring), 26-27.
>   Mentions The Spanish Earth.

44 _____. "This Quarter's Films." Sight and Sound, 15 (Autumn), 96-98.
 Reviews film version of The Searching Wind. The film's documentary theme is marred by its overdramatization. The film is thus a "curious mixture of honesty and domestic melodrama."

45 MOREHOUSE, WARD. "Hellman's Another Part of the Forest Is a Fascinating and Powerful Drama." New York Sun (21 November).
 "Another Part of the Forest is full-bodied, vibrant theater, theater that Lillian Hellman can write. She has now done the trick five times out of six."

46 MULVEY, KAY. "Hollywood." Woman's Home Companion, 73 (September), 10.
 Brief comments about Mulvey's "unofficial technical" advice for filming scenes of The Searching Wind. Photo from the film.

47 NATHAN, GEORGE JEAN. Review of Another Part of the Forest. New York Journal American (2 December).
 Hellman's talent postures as genius. Her attempts at hate and avarice in Strindberg's manner result in over-wrought melodrama close at times to travesty.
 Reprinted with additional material, 1947.17.

48 NEW YORK THEATRE CRITICS' REVIEWS, 1946. Vol. 7. New York: Critics' Theatre Reviews, pp. 247-50.
 Reprints reviews of Another Part of the Forest from New York daily newspapers for 21 November 1946 (22 November 1946 for PM): New York Herald Tribune, PM, New York Times, New York Journal American, Daily News, New York World-Telegram, New York Sun, New York Post.

49 PHELAN, KAPPO. Review of Another Part of the Forest. Commonweal, 45 (6 December), 201-202.
 Hellman is more interested in melodramatizing specific examples of the Hubbards' evil rather than exploring that evil's root or cause. Another Part of the Forest ends up, therefore, as a "sordid, silly 'shocker,'" despite effective direction by Hellman and superb performances by its cast.

50 PLATT, DAVID. "Hellman's Thoughtful Anti-Fascist Film." Daily Worker (2 July), p. 11.
 Reviews screen version of The Searching Wind. It is a "thoughtful indictment of the appeasement policy that

1946

helped to bring about world war two." But Hellman does
not state frankly "that at the bottom of Alex Hasen's [sic]
political struggle was fear of the Soviet Union, fear of
the working classes, that he was faithfully carrying out
State Department policy--a policy of opposition instead of
collaboration with the Soviet Union to halt aggression.
Failure to even mention the Soviet Union as the chief
bulwark against fascism weakens the film's indictment of
those Americans in responsible posts who betrayed our
national interests. It limits the value at a time when men
like Alex Hasen [sic] are still preparing the ground for
another blood bath." Photo.

51 PRYOR, THOMAS M. "At Peace with the World." New York Times
(7 July), section 2, p. 3.
Discussion with Hellman relating to her playwriting
method, critics' reactions to the recently released film
version of The Searching Wind, and her objections to The
North Star.

52 SCHNEIDER, ISIDOR. Review of Another Part of the Forest.
New Masses, 61 (24 December), 28-29.
Commends Hellman's direction of her own play but challenges the "oversimplified" characterizations which lead
to "oversimplified history." It is erroneous for Hellman
to equate Marcus and Ben Hubbard with capitalism and to
omit both inward conflict and the general conflict of good
and evil.

*53 SHROPSHIRE, ANNE W. "The Plays of Lillian Hellman: A Study
in Contemporary Drama." Master's thesis, English,
University of Kentucky.
Cited in Emerson and Michael, Southern Literary Culture:
A Bibliography of Masters' and Doctors' Theses, 1979.10.

54 SILLEN, SAMUEL. "Lillian Hellman's Another Part of the
Forest." Daily Worker (25 November), p. 11.
Hellman's play is compelling and powerful, and she has
directed it with force. After the tension of the first two
acts, however, the reversals of fortune in the final section of the play take on a falsely melodramatic air. "Here
the play may be paying the penalty for failing to develop
or even to suggest a counterforce to evil."

55 SUTHERLAND, ANNE C., and BEULAH C. RATHBUN, eds. The Dramatic
Index for 1945. Boston: F. W. Faxon Company, pp. 101, 194;
appendix, p. 26.
Lists articles on Hellman and The Searching Wind.

*56 TURNER, CORA E. "Parent-Child Conflict in Selected American
       Dramas, 1919-1939." Master's thesis, English, University
       of Florida.
           Includes Hellman. Cited in Emerson and Michael,
       Southern Literary Culture: A Bibliography of Masters' and
       Doctors' Theses, 1979.10.

 57 VON WIEN, FLORENCE. "Playwrights Who Are Women." Independent
       Woman, 25 (January), 12-14.
           Says Hellman is the outstanding woman playwright "whose
       fame at forty has spread all over the world and ranks her
       with our best American playwrights." Briefly surveys her
       work, calling Watch on the Rhine her best play and "the
       best anti-Fascist play yet written." Photos of Hellman and
       a scene from Watch on the Rhine. (Independent Woman later
       changed its name to National Businesswoman.)

 58 WATTS, RICHARD, JR. "Lillian Hellman's New Play is Fascinat-
       ing Drama." New York Post (21 November).
           Reviews Another Part of the Forest. Believes it sur-
       passes all her previous plays "in sheer, overwhelming in-
       tensity of interest. It is also a brilliant, distinguished
       work, of enormous power and impact, but its deadly, ser-
       pent-like fascination is its most irresistable feature."

 59 WHITEBAIT, WILLIAM. "The Movies." New Statesman and Nation,
       32 (24 August), 133.
           Reviews the film version of The Searching Wind. Says
       the film makes the audience "stir painfully under the
       eiderdown of the play."

 60 WRIGHT, BASIL. Review. Spectator, 177 (23 August), 191.
           Reviews the film version of The Searching Wind.

 61 YOUNG, STARK. Review of Another Part of the Forest. New
       Republic, 115 (16 December), 822.
           Another Part of the Forest fails generally because all
       the violence and lurid vehemence do not stem from within
       the characters. Instead, Hellman heaps external events
       into "rank melodrama, with an innate lack of essential
       dignity and thrust."

                              1947

  1 ANON. "The News of Radio." New York Times (26 December), p.
       30.
           Announces that The Little Foxes will be broadcast as

                              123

1947

the special 100th radio presentation of "Theatre Guild on the Air," with Agnes Moorehead as Regina.

2 ATKINSON, BROOKS. Broadway Scrapbook. New York: Theatre Arts, Inc., pp. 107-10, 192-95, 222, 255-57.
Reprints Atkinson's New York Times Sunday reviews of The Little Foxes, Watch on the Rhine, and Another Part of the Forest. See 1939.9, 1941.23, and 1946.14. Note: review of The Little Foxes, incorrectly dated in this volume as 25 February 1939, is reprinted from the New York Times of Sunday, 26 February 1939.
This collection reprinted 1970.7.

3 BARRY, IRIS. "In Search of Films." Sight and Sound, 16 (Summer), 65-67.
Briefly mentions These Three.

4 BENTLEY, ERIC. "Broadway and Its Intelligentsia." Harper's Magazine, 142 (March), 211-21.
Notes that audiences at Another Part of the Forest laugh, not inappropriately, "at some of the most hideous moments in Miss Hellman's play." The play, like The Little Foxes, "is Grand Guignol in the guise of realism." See 1953.9.

5 BEYER, WILLIAM. "The State of the Theatre: Midseason Highlights." School and Society, 65 (5 April), 250-52.
Includes a review of Another Part of the Forest. Beyer attacks Hellman's intention to fashion a trilogy about the Hubbards as "pretentious nonsense." Villainy, when belabored, becomes surprisingly dull. From the start of Another Part of the Forest, Hellman "piles on contrived villainies including the papers, robberies, insanity, torture, lechery, more papers, even a leer at incest, at such a preposterous rate that, being unconvinced, we were utterly bored, all of which makes for an uninspired evening."

6 CALTA, LOUIS. "Hellman Returns from Paris." New York Times (26 August), p. 26.
Report on Hellman's return from Paris, where she participated in a UNESCO conference attended by people in the theater arts.

7 CLARK, BARRETT H., and GEORGE FREEDLEY, eds. A History of Modern Drama. New York and London: D. Appleton-Century Company, Inc., pp. 644, 721, 728-29.

Brief discussions of Hellman's plays (pp. 728-29) and other passing references. Considers The Little Foxes the most satisfying of Hellman's dramas through The Searching Wind. "Despite her moral bias, and her decidedly Communist sympathies, Miss Hellman promises to write plays that may be even more effective and moving than any she has yet given us, because among other things she is learning that social criticism is useful largely to the extent to which it is not added to, but inherent in, the works which attempt to drive it home."

8 COLLINGE, PATRICIA. "Another Part of the Hubbards Or, When They Were Even Younger." New Yorker, 27 (15 March), 29-30.
    Parody of the Hubbard plays by the actress who played Birdie in the original production of The Little Foxes.
    Reprinted in Twentieth-Century Parody, edited by Burlington Lowrey. See 1960.29.

9 GAGEY, EDMOND. Revolution in American Drama. New York: Columbia University Press, pp. 126, 137-38, 142, 268.
    Brief discussions of The Children's Hour, The Little Foxes and Watch on the Rhine.

10 GASSNER, JOHN. "The Theatre Arts." Forum, 107 (January), 78-83.
    Reviews Another Part of the Forest. Gassner praises the play highly, calling it "another episode in Miss Hellman's retelling of Gustavus Myer's History of Great American Fortunes." The play belongs to an unusual genre, the "joyless comedy," which goes back to such dark comedies as Measure for Measure, The Winter's Tale, and Volpone. But the play's resolution is mechanical.

11 _____. "The Theatre Arts." Forum, 107 (February). 172-77.
    Brief but interesting comments on Another Part of the Forest. Since the Hubbards ultimately do each other in, they are essentially comic characters, not Strindbergian ones. Hellman exerts too much energy on the "piteous characters who contaminate the sultry comic mood with intimations of heavier content than the play can carry validly. But like O'Neill, although in a radically divergent mode, Lillian Hellman dramatizes by locating the dynamite in the ego and putting a spark to it."

12 _____, ed. Best Plays of the Modern American Theatre. New York: Crown, pp. 641-82.

1947

         Includes text of <u>Watch on the Rhine</u>, with introductory comments. Questions Hellman's assertion that she begins with persons, not with political ideas.

13 GILDER, ROSAMOND. "New Year, New Plays." <u>Theatre Arts</u>, 31 (January), 12-23.
         Reviews <u>Another Part of the Forest</u>. Hellman's characterizations, though extreme to the point of caricature, are "so infused with passion that they become horribly alive." The trappings of melodrama are present but they are "still acceptable symbols of power and Miss Hellman uses them adroitly for the purpose of riveting attention and raising the audience's blood pressure." Photo from the play, p. 14.

14 GREEN, E. M. Review. <u>Theatre World</u>, 43 (January), 36.
         Reviews <u>Another Part of the Forest</u>.

*15 MANGUM, VALERIE. "American Attitudes toward War as Reflected in American Drama, 1773-1946." Ph.D. dissertation, University of Texas at Austin.
         Listed in <u>American Doctoral Dissertations</u>.

16 MANTLE, BURNS, ed. <u>The Best Plays of 1946-47</u>. New York: Dodd, Mead and Company, pp. 10, 163-203, 402, 443, 503, 515, 517-19.
         Condenses <u>Another Part of the Forest</u>; relates the play to the time sequence of <u>The Little Foxes</u>; quotes Hellman on writing the sequel. Production data for <u>Another Part of the Forest</u>.

17 NATHAN, GEORGE JEAN. <u>The Theatre Book of the Year, 1946-1947</u>. New York: Alfred A. Knopf, pp. x-xx, 201-204.
         Foreword includes discussion of objections by Hellman and others to the decorum of several members of the New York Drama Critics' Circle. Also assesses Hellman's six plays through <u>Another Part of the Forest</u>, which tries to imitate Strindbergian hate and malice but ends up as a travesty of overwrought melodrama. Hellman is "guilty of some pretty shameless character hokum." <u>See</u> 1946.47.

18 SUTHERLAND, ANNE C., and BEULAH C. RATHBUN, eds. <u>The Dramatic Index for 1946</u>. Boston: F. W. Faxon Company, pp. 18-19, 117, 152, 232.
         Cites miscellaneous items and reviews of <u>Another Part of the Forest</u>, <u>The Searching Wind</u> (film version), and <u>The Little Foxes</u>.

19 WATTS, RICHARD. "The Art of Melodrama." Go Magazine, 11
    (January), 35-36.
        Considers the two Hubbard plays probing social studies.
    Another Part of the Forest clarifies Hellman's intentions
    of The Little Foxes.

20 WYATT, EUPHEMIA VAN RENSSELAER. Review of Another Part of the
    Forest. Catholic World, 164 (January), 360-61.
        Inconclusive review praises the acting and summarizes
    the plot. Calls Another Part of the Forest "a melodramatic
    study of villainy," with the foxes back in the same vine-
    yards.

21 ZOLOTOW, SAM. "Saturday Closing for Hellman Play." New York
    Times (23 April), p. 32.
        Comments on impending closing of Another Part of the
    Forest as indicative of a Broadway "slump."

1948

1 AGEE, JAMES. "Films." Nation, 166 (19 June), 697-98.
        Includes brief remarks on the screen version of Another
    Part of the Forest. Says the "saber-toothed" Hellman play
    has resulted in an "unusually good hybridization of stage
    and screen drama."
        Reprinted in Agee on Film: Reviews and Comments. See
    1958.1, 1964.1, 1966.1.

2 ANON. "Cinema: Another Part of the Forest." Time, 51 (31
    May), 86.
        Another Part of the Forest "has been screened with a
    Broadway kind of incisiveness. It isn't in any sense a
    movie; but . . . it is a nearly perfect example of how to
    film a play." Still.

3 ANON. "Half-Grown Foxes." Newsweek, 31 (31 May), 73.
        Calls the film version of Another Part of the Forest a
    successful and cinematic adaptation of the play. Still.

4 ANON. "Movie of the Week: Another Part of the Forest." Life,
    24 (31 May), 63-64, 67.
        Short review, with photos, of Another Part of the Forest
    on screen. A parade and a Klan raid have been added and
    improve on the play. "Result: a tiptop drama of evildoers
    who find real pleasure in their work."

1948

5 BARNES, HOWARD. "Dynastic Skullduggery." <u>New York Herald Tribune</u> (19 May), p. 17.
   <u>Another Part of the Forest</u> has been filmed with remark-able integrity. The screen version is as corrosive as the play in its portrayal of greed and decadence.

6 _____. "Two Stage Hits Here Again on Screen." <u>New York Herald Tribune</u> (23 May), section 5, p. 1.
   Reviews the screen adaptation of <u>Another Part of the Forest</u>. The film version "has a tendency to wander away from the tragic core of the work, while the climax has none of the terrifying effect of the original."

7 BRANDEN, ELSA. Review. <u>Photoplay</u>, 33 (July), 23.
   Review, with photos, of film version of <u>Another Part of the Forest</u>.

8 CUNNINGHAM, R. R. "The Japanese Cinema To-Day." <u>Sight and Sound</u>, 17 (Spring), 16-18.
   Notes the popularity in Japan of the film version of <u>Watch on the Rhine</u>.

*9 DESSLER, HAROLD. "Lillian Hellman: An Evaluation." Master's thesis, English, University of North Carolina at Chapel Hill.
   Cited in Emerson and Michael, <u>Southern Literary Culture: A Bibliography of Masters' and Doctors' Theses</u>, 1979.10.

10 HARTUNG, PHILIP T. "Theater-into-Cinema." <u>Commonweal</u>, 48 (4 June), 185-86.
   Reviews <u>Another Part of the Forest</u> as one of three newly released films based on plays. The Hubbards are per-haps the most despicable family ever to appear on film. The story's lack of action prevents the film from being sufficiently cinematic but <u>Another Part of the Forest</u> deserves audience attention as a thoughtful study of post-Civil War economics and base human motivation.

11 HATCH, ROBERT. "Movies: Broadway in Hollywood." <u>New Republic</u>, 118 (7 June), 29.
   Review of <u>Another Part of the Forest</u> (film). The play is not one of Hellman's successes because there is no real drama; evil, if it is to serve as a theatrical motif, "must have something besides itself to grind upon." The film retains the play's flaws, but, like the play, offers a field day for actors. It is worth seeing for its per-formances "and perhaps as a memorable example of the poi-son that can be distilled from the Southern vernacular."

12 McCARTEN, JOHN. "The Current Cinema." New Yorker, 24 (29
    May), 66-67.
        Reviews Another Part of the Forest (film). The adapta-
    tion is faithful to the play but the unrelieved villainy of
    the Hubbards becomes monotonous; the acting is pedestrian.

13 NAGELBERG, MUNJON MOSES, ed. Drama in Our Time. New York:
    Harcourt Brace, 478 pp.
        Includes text of Watch on the Rhine, with comments.

14 NOBLE, PETER. "Stroheim--His Work and Influence." Sight and
    Sound, 16 (Winter 1947-48), 163-66.
        Brief mention of The North Star.

15 P.[RYOR], T.[HOMAS] M. "The Screen." New York Times (19
    May), p. 30.
        Reviews film adaptation of Another Part of the Forest.
    Commends the script by Vladimir Pozner for preserving the
    essence of Hellman's play and Michael Gordon's direction
    for its fluidity. Hellman's fascinating drama is compel-
    lingly entertaining as a film. Her statements about the
    misuses of ill-gotten wealth are as applicable to our own
    time as to the period of her tale.

16 PRYOR, THOMAS M. "Reviews in Brief." New York Times (23
    May), section 2, p. 1.
        Brief, laudatory remarks on the screen adaptation of
    Another Part of the Forest.

17 SPILLER, ROBERT E., et al., eds. Literary History of the
    United States. Vol. 2. New York: Macmillan, pp. 1314,
    1330.
        Brief discussion of Hellman's plays. Despite their
    theatrical dexterity and popular and critical success,
    Hellman's plays (through Another Part of the Forest) suffer
    from "a propagandistic element which makes it difficult to
    take her artistic pretensions with full seriousness."
    Written by Joseph Wood Krutch. See also Spiller et al.:
    1953.29, 1963.57, 1974.41.

18 _____. Literary History of the United States. Vol. 3.
        Bibliography. New York: Macmillan, p. 161.
        Brief mention of Hellman, whose dramatic productions
    "may be represented by" The Children's Hour, The Little

1948

Foxes, and Watch on the Rhine. See also Spiller et al.:
1953.30, 1963.56, 1972.37, 1974.40.

19 SUTHERLAND, ANNE C., and BEULAH C. RATHBUN. The Dramatic
Index for 1947. Boston: F. W. Faxon Company, pp. 21, 143;
appendix, pp. 40, 43, 50.
Cites items related to Hellman and Another Part of the
Forest. Also notes editions of her plays published in
1948.

*20 WEINGARTER, JOSEPH A. Modern American Playwrights, 1918-1948:
A Bibliography. New York: Privately Printed.
Cited by E. Hudson Long, in American Drama from Its
Beginnings to the Present. See 1970.26.

*21 WILLINGHAM, JOHN R. "Social Problems in American Drama from
1930 to 1940." Master's thesis, English, North Texas
State University.
Includes Hellman. Cited in Emerson and Michael,
Southern Literary Culture: A Bibliography of Masters' and
Doctors' Theses, 1979.10.

1949

*1 AFANAS'EV, O. "O 'dobrykh' i 'zlykh' plantorakh (Ledi i
dzhentl'meny)" [About "good" and "evil" planters (Ladies
and gentlemen)]. Teatre (no. 12), pp. 95-98.
Discusses Russian production of Another Part of the
Forest (retitled Ladies and Gentlemen). Cited in Valentina
Libman, Russian Studies of American Literature, 1969.31.

2 ANON. "Hellman Week on Broadway." Cue (1 October), 14-15.
Article and photos on the impending, consecutive openings of Montserrat and Regina.

3 ANON. "Hundreds Named as Red Appeasers." New York Times (9
June), p. 5.
California State Senate Committee on Un-American
Activities names Hellman and several hundred others as
followers of the Communist party line.

4 ANON. Item. Vogue, 114 (1 November), 110.
Photo from Montserrat, with brief comments.

5 ANON. "Moscow Acclaims a Hellman Play." New York Times (18
October), p. 34.

News report on the "distinguished premiere" at the
Moscow Drama Theatre of <u>Another Part of the Forest</u> (re-
named <u>Ladies and Gentlemen</u>). The article notes that the
production was on "an extremely high professional level"
and drew more than a dozen curtain calls following the
five-hour performance.

6 ANON. "Moscow Likes Hellman Play." <u>New York Times</u> (17
   October), p. 19.
      Reuters dispatch noting the Moscow Drama Theatre opening
   of <u>Another Part of the Forest</u>, under the title of <u>Ladies
   and Gentlemen</u>, before "a packed house."

7 ANON. "National Affairs: Peace: Everybody Wars over It."
   <u>Newsweek</u>, 33 (4 April), 19-22.
      Reports on the Cultural and Scientific Conference for
   World Peace, held at the Waldorf-Astoria Hotel, and the
   controversy involving Hellman and Norman Cousins. Photo.

8 ANON. "The New Season, 1949-1950." <u>Theatre Arts</u>, 33
   (October), 14.
      Mentions forthcoming production of <u>Montserrat</u>; large
   photo of Hellman.

9 ANON. "Red Rumpus: The Russians Get a Big Hand from U.S.
   Friends." <u>Life</u>, 26 (4 April), 40, 43.
      Reports on the Cultural and Scientific Conference for
   World Peace, smearing, among others, Hellman, Albert
   Einstein, Arthur Miller, Norman Mailer, and Dorothy Parker.
   Features photo of Hellman laughing at what the article
   calls "pro-communist propaganda" remarks by conference
   host Harlow Shapely. The continuation of the article, p.
   43, is headed: "Dupes and Fellow Travellers Dress Up
   Communist Fronts." Hellman is pictured again, along with
   numerous other celebrities, all of whom, the report states,
   "have persistently lent their names to organizations
   labeled by the U.S. Attorney General or other government
   agencies as subversive. . . . Innocently or not, they
   accomplish quite as much for the Kremlin in their glamorous
   ways as a card holder does in his drab toil."

10 ANON. Review of <u>Montserrat</u>. <u>Christian Science Monitor</u> (5
    November).
       Finds <u>Montserrat</u> a "heavy, stilted" play.

11 ANON. "Soviet Paper Finds Hellman Play Fails." <u>New York
    Times</u> (13 November), section 1, p. 83.

1949

Report on criticisms leveled at the Russian production
of Another Part of the Forest by Soviet Art: Hellman's
play merely portrays a conflict between two swindlers,
instead of depicting a sufficiently scornful exposé of the
capitalist system.

12 ANON. "Theater: Montserrat." Newsweek, 34 (7 November), 80-
81.
Review finds Montserrat a disappointment. The play's
faults, especially its monotonous device of giving each
hostage his "moment of special pleading," seems inherent
in Roblès's original version.

13 ANON. "The Theater: New Musical Play in Manhattan." Time,
54 (14 November), 46.
Although Regina tends to treat Hellman's Hubbards
comically, "it is an exhilarating and enjoyable show."

14 ANON. "The Theater: New Play in Manhattan." Time, 54 (7
November), 79-80.
Review of Montserrat. The play is frequently talky but
is also effectively melodramatic. Hellman's sharpness and
bite are much in evidence, especially in the sardonic
characterization of Izquierdo.

15 ANON. "Theater: Regina." Newsweek, 34 (14 November), 84-85.
Generally positive review of Regina.

16 ANON. "Venezuelan Venture." Theatre Arts, 33 (November), 44-
47.
Photographic essay on costume designer Irene Sharaff,
emphasizing her work for Montserrat. Photos include
Hellman, Sharaff, actors in the production.

17 ATKINSON, BROOKS. "At the Theatre." New York Times (31
October), p. 21.
Review of Montserrat criticizes the absence of motivation, excessive carnage on stage, and "monotonous" direction by Hellman.

18 _____. "At the Theatre." New York Times (1 November), p. 32.
Review of Regina. Although Blitzstein has written a
brilliant score, The Little Foxes has been softened and
made less melodramatic. Whatever has been added to
Hellman's play "does not compensate for the loss in force,
belligerence and directness."

19 ____. "Musical Experiment." New York Times (13 November), section 2, p. 1.

Calls Regina a "notable experiment that does not succeed." The work is a modern opera which would not seem to be the proper form for The Little Foxes, "a realistic study of character representing a specific social point of view."

20 BARNES, HOWARD. "Brilliant Adaptation." New York Herald Tribune (31 October), p. 10.

Praises Hellman's adaptation of Montserrat highly. The work is conversational and repetitious, but "to the great credit of Miss Hellman, she has made it frequently eloquent in her translation and remarkably full of action in her staging."

21 ____. "The Play: Little Musical Foxes." New York Herald Tribune (1 November), p. 18.

Regina presents the "malevolent Hubbard clan singing and sometimes dancing their way through the baleful scenes which made the original play one of the memorable events of the modern theatre. . . . The musical embellishments have not illuminated the Hellman work." Generally, the dramatic impact of "a fine tragedy" has been lost.

22 BEAUFORT, JOHN. Review of Regina. Christian Science Monitor (5 November).

Praises Regina highly.

23 BERNSTEIN, LEONARD. "Prelude to a Musical." New York Times (30 October), section 2, pp. 1, 3.

Discusses Regina, on the eve of its Broadway premiere. The musical adaptation of The Little Foxes represents Marc Blitzstein's apex, a summation of what he has been trying to do. The ugly dealings of Hellman's play and the dependence of the plot on talk of schemes, percentages, and deaths would appear to deny musical possibilities. Yet, Blitzstein's musical treatment is inventive, urbane, and dramatically appropriate for Hellman's characters.

24 BOLTON, WHITNEY. "'Foxes' Loses Something in Transition to Opera." New York Morning Telegraph (2 November).

The Little Foxes loses much of its brutality in Marc Blitzstein's adaptation, Regina.

25 ____. "Montserrat Not Quite Perfect." New York Morning Telegraph (1 November).

The typical Hellman astringency is present in Montserrat.

1949

26 BRON[STEIN, ARTHUR]. Review of Regina. Variety (2 November).
        Finds Regina a "highly intriguing and meritorious work"
   musically and thematically, though the opera "isn't likely
   to be boxoffice on Broadway."

27 BROWN, JOHN MASON. "With and Without Music." Saturday
   Review, 32 (19 November), 53-55.
        Combined review of Montserrat and Regina. Argues that
   Hellman generally reaches her moral conclusions through the
   contrived and taut means associated with melodrama. "She
   has never been one to show Beauty without the Beast."
   Montserrat, poorly directed by Hellman, is a repetitious
   and static bore. Blitzstein's adaptation of Little Foxes
   receives an admirable production, but the music of Regina
   "undoes the very thing Miss Hellman had done well. It
   interrupts the action, annihilates the illusion and
   destroys the suspense." The Little Foxes should have been
   left alone.

*28 BURKE, WILLIAM M. "American Playwrights' Treatment of War,
   1914-1949." Ph.D. dissertation, American Studies,
   University of Pennsylvania.
        Discusses Watch on the Rhine and The Searching Wind.
   Cited in Emerson and Michael, Southern Literary Culture: A
   Bibliography of Masters' and Doctors' Theses, 1979.10.

29 CASSIDY, FREDERIC GOMES, ed. Modern American Plays. New
   York: Longmans, Green, 501 pp.
        Includes text of Watch on the Rhine, with comments.

30 CHAPMAN, JOHN. "The Little Foxes Loses Its Wallop in New
   Musical Version, Regina." New York Daily News (1
   November).
        Criticizes Marc Blitzstein's adaptation of The Little
   Foxes. The music interferes with the plot of "what used
   to be a good play."

31 _____. "Montserrat a Brutal Melodrama." New York Daily News
   (31 October).
        Praises the adaptation of Montserrat by Hellman, "the
   most uncompromising and hardest-headed of women dramatists."

32 CLURMAN, HAROLD. "Theatre: Roblès, Hellman, Blitzstein."
   New Republic, 121 (5 December), 21-22.
        Reviews Montserrat and Regina. Clurman objects to
   Hellman's imposition of realistic style and atmosphere on
   Montserrat and to her error in believing that she was

adapting a "revolutionary" play. Contrastingly, Marc Blitzstein's Regina is "an interesting attempt to extend the limitations and conventions of our stage beyond the flat statement of journalistic naturalism and the merely decorative theatricality of our musical comedy and operetta." Blitzstein does not sufficiently depart from the Hellman material but his musical drama should be seen by true theater lovers.

33 COLEMAN, ROBERT. "Montserrat Well Acted But Script Is Bumpy." New York Daily Mirror (31 October).
Finds the script of Montserrat "uneven and insufficiently motivated."

34 _____. "Regina Is an Arresting Adaptation of Foxes." New York Daily Mirror (1 November).
Finds Regina an interesting experiment that "aims well even when it misses."

35 CURRIE, GEORGE. "Theater." Brooklyn Eagle (1 November).
Finds Regina an interesting but flawed experiment.

36 DASH, THOMAS R. Review of Montserrat. Women's Wear Daily (31 October).
Calls Montserrat a significant, vital, and revealing play.

37 _____. Review of Regina. Women's Wear Daily (1 November).
Calls Regina a work of "inspired art."

*38 EMEL'IANOV, B. "Mnimoe razoblachenie (Ledi i dzhentl'meny)" [A pretended unmasking (Ladies and Gentlemen)]. Sovetskoe iskustsvo (12 November).
Discusses Moscow production of Another Part of the Forest (retitled Ladies and Gentlemen). Cited in Valentina Libman, Russian Studies of American Literature, 1969.31.

39 FIELD, ROWLAND. "Musical Drama." Newark Evening News (1 November), p. 58.
Considers Regina a thrilling adaptation of The Little Foxes.

40 FUNKE, LEWIS. "News and Gossip Gathered on the Rialto." New York Times (30 January), section 2, p. 1.
Notes Hellman's progress on Montserrat.

41 GARLAND, ROBERT. "Grand Grand Opera, An Excellent Show." New York Journal American (1 November).

1949

        Strongly approves of <u>Regina</u>. "When words are too melo-
dramatic to be spoken, they are better sung. Thus it is
with <u>The Little Foxes</u>. Without the composer's comple-
mentary setting, the nasty Alabama Hubbards are no more
than talky pre-Tennessee Williams samples of Southern
Discomfort at its most discomforting. Only Regina has
character."

42   . Review of <u>Montserrat</u>. <u>New York Journal American</u> (31
October), p. 8.
        Says there must be more to <u>Montserrat</u> than Hellman, as
adapter and director, gets out of it, but the play is
nevertheless grim and fascinating.

43 GASSNER, JOHN. "The Theatre Arts." <u>Forum</u>, 112 (December),
337-40.
        Reviews <u>Montserrat</u> and <u>Regina</u>. <u>Montserrat</u> illustrates
the contemporary theater's reluctance to depart from well-
made realism. The minds and pasts of Montserrat and the
hostages should have been presented expressionistically,
through a full use of theatricality, not tight dramaturgy.
Hellman's direction of her own adaptation is "pedestrian."
<u>Regina</u>, though expert, clever, and interesting, diminishes
the power of <u>The Little Foxes</u>.

44 GIBBS, WOLCOTT. "The End and the Means." <u>New Yorker</u>, 25 (5
November), 62, 64.
        Review of <u>Montserrat</u>. Hellman and Roblès make their
point that "a dedicated revolutionary is justified in
betraying his country and sacrificing six innocent lives
for the ultimate good of the cause," but they set up
"highly special circumstances to prove general theories."
The hero spouts "virtuous nonsense" in this contrived,
hollow play.

45   . "The Theatre: Boston, Alabama, and Johannesburg."
<u>New Yorker</u>, 25 (12 November), 54-59.
        Includes review of <u>Regina</u>. Marc Blitzstein has done a
surprisingly able job of transforming <u>The Little Foxes</u> into
an opera. His primary addition has been "a troupe of Negro
singers, servants on the Hubbard estate, who . . . provide
an innocent contrast to the depravity of their white
masters and . . . introduce a note of aboriginal, or at any
rate non-capitalistic, gaiety into the score."

46 GRAHAM, VIRGINIA. "The Cinema." <u>Spectator</u>, 182 (4 March),
287.

Praises the film version of <u>Another Part of the Forest</u>.
Hellman has the ability to invest her characters "with
every deadly sin without straining one's credulity."

47 GREEN, E. M. Item. <u>Theatre World</u>, 45 (December), 28.
On <u>Regina</u> and <u>Montserrat</u>.

48 HAWKINS, WILLIAM. "Montserrat Hits Like 'Quake." <u>New York
World-Telegram</u> (31 October).
Considers Hellman's adaptation and direction of
<u>Montserrat</u> shattering in their impact.

49 _____. "<u>Regina</u> Is Exciting Musical Exposition." <u>New York
World-Telegram</u> (1 November).
Highly favorable review of <u>Regina</u>. "It is the most
exciting musical theater I know since <u>Rosenkavalier</u>."

50 JOHNSON, HARRIET. "Music: The Musical Aspects of <u>Regina</u>."
<u>New York Post</u> (1 November).
Generally praises Blitzstein's music as a vehicle for
the work.

51 KRACAUER, SIEGFRIED. "National Types as Hollywood Presents
Them." <u>Public Opinion Quarterly</u>, 13 (Spring), 53-72.
Mentions <u>The North Star</u> in a section devoted to the film
image of Russia in wartime.
Reprinted in <u>The Movies: An American Idiom</u>, ed. Michael
McClure. <u>See</u> 1971.22.

52 LAWSON, JOHN HOWARD. <u>Theory and Technique of Playwriting and
Screenwriting</u>. New York: G. P. Putnam's Sons, 464 pp.
Reprints 1936.52 with additional material on writing
for film. <u>Theory and Technique of Playwriting</u>, excluding
film section, reprinted 1960, Hill and Wang Dramabook edition. <u>See</u> 1960.47.

53 MARSHALL, MARGARET. "Drama." <u>Nation</u>, 169 (12 November), 478.
Combined reviews of <u>Montserrat</u> and <u>Regina</u>. <u>Montserrat</u>
"touches upon all the themes that are so dear to the hearts
of leftists committed to the class struggle," and these
themes have lost any freshness they once had. The play is
contrived and dated, but this adaptation "shows the hand of
an experienced and skillful worker in the theater." Music
ill suits the Hubbards in <u>Regina</u>; "the little foxes tend to
seem more funny than fierce."

1949

54 MOREHOUSE, WARD. "Broadway After Dark: Visit with Miss
    Hellman." New York Sun (16 December).
        Interview, especially on Montserrat and Regina. Photo.

55 _____. Matinee Tomorrow. New York: McGraw Hill, pp. 248-49,
    261, 267, 269, 274, 290.
        Several references to Hellman's critical reputation, her
    early career, and her feud with Tallulah Bankhead. Praises
    her work highly. Photo.

56 _____. Review of Montserrat. New York Sun (31 October).
        Calls Montserrat grim and harrowing, but finally disap-
    pointing.

57 _____. Review of Regina. New York Sun (1 November).
        Considers Regina a fascinating experiment that retains
    the power of The Little Foxes.

58 [MORRISON,] HOBE. Review of Montserrat. Variety (2
    November).
        Calls the play "a powerful but heavy drama with limited
    boxoffice appeal."

59 NATHAN, GEORGE JEAN. "Still Another Stage Battlecry for
    Freedom." New York Journal American (7 November), p. 24.
        Reviews Montserrat, "a play that consumes two hours to
    inform us that liberty and freedom are considerable posses-
    sions and that they are not to be had without some sacri-
    fice."
        Slightly revised, 1950.13.

60 NEW YORK THEATRE CRITICS' REVIEWS, 1949. Vol. 10. New York:
    Critics' Theatre Reviews, pp. 237-40, 244-47.
        Reprints reviews of Montserrat from New York daily news-
    papers for 31 October 1949 and reviews of Regina from the
    same newspapers for 1 November 1949: New York Sun, New
    York World-Telegram, New York Post, New York Journal
    American, New York Herald Tribune, New York Times, Daily
    Mirror, Daily News.

61 NICOLL, ALLARDYCE. World Drama: From Aeschylus to Anouilh.
    New York: Harper and Row.
        General discussion of Hellman in a section entitled
    "Current American Realism." In her plays of the 1930s and
    early 1940s, "she stands about midway between the social
    playwrights and those realistic writers who are intent upon
    depiction of character."
        Revised 1976.85.

62 PARKE, RICHARD. "Our Way Defended to 2,000 Opening 'Culture'
    Meeting." New York Times (26 March), 1, 3.
        Reports on controversial Cultural and Scientific Con-
    ference for World Peace in New York. Cites Hellman's
    criticisms of Norman Cousins and Sidney Hook.

*63 PARRISH, JAMES A. "A Study of the Plays of Lillian Hellman."
    Master's thesis, English, Florida State University.
        Cited in Emerson and Michael, Southern Literary Culture:
    A Bibliography of Masters' and Doctors' Theses, 1979.10.

64 PHELAN, KAPPO. "The Stage and Screen: Montserrat."
    Commonweal, 51 (18 November), 179-80.
        Calls Montserrat an absorbing play, "an occasion for
    gratitude rather than wrestling analysis." The hero, how-
    ever, has little to say: "His author has sadly tried to
    build a man rather than the illusion of a man, which, for
    the theatre, is nonsense of course, and a most mistaken use
    of a useful medium. . . . And until I can see the play
    again, or read it, I do not feel capable of tracing the
    existentialist line which unquestionably motivates the
    finale: the fact that Montserrat seems only to descend into
    humanity in his author's eyes."

65 _____. "The Stage and Screen: Regina." Commonweal, 51 (2
    December), 238.
        Objects, in a review of Regina, to the comic treatment
    of some of the most serious characters in The Little Foxes,
    especially Ben and Leo; but, overall, finds Regina an
    exciting and intriguing opera.

66 POLLOCK, ARTHUR. "Theater 'Strikes Gold' in Blitzstein's
    Regina." New York Daily Compass (2 November).
        Praises Regina highly.

67 _____. "Theater Time." New York Daily Compass (31 October),
    p. 18.
        Montserrat is "a thrilling play," although the acting
    and direction are not all they might be.

68 SCHNEIDER, ALAN, and MICHAEL LAURENCE. Letters to the Drama
    Editor. New York Times (30 October), section 2, p. 3.
        Two responses to Hellman's comments about directing in
    an interview with Murray Schumach, New York Times, 23
    October. See 1949.69.

69 SCHUMACH, MURRAY. "Miss Hellman Discusses Directors." New
    York Times (23 October), section 2, pp. 1, 3.

Interview (a week before the opening of Montserrat, which Hellman adapted and directed) in which she discusses her reasons for directing her own plays.

70 SHERWOOD, ROBERT E. "Footnote to a Preface." Saturday Review, 32 (6 August), 130-35.
Reminiscence of Sherwood's early days in the theater. Brief mention of Hellman, with photo (p. 132).

71 SHIPLEY, JOSEPH T. "On Stage." New Leader (26 November).
Montserrat is gripping in concept but anticlimactic. "The tension grows less, not greater, as one by one the innocents are shot."

72 _____. Review of Regina. New Leader (31 December).
Considers the musical adaptation of The Little Foxes "the early high point of the season."

73 SMITH, C. "Regina: Yet Another Opera on Broadway." Musical America, 69 (1 December), 9.
Reviews Regina.

74 TAUBMAN, HOWARD. "Good Opera Need Not Be Grand Opera." New York Times Magazine (11 December), pp. 14-15, 44-45.
Discusses the ways in which certain musicals of the 1940s, including Regina, attempt to fuse music and action into integrated works. Marc Blitzstein's music helps to bring the atmosphere of the outside world into "contrast with the inbred Hubbards." Regina should be judged as "an independent theatre piece," not strictly in comparison to The Little Foxes.

75 THOMAS, MARGARET LEE. "Lillian Hellman, A Contemporary Dramatist." Master's thesis, English, Columbia University.
Discusses Hellman's plays through Another Part of the Forest.

76 THOMSON, VIRGIL. "Music in Review." New York Herald Tribune (13 November), section 5, p. 6.
Though musically ambitious, Regina is successful chiefly "through the dramatic power" of The Little Foxes. Marc Blitzstein's music is primarily "ironic interpolation."

77 _____. "The Music: Not Quite an Opera." New York Herald Tribune (1 November), p. 18.
Reviews Regina as musical theater. While there are moments of musical interest, "by and large the tonal

habiliment of the script, as performed, is raucous in sound, coarse in texture, explosive, obstreperous and strident."

78 WATTS, RICHARD, JR. "Montserrat, Tragic Play." New York Post (31 October).
      Considers Montserrat a play of "striking philosophical interest." It is thoughtful and provocative rather than emotionally shattering.

79 ____. "A Musical Version of Little Foxes." New York Post (1 November).
      Considers Regina an intelligent and imaginative adaptation of The Little Foxes but doubts that Marc Blitzstein's music improves emotionally upon "what was virtual perfection in its own realistic medium."

80 WHITEBAIT, WILLIAM. "The Movies." New Statesman and Nation, 37 (5 March), 225.
      Considers the screen version of Another Part of the Forest a waste of Hellman's talents.

81 WYATT, EUPHEMIA VAN RENSSELAER. "Theater." Catholic World, 170 (December), 227-29.
      Reviews Montserrat and Regina. Montserrat, whose chief purpose appears to be punishment of the audience, is a "two-act horror drama" in which the cowards have the best roles. Hellman has squandered her time on the Robles play. In Regina, the Hubbards "snarl all the nastier" through Blitzstein's score. Regina herself, in Jane Pickens's performance, lacks any humanity, Birdie resembles an escapee from a psychopathic ward, and Leo "hops about like a harlequin." Only the roles of Ben and Alexandra approach reality.

82 ZOLOTOW, SAM. "Regina, Musical, Will Open Tonight." New York Times (31 October), p. 21.
      Lists cast, production personnel, and other information concerning Marc Blitzstein's musical adaptation of Little Foxes.

1950

1 ANON. Review of The Children's Hour. The Times [London] (22 November), p. 10a.
      Says The Children's Hour fails as an attempt at tragedy but remains an exciting melodrama which treats "a

1950

censorable theme with courage, with sincerity, and with
moving theatrical effect." (Production at New Boltons
Theatre.)

2 ANON. Review of Montserrat. Theatre Arts, 34 (January), 10.
Hellman's adaptation of Montserrat "seems much more
obvious than her usual product, more tricked-up with trans-
parent devices to arouse pathos." The dramatic situation
is unmoving and one sided, bearing little relevance to
genuine moral dilemmas. Photos of Hellman and a scene from
the play.

3 ANON. Review of Regina. Theatre Arts, 34 (January), 12.
Assesses Regina.

4 ANON. "The State of the Theatre: The Strindberg Heritage."
School and Society, 71 (14 January), 23-28.
Analyzes Regina and Montserrat, asserting that Hellman
is among Strindberg's American disciples. The Little
Foxes "gains nothing by being translated into another
medium." The unfolding of Montserrat is "static and flatly
intellectual rather than emotionally compelling."

5 BLUM, DANIEL. A Pictorial History of the American Theatre,
1900-1950. New York: Greenberg, passim.
Numerous brief references and photos from the plays.

*6 BURKE, WILLIAM. "American Playwrights' Treatment of War,
1914-1949." Ph.D. dissertation, University of Pennsylvania.
Listed in American Doctoral Dissertations.

7 CHAPMAN, JOHN, ed. The Burns Mantle Best Plays of 1949-50.
New York: Dodd, Mead and Company, pp. 5, 6, 358-59, 400-
403.
Cast information and brief comments on Montserrat and
Regina.

8 DAVIS, OWEN. My First Fifty Years in the Theatre. Boston:
Walter H. Baker Company, pp. 125-26.
Cites Hellman for writing "the best scene in the modern
drama," the confrontation of Karen and Martha with Mrs.
Tilford in The Children's Hour.

9 GILDER, ROSAMOND, HERMINE RICH ISAACS, ROBERT M. MacGREGOR,
and EDWARD REED, eds. Theatre Arts Anthology. New York:
Theatre Arts Books, Robert M. MacGregor, pp. 124, 649-51.

Reprints 1941.49. Hellman is also briefly mentioned in
a piece entitled "Playwrights and Playwriting" by Howard
Lindsay (p. 124).

*10 HAGAN, ROBERT. "The Influence of the Well-Made Play upon
American Playwriting." Ph.D. dissertation, Case Western
Reserve University.
Listed in Comprehensive Dissertation Index.

11 KEOWN, ERIC. "At the Play." Punch, 219 (6 December), 562.
Maintains that the "delicate London production of The
Children's Hour makes one regret again the intransigence
of the Lord Chamberlain which still denies it a public
stage. . . . Here is a piece by which any thinking adult
must be moved."

12 MARSHALL, MARGARET. "Theater Chronicle." Partisan Review,
17 (January), 76-79.
Reviews Montserrat and Regina. The ostensible message
of Montserrat "is that the end justifies the means, and on
this level it conveys no conviction or belief, is intellectually stale and mechanically contrived. The real pur-
port of the piece is quite different and, I am sure, quite
unintended. Montserrat is a ruthless assault on the sensi-
bilities and on humane values. Izquierdo is its hero, and
its real message is not that cruelty is sometimes necessary
for the achievement of a good but that the power to inflict
or withhold cruelty, and the wielders of such power, are
fascinating and enviable." Says Marc Blitzstein's Regina
makes the Hubbards appear ridiculous. In The Little Foxes,
they were convincing; in Regina, they are merely caricatures.

13 NATHAN, GEORGE JEAN. The Theatre Book of the Year, 1949-1950.
New York: Alfred A. Knopf, pp. 63-71, 77-80.
Reviews Montserrat (slightly revised version of
1949.59). Also discusses Regina: Most of the production's
interest exists in its performance and staging. Marc
Blitzstein's music "confuses shrillness with emotional
intensity."

14 _____. "The Theatre: Two Musical Dramas." American Mercury,
70 (February), 169-73.
Declares Regina unsuccessful for several reasons. Marc
Blitzstein confuses "mere stuntiness with real artistic
achievement" in his transformation of The Little Foxes
into opera.

1950

15 SUTHERLAND, ANNE C., and RUTH H. COOMBS. The Dramatic Index
      for 1948. Boston: F. W. Faxon Company, pp. 21, 144;
      appendix, pp. 48, 62.
          Cites reviews of the movie version of Another Part of
      the Forest. Also notes editions of Hellman plays published
      in 1948.

16 TREWIN, J. C. "Our Critic's First-Night Journal."
      Illustrated London News, 217 (9 December), 962.
          Brief, laudatory comments about the production of The
      Children's Hour at New Boltons, one of the London club
      theaters. This "production should cause the Lord
      Chamberlain to revoke a former ban on a strong, sincere
      drama."

*17 TURNER, CLARENE A. "The Decade of Social Protest in the
      American Drama, 1929-1939." Master's thesis, English,
      Southern Methodist University.
          Includes plays by Hellman. Cited in Emerson and
      Michael, Southern Literary Culture: A Bibliography of
      Masters' and Doctors' Theses, 1979.10.

                           1951

1 ANON. "Drama Still Alive, Stage Experts Say." New York
      Times (2 December), p. 85.
          Quotes Hellman's remarks at a Harvard panel discussion
      on the state of the serious theater.

2 ANON. Review of The Autumn Garden. Christian Science
      Monitor (17 March).
          Objects to the absence of positive characters in the
      play. Hellman presents a "slanted view" of American
      society. "Aware that the drama can be a powerful weapon
      in the war of ideas, playwrights who enjoy the freedoms of
      a democracy may usefully reflect to what extent" they may
      be contributing "to Moscow's arsenal."

3 ANON. Review of The Autumn Garden. Newsweek, 37 (19 March),
      84.
          Says Hellman has in this instance "written about people
      for their own sake, without any 'message' in the conven-
      tional sense." The Autumn Garden brings vividly to life a
      group of middle-aged people who are revealed in "their
      frustration and futile rebellion." The play's conclusion
      is not especially profound.

4 ANON. "The Theater." Time, 57 (19 March), 51-52.
     Reviews The Autumn Garden. Hellman's character por-
traits, "without being unsympathetic, are adultly uncompromising." The play utilizes the "relaxed Chekhovian
method without his unifying lyrical mood." The Autumn
Garden contends that people are the products of their past
actions and the play's point--"that lack of character is
also fate--is sharply driven home."

5 ATKINSON, BROOKS. "First Night at the Theatre." New York
     Times (8 March), p. 36.
     Review of The Autumn Garden, in which Hellman is saying
that middle-aged people bear responsibility for the sort of
people they have become. The past cannot be escaped. Aimless in mood, The Autumn Garden depends upon Chekhov for
its form. Its characterizations are brilliantly drawn and
eminently actable, but the play, like its characters, tends
to be "boneless and torpid."

6 _____. Review of The Autumn Garden. New York Times (18
     March), section 2, p. 1.
     Sunday review finds The Autumn Garden "a scrupulous
drama," in which Hellman gives the impression that she is
leaving her characters to their own devices. Artistically
fascinating though the characters may be, they infect the
play with their own malaises. In most respects, The Autumn
Garden is Hellman's "most discerning drama."

6a BAZIN, ANDRÉ. "A Final Word About Depth of Focus." Cahiers
     du Cinéma, 1 (April).
     Discusses William Wyler's placement of the metal box, in
his direction of the film version of The Little Foxes, in
order to show how the single-shot sequence can improve
upon montage. See 1971.13.

7 BOLTON, WHITNEY. "Hellman's Autumn Garden Fascinating,
     Brilliant Study." New York Morning Telegraph (9 March).
     Calls The Autumn Garden a fascinating and occasionally
puzzling play.

8 BROWN, JOHN MASON. "Seeing Things: A New Miss Hellman."
     Saturday Review, 34 (31 March), 27-29.
     Praises The Autumn Garden and comments at some length
upon Hellman's shift from an Ibsenite approach to a
Chekhovian one. She is now more concerned with the
revelation of inward crises of her characters than with
outward climaxes.

1951

9   CHAPMAN, JOHN. "Hellman's Autumn Garden Meaty Comedy Played
    by Flawless Cast." New York Daily News (8 March).
        Reviews The Autumn Garden. Considers it a kindly, pro-
    found, intelligent "comedy" with a remarkable cast.

10   _____, ed. The Best Plays of 1950-51. New York: Dodd, Mead
    and Company, pp. 11, 43, 125-54, 306, 355, 379, 388-92.
        Condenses The Autumn Garden. Calls it a Chekhovian
    comedy and Hellman's best play. "It looks rather affec-
    tionately upon the sad and funny frailties of the human
    being." Production information.

11   CLURMAN, HAROLD. "Director's Explanation." New York Times
    (22 April), section 2, p. 3.
        Letter to the drama editor explaining the character of
    Sophie in The Autumn Garden.

12   _____. "Lillian Hellman's Garden." New Republic, 124 (26
    March), 21-22.
        Clurman, who directed the Broadway production of The
    Autumn Garden, reviews the play, which has "the density of
    a big novel." The characters are more representative of
    most of us than we care to believe, for Hellman is saying
    "that each of our lives constitutes a decisive act, and
    that when the chain of these acts reaches a certain point--
    around the middle years--no sudden movement of our will is
    likely to alter the shape and meaning of what we have
    made." The Autumn Garden is the subtlest and most probing
    of Hellman's works. Witty, lucid, and dramatic, its one
    limitation lies in Hellman's failure to consider her
    characters worthy of her (or our) love. She "is a fine
    artist; she will be a finer one when she melts."
        Reprinted 1958.5 and 1960.26.

13   COLEMAN, ROBERT. "Autumn Garden Harps on Depressing Theme."
    New York Daily Mirror (8 March).
        Review of The Autumn Garden. Says Hellman has few peers
    at portraying "human meanness, loneliness and frustration."
    But in this play her characters appear to be puppets that
    she manipulates "too obviously and futilely."

14   DARBY, EILEEN. Review of The Autumn Garden. Theatre Arts,
    35 (May), 18.
        The Autumn Garden "is almost Lillian Hellman's finest
    play." Its omission of one "single redeeming character who
    might leave us with a glimmer of hope" is a mistake. While
    Hellman's characterizations represent her at her finest,
    one does wish that she had been more compassionate.

15 DASH, THOMAS R. Review of <u>The Autumn Garden</u>. <u>Women's Wear</u>
    <u>Daily</u> (8 March).
        In this play, Hellman is "in a much more mellow mood."
    The Chekhovian play is her forte.

16 DOWNER, ALAN S. <u>Fifty Years of American Drama, 1900-1950</u>.
    Chicago: Henry Regnery Company, pp. 60-61, 137, 139-41.
        Hellman's portrait of the Hubbards "has not been
    equalled on our stage for its effective combination of
    brutality and pathos." In <u>Watch on the Rhine</u> and <u>The</u>
    <u>Searching Wind</u>, Hellman permits her convictions about the
    war to overwhelm her dramatic structure and to divide her
    attention "between human motives and political commentary."
    <u>The Autumn Garden</u>, structurally and thematically, is her
    most original play. "Humanely, it reveals the nature of
    our life, of our means to grace."

17 DRUTMAN, IRVING. "Author's Problem--What to Do After Play
    Opens?" <u>New York Herald Tribune</u> (18 October), section 4,
    p. 2.
        Hellman discusses the writing of <u>The Autumn Garden</u> and
    the letdown she experiences after the play's Broadway
    opening.

18 FIELD, ROWLAND. Review of <u>The Autumn Garden</u>. <u>Newark Evening</u>
    <u>News</u> (8 March).
        Negative review; calls the play "literate but limp."

19 GASSNER, JOHN. "Entropy in the Drama." <u>Theatre Arts</u>, 35
    (September), 16-17, 73.
        Surveys possible reasons for critical reservations
    regarding <u>The Autumn Garden</u>. Gassner praises the deft,
    sure manner in which Hellman--"stern moralist always, our
    hanging-judge of the American theatre"--made her thematic
    points. But audiences and critics never knew where
    Hellman stood and, especially, what she stood <u>for</u> in this
    play: "Miss Hellman, possibly infected with the under-
    standable despair of the intelligentsia, or possibly
    straining for a symbolic but discreetly attenuated repre-
    sentation of the failures of society, made her indictment
    too general to be entirely effective, and her resolution
    too dubious to be satisfying." The style of <u>The Autumn</u>
    <u>Garden</u> "was Hellman's, not Chekhov's in the least."

20 GILDER, ROSAMOND. "Broadway Highlights." <u>Drama</u>, New Series,
    no. 22 (Autumn), 16-20.

1951

Includes comments on The Autumn Garden (New York production). It is "less closely knit, less violent and
forthright than most of Miss Hellman's writing."

21 GILROY, HARRY. "Lillian Hellman Drama Foregoes a Villain."
New York Times (25 February), section 2, pp. 1, 3.
Interview with Hellman on the writing of The Autumn
Garden shortly before the play's Broadway opening.

22 GUERNSEY, OTIS. "The Theaters: Some Leaves are Golden." New
York Herald Tribune (8 March), p. 18.
Muted review of The Autumn Garden finds "good theater"
within Hellman's "scattered script." Hellman "has taken
another look at the South (though these people could come
from anywhere), this time without an edge in her words.
Her work is rounded, diffuse and sometimes almost shallow,
but it provides a suitable gallery for a company" of experienced performers.

23 HAWKINS, WILLIAM. "Autumn Garden Is Rich and Mellow." New
York World-Telegram and The Sun (8 March).
Reviews The Autumn Garden; finds it an engrossing play
which will give audiences the feeling of "being distinctly
superior to the people on the stage."

24 KERR, WALTER. "The Stage: The Autumn Garden." Commonweal,
53 (6 April), 645.
The Autumn Garden is a fascinating play so long as
Hellman probes her characters for their failure "to live
in the moment and to recognize the moment as the absolute
condition" of their lives. The play's difficulty lies in
her determination to handle her themes through multiple
examples, resulting in repetitiousness and a lack of
balance. The Autumn Garden might have succeeded as tragedy
had it been the study of one man.

25 LAMBERT, GAVIN. "Portrait of an Actress: Bette Davis." Sight
and Sound, 21 (August-September), 12-19.
Contains several references to Davis roles in screen
adaptations of The Little Foxes and Watch on the Rhine.
Photos.

26 LANGNER, LAWRENCE. The Magic Curtain. New York: E. P.
Dutton and Company, Inc., p. 440.
Briefly mentions Hellman as one of a group of American
playwrights of the highest rank.

1951

27 LARDNER, JOHN. "The Theatre: The First Team Takes Over."
    New Yorker, 27 (17 March), 52-54.
         Review of The Autumn Garden. Viewers may miss the
    "emotional zing" and violence of Hellman's mood in the
    earlier plays. Her dialogue and organization remain sharp
    ꞏ and accurate but she shows signs of having mellowed in her
    attitude toward her characters. "The important thing is
    that Miss Hellman, writing without the cold fury of former
    times, continues to show more intelligence and craftsman-
    ship than almost any other present-day playwright."

*28 LEE, FLORA M. S. "The Forces of Evil in the Plays of Lillian
    Hellman." Master's thesis, English, Hardin-Simmons
    University.
         Cited in Emerson and Michael, Southern Literary Culture:
    A Bibliography of Masters' and Doctors' Theses, 1979.10.

29 McCLAIN, JOHN. "Play at Coronet Beautifully Set." New York
    Journal American (8 March).
         Reviews The Autumn Garden. Finds the writing stimulat-
    ing and assured but has some reservations about Hellman's
    attempt to juggle too much at once. Notices similarities
    to The Cherry Orchard.

30 MARSHALL, MARGARET. "Drama." Nation, 172 (17 March), 257.
         Review of The Autumn Garden. Hellman's competence and
    humor serve her well but it is difficult to dramatize bore-
    dom and futility. The plot "tends to be unconvincing when
    it is most like action and boring when it is most con-
    vincing."

31 [MORRISON,] HOBE. Review of The Autumn Garden. Variety (14
    March).
         Considers The Autumn Garden a thoughtful, probing, but
    diffuse play.

32 NATHAN, GEORGE JEAN. "Miss Hellman Buries the Middle-Aged."
    New York Journal American (19 March), p. 14.
         Assesses The Autumn Garden as a "diffuse and somnambu-
    listic play" whose theme gets lost somewhere in the script.
    The characters are primarily "comic figures pulled into
    tragic postures at the end of wires manipulated by a puppet
    master dressed in the blouse of Turgenev and the hat of
    Chekhov." Their fate is a mindlessness arbitrarily imposed
    by Hellman. What she may believe to be complex characteri-
    zations profoundly analyzed are simpleminded people
    illuminated "with a small pocket flashlight."
         Reprinted 1951.33.

1951

33 _____. The Theatre Book of the Year, 1950-51. New York:
   Alfred A. Knopf, pp. 241-44.
      Reprints 1951.32.

34 NEW YORK THEATRE CRITICS' REVIEWS, 1951. Vol. 12. New York:
   Critics' Theatre Reviews, pp. 325-27.
      Reprints reviews of The Autumn Garden from New York
   daily newspapers for 8 March 1951 (New York Journal
   American, New York World-Telegram and The Sun, New York
   Times, New York Herald Tribune, New York Post, Daily
   Mirror, Daily News).

35 POLLOCK, ARTHUR. "The Autumn Garden Is Miss Hellman in a
   Pessimistic Mood." New York Daily Compass (9 March).
      Negative review.

36 S., F. Review of The Children's Hour. Theatre World, 47
   (January), 6.
      Praises the English production of The Children's Hour
   at the New Boltons Theatre Club.

37 SCHUTTE, LOUIS H., and LEWIS HOWARD. Letters to the Drama
   Editor. New York Times (13 May), section 2, p. 3.
      Conflicting opinions of The Autumn Garden.

38 SHEAFFER, LOUIS. "Curtain Time." Brooklyn Eagle (8 March),
   p. 4.
      Praises The Autumn Garden as "a compassionate piece of
   work, rich in understanding."

39 SHIPLEY, JOSEPH. "On Stage: Hellman Drags, Herbert Soars."
   New Leader (19 March).
      Dismisses The Autumn Garden as "an unattractive hodge-
   podge."

40 WATTS, RICHARD, JR. "Lillian Hellman's Latest Drama." New
   York Post (8 March).
      Reviews The Autumn Garden as an adult, interesting
   drama which "lacks the biting and overwhelming theatrical
   power that we have come to expect" from Hellman. The
   characters are believable, average people but they never
   acquire genuine dramatic interest.

41 WYATT, EUPHEMIA VAN RENSSELAER. "Theater." Catholic World,
   173 (April), 67-68.
      Review of The Autumn Garden. Hellman has created "real
   people" living through the critical period of middle age.

Thematically, the play resembles Pinero's The Second Mrs. Tanqueray.

1952

1 ANON. "Lillian Hellman Balks House Unit." New York Times (22 May), p. 15.
   News report of Hellman's appearance before the House Un-American Activities Committee. Quotes Hellman's letter to the committee.

2 ANON. Review of Montserrat. The Times [London] (9 April), p. 6d.
   Criticizes Montserrat for not concentrating on the mind and moral dilemma of the idealistic captain. Instead, the audience experiences a moral dilemma of its own: "How far should we give ourselves up to the enjoyment of prolonged torture simply for the sake of easy theatrical excitement?" Photo, p. 10d. (Production at Lyric Theatre, Hammersmith.)

3 ANON. "Theater: The Children's Hour." Newsweek, 40 (29 December), 40.
   Review praises The Children's Hour revival highly. Even in the third act, which shifts attention from the sadistic child in order to focus upon the victims and a melodramatic resolution, The Children's Hour represents "theatrical writing at its most effective."

4 ANON. The Theater: Meeting-Goer." Time, 59 (2 June), 74.
   Innuendo-filled report on Hellman's appearance before the House Un-American Activities Committee. Photo.

5 ANON. "The Theater: Old Play in Manhattan." Time, 60 (29 December), 55.
   Review of The Children's Hour. The play, after eighteen years, remains "vivid and powerful." It explores such issues as the awful power of gossip and the "psychopathic nature of evil." The final scene assumes, "emotionally and morally, a sense of the tragic."

6 ATKINSON, BROOKS. "At the Theater." New York Times (19 December), p. 35.
   The revival of The Children's Hour suggests that, good as it originally was, the play may in fact have grown in stature. The story has particular relevance to a time

1952

when lives are being destroyed by slander. Hellman "has
never written so tersely or accurately."

7   _____. "Children's Hour." New York Times (28 December),
       section 2, p. 1.
          Sunday analysis of The Children's Hour revival. The
       production makes almost everything on Broadway appear
       "trifling and irrelevant." Hellman had a terrible tale to
       tell in 1934. "What we have learned about slander in the
       meantime confirms the clarity of her thinking and the vio-
       lence of her feeling on the threshold of her career
       eighteen years ago."

8   BANKHEAD, TALLULAH. Tallulah. New York: Harper and Brothers,
       pp. 21, 23, 25, 35, 103, 106, 229, 237-59, 283, 290, 304-
       305.
          Autobiography of the actress who originated the role of
       Regina Giddens. Contains numerous references to The Little
       Foxes and to Hellman. Considerable attention is given to
       the well-publicized feud with Hellman over the Russian
       invasion of Finland. Photos of Bankhead as Regina.

9   BEAUFORT, JOHN. "Tragic Children's Hour." Christian Science
       Monitor (27 December).
          Hellman's preoccupation with the problem of evil has
       lost none of its shattering effect in The Children's Hour.
       The revival shows again that it is a soundly crafted play.

10   BOLTON, WHITNEY. "Stage: Children's Hour Still Taut, Powerful
       Drama." New York Morning Telegraph (20 December).
          The play is as "crisp and tragic" as it was in 1934.

11   BROWN, IVOR. "At the Theatre." London Observer (13 April),
       p. 6.
          Reviews the London staging of Montserrat. Hellman's
       adaptation from the French "must certainly be deemed, as an
       American once said of Matthew Arnold, 'nowhere to go for a
       laugh.' It provides two hours of agonized suspense with
       Spanish atmospherics and acute, distinguished performance."

12   CHAPMAN, JOHN. "Revival of The Children's Hour Strong in Plot,
       Weak in Acting." New York Daily News (19 December).
          Review of The Children's Hour revival. The "melodra-
       matic tragedy" remains "taut and vigorous--but, after all
       it isn't a classic." It requires better acting than it is
       receiving in this production.

13 COMMITTEE ON UN-AMERICAN ACTIVITIES. "Communist Infiltration of the Hollywood Motion-Picture Industry." Hearings before the Committee on Un-American Activities, House of Representatives, 82nd Congress, Second Session. Part VIII (19-21 May). Washington, D.C.: U.S. Government Printing Office, pp. 3541-49.
   Includes Hellman's correspondence with the committee and her testimony of 21 May 1952.

14 DARLINGTON, W. A. "London Letter." New York Times (11 May), section 2, p. 3.
   Reviews London production of Montserrat. Believes the play's power "gradually dissipates itself in monotony."

15 DASH, THOMAS R. Review of The Children's Hour. Women's Wear Daily (19 December).
   The Children's Hour "remains one of the best constructed and most meaningful plays of the modern theatre."

16 DRUTMAN, IRVING. "The Children's Hour Is Here Again." New York Herald Tribune (14 December), section 4, p. 1.
   Article and photos of the impending revival of The Children's Hour.

*17 EDYVEAN, ALFRED R. "A Critical Appraisal of American Dramas (1935-1949) in the Light of the Christian View of Man." Ph.D. dissertation, English, Northwestern University.
   Discusses Watch on the Rhine. Cited in Emerson and Michael, Southern Literary Culture: A Bibliography of Masters' and Doctors' Theses, 1979.10.

18 FIELD, ROWLAND. Review of The Children's Hour. Newark Evening News (19 December).
   It remains a splendid and rewarding play. Hellman's direction of this production is "most satisfying."

19 FREEDLY, GEORGE. "Off Stage--and On." New York Morning Telegraph (26 December).
   Calls The Children's Hour, in its New York revival, a "sturdy," adult, and exciting play.

20 GABRIEL, GILBERT. "Behind the Asbestos Curtain." Nation, 174 (28 June), 625-28.
   Hellman alone, of the most recent group of theater people to appear before the House Un-American Activities Committee, "did the theater no disservice." She spoke "with exceptional dignity."

1952

21　GILROY, HARRY. "The Bigger the Lie." New York Times (14
　　December), section 2, pp. 3, 4.
　　　　Interview with Hellman on the eve of the Broadway re-
　　vival of The Children's Hour. She comments on a number of
　　matters connected with the play and the new production,
　　noting that, to her, "'this is really not a play about
　　lesbianism, but about a lie.'"

22　HAWKINS, WILLIAM. "Children's Hour at 18, Still Shocks."
　　New York World-Telegram and the Sun (19 December).
　　　　Says The Children's Hour revival shows that the play
　　passes the test of time and remains as shattering as it was
　　in 1934. "It seems that Lillian Hellman has always written
　　with fire and shrewdness."

23　HOPE-WALLACE, PHILIP. "Last Night at the Theatre."
　　Manchester Guardian (10 April), p. 5.
　　　　Claims, in a critical review of the London production
　　of Montserrat, that "the dilemma of the poor young captain
　　is perfunctorily stated, without variations."

24　KERR, WALTER F. "The Theaters: The Children's Hour." New
　　York Herald Tribune (19 December), p. 18.
　　　　Finds The Children's Hour revival somewhat slack, par-
　　ticularly in Hellman's direction of Patricia Neal as Martha
　　Dobie. The play itself "remains a remarkably shrewd and
　　incisive melodrama."

25　KIRCHWEY, FREDA. "How Free Is Free?" Nation, 174 (28 June),
　　615-18.
　　　　Applauds Hellman's statements to the House Un-American
　　Activities Committee as a "hopeful omen" in the current
　　"American witch hunt."

26　LAMBERT, J. W. "Plays in Performance." Drama, New Series,
　　no. 26 (Autumn), 17-20.
　　　　Includes brief assessment of the English production of
　　Montserrat: "a cruel and rather unsatisfying play."

27　M., H. G. Review of Montserrat. Theatre World, 48 (May), 18.
　　　　Reviews English production, at the Lyric Theatre,
　　Hammersmith, of Montserrat, with Richard Burton in the
　　title role. The play is a searing melodrama in a romantic
　　setting; it "remains on the Grand Guignol plane" but vivid
　　acting prevents it from being anticlimactic.

28 McCLAIN, JOHN. "A Welcome, Though Gruesome, Addition." New
York Journal American (19 December).
Considers The Children's Hour revival a compelling
evening of theater. Objects to early indications by
Patricia Neal, in the role of Martha, that she has "an
unnatural affection for" Karen.

29 [MORRISON,] HOBE. Review of The Children's Hour. Variety
(24 December).
Although Hellman's direction of The Children's Hour
revival is "possibly not as firm as Shumlin's original,"
the play remains taut and exciting. It "has acquired a
stimulating quality of contemporary significance."

30 NEW YORK THEATRE CRITICS' REVIEWS, 1952. Vol. 13. New York:
Critics' Theatre Reviews, pp. 151-53.
Reprints reviews of The Children's Hour revival from
New York daily newspapers for 19 December 1952 (New York
Herald Tribune, New York Post, New York Times, New York
World-Telegram and The Sun, Daily News, New York Journal
American, Daily Mirror).

31 P., R. "Regina Returns in Concert Form." New York Times (2
June), p. 25.
Revival in concert form of Regina, with Hellman serving
as narrator.

32 SHEREK, HENRY. "Audiences--English and American." Drama,
New Series, no. 24 (Spring), 16-17.
Brief references to The Children's Hour and its London
censorship problems. Refers to it as "a fine play."

33 SUTHERLAND, ANNE C., and JOHN F. SHEA, eds. The Dramatic Index
for 1949. Boston: F. W. Faxon Company, pp. 21, 155-56,
228, 290; appendix, pp. 44, 55.
Cites reviews of Montserrat and Regina, items related
to Hellman, and editions of her plays published in 1949.

34 TYNAN, KENNETH. "Plays." Spectator, 188 (18 April), 512.
Argues, in an unsympathetic review of the London production of Montserrat, that "the alarming point is that
Miss Hellman sees no need to defend her hero's callous
taciturnity. To her mind the end is well worth the means,
and her childish assumption that we shall accept
Montserrat, without further argument, as a sympathetic and
honorable idealist made my spine prickle with frustrated
rage."

1952

35 WATT, DOUGLAS. "Musical Events: Reunion." New Yorker, 28
    (14 June), 103-105.
        Lengthy, interesting review of Regina, revived in con-
    cert form with Hellman reading comments to set the various
    scenes. Argues that Regina failed in its original Broadway
    production because its "musical technique was too advanced
    for Broadway" and because audiences expected Broadway
    musicals to contain a love interest. Defends Blitzstein's
    adaptation.

36 WATTS, RICHARD, JR. "The Children's Hour Scores Again." New
    York Post (19 December).
        Considers the revival of The Children's Hour a welcome
    reminder of the play's tragic power. Hellman's vast tech-
    nical skill and probing intelligence combine here with her
    ability to write strong acting roles. The current produc-
    tion makes The Children's Hour once again "the drama of the
    season."

37 WINCHELL, WALTER. "Children's Hour Revival a Spellbinder as
    in '34." New York Daily Mirror (19 December).
        Reprints the Daily Mirror review of the original pro-
    duction of The Children's Hour (1934.19), with parentheti-
    cal information added regarding the cast of the 1952
    revival. Introductory paragraph states that the revival
    is equally spellbinding; concluding paragraphs refer to
    These Three and say the play is still "great drama."

1953

1   ANON. "Chicago Sees Children's Hour." New York Times (10
    November), p. 39.
        Item noting the first performance in Chicago of The
    Children's Hour, long banned from the stage by police
    censors.

2   ANON. "Comeback." Time, 61 (13 April), 79-80.
        Compares the successful New York City Center revival of
    Regina with the original production. Notes improvements
    made by Marc Blitzstein in his original adaptation of The
    Little Foxes.

3   ANON. "M'Carthy Calls 23 for Book Inquiry." New York Times
    (28 June), section 1, p. 33.
        Reports on the possible summoning of Hellman and others
    to testify on the State Department's overseas libraries and

information centers, under investigation by Senator Joseph McCarthy.

4   ANON. "Music: Regina at the Opera." Newsweek, 41 (13 April), 96.
    Reviews Regina revival. Discusses the original (1949) controversy over whether or not The Little Foxes should have been set to music.

5   ANON. "An Overture to The Little Foxes." The Times [London] (31 August), p. 3f.
    Announces impending opening by Liverpool Repertory Company of Another Part of the Forest; discusses the play's relationship to The Little Foxes.

6   ANON. Review of Another Part of the Forest. The Times [London] (4 September), p. 10a.
    Reviews Liverpool Repertory production of Another Part of the Forest. The melodramatic formula used in The Little Foxes here "runs an ingeniously contrived course, now brilliantly skirting the edge of absurdity, now toppling over." In the earlier play, Regina's viciousness turned the blood cold. "Now we merely wonder that so much transpontine villainy should run in the veins of the same family."

7   ANON. "Theater." Life, 34 (19 January), 51, 54.
    Review, with photos, of The Children's Hour revival on Broadway. Modern audiences, "more familiar with the facts of abnormal psychology" than those viewing the play in its original production, may find the play less shocking now and exceedingly melodramatic. "But as an exposure of the evils of character assassination, which are always at large, the play is remarkably timeless and valid."

8   BENTLEY, ERIC. "Hellman's Indignation." New Republic, 128 (5 January), 30-31.
    Review of The Children's Hour revival. Bentley criticizes the play and Hellman's direction of the production. The Children's Hour attempts to tell two stories: "The first is a story of heterosexual teachers accused of Lesbianism; the enemy is a society which punishes the innocent. The second is a story of Lesbian teachers accused of Lesbianism; the enemy is a society which punishes Lesbians." The revelation that one of the teachers is lesbian confuses the moral issues Hellman has raised earlier and cheats the audience that has begun to share in the playwright's indignation.
    Reprinted 1954.2.

1953

9 _____. In Search of Theater. New York: Alfred A. Knopf, pp.
9, 49.
Comments on Another Part of the Forest, calling it
neither original nor profound. "It is a pretty good play"
in the theater but it reveals a few exciting moments, not
life. "At some of the most hideous moments in Miss
Hellman's play the audience laughs, and is not altogether
wrong in doing so. Like The Little Foxes, Another Part of
the Forest is Grand Guignol in the guise of realism."
Bentley also notes, in discussing several Anouilh plays
(before The Lark), that "Anouilh resembles Lillian Hellman
rather than Strindberg, whose sharpness is a sharpness of
vision." See 1947.4.

10 BEYER, WILLIAM H. Review of The Children's Hour. School and
Society, 77 (21 February), 117-19.
Says the revival of The Children's Hour reminds the
audience of the way in which McCarthyism has become
established government procedure. But The Children's Hour,
like the Hellman plays that followed, treats socially significant themes with "the sledge hammer of melodramatics,
finishing off with slick, psychological chisel carving."

11 BLOOMGARDEN, KERMIT. "The Pause in the Day's Occupation."
Theatre Arts, 37 (May), 33.
Bloomgarden discusses the performance history of The
Children's Hour through the 1952 revival, which he produced
for Broadway. Photo of Hellman.

12 CALTA, LOUIS. "Double Jeopardy Slated for Rialto." New York
Times (7 March), p. 12.
Round-up of theater news notes criticism by the Boston
Herald of the continuing ban of The Children's Hour in
that city.

13 EYER, RONALD. "Blitzstein's Regina Revived at City Center."
Musical America, 73 (15 April), 5.
Generally positive review of Regina revival.

14 GIBBS, WOLCOTT. "The Theatre: No Pause." New Yorker, 28 (3
January), 30.
Review of The Children's Hour. The revival concludes
with the suggestion of a public apology and financial
restitution. In this respect, something has been lost--
"shock, or pity, or a real sense that no guilt can ever be
paid for or forgiven." Theatrical contrivances notwithstanding, Hellman "has written one of the most honest,
perceptive, distinguished plays of our time."

15 HAGGIN, B. H. "Music." Nation, 177 (8 August), 118-19.
    Reviews New York City Opera production of Regina. The
    composer attempts to "use his gift for musical shows to
    cover his lack of the gift required to set The Little Foxes
    to music."

16 HAYES, RICHARD. Review of The Children's Hour. Commonweal,
    57 (16 January), 377.
    The Children's Hour is relevant as a rejection of
    McCarthyism. What should also be emphasized "is the im-
    mense theatricality of the work--the sheer, exhilarating
    sense it conveys of a positive dramatic talent, of a play-
    wright who is not afraid to calculate her exits and en-
    trances, to drop her curtains at a provocative moment, or
    to expose her characters to passion and violence."

17 HEWES, HENRY. "Broadway Postscript." Saturday Review, 36
    (10 January), 30.
    Criticizes the revival of The Children's Hour. The
    pacing of Hellman's direction is poor and the play is
    filled with improbabilities and "puppet characters."

18 ____. "Broadway Postscript." Saturday Review, 36 (4 April),
    41-42.
    Discusses the impending revival of Regina at the New
    York City Center.

19 HINTON, JAMES, JR. "Regina: Broadway in the Opera House."
    Reporter, 8 (23 June), 36-37.
    Speaks highly of the recent entry of Regina into the
    New York City Opera's repertoire. It is "a tragic opera
    of uncompromising musical seriousness," despite the occa-
    sional problems caused by the terseness and hardness of
    Hellman's original play.

20 KARMAN, RITA. Letter to the Drama Editor. New York Times (1
    February), section 2, p. 3.
    Denies validity of a comparison between the theme of
    The Children's Hour and current politics.

21 KOLODIN, IRVING. "Music to My Ears." Saturday Review, 36
    (18 April), 33.
    Reviews New York City Center revival of Regina. The
    introduction of music into The Little Foxes tends to be an
    intrusion on the fast-paced action, but the opera is worth
    the company's efforts.

1953

22 LeROY, MERVYN. "What Makes a Good Screen Story?" in his It
    Takes More Than Talent. New York: Alfred A. Knopf, Inc.,
    pp. 38-41.
         Cynical reference to Another Part of the Forest as a
    beautifully done "critics' picture," which few people
    wanted to see. "They needed a talking mule in Another
    Part of the Forest."
         Reprinted 1964.13.

23 MARSHALL, MARGARET. Review of The Children's Hour. Nation,
    176 (3 January), 18-19.
         The Children's Hour has its fascination as a clinical
    study of the child as monster, but the play is neither con-
    vincing nor moving because the adults and other children
    are too conveniently "suited to the monster's purposes."

24 MORRIS, LLOYD. Curtain Time. New York: Random House, pp.
    337, 353-54.
         Briefly surveys Hellman's major plays. Photo of
    Tallulah Bankhead as Regina Giddens.

25 NATHAN, GEORGE JEAN. "Gossip Column." New York Journal
    American (11 January), p. 20L.
         Reviews revival of The Children's Hour. Relates its
    fascinating theme of gossip to The School for Scandal,
    Othello, and other plays. It is better by miles than any
    other American play on Broadway this season, although the
    fact that Mary whispers her charges is bothersome. See
    also 1953.26.

26 _____. The Theatre in the Fifties. New York: Alfred A.
    Knopf, pp. 49-52.
         Discusses The Children's Hour in the context of the 1952
    revival. The play retains its power and intelligent re-
    straint, although Hellman ought not to have had Mary
    whisper the lie to her grandmother. Everything in this
    child's character would make her want to speak her accusa-
    tions openly. "It is not the child that is hesitant about
    articulating them; it is the playwright" who has qualms.
    See also 1953.25.

27 SARGEANT, WINTHROP. "Musical Events." New Yorker, 29 (17
    October), 112-13.
         Brief review of New York City Center production of
    Regina. Hellman's "singularly unpleasant characters do not
    fit very well into opera." They are obsessed with greed
    "and greed is not ordinarily something that one sings
    about."

28 S.[CHONBERG], H.[AROLD] C. "City Center Offers Blitzstein
    Opera." New York Times (10 October), p. 12.
        Generally negative review of the City Center Opera
    revival of Regina. Claims that the opera has a powerful
    libretto and that "the libretto manages to dwarf the
    music," perhaps because Marc Blitzstein was awed by the
    Hellman source.

29 SPILLER, ROBERT E., et al., eds. Literary History of the
    United States. Revised edition in one volume. New York:
    Macmillan, pp. 1314, 1330.
        Reprints the Hellman material of the 1948 edition,
    volume 2. See 1963.57 and 1974.41.

30 _____. Literary History of the United States: Bibliography.
    Second edition. New York: Macmillan, p. 161.
        Reprints the Hellman reference of the 1948 edition.
    See 1963.56, 1972.37, and 1974.40.

31 TAUBMAN, HOWARD. "At the Opera: Regina." New York Times (3
    April), p. 18.
        Praises Regina, in its New York City Center Opera pro-
    duction, highly. Marc Blitzstein's book loses little of
    the Hellman drive.

32 _____. "From Play into Opera." New York Times (12 April),
    section 2, p. 7.
        Discusses the triumphant revival of Regina at the New
    York City Center. Compares the production to the original
    Broadway version of 1949 and to The Little Foxes.

33 WEST, DOROTHY HERBERT, and DOROTHY MARGARET PEAKE, comps.
    Play Index, 1949-52. New York: H. W. Wilson Company, p.
    79.
        Lists Hellman plays in anthologies.

34 WYATT, EUPHEMIA VAN RENSSELAER. "Theater: The Children's
    Hour." Catholic World, 176 (February), 388.
        Says the Broadway revival of The Children's Hour "sends
    one fairly staggering from the theater." Since World War
    II, we have seen the terrible damage of propaganda and the
    "brutal impact of false testimony" from Goebbels to the
    Soviet trials. Such happenings give the play additional
    power. The play barely misses being a "great tragedy be-
    cause there is a lack of any spiritual development in
    Karen."

1954

1 BENTLEY, ERIC. "The American Drama (1944-1954)," in his The Dramatic Event. New York: Horizon Press, pp. 244-62.
  Refers to political implications of The Children's Hour (pp. 257-58) and to The Autumn Garden as one of the best plays of the period surveyed (p. 254). Maintains that The Children's Hour represents a "dangerous and now . . . obsolescent type of liberalism."
  Reprinted 1965.3 and 1967.10.

2 _____. "Lillian Hellman's Indignation," in his The Dramatic Event. New York: Horizon Press, pp. 74-77.
  Reprint of 1953.8.

*3 BUSFIELD, ROGER M., JR. "From Idea to Dialogue: An Analysis of the Playwriting Process as Derived from the Non-Dramatic Writings of a Selected Group of Successful Dramatists, 1899-1950." Ph.D. dissertation, English, Florida State University.
  Includes Hellman in the group of discussed dramatists. Cited in Emerson and Michael, Southern Literary Culture: A Bibliography of Masters' and Doctors' Theses, 1979.10.

4 FARRELL, ISOLDE. "Literature and Arts: Religious Themes in the Theatre." America, 90 (23 January), 420-21.
  Reviews Paris production of Anouilh's L'Alouette (The Lark). The play is superficially clever but empty. "Anouilh's standard of values is obvious: he prefers Jeanne's temporal triumph at Rheims to her true triumph in martyrdom."

5 GASSNER, JOHN. The Theatre in Our Times. New York: Crown Publishers, Inc., pp. 6, 11, 78, 119, 286, 370, 405-406, 450, 579.
  Brief but interesting allusions to Hellman and her plays, with longer consideration of The Children's Hour (pp. 405-406). That play's flaws derive from Pinero but few American plays of recent years possess such power.

6 KAEL, PAULINE. "Morality Plays Right and Left." Sight and Sound, 24 (October-December), 67-73.
  Brief mention of The North Star as a film that depends upon melodrama for its political point.
  Reprinted in I Lost It at the Movies. See 1965.11 and 1966.30.

7 LEARY, LEWIS, comp. Articles on American Literature 1900-1950. Durham, N.C.: Duke University Press, p. 137.

Lists two articles on Hellman: Barrett Clark, 1944.16, and Edith Isaacs, 1944.31.

8 S.[HANLEY], J.[OHN] P. "Theatre: Montserrat." New York Times (26 May), p. 34.
    Calls the off-Broadway revival of Montserrat a futile attempt to impress audiences with the play's qualities, overlooked five years earlier on Broadway. "The theme is grim and it might succeed as theatre only with a flawless production and performances."

1955

1 ANON. "Authors in Action." Time, 45 (12 March), 55.
    Includes a report on Hellman's trip to Russia, written in Time's innuendo style. Photo of Hellman.

2 ANON. "Bohemian Nights in New York." The Times [London] (7 February), p. 11b.
    Brief reference to The Little Foxes.

3 ANON. "The Theater: A Fiery Particle." Time, 66 (28 November), 76-78, 81-82, 84.
    Cover story on Julie Harris, appearing as Joan of Arc in The Lark. Contains numerous references to Hellman's adaptation of Anouilh's play, which is called "intellectual theater at close to its best." Photos of Harris in scenes from the play and with Hellman.

4 ANON. "Theater: A Joan with Gumption." Newsweek, 46 (28 November), 110.
    Reviews of The Lark. "Writer Lillian Hellman and actress Julie Harris make the heroine a crop-haired, sensible little warrior who leads an army to victory because she has more gumption and go than the men of her time. She is less a press-agent symbol than an exalted gamin who understands the weaknesses of the men she inspires." Related feature story on Julie Harris appears on the same page. Photo from the play.

5 ANON. "Theater: Julie as a Memorable Joan." Life, 39 (12 December), 113-14, 116.
    Brief comments acclaiming The Lark as an expert adaptation, an example of "American theater at its distinguished best," with photos from the production.

1955

6　ATKINSON, BROOKS. "New Joan of Arc." New York Times (27
　　　November), section 2, p. 1.
　　　　　Analyzes The Lark. Hellman's adaptation is superior to
　　　Fry's version of Anouilh's play. "She has an instinct for
　　　the forthright statement."

7　____. "Theatre: St. Joan with Radiance." New York Times
　　　(18 November), p. 20.
　　　　　Review of The Lark. Hellman's adaptation has added
　　　theatrical life to the drama that seemed little more than
　　　an intellectual exercise in Fry's version.

8　BEAUFORT, JOHN. Review of The Lark. Christian Science
　　　Monitor (26 November).
　　　　　Analyzes Broadway production of The Lark.

9　BENTLEY, ERIC. The Playwright as Thinker. New York: Meridian
　　　Books, pp. 8-16.
　　　　　Reprint of 1946.19.

10　____. "Theatre." New Republic, 133 (5 December), 21.
　　　　　Review of The Lark discusses Hellman's adaptation in
　　　relation to Anouilh's version and Shaw's St. Joan.
　　　Hellman, through a brief deletion, tries in the final
　　　scene "to rescue Joan from Anouilh. She inserts a little
　　　speech of her own to guarantee that Joan, lost to saint-
　　　hood . . . may be at least a good girl. She goes back
　　　into the body of the text and slashes the inquisitor's
　　　speeches so that our audiences will never find out what
　　　Anouilh meant to convey." The New York production is
　　　visually a grand show. With Julie Harris in the midst of
　　　it, anyone interested in theater will enjoy The Lark,
　　　"especially those who are not interested in Joan of Arc,
　　　history in particular, or truth in general."

11　BOLTON, WHITNEY. "Stage Review." New York Morning Telegraph
　　　(19 November).
　　　　　Considers The Lark great theater. Hellman's English
　　　translation soars.

12　BOURJAILY, VANCE. "Theatre Uptown." Village Voice, 1 (7
　　　December), 10.
　　　　　Reviews The Lark. In Hellman's adaptation, Anouilh's
　　　play is "more often interesting than not" but the work
　　　fails to conclude satisfactorily. It is, though, the most
　　　distinguished production of the Broadway season, primarily
　　　because of the performance of Julie Harris as Joan of Arc.

13 CHAPMAN, JOHN. "Julie Harris Simply Magnificent in a Beautiful Drama, The Lark." New York Daily News (18 November).
Considers The Lark a triumph. This version tells Joan's
story from two viewpoints: history's and Joan's.

14 COLEMAN, ROBERT. "The Lark Proves Spell-Binding, Witty."
New York Daily Mirror (18 November).
Calls The Lark a distinguished contribution to the
Broadway season. Hellman's adaptation is "excellent."

15 COTES, PETER. "A Golden Age." Plays and Players, 2
(February), 5.
Mentions Hellman's "masterpiece," The Children's Hour,
as a play still banned in England.

16 DASH, THOMAS R. Review of The Lark. Women's Wear Daily (18
November).
Hellman's adaptation "has verbal sinew, intellectual
pith and integrity."

17 FIELD, ROWLAND. "Joan Lives Again." Newark Evening News (18
November).
Review of The Lark. Hellman's new approach to Joan sees
her "as a symbol of almost happy confrontment with martyrdom." The tragic nature of her story is not lessened.

18 GAVER, JACK, ed. Critics' Choice: New York Drama Critics'
Circle Prize Plays 1935-1955. New York: Hawthorn Books,
pp. 13, 201-42.
Cites (p. 13) the controversy that arose when the New
York Drama Critics' Circle award for best play went in
1935 to The Old Maid, instead of to The Children's Hour.
Introduces the complete text of Watch on the Rhine (pp.
201-42) by noting that Watch won for Hellman the Critics'
Circle prize that eluded her in 1939, when The Little Foxes
could not garner the necessary number of votes. Gaver considers Foxes the better play.

19 GIBBS, WOLCOTT. Review of The Lark. New Yorker, 31 (3
December), 112, 117-18.
The adaptation's narrative device is effective and intelligent, offering "the best possible opportunity to conduct a fine running debate on many problems of church and
state." Less romantic than Shaw's "eloquent mystic,"
Anouilh's Joan is apt to be remembered as "a practical
patriot."

1955

20   HATCH, ROBERT.   Review of The Lark.   Nation, 181 (3 December),
     485-86.
         The adaptation is "at once a clever and a deeply-felt
     work of theater craft."   But The Lark is too cheerfully
     sentimental and Joan remains an intangible, spritely
     figure.

21   HAWKINS, WILLIAM.   "Julie Harris Captures Inner Beauty of
     Joan."   New York World-Telegram and the Sun (18 November).
         Finds the construction of the second half of The Lark
     excessively elaborate but considers the adaptation and the
     production "crisp and shining."

22   HAYES, RICHARD.   "The Stage: The Lark."   Commonweal, 63 (23
     December), 304-305.
         Compares Hellman's adaptation of The Lark to other
     works about Joan of Arc.   The performance of Julie Harris
     is delicate, touching, exact, though, "for all her sharp
     sense of 'good theater,' Miss Hellman seems to me to have
     reduced the play to a genteel muddle."

23   HEWES, HENRY.   "Broadway Postscript: Saint Julie."   Saturday
     Review, 38 (3 December), 38.
         Review of The Lark.   "Adapter Lillian Hellman has weeded
     out most of the intellectual asides, chopped up the long
     speeches, deleted the perhaps too familiar action in which
     Joan recognizes the Dauphin in disguise, improved the fre-
     quently facetious and loose construction and given the
     ending an audience-satisfying emotional touch."   Yet one
     must regret the pruning.   The play is less provocative than
     Anouilh's version and, in fact, "less fertile in ideas than
     such a fine drama as her own The Autumn Garden."   This
     adaptation, through Hellman's omissions or rephrasing, suc-
     ceeds "by being real, not by being, as Anouilh aspired,
     'truer than the real thing.'"

24   KERR, WALTER.   How Not to Write a Play.   New York: Simon and
     Schuster, pp. 23, 25, 33, 53.
         Several references to Hellman.   Argues that the theatri-
     cality and somewhat concealed social content of The Little
     Foxes emanate from Ibsen.   With Watch on the Rhine, Hellman
     "engineered a beginning compromise: the political intention
     remains paramount and in strong focus, but the characteri-
     zation has taken on the more delicate hues of twilight."
     The transition is completed in The Autumn Garden, where the
     social comment is "almost obscured, the characterization is
     ruefully Chekhovian, the mood of the play is the principal
     guide to its meaning."

25 _____. "Theater: A Brisk New Joan." New York Herald Tribune
(27 November), section 4, pp. 1, 3.
Sunday analysis of The Lark. Anouilh and Hellman portray Joan with a fresh slant. The special inspiration of
The Lark "is to show a divine mission being battered out
with exclusively human tools." It may be excessive, however, to view Joan as "'the natural man,' a role for which
this voice-driven firebrand seems an unlikely candidate."
Hellman's dialogue is "barbed, bracing, wholly contemporary."

26 _____. "Theater: The Lark." New York Herald Tribune (18
November), p. 12.
A woman dramatist has created "the first really tough-
minded Joan of Arc. Lillian Hellman is, of course, only
the adapter of Jean Anouilh's The Lark. But that 'only'
may be misleading. I have a strong suspicion that a great
deal of the biting briskness, the cleaver-sharp determination, the haughty and hardheaded candor of this Joan comes
from the pen of the lady who carved out, and carved up,
The Little Foxes."

*27 KULAKOVSKAIA, I. "Lilian Khellman." Sovetskaia kul'tura (19
July).
Cited in Valentina Libman, Russian Studies of American
Literature, 1969.31.

28 KUNITZ, STANLEY, ed. Twentieth Century Authors, First Supplement. New York: Wilson, pp. 432-33.
Updates 1942.26 through Hellman's appearance before the
House Un-American Activities Committee. Includes list of
her works from 1943 and several references to works about
her.

29 LEWIS, THEOPHILUS. "Theatre: The Lark." America, 94 (24
December), 363-64.
Although one cannot be certain about the extent of her
changes in The Lark, "it can be safely assumed that whatever changes Miss Hellman made were improvements, for the
drama faithfully reflects the mystery and glory of Joan's
career, the tragedy of her trial and the integrity of her
character."

30 McCLAIN, JOHN. "Julie Depicts a Vital Joan." New York
Journal American (18 November).
Praises the earthiness and idiomatic speech of Hellman's
adaptation.

1955

31 MANNES, MARYA. "Three Playwrights Compliment Their Audi-
       ences." Reporter, 13 (29 December), 21-32.
          Calls The Lark one of the best plays of the Broadway
       season. Joan, "thanks to Anouilh and Hellman," consistent-
       ly retains her gamin vitality and the "earthy shrewdness
       of the peasant until the moment of her collapse and recan-
       tation before Cauchon."
          Reprinted in George Oppenheimer, The Passionate Play-
       goer, 1958.13 and 1962.38.

32 [MORRISON,] HOBE. "Shows on Broadway." Variety (23
       November).
          Calls The Lark an emphatic success.

33 NATHAN, GEORGE JEAN. "Hark, Hark." New York Journal American
       (3 December).
          On The Lark.

34 NEW YORK THEATRE CRITICS' REVIEWS, 1955. Vol. 16. New York:
       Critics' Theatre Reviews, pp. 206-208.
          Reprints reviews of The Lark from New York daily news-
       papers for 18 November 1955 (New York Times, New York
       Herald Tribune, New York Post, Daily Mirror, New York
       World-Telegram and the Sun, New York Journal American, and
       Daily News).

35 PECK, SEYMOUR. "The Maid in Many Guises." New York Times
       Magazine (4 December), p. 28.
          Photo-essay on the popularity of Joan of Arc as a
       dramatic heroine. Quotes Hellman on Shaw's Joan and her
       own: "Lillian Hellman sees the Shaw Joan as 'deeply
       religious, a big, healthy, sensible girl, a sort of
       peasant type.' In The Lark Miss Hellman and Anouilh have
       made Joan 'gayer, more fragile, less saintly.' Joan in
       The Lark believes positively in man's own strength and
       courage."

36 PROUSE, DEREK. "Notes on Film Acting." Sight and Sound, 24
       (Spring), 174-80.
          Discusses the actors' submission of their personalities
       to their roles in the screen version of The Little Foxes,
       in which the relationships to be exposed depend not so
       much on "subtle, mutually affecting interplay of character"
       as on "patterns of settled rejection." Photo.

37 SCHUMACH, MURRAY. "Shaping a New Joan." New York Times (13
       November), section 2, pp. 1, 3.

1956

Discussion with Hellman of her adaptation of The Lark, during its Boston tryout. Hellman stresses Joan's principles rather than Anouilh's emphasis on feminine vanity.

38 SIEVERS, W. DAVID. Freud on Broadway. New York: Hermitage House, pp. 17, 94, 279-89, 397, 450, 452.
    Sievers seeks Freud in American drama and finds him everywhere, resulting in curious conclusions about Hellman's plays: "Although there is no reference to the psychodynamics which are responsible for Martha's latent inversion, The Children's Hour is nevertheless a daring step forward in the theatre's humanizing power to create understanding and empathy for unconscious deviation as a tragic flaw rather than a loathsome anomaly"; "[Julie Rodman in Days to Come] is Hedda Gabler without even the compassion that Ibsen evokes from his neurotic heroine"; "[Regina] has identified herself so completely with the male Hubbards that she expresses a hint of Lesbianism by her curiosity over the lovely women in Chicago"; "At the end [of The Little Foxes] Regina gaily leaves for Chicago"; "Even Ben and Oscar are treated as hired help by their father [in Another Part of the Forest]. . . . Little wonder, then, that Oscar and Ben found it necessary in the other play to release their Oedipally engendered hostility on whomever they could find as substitutes for their autocrat father"; and so on.

39 WATTS, RICHARD, JR. "A Stirring Play About Joan of Arc." New York Post (18 November).
    Praises all aspects of The Lark and the production but reserves the "most enthusiastic credit" for Hellman's adaptation. "By occasional changes and omissions in text and the general straightforwardness and force of her style, she has made The Lark stand in its own right and power."

1956

1 ANON. "Candide, Indeed!" Newsweek, 48 (10 December), 77.
    Says Candide should never have been adapted for the stage. "Lillian Hellman is concerned with saving as much as possible of Voltaire's knife in the back of eighteenth-century optimism—and nobody will ever know why she was so concerned."

2 ANON. "New Musical Version of Candide." The Times [London] (12 December), p. 5a.

1956

Reviews the New York production of <u>Candide</u>. The score
is wonderful and the production is finally triumphant, but
Hellman's libretto fails to convey Voltaire's irony and
bite. "There is a lack of dramatic vitality astonishing
for a dramatist of Miss Hellman's powers. There are sardonic flashes and frequently bright lyrics but the total
effect of the libretto is sadly disappointing."

3 ANON. "New Operetta in Manhattan." <u>Time</u>, 68 (10 December),
70.
Reviews <u>Candide</u>. Hellman's libretto is foreign to
Voltaire's tone. Where he is diabolical, she is humani-
tarian.

4 ANON. Review of <u>The Children's Hour</u>. <u>Plays and Players</u>, 4
(November), 10, 16.
Reviews production of <u>The Children's Hour</u> at the Arts
Theatre, London. Calls the play contrived, with simplified
characters. Lillian Hellman is uncertain about her theme.
Photos.

5 ANON. Review of <u>The Children's Hour</u>. <u>The Times</u> [London] (20
September), p. 5f.
<u>The Children's Hour</u> is a smooth and expressive play.
Hellman takes a good deal of time to establish Mary's
viciousness and the deliberate method of the playwright
pays dividends later on, despite the drama's contrivances.
But this production at the Arts Theatre is receiving
spiritless performances, thus making the play "seem almost
preternaturally slow."

6 ANON. Review of <u>The Lark</u>. <u>Theatre Arts</u>, 40 (January), 18-19.
Calls <u>The Lark</u> a literate and forceful adaptation. The
play's "framework is cerebral," but the character of Joan
is not. "This Joan is a man [<u>sic</u>] of action." Lists
cast and production credits. Photos.

7 ANON. "Television Next Week." <u>Nation</u>, 183 (15 December),
527.
Notes the impending television production of <u>The Little</u>
<u>Foxes</u>, scheduled to be telecast (16 December) on the
"Hallmark Hall of Fame," starring Greer Garson and Franchot
Tone. This new production of Hellman's "highly-charged
parable" represents "an admirable way to begin exploding
the blacklist terror."

8 ATKINSON, BROOKS. "Musical <u>Candide</u>." <u>New York Times</u> (9
December), section 2, p. 5.

Review of Candide. Commends Hellman's faithful preservation of Voltaire's assult on optimism.

9 _____. "The Theatre: Candide." New York Times (3 December), p. 40.
Calls Candide "a brilliant musical satire." Hellman's Candide is more the disillusioned hero than Voltaire's blithering idiot.

10 BERNSTEIN, LEONARD. "Colloquy in Boston." New York Times (18 November), section 2, pp. 1, 3.
Reflections on Candide, prior to its New York premiere, with references to Hellman's adaptation of Voltaire.

11 BOLTON, WHITNEY. "Candide Brilliant, Compelling Show." New York Morning Telegraph (3 December).
Laudatory review of Candide.

12 CHAPMAN, JOHN. "Candide an Artistic Triumph: Bernstein's Score Magnificent." New York Daily News (3 December).
Considers Candide the best light opera since Richard Strauss's Der Rosenkavalier. Hellman "has fashioned a strong, clear and humorous libretto."

13 CLURMAN, HAROLD. Review of Candide. Nation, 183 (15 December), 527.
Criticizes Candide as indecisive in purpose. "Lillian Hellman's tart realism of mind and capacity for sharp statement sometimes serve to focus attention on the point of the enterprise and sometimes--because of the spectacular, extravaganza-like nature of the show--strike one as a wicked intrusion."

14 COGLEY, JOHN. Report on Blacklisting: Part I: Movies. New York: Fund for the Republic, Inc., pp. 96, 100-101, 170, 274.
Quotes Hellman's letter to the House Un-American Activities Committee and lists her screen credits to 1949. Reprinted 1972.12. Also excerpted as "The Mass Hearings," in The American Film Industry, ed. Tino Balio. See 1976.16.

15 COLEMAN, ROBERT. "Musical Candide Is Distinguished Work." New York Daily Mirror (3 December).
Praises Candide as a "colorful and cynical musical." Hellman's libretto is "fairly true to the original."

1956

16 DAVIS, MAC. <u>Jews at a Glance</u>. New York: Hebrew Publishing
    Company, p. 60.
    Adulatory sketch of Hellman, in a collection of 114
    brief biographies of eminent Jews. Drawing by Sam
    Nisenson.

17 DONNELLY, TOM. "Best Musical News of Year Is Found in New
    Candide." <u>New York World-Telegram and The Sun</u> (3
    December).
    Review of <u>Candide</u>. Finds the play uneven but brilliant
    in certain areas. Hellman's "book tends to be vague and
    meandering," but she provides a number of sardonic flashes
    and the basis for "an almost continuously stimulating
    show."

18 FIELD, ROWLAND. "<u>Candide</u> Tedious." <u>Newark Evening News</u> (3
    December).
    Negative review.

19 GASSNER, JOHN. <u>Form and Idea in Modern Theatre</u>. New York:
    Dryden Press, pp. 84, 256.
    Brief references to the realistic mode of <u>The Little</u>
    <u>Foxes</u>.
    Revised edition reprints same material. <u>See</u> Gassner's
    <u>Directions in Modern Theatre and Drama</u>, 1965.8.

20 GIBBS, WOLCOTT. "The Theatre: Voltaire Today." <u>New Yorker</u>,
    32 (15 December), 52-54.
    Review of <u>Candide</u>. "It is hard to see how so formidable
    a collection of talent could turn out a work only inter-
    mittently satisfactory." Hellman's book, "though perhaps
    a little elfin here and there, also has its humor and, of
    course, the high technical competence for which she has
    always been noted." It is, on the whole, "an admirable
    and intelligent dramatization," though not "one of the
    great theatrical offerings of our time."

21 GRIFFIN, ALICE. "Books:--of a Different Feather." <u>Theatre</u>
    <u>Arts</u>, 40 (May), 8-10.
    Reviews published editions of Christopher Fry's transla-
    tion of Anouilh's <u>The Lark</u> and Hellman's adaptation of the
    same play. Says Fry's is a fairly close translation, while
    Hellman's version is a much freer, shorter adaptation.
    "Her ending is different, and her expedient adaptation,
    while doubtless more appealing to the average American
    theatre-goer, lacks the spirit and tone of Anouilh's
    original, while Fry has captured these qualities." Fry is
    ironic and appeals to the head; Hellman is romantic and

appeals to the heart. Fry is saying that "man himself, as
man, with all his faults but his glory too, will prevail
despite the attempts of those who would sacrifice humanity
to the Idea." Hellman, less complex and original, is saying that "man's courage, as characterized by Joan, will
prevail despite efforts to destroy it."

22 GRIFFITH, RICHARD. Samuel Goldwyn: The Producer and His
    Films. New York: Museum of Modern Art Film Library, 48
    pp.
        Discusses Goldwyn's films, including These Three, Dead
    End, and The Little Foxes. Also lists credits for The
    Dark Angel and The North Star. Contains interesting
    observations on the relationship of drama and film (in
    the discussion of These Three). Says Hellman's screenplay
    for These Three improves upon The Children's Hour "in
    solidity and conviction."

23 HAYES, RICHARD. "The Stage: Mr. Bernstein Cultivates His
    Garden." Commonweal, 65 (28 December), 333-34.
        Review of Candide. Commends Leonard Bernstein's score
    but seriously faults Hellman's libretto. What most pre-
    vents Hellman from effectively dramatizing Voltaire "is
    the temperament she shares so articulately with our soci-
    ety. Where Voltaire was passionate and disabused, we--in
    the person of Miss Hellman--are recriminatory and didactic;
    where Candor and Reason sufficed for him, we insist also
    on Will; a world which he saw under the mysterious dispen-
    sations of folly and chance, we interpret in the dry light
    of the Moral Imperative. Miss Hellman, as librettist, may
    take the liberty of interpolating incident; it is her re-
    ductions of feelings and thought which cause so much pain."

24 HEWES, HENRY. Review of Candide. Saturday Review, 39 (22
    December), 34-35.
        This adaptation is "a beautiful bore." Hellman's
    libretto wavers. "Her comedy seems labored, her attitude
    towards the total work unclear. One suspects she sides
    with Martin in his statement that we live in the worst of
    all possible worlds." But this contradicts Voltaire as
    well as the spirit of musical comedy.

25 HEWITT, ALAN. "The Lark: Theatrical Bird of Passage."
    Theatre Arts, 40 (March), 63-64, 96.
        Compares the Anouilh, Fry, and Hellman versions of The
    Lark. Hellman has made numerous shifts in Anouilh's play,
    resulting in a bolder, "less intellectual, more obviously
    theatrical" work. Her adaptation is disappointing,

1956

however. It lacks a sense of humor, simplifies "the cross-
currents of debate," and appeals to the emotions of the
audience.

26 [HUMPHRIES,] CLEM. Review of The Children's Hour. Variety
(3 October), p. 82.
Reviews the production of The Children's Hour at the
"private" Arts Theatre Club, London, because of the continuing ban against the play. Finds it a pallid production, lacking the original shock value.

27 KEOWN, ERIC. "At the Play." Punch, 231 (26 September), 386.
Reviews the London restaging of The Children's Hour as
a "flabby production" which has been miscast and does not
move us in the least. Recalls the 1950 London production,
which was "gripping as drama and strangely wise in human
understanding."

28 KERR, WALTER. "Theater: Candide." New York Herald Tribune
(3 December), p. 10.
Three of the theater's most talented people--Hellman,
Leonard Bernstein, and Tyrone Guthrie--have turned Candide
into a "really spectacular disaster." Hellman's libretto
lacks the humor and snappish wit necessary for satire.
Instead, it is "academic, blunt and barefaced."

29 _____. "Voltaire's Candide and a Light Opera." New York
Herald Tribune (23 December), section 4, p. 1.
Sunday analysis of Candide. Negative assessment.

30 KRONENBERGER, LOUIS, ed. The Best Plays of 1955-1956. New
York: Dodd, Mead and Company, pp. 11-12, 189-213, 362, 402,
405, 415, 418-20, 426.
Condenses The Lark. Finds Hellman's adaptation
"trenchant," although the play is never really fused.
Production information.

31 LAMBERT, J. W. "Plays in Performance." Drama, New Series,
no. 43 (Winter), 18-23.
Includes brief comments on Arts Theatre (London) production of The Children's Hour. Calls the play "a passable
piece of contrivance."

32 McCARTHY, MARY. Sights and Spectacles, 1937-1956. New York:
Farrar, Straus, and Cudahy, pp. 81, 91.
Reprint of 1946.40. Contains one additional reference
to Hellman.
Reprinted 1963.45.

174

33 _____. "Theatre: The Reform of Dr. Pangloss." New Republic,
135 (17 December), 30-31.
Criticizes Candide, calling it "a sad fizzle which is
more like a high school pageant than a social satire."
Hellman and her collaborators have removed all the pessimism from Voltaire's tale. "A bowdlerized Candide, a
Candide that cannot afford to be candid is a contradiction
in terms."

34 McCLAIN, JOHN. "Fine, Bright--But Operetta Lacks Spark."
New York Journal American (3 December).
Reviews Candide as an ambitious and occasionally brilliant musical that doesn't "quite score." Hellman's book
is "bright."

35 M.[AJESKI], F., JR. "Bernstein Writes Operetta Score."
Musical America, 76 (15 December), 26.
Reviews score of Candide; briefly mentions Hellman.

36 NEW YORK THEATRE CRITICS' REVIEWS, 1956. Vol. 17. New York:
Critics' Theatre Reviews, pp. 176-80.
Reprints reviews of Candide from New York daily news-
papers for 3 December 1956 (Daily News, New York Post, New
York Journal American, Daily Mirror, New York Herald
Tribune, New York Times).

37 O'CONNOR, FRANK. "Saint Joans, from Arc to Lark." Holiday,
19 (March), 77, 88-89.
Compares the historical Joan of Arc with some of her
literary and dramatic incarnations. "Now, in The Lark, M.
Anouilh turns her into a member of the French Underground,
and I nearly jumped out of my seat when the Inquisitor
described Joan as an example of 'Natural Man.' That, I am
sure, must be Miss Hellman chiming in. The lesson is
plain. We all read ourselves into the part of Joan."

38 O'FLAHERTY, VINCENT. "St. Joan Wouldn't Know Herself."
America, 95 (28 April), 109-10.
Calls the Joan of The Lark "an imposter." Anouilh and
other dramatists who write about Joan of Arc fail to con-
sult history and ignore the fact that Joan "was sent by
the King of Heaven" to do His work. "Living and dying,
she makes sense only as a daughter of the Church and in a
Catholic context."

39 PECK, SEYMOUR. "Broadway Goes Song-and-Dance." New York
Times Magazine (4 November), p. 28.

1956

Photos, with brief comments, of impending Broadway musicals, including Candide.

40 SAVERY, RANALD. "Echoes from Broadway." Theatre World, 52 (January), 34.
    Reviews The Lark.

41 S.[TEPHENS], F.[RANCES]. Review of The Children's Hour. Theatre World, 52 (November), 7.
    Reviews production of The Children's Hour at the Arts Theatre, London. Says the play is badly dated. "In these days such a child would long since have been in the hands of a psychiatrist, while the schoolmarms' future would surely not be ruined." In this production Martha displays a sense of guilt too early in the play.

42 TAUBMAN, HOWARD. "Broadway and TV." New York Times (16 December), section 2, p. 9.
    Praises Candide highly, particularly its musical score.

43 TREWIN, J. C. "The World of the Theatre." Illustrated London News, 229 (6 October), 566.
    Maintains, in a mostly favorable review of the London production of The Children's Hour, that "it is an honest drama that is, as much as anything, a violent assault upon the dangers of malicious gossip."

44 TYNAN, KENNETH. "At the Theatre." London Observer (23 September), p. 11.
    Reviews London production of The Children's Hour. The play "retains enormous historical interest as the germ from which sprang so many other successes, among them The Bad Seed and The Crucible." But Tynan agrees with Mary McCarthy, who has alluded to Hellman's "'oily virtuosity.'" See 1946.40. The play is finally a candid, moral study of human behavior that less discriminating audiences will enjoy.

45 WATTS, RICHARD, JR. "Voltaire's Candide as an Operetta." New York Post (3 December).
    Considers Candide a laudable venture but finds little of Voltaire's bite and pungency retained in Hellman's libretto.

46 WYATT, EUPHEMIA VAN RENSSELAER. "Theater: The Lark." Catholic World, 128 (January), 308-309.
    Hellman has removed all traces of Gallicism from Anouilh's The Lark. History is distorted by the play, with

The Lark going one step further than St. Joan. Shaw tried
to show Joan as the first Protestant; Anouilh associates
her with "Natural Man."

1957

1 ANON. "400 Writers Hold First U.S. Meeting." New York Times
(7 May), p. 29.
   Cites Hellman's remarks on "emotional problems of
writers" at a conference sponsored by the Authors' Guild
of America.

2 ANON. "The Lark by Jean Anouilh, Adapted by Lillian Hellman."
Theatre Arts, 41 (March), 33-56.
   The complete text of The Lark, with production credits
and photos.

3 ANON. "Television Play: Another Part of the Forest." The
Times [London] (17 January), p. 3e.
   Reviews English television production of Another Part of
the Forest. The characters appear inhuman; except for
Lavinia, they are motivated solely by malice and selfish-
ness. "But the reasons for this inhumanity are so dramatically presented, and its range of expression is so wide,
that the play makes an authentic comment on the origins of
violence."

4 COLIN, SAUL. "Plays and Players in New York." Plays and
Players, 4 (January), 31.
   Mentions New York production of Candide.

5 CLURMAN, HAROLD. The Fervent Years: The Story of the Group
Theatre and the Thirties. New York: Hill and Wang, pp.
237, 261, 281, 287.
   Reprint of 1945.4, with an epilogue (1945-1955) containing two additional, brief references to Hellman.

6 DRIVER, TOM F. Review of Candide. Christian Century, 74 (6
February), 171.
   The moralism of this version of Candide "falls into the
'if only' variety and therefore must strike us nowadays
as somewhat irrelevant." This production offers "an
awfully long trip for such a short philosophy."

7 FERGUSON, PHYLLIS. "Women Dramatists in the American Theatre,
1901-1940." Ph.D. dissertation, University of Pittsburgh.

1957

Includes Hellman, Susan Glaspell, Rachel Crothers, and others. Dissertation Abstracts International, 18:230-31.

8 GASSNER, JOHN. "Hellman, Lillian," in The Oxford Companion to the Theatre. Second edition. Edited by Phyllis Hartnoll. London: Oxford University Press, p. 361.
    Concise profile of Hellman's career through Another Part of the Forest. See 1967.22.

9 ____. "The Possibilities and Perils of Modern Tragedy." Tulane Drama Review, 1 (June), 3-15.
    Refers briefly to The Children's Hour as a play that fills a place in the American theater without fitting into the pigeonhole of tragedy.
    Reprinted in Theatre and Drama in the Making, Vol. 2. Edited by Gassner and Ralph Allen. See 1964.9.

10 KOLODIN, IRVING. "Candied Candide." Saturday Review, 40 (23 February), 49.
    Critical review of the Candide recording. Mentions Hellman in passing.

11 KRONENBERGER, LOUIS, ed. The Best Plays of 1956-1957. New York: Dodd, Mead and Company, pp. 27, 29, 148-49, 340, 384, 388, 397-402, 404, 408.
    Condenses Candide, citing it as a "medley of the brilliant, the uneven, the exciting, the earthbound, the adventurous and the imperfectly harmonized." Production data.

12 KRUTCH, JOSEPH WOOD. American Drama Since 1918. Revised edition. New York: George Braziller, Inc., pp. 130-33, 319.
    Revised edition of 1939.28. Hellman material is identical, except for one brief mention of Watch on the Rhine (p. 319) in a chapter added for this edition.

13 MANNES, MARYA. Review of Candide. Reporter, 16 (24 January), 35.
    Praises music, lyrics, production, but criticizes Hellman's book: "It is a little surprising that a dramatist as brilliant as Lillian Hellman has somehow blunted Voltaire's cutting edge, that her sense of timing--so flawless in drama--should falter in this book."

14 WYATT, EUPHEMIA VAN RENSSELAER. Review of Candide. Catholic World, 184 (February), 384-85.
    "With sanguine temerity, Miss Lillian Hellman has appropriated the characters appearing in Part I of

178

Candide, and . . . she has woven a story with a continuity
that only those who remember the original can evaluate."

1958

1 AGEE, JAMES. Agee on Film: Reviews and Comments. New York:
   McDowell, Obolensky, Inc., pp. 53, 55-58, 65-67, 206, 305.
      Reprints Agee's comments on Hellman films: Watch on the
   Rhine, The North Star, The Searching Wind, Another Part of
   the Forest. See 1943.2, 3, 4; 1946.1; 1948.1.
      Reprinted 1964.1 and 1966.1.

2 ANON. "The Front Page." Sight and Sound, 27 (Winter 1957-
   58), 111.
      Brief mention of Dead End (film).

3 BLUM, DANIEL. A Pictorial History of the Talkies. New York:
   Grosset and Dunlap, 318 pp.
      Includes photos from Hellman films.

4 BUSFIELD, ROGER M., JR. The Playwright's Art: Stage, Radio,
   Television, Motion Pictures. New York: Harper and
   Brothers, pp. 39, 92, 127.
      Quotes Hellman on dialogue writing. Also cites Owen
   Davis on The Children's Hour. See 1950.8.

5 CLURMAN, HAROLD. Lies Like Truth. New York: Macmillan, pp.
   10, 38, 44, 45, 47-49, 258-67.
      Reprints review of The Autumn Garden (1951.12). Also
   discusses production of Montserrat which Clurman directed
   for the Habimah company in Israel (1949). Clurman calls
   the play "a heroic tragedy," in which choosing the manner
   of one's death becomes "the touchstone as to the kind of
   life one has chosen to live." Several other brief
   references to Hellman.
      Reprinted 1960.26.

6 DOWNES, EDWARD. "Louise Parker Bows as Addie in Regina."
   New York Times (3 May), p. 10.
      Brief assessment of Parker's debut as Addie in New York
   City Opera Company production of Regina.

7 EWEN, DAVID. Complete Book of the American Musical Theater.
   New York: Henry Holt and Company, pp. ix, 36-37, 42-43,
   188.
      Discusses Regina and Candide. Ewen, quoting reviewers,
   says of Candide: "It was rather to the spirit of Voltaire,

than to the letter, that Lillian Hellman was not altogether true." The indictment of society in The Little Foxes, which provides similar strength in Regina, "is not thundered from a soapbox but lies implicit in the tragedy of a family consumed by its own vices."
Revised 1959.6 and 1970.13.

8 GILLETT, JOHN. "Cut and Come Again!" Sight and Sound, 27 (Summer), 258-60.
Discusses the excisions made in The North Star, released as Armoured Attack. The film is another victim of the Cold War with Russia.

9 GRENIER, CYNTHIA. "Joris Ivens." Sight and Sound, 27 (Spring), 204-207.
References to The Spanish Earth.

10 KNEPLER, HENRY. "The Lark, Translation vs. Adaptation: A Case History." Modern Drama, 1 (May), 15-28.
Compares in detail the Christopher Fry and Hellman versions of Anouilh's L'Alouette. Important differences exist in dramatic technique and matters related to sex and religion. The distinct approaches to the use of the flashback underscore the contrasting methods of Hellman and Fry generally. Hellman simplifies "structure, characters and language, and has in the process removed much of the sophistication and originality" of the original play. But in her ending she finds a rough equivalent for Anouilh's intentions, "one that will have an effect on her audience somewhat comparable to the effect of the original." Hellman knows that in American drama "it is better to settle on the side of furtive tears than to stray toward self-conscious smiles."

11 MERSAND, JOSEPH, ed. Guide to Play Selection. Second edition. New York: Appleton-Century-Crofts, Inc., pp. 24, 27, 42, 47.
Lists Hellman plays, with brief summaries, acting editions, and fees.

*12 OBRAZTSOVA, A. "Dramaturgiia Lilian Khellman," in P'esy [Plays]. Moscow, 1958, pp. 3-25.
Introduction to Russian edition of Hellman's plays. Cited in Valentina Libman, Russian Studies of American Literature, 1969.31.

13 OPPENHEIMER, GEORGE, ed. The Passionate Playgoer. New York: Viking Press, pp. 227, 250, 294-301, 534, 592-95.

1958

Reprints Marya Mannes's review of The Lark. Saturday Review (29 December 1955). See 1955.31. Also reprints Hellman's "Introduction" to Four Plays (New York: Random House, 1942). Other brief references.
Reprinted 1962.38.

*14 RUSSELL, HELEN. "Social Satire as Depicted by American Women Playwrights." Ph.D. dissertation, Theater, University of Denver.

Hellman is represented. Cited in Emerson and Michael, Southern Literary Culture: A Bibliography of Masters' and Doctors' Theses, 1979.10. Also listed in American Doctoral Dissertations as completed in 1959.

15 SARGEANT, WINTHROP. "Musical Events." New Yorker, 34 (26 April), 79-82.

Reviews New York City Opera production of Regina. Says Marc Blitzstein's score "is constantly overwhelmed by the drama it is attached to." The grisly aspects of The Little Foxes are not "well suited to operatic treatment."

16 TRIMBLE, LESTER. "Music." Nation, 186 (3 May), 399-400.

Reviews New York City Opera Company production of Regina. The work tries to be opera and Broadway at the same time. Marc Blitzstein has retained "more text [of The Little Foxes] than a normal libretto would contain."

17 WALBRIDGE, EARLE F. "Films A Clef [sic]." Films in Review, 9 (March), 113-25.

Article on real people represented in a number of films, including These Three. Discusses as the source of The Children's Hour "The Great Drumsheugh Case," discovered and described by William Roughead in Bad Companions (1931). Walbridge claims that his letter to the Saturday Review (16 March 1935) objecting to Hellman's statement that the play "'came out of her head'" was instrumental in the play's being denied a Pulitzer Prize. These Three, he says, was bowdlerized to such a degree that the two teachers (named Pirie and Woods) in Roughead "would not have recognized themselves." See 1935.54.

18 WRIGHT, EDWARD A. A Primer for Playgoers. Englewood Cliffs, N.J.: Prentice-Hall, p. 61.

Mentions that The Little Foxes has been called both comedy and melodrama. Wright says it belongs to the latter category.

1959

*1 ANON. Celebrity Register. International Celebrity Register
Ltd., U.S. edition, p. 337.
Cited by Norma Olin Ireland, Index to Women of the
World, 1970.19, p. 236.

2 ANON. Review of Candide. London Observer (3 May), Leisure
Section, p. 5.
Praises Candide's "superior ingredients," including
Hellman's book.

3 BOWERS, FAUBIAN. Broadway, U.S.S.R. New York: Thomas Nelson
and Sons, pp. 61, 75, 89-93.
Discusses Russian production of The Autumn Garden during
the 1957-58 season. Changes in the text were substantial
and disturbing. "In Moscow, Nick Denery returns from
Germany with a German maid. Sophie, a refugee from
Germany, who works as a maid in the boarding house, is
turned into a French girl. This removes the Jewish element
and changes the accent from kindliness to exploitation of
servants imported from Europe."

4 BRUSTEIN, ROBERT. "Why American Plays Are Not Literature."
Harper's Magazine, 219 (October), 167-72.
Briefly mentions Hellman as a contributor to an "intel-
lectual ferment" no longer present in American drama.
Reprinted in Writing in America, ed. John Fischer and
Robert Silvers (see 1960.24), and in Discussions of Modern
American Drama, ed. Walter Meserve (see 1965.17).

5 CLURMAN, HAROLD, ed. Famous American Plays of the 1930s.
The Laurel Drama Series. New York: Dell Publishing Co.,
p. 10.
Clurman's introduction cites The Little Foxes as a
major play of the 1930s.

6 EWEN, DAVID. Complete Book of the American Musical Theater.
Revised edition. New York: Holt, Rinehart and Winston,
pp. ix, 36-37, 42-43, 188.
Reprints material on Regina and Candide from 1958.7.
Revised 1970.13.

7 GILLETT, JOHN. "The Survivors." Sight and Sound, 28 (Summer
and Autumn), 150-55.
Brief mention of Dead End (film).

8 HEWITT, BARNARD. Theatre U.S.A., 1668-1957. New York:
      McGraw Hill, pp. 415-17, 424, 479.
         Discusses The Little Foxes, with brief references to
      other Hellman plays. Reprints most of Richard Watts's
      review of The Little Foxes, from the New York Herald
      Tribune of 16 February 1939. See 1939.43.

9 MARCORELLES, LOUIS. "André Bazin." Sight and Sound, 28
      (Winter 1958-59), 30.
         Tribute to film critic André Bazin, noting as his major
      contribution to film aesthetics his analysis of deep-focus
      photography, as used by William Wyler in The Little Foxes.

10 PARMENTER, ROSS. "Opera: Regina Returns." New York Times
      (20 April), p. 36.
         Reviews New York City Opera production of Regina.
      Praises the work as one "worthy of remaining in the reper-
      tory."

11 PRYOR, WILLIAM. "An Examination of the Southern Milieu in
      Representative Plays by Southern Dramatists, 1923-1956."
      Ph.D. dissertation, Florida State University.
         Includes Hellman. Dissertation Abstracts International,
      20:674.

12 RICE, ELMER. The Living Theatre. New York: Harper and
      Brothers, pp. 59, 126, 162, 206, 207.
         Passing references to Hellman.

13 SHARPE, ROBERT BOIES. Irony in the Drama. Chapel Hill:
      University of North Carolina Press, pp. 163, 190-91.
         Classifies Hellman as a dramatist who belongs in a line
      of "individuals and moralists" descending from Ibsen, by
      way of Shaw and O'Neill. This group of playwrights differs
      from the other primary line of modern dramatists
      (Strindberg, Brecht, Williams), which tends to be "morally
      defiant."

14 SOBEL, BERNARD, ed. The New Theatre Handbook and Digest of
      Plays. New York: Crown Publishers, Inc., pp. 110-11, 355,
      428.
         Brief biographical sketch of Hellman through Candide
      (p. 355). Brief synopsis of The Little Foxes (p. 428).
      Much fuller synopsis of The Children's Hour (pp. 110-11).

15 STERN, RICHARD G. "Lillian Hellman on Her Plays." Contact,
      3 (1959), 113-19.

1960

> Interview with Hellman while she served as Visiting
> Lecturer in the English Department at the University of
> Chicago. She discusses her progress on what was to become
> Toys in the Attic, citing specific details of plot and
> character. Hellman also comments on The Little Foxes and
> notes that, to her, "most villains are funny," including
> Regina. "I thought Birdie was silly. I was amazed to
> wake up and find that people thought Birdie was a touching
> character." (Tape of this interview is at Harper Library
> of the University of Chicago.)

1960

1 ANON. "Academy Elects 116." New York Times (12 May), p. 22.
   Announces election of Hellman to the American Academy
   of Arts and Sciences.

2 ANON. "The Autumn Garden." The Times [London] (2 March),
   p. 13e.
   Reviews production for English television of The Autumn
   Garden, heretofore unproduced in England. We are in
   familiar Hellman territory at the start, with "a moulder-
   ing Southern mansion, faded and melancholy, [and] a
   variety of strange, vague characters drifting through their
   aimless and neurotic lives." It is a consistently interesting play, but "somehow too smooth, too neat, too insu-
   lated from life."

3 ANON. "Broadway Plays to Be Filmed." The Times [London] (2
   August), p. 11e.
   Says William Wyler has bought screen rights for Toys in
   the Attic.

4 ANON. "Broadway Success for London." The Times [London] (16
   September), p. 16f.
   Announces London opening of Toys in the Attic, a play
   whose action "takes place in an old mansion in the Deep
   South [sic]."

5 ANON. "English Finesse in an American Play." The Times
   [London] (11 November), p. 16a.
   Reviews London production of Toys in the Attic, at the
   Piccadilly Theatre. Hellman "probes cleverly into the
   mental, sexual and moral wounds of two families related by
   marriage but we may well feel that her approach is somewhat too clinical." Her characters tend to become her

patients and she forgets at times that they are also human beings.

6   ANON. "Hellman, Lillian." Current Biography, 1960. New York: H. W. Wilson Company, pp. 186-87.
    Biographical sketch of Hellman through Toys in the Attic. Cites brief comments by drama critics regarding specific plays. Lists additional references in Who's Who in America, etc. Photo.

7   ANON. "Lillian Hellman to Be Lecturer." New York Times (31 July), p. 48.
    Notes Hellman's appointment as Visiting Lecturer in English at Harvard for the spring 1961 semester.

8   ANON. "Second Film of Hellman Play." The Times [London] (22 September).
    Says William Wyler plans to refilm The Children's Hour with Doris Day and Katharine Hepburn.

9   ANON. "Theater." Life, 48 (4 April), 53-54, 56, 58.
    Review, with photos, of Toys in the Attic which confirms Hellman's "position as the world's foremost playwright." She is able to look probingly at people in trouble without lapsing into the luridly psychological approach so common today.

10 ANON. "The Theater: Toys in the Attic." Time, 75 (7 March), 50.
    Praises the play for the reappearance of Hellman's mordant power, coupled with a more probing and wide-ranging view of character. "She has passed from human greed to something at times no prettier but much more universalizing: human need, the ego's fierce need to be needed and be loved, and hence its ugly need, when failed, to hurt or betray or destroy."

11 ANON. "Theater: Triumph for Starkness." Newsweek, 55 (7 March), 89.
    Review of Toys in the Attic calls Hellman's sense of characterization and lean style "as acute as ever," although the play is not one of her best. The "unexpected monstrosity" of the characters resembles behavior in the plays of Williams, but the members of Hellman's Berniers family are "more recognizable people."

1960

12   ANON. "Toys in the Attic." Theatre World, 56 (December),
     13-18.
          Photos (with brief comments) from the London production
     of Toys in the Attic, starring Diana Wynyard and Wendy
     Hiller.

13   ANON. "The Unpredictable Miss Hellman." The Times [London]
     (9 November), p. 8e.
          Interview with Hellman during her stay in London for
     Toys in the Attic rehearsals. Topics include Candide, the
     well-made play, differences in Broadway and London produc-
     tion methods. Says Hellman "has resolutely eluded the sort
     of neat pigeonholing operation which generally, sooner or
     later, overtakes every writer whose individuality is
     strongly marked in all he does." Photo.

14   ASTON, FRANK. "Toys in the Attic Takes Apart Lives of Five."
     New York World-Telegram and The Sun (26 February).
          Review of Toys in the Attic. Calls it the "most
     hellishly hypnotic drama" of a brilliant social vivisec-
     tionist.

15   ATKINSON, BROOKS. "One Revue: One Play." New York Times (6
     March), section 2, p. 1.
          Sunday review of Toys in the Attic. Appreciates the
     "dramatic candor" of the play, once its preliminary en-
     tanglements have been established, but finds it to be one
     of Hellman's "minor works."

16   _____. "Theatre: Hellman's Play." New York Times (26
     February), p. 23.
          Toys in the Attic can use a little more of Hellman's
     "familiar talent for putting things together neatly."
     Only toward the close of the second act do the characteri-
     zations and Hellman's "hard-headed knowledge of the intri-
     cacies of human relationships" mesh into thematic focus.
     But the play "will do until something more independent and
     adult comes along."

17   BLUM, DANIEL. Theatre World, Season 1959-60. New York:
     Chilton, pp. 69-70.
          Credits and photos of the Broadway production of Toys
     in the Attic.

18   BOLTON, WHITNEY. "Hellman Welcome with Toys in the Attic."
     New York Morning Telegraph (27 February).
          Calls Toys in the Attic a brilliant play, though not
     Hellman's best.

19 BOULTON, MARJORIE. The Anatomy of Drama. London: Routledge
    and Kegan Paul, pp. 10, 50.
        Cites The Children's Hour as one of numerous plays that
    have suffered at the hands of British censors; calls the
    ending of the play "tragic."

20 BRAHMS, CARYL. Review of Toys in the Attic. Plays and
    Players, 8 (December), 11.
        Snide review of the London production of Toys in the
    Attic. Calls casting of Wendy Hiller and Diana Wynyard
    as the Berniers sisters monumentally inappropriate. Their
    real talents are buried, along with, perhaps, "the bones
    of a very good play."

21 BRANDON, HENRY. Interview with Arthur Miller. Sunday Times
    [London] (20 March).
        See 1962.12.

22 BRIEN, ALAN. "Plays." Spectator, 205 (18 November), 782-83.
        Ridicules Toys in the Attic, in its London production,
    as "an anthology of bathos." Finds echoes of Inge, Miller,
    and Williams--"all the bruised-purple passages from the
    laureates of self pity."

23 BRUSTEIN, ROBERT. "The Play and the Unplay." New Republic,
    142 (14 March), 22-23.
        Reviews Toys in the Attic. Precisely because Hellman
    is "a playwright in the original sense of the word, a
    maker or fashioner of plays," Toys in the Attic "never
    seems more than a moderately interesting play." Except
    for Albertine Prine, the characters have no life beyond
    their dramatic function. Hellman's "new flirtation with
    Freudianism" distracts her from the savage indignation
    which distinguishes her earlier plays. The incestuous
    theme is simplistic and unnecessary. Hellman is on much
    more original ground in her examination of the "organic
    effect of money on people's lives." But the "play's theme
    --that 'there's something sad in people not liking what
    they want when they get it'--is one that comes perilously
    close to homily."

24 _____. "Why American Plays Are Not Literature," in Writing
    in America. Edited by John Fischer and Robert Silvers.
    New Brunswick, N.J.: Rutgers University Press, pp. 46-60.
        Reprint of 1959.4.

25 CHAPMAN, JOHN. "Miss Hellman's Toys in the Attic Vigorous and
    Absorbing Drama." New York Daily News (26 February).
        Praises Toys in the Attic highly.

1960

26 CLURMAN, HAROLD. Lies Like Truth. New York: Grove Press;
     London: Evergreen Books, pp. 10, 38, 44, 45, 47-49, 258-67.
     Reprint of 1958.5.

27 _____. "Theatre." Nation, 190 (19 March), 261-62.
        Review of Toys in the Attic. Articulates the play's
     various themes, relating the role of self-deception in
     human lives to that subject as presented in The Autumn
     Garden. These themes are, however, jumbled and confused
     by the play's narrative and by irrelevant, lurid violence
     and melodrama. Toys in the Attic is "signally well written
     with that combination of selective realism and subtly
     rhetorical phrasing which gives Miss Hellman's dialogue a
     distinction approaching nobility."

28 COLEMAN, ROBERT. "Toys in the Attic Sure-Fire Hit." New
     York Daily Mirror (26 February).
        Considers Toys in the Attic "the best shocker since
     Tennessee Williams' Sweet Bird of Youth."

29 COLLINGE, PATRICIA. "Another Part of the Hubbards Or, When
     They Were Even Younger," in Twentieth-Century Parody.
     Edited by Burlington Lowrey. New York: Harcourt, Brace
     and Company, 182-88.
        Reprint of 1947.8. Also briefly mentioned in Preface
     to this collection by Nathaniel Benchley (p. xiv).

30 CRAIG, H. A. L. "Red Roses for O'Casey." New Statesman, 60
     (19 November), 782.
        Belittles Toys in the Attic as a boring play based on
     "the cliché of Southern heavy drama concealment: a con-
     cealed homosexuality, concealed lesbianism, concealed
     hatred, colour, castration, impotence. Faulkner does it
     with genius. Tennessee Williams with talent. But when
     Miss Hellman's moment of truth arrives--concealed incest--
     she manages it with no more dramatic push than a tea
     trolley." Her characters are merely servants of the well-
     made play.

31 DASH, THOMAS R. "Toys in the Attic Should Bring One Playtime
     Thrill." Women's Wear Daily (26 February).
        Positive review of Toys in the Attic: "a penetrating and
     probing play."

32 DRIVER, TOM F. "Puppet Show: Toys in the Attic." Christian
     Century, 77 (27 April), 511-12.
        Hellman's skill with melodrama proved effective in the
     early plays, when she applied her technique to social

propaganda plays. But in Toys in the Attic the connections
to real life have been severed, leaving us with undeveloped
social themes (greed, racial equality) and hollow characters.

33 DUSENBURY, WINIFRED. The Theme of Loneliness in Modern
American Drama. Gainesville: University of Florida Press,
pp. 134-54, passim.
Discusses The Little Foxes and Another Part of the
Forest, along with A Streetcar Named Desire and other
plays, as "Southern" works. "Although the theme of tragic
loneliness is carried by Birdie, at the end it is the
powerful Regina who pleadingly asks her daughter to sleep
with her because of fear of being alone." All the Hubbards
are cut off from positive human contacts in their town.
"To some extent John Bagtry and Ben Hubbard are contrasted
as are the women in the two families. . . . John's loneliness is tragic, as is Birdie's; but Lillian Hellman con-
vinces her audiences that there is also tragedy in belong-
ing to nothing but business."

34 FELHEIM, MARVIN. "The Autumn Garden: Mechanics and Dialec-
tics." Modern Drama, 3 (Summer), 191-95.
Considers The Autumn Garden a significant departure for
Hellman in its structure, themes, and character development. No American play is more completely Chekhovian. In
its presentation of "nostalgia for a no-longer existent
past and the individual's frustrating search for love and
the meaning of life," The Autumn Garden most resembles
The Three Sisters. The kind of drama depicted here--
artistic and moral, not merely psychological (as in
Williams) or sociological (as in Miller)--"is the only kind
which makes for modern tragedy."

35 FIELD, ROWLAND. "New Hellman Play Incisive." Newark Evening
News (26 February).
Considers Toys in the Attic a gripping and incisive
drama of family maladjustment.

36 GASSNER, JOHN. "Broadway in Review." Educational Theatre
Journal, 12 (May), 113-21.
Reviews Toys in the Attic. Compassion guides Hellman's
hand "so that she performs surgery on her characters instead of summarily decapitating them." One of Hellman's
gifts is her ability to show that "dreadful things are
done by the onstage characters out of affectionate
possessiveness, rather than out of ingrained villainy.
Although the author's corresponding view of life is ironic

and is trenchantly expressed, there is no gloating over
human misery, no horror-mongering, no traffic with sensationalism in Toys in the Attic. And, unlike some well-
known contemporary playwrights here and abroad, Miss
Hellman has proved once more that she can deal with human
failure without falling in love with it herself."
Reprinted 1968.11.

37 _____. "Broadway in Review." Educational Theatre Journal,
12 (October), 221-30.
Briefly mentions Toys in the Attic as Gassner's choice
for the Pulitzer Prize.

38 _____. "Playwrights of the Period." Theatre Arts, 44
(September), 19-22, 69, 71.
Discusses American playwriting of the 1930s. Only
Hellman, who relied on nothing "but her own strong mind
and will," continued to write with power beyond that
period. For many of the dramatists of the 1930s used
social faith as a crutch, in the way that later writers
were to use psychopathology, and "when the crutch slipped
from under the armpit, the playwright stumbled."
Reprinted 1968.11.

39 _____. Theatre at the Crossroads. New York: Holt, Rinehart
and Winston, pp. 132-39, 247-49.
Analyzes Hellman's playwriting career, particularly in
the context of her changes in style in The Autumn Garden.
"Comprehensiveness did not lessen her power and a compas-
sionate viewpoint would not blunt the edge of her writing.
The Autumn Garden, in 1951, spoke better for her than for
the decade." Gassner also comments favorably on Toys in
the Attic and praises Hellman's fascinating "theatricaliza-
tion of reality" in The Lark (although he objects to
Anouilh's basic structure).

40 HEWES, HENRY. "Broadway Postscript: Love in the Icebox."
Saturday Review, 43 (12 March), 71-72.
Review of Toys in the Attic praises Hellman's tough,
literate "concern for catching the quality of life as she
sees it," even if that concern prevents us from sympathiz-
ing with her characters. Typical Hellman elements combine
with Chekhovian and Brechtian touches in order to portray
the most selfish aspects of "love" and their destructive
influence on others.

41 HOBSON, HAROLD. "Theatre." Sunday Times [London] (13
November), p. 35.

Negative review of the London production of Toys in the Attic. Hellman "has chosen to write on a Tennessee Williams theme in an Agatha Christie style. But she has neither Mrs. Christie's cunning, nor Mr. Williams' authentic, if hysterical, passion."

42 HOPE-WALLACE, PHILIP. "Last Night at the Theatre." Manchester Guardian (11 November), p. 11.
     Argues, in a review of the London production of Toys in the Attic, that "Miss Hellman strips away the self-deception with a hand not always as cunning as it was in The Little Foxes. We are more curious, than involved, in the acting."

43 KEOWN, ERIC. "At the Play." Punch, 239 (16 November), 716-17.
     Reviews Toys in the Attic (London production). Condemns the play as a humorless, pretentious study of dreary people. The production ought to have been mounted as melodrama, which appears to be the drama's true level; then, at least, it might have acquired some emotional life.

44 KERR, WALTER. "First Night Report: Toys in the Attic." New York Herald Tribune (26 February), p. 12.
     Toys in the Attic contains "straightforward, uncompromised writing" and dramatic materials that unfold subtly and firmly. It is an ugly tale but audiences will be grateful for its having been told.

45 _____. "Lillian Hellman Whets the Knife of Language." New York Herald Tribune (6 March), section 4, pp. 1, 3.
     Analyzes Toys in the Attic, "a play about the failure to change, a dark and despairing playground on which eternal children whither and die." Hellman, whose "body of work exceeds Miller's in volume and Inge's in force," writes with lucid control; her language in Toys in the Attic "has precisely the same power to slice deeply into flesh as it did when Regina Hubbard was a girl." It reminds us, with a jolt, that contemporary American drama does not belong only to Miller, Williams, or Inge.
     Slightly revised 1963.39.

46 KRONENBERGER, LOUIS, ed. The Best Plays of 1959-60. New York: Dodd, Mead and Company, pp. 17, 157-82, 322, 369, 383-88, 390-91, 396.
     Condenses Toys in the Attic, praising it for its insight, power, and writing. Production data.

1960

47 LAWSON, JOHN HOWARD. Theory and Technique of Playwriting.
     Dramabook edition. New York: Hill and Wang, pp. xxvi-
     xxvii, 223, 263-66.
        Reprints 1936.52 with a new introduction in which Lawson
     discusses major shifts in dramatic literature to 1960.
     Hellman is mentioned in the introduction; material on The
     Children's Hour remains the same. Reprinted in this edi-
     tion 1961, 1964, 1965, 1967, 1968, 1969.

48 LEWIS, THEOPHILUS. "Theatre: Toys in the Attic." America,
     103 (28 May), 323.
        Calls the play "a tawdry tale," which lacks the "dra-
     matic drive or social illumination" of Hellman's earlier
     plays. The material of Toys, which we tend to associate
     with that of Tennessee Williams, is skillfully and deli-
     cately presented, however, because Hellman always respects
     the dignity of drama and the maturity of her audience.

49 McCLAIN, JOHN. "Top Writing--Top Acting." New York Journal
     American (26 February).
        Review of Toys in the Attic. Resents plays about
     decadent southern families but admires the persuasive
     force of Hellman's writing.

50 MANNES, MARYA. "Miss Hellman's 'Electra.'" Reporter, 21 (31
     March), 43.
        Highly favorable review of Toys in the Attic. Compares
     Hellman's material with that of Tennessee Williams. Her
     economy, discipline and "consistent integrity" in not
     striving for shock effect distinguish her from Williams.
     Although he is "more a master of verbal music," the dif-
     ference between them seems to be one between "a deep but
     controlled involvement" (Hellman) and "a dark obsession"
     (Williams).

51 MOREHOUSE, WARD. "'These Full Lean Years!'" Theatre Arts, 44
     (September), 10-14, 71-73.
        Reminiscences of the theater of the 1930s, with
     references to The Children's Hour, The Little Foxes, and
     Hellman's feud with Tallulah Bankhead. Photo of Bankhead
     as Regina Giddens.

52 [MORRISON,] HOBE. Review of Toys in the Attic. Variety (2
     March).
        Finds Toys in the Attic "a gripping melodrama about the
     corrosive effect of possessiveness."

53 NANNES, CASPAR. <u>Politics in the American Drama</u>. Washington, D.C.: Catholic University of America Press, pp. 24, 139, 142-44, 150, 168, 170-71, 221, 224-25.
Several brief references to Hellman, with more detailed discussions of <u>The Searching Wind</u> (pp. 142-44) and <u>Watch on the Rhine</u> (pp. 170-71).

54 <u>NEW YORK THEATRE CRITICS' REVIEWS, 1955</u>. Vol. 21. New York: Critics' Theatre Reviews, pp. 345-48.
Reprints reviews of <u>Toys in the Attic</u> from New York daily newspapers for 26 February (<u>New York World-Telegram and The Sun</u>, <u>New York Mirror</u>, <u>New York Journal American</u>, <u>New York Times</u>, <u>New York Post</u>, <u>Daily News</u>, <u>New York Herald Tribune</u>).

55 OPPENHEIMER, GEORGE. "On Stage." <u>Newsday</u> (9 March).
Considers <u>Toys in the Attic</u> a "rich and rewarding shock treatment administered to a sick season."

56 PECK, SEYMOUR. "Lillian Hellman Talks of Love and 'Toys.'" <u>New York Times</u> (21 February), section 2, p. 3.
Interview with Hellman during the Boston tryout of <u>Toys in the Attic</u>. Includes her observations on the reception of <u>The Little Foxes</u>, her dissatisfaction with the ending of <u>The Children's Hour</u>, and the gestation of <u>Toys in the Attic</u>.

*57 SMIRNOV, B. A. "Traditsii russkoi klassicheskoi dramy i dramaturgiia Lilian Hellman" [The tradition of Russian classical drama and the plays of Lillian Hellman], in <u>Zapiski o teatre</u> [Notes about the theater]. Leningrad, Moscow, 1960, pp. 284-305.
Cited in Valentina Libman, <u>Russian Studies of American Literature</u>, 1969.31.

58 S.[TEPHENS], F.[RANCES]. Review of <u>Toys in the Attic</u>. <u>Theatre World</u>, 56 (December), 9, 13-19.
Reviews London production of <u>Toys in the Attic</u>. Expresses considerable disappointment with the all-English company and with the play itself. The production fails to clarify the psychological background to the relationship between the sisters and Julian. Numerous photos from the production (pp. 13-18).

59 TALLMER, JERRY. "Theatre Uptown: Burnt Offering." <u>Village Voice</u>, 5 (2 March), 9-10.
Reviews <u>Toys in the Attic</u>, the first American play to open on Broadway since <u>A Raisin in the Sun</u> "with characters

1960

so sufficiently founded in personal truth as to make us
give even the slightest damn as to why they are not perhaps completely fulfilled in truth."

60 THORP, WILLARD. American Writing in the Twentieth Century.
    Cambridge, Mass.: Harvard University Press, pp. 65, 75,
    96-97.
        Says Hellman's plots are carefully constructed but not
    "'well-made' in the manner of Scribe and Sardou. She
    delights in strong situations which in other hands might
    have been shaped into melodrama rather than tragedy." She
    is an ironist as well as a specialist in evil in people's
    lives.
        Reprinted 1963.59.

61 TREWIN, J. C. "The World of the Theatre: Deep Down."
    Illustrated London News, 237 (26 November), 964.
        Reviews London production of Toys in the Attic.
    Hellman's answers to the questions she raises result in
    almost "a parody of the sultrier Deep South drama." The
    play has been overcharged and overwritten.

62 TYNAN, KENNETH. "At the Theatre." London Observer (13
    November), p. 30.
        Writes, in a review of the London production of Toys in
    the Attic, that "the play is not Miss Hellman's best; the
    characters spend too much time advising and describing
    each other in aphorisms frequently portentous and too
    little time making real dramatic contact with each other."

63 _____. Review of Toys in the Attic. New Yorker, 36 (5
    March), 124-25.
        Praises the play for its "dedicated professionalism,"
    for returning the drama to its original purpose: the
    analysis of "how and why we suffer." But Toys in the
    Attic "changes horses in midstream. It starts out as an
    inquiry into the moral consequences of wealth and ends up
    as a treatise on abnormal psychology. . . . Miss Hellman
    is a wonderful woman but I prefer her when she is not try-
    ing to write on two levels at the same time."

64 WATTS, RICHARD, JR. "Two on the Aisle: Lillian Hellman's
    Striking Drama." New York Post (26 February).
        Reviews Toys in the Attic. Finds the play stunning in
    its theatrical power and ugly candor. At first reminiscent
    of the plays of Tennessee Williams, Toys in the Attic
    utilizes more subtle, devious and complex methods.

65 ZOLOTOW, SAM. "Toys in the Attic, Fiorello! Cited." New
York Times (20 April), p. 44.
Reports the naming of Toys in the Attic as best American
drama of the 1959-60 season by the New York Drama Critics'
Circle. Photo from the play.

1961

1 AARON, DANIEL. Writers on the Left. New York: Harcourt,
Brace & World, 460 pp.
Brief reference to Hellman. Quotes Albert Maltz on in-
consistent political reactions to Watch on the Rhine in
New Masses reviews. See 1946.42.
Reprinted 1965.1 (Avon Books) and 1969.1 (Avon Books,
Discus Edition).

2 ADLER, JACOB H. "The Rose and the Fox: Notes on the Southern
Drama," in South: Modern Southern Literature in Its
Cultural Setting. Edited by Louis D. Rubin, Jr., and
Robert D. Jacobs. Garden City, N.Y.: Doubleday, pp. 349-
75.
Analyzes the plays of Hellman and Williams which are
about the South. Adler finds numerous parallels and contrasts in their work, particularly in the use of the
southern environment, the conflict between cultural ideals
and harsh reality, and the presence of sex and money as
symbols of power. For all Hellman's gifts, she lacks
Williams's complexity and symbolism. Her characters (such
as the Hubbards) are often fascinating, but exist only at
one level; her southern settings and characters (as in
Autumn Garden) do not finally reveal characteristically
southern themes. Williams is the profounder of the two
for he possesses a "wider variety of technique and a far
greater ability to make characters function both as
characters and as multiple symbols."

3 ANON. "The Adults' Hour." Newsweek, 58 (7 August), 77.
Feature article on the remaking of The Children's Hour
as a film.

4 ANON. "Awards Made for Arts." New York Times (30 March), p.
21.
Names Hellman as recipient of a Brandeis University
Creative Arts Award.

5 ANON. "Brandeis U. Honors 9 in Creative Arts." New York
Times (11 June), p. 63.

1961

      Brief report on dinner at which Hellman received the
Theatre Arts Medal, one of nine Creative Arts Awards for
1961 given by Brandeis University.

6 ANON. "The Complete Text of Toys in the Attic by Lillian
    Hellman." Theatre Arts, 45 (October), 25-26.
      Comments briefly on Hellman's career. Praises her as
    "a superb craftsman, a writer of great integrity and in-
    tense vitality." Prints the entire script of Toys in the
    Attic with production credits and photos.

7 ANON. "Dashiell Hammett, Author, Dies; Created Hard-Boiled
    Detectives." New York Times (11 January), p. 47.
      Obituary of Hammett records highlights of his career,
    noting that at his death he had been the house guest of
    Hellman, who would speak at the funeral service.

8 ANON. "Hammett Eulogized by Lillian Hellman." New York
    Times (13 January), p. 29.
      Brief report on Hammett's funeral service, with excerpt
    from Hellman's eulogy.

9 ANON. "Hammett's Will Filed." New York Times (7 February),
    p. 66.
      Mentions Hellman being named Hammett's literary
    executor and executor of his estate.

10 ANON. "Kennedy Doctor Widens Activity." New York Times (20
    April), p. 23.
      Names Hellman as one of six recipients of achievement
    awards from the Women's Division of the Albert Einstein
    College of Medicine of Yeshiva University.

11 BALLIETT, WHITNEY. "Off Broadway: Martyrs and Misery." New
    Yorker, 36 (21 January), 68-70.
      Negative review of Montserrat revival at the Gate
    Theatre. Criticizes Hellman's adaptation as "one of those
    Gallic seminars in which a moral question is talked to
    death, with occasional time-outs for illustrative but in-
    effectual action."

12 BRIGGS, JOHN. Leonard Bernstein: The Man, His Work and His
    World. Cleveland and New York: World Publishing Company,
    pp. 151, 195-201.
      Portrait of Leonard Bernstein refers to his collabora-
    tion with Hellman and others on Candide. Quotes Richard
    Wilbur on the play's failure: "'There was no single
    villain. Lillian Hellman doesn't really like musicals.

Lenny's music got more and more pretentious and smashy--
the audience forgot what was happening to the characters.
Lillian's book got to be more connective tissue. And I
was inclined to be too literary and stubborn.'" Also reprints Bernstein's "Colloquy in Boston." See 1956.10.

13 CALTA, LOUIS. "Arts Medal Goes to Miss Hellman." New York
     Times (11 March), p. 15.
        Announces the naming of Hellman as winner of the
     Brandeis University Creative Arts Medal. Also mentions
     that Hellman has completed one act of a new play promised
     to Kermit Bloomgarden for production. A related note else-
     where in this compilation of theater news states that
     Hellman has agreed to serve on a committee to ensure the
     continuance of Joseph Papp's New York Shakespeare Festival,
     in Central Park.

14 CERF, BENNETT. "Lillian Hellman," in his edition of Four
     Contemporary American Plays. New York: Vintage Books, p.
     385.
        Summarizes Hellman's career. Calls her "tough, un-
     yielding, brilliant," capable of understanding and compas-
     sion. Says her career has been marked by a limitless
     capacity for work and a constant striving for perfection.
     Includes complete text of Toys in the Attic (pp. 207-93).

*15 CRANE, JOSHUA. "A Comparison of G. B. Shaw's Saint Joan and
     Lillian Hellman's Adaptation of The Lark by Jean Anouilh."
     Master's thesis, English, University of Florida.
        Cited in Emerson and Michael, Southern Literary Culture:
     A Bibliography of Masters' and Doctors' Theses, 1979.10.
     Also cited by Manfred Triesch, in The Lillian Hellman
     Collection at the University of Texas, p. 98. See
     1966.46.

16 DOWNER, ALAN S. Recent American Drama. University of
     Minnesota Pamphlets on American Writers, no. 7.
     Minneapolis: University of Minnesota Press, pp. 41-42.
        Hellman takes a "fresh and realistic" look in Toys in
     the Attic at the corrupting potential of conventional
     love. Julian's life is "shattered by a force unknown to
     the artist-sociologist or the artist-psychologist, by a
     force known only to the artist-moralist, the force of
     evil." And that force is embodied in Carrie, "no capital-
     ist dragon, no Satan lusting for revenge, no more incestu-
     ous than Ferdinand of The Duchess of Malfi. She is what
     evil must always be, the other side of good, tragic
     because she cannot know of her enslavement, because she

1961

can never have the opportunity to escape. She is the most
memorable figure of a memorable work."

17   ESTRIN, MARK W. "An Evil World Well-Made: The Plays of
     Lillian Hellman." Master's thesis, English, Columbia
     University.
          Analyzes Hellman's dramas through Toys in the Attic.

18   EWEN, DAVID. The Story of America's Musical Theater.
     Philadelphia and New York: Chilton Company, p. 236.
          Concise discussion of Regina, Marc Blitzstein's musical
     drama based on Hellman's "bitter, vitriolic play about a
     decaying Southern family." Regina is shattering, an "over-
     whelming tragedy about a deceitful, avaricious, hate-torn
     family destroyed by its own vices."
          Reprinted 1968.8.

19   GREEN, GORDON. "The Propaganda Play." Modern Drama, 4 (May),
     429-30.
          Briefly mentions Hellman.

20   HYAMS, JOE. "Children's Hour Not for Children." New York
     Herald Tribune (30 July).
          On refilming The Children's Hour.

21   KNEPLER, HENRY. "Translation and Adaptation in the Contem-
     porary Drama." Modern Drama, 4 (May), 31-41.
          Compares flashback techniques used by Hellman in her
     adaptation of The Lark with those of Christopher Fry in
     his translation of the same play. Knepler prefers
     Hellman's method, which he finds subtle, profound, and
     illustrative of his basic argument: contemporary plays
     should be adapted with the recognition that the drama is
     a communal experience; they should therefore be translated
     in terms of the stage environment of the new country and
     should be permitted to depart from the literalness of the
     source.

22   LAMBERT, J. W. "Plays in Performance." Drama, New Series,
     no. 60 (Spring), 20-26.
          Includes strongly negative comments about Toys in the
     Attic, based on its London production.

23   LEWIS, THEOPHILUS. "Theatre: Montserrat." America, 104 (28
     January), 577.
          Review of the Gate Theatre revival calls the acting
     more resourceful than that of the original Broadway produc-
     tion. Hellman's adaptation transforms Montserrat from an

historical drama with a religious slant into "an intellectual horror play" that is taut and suspenseful.

24 LOVELL, JOHN, JR. <u>Digests of Great American Plays</u>. New York: Crowell, pp. 321-24, 349-52.
    Comments on and synopsizes <u>The Little Foxes</u> and <u>Watch on the Rhine</u>.

25 MILLER, JORDAN Y. <u>American Dramatic Literature</u>. New York: McGraw-Hill, pp. 87-131.
    Anthologizes <u>The Little Foxes</u>, with critical introduction and questions for study. Calls the play "one of the finest examples of the craft of playmaking combined with the qualities of excellent realistic drama." <u>The Little Foxes</u> is not melodrama, but it is "a melodramatic play."

*26 OBRAZTSOVA, A. "<u>Slomannye igrushki</u> (<u>Igrushki na cherdake</u>)" [Broken toys (Toys in the Attic)]. <u>Teatre</u> (no. 3), pp. 186-88.
    Cited in Valentina Libman, <u>Russian Studies of American Literature</u>, 1969.31.

27 TAUBMAN, HOWARD. "Theatre: <u>Montserrat</u>." <u>New York Times</u> (9 January), p. 30.
    Praises the Gate Theatre Repertory Company's revival of the play. The plotting, characterization, and moral concerns of <u>Montserrat</u> bear the typical Hellman stamp.

28 TYNAN, KENNETH. <u>Curtains</u>. New York: Atheneum, pp. 257, 362, 363, 430.
    Brief references to Hellman.

29 WHITING, FRANK M. <u>An Introduction to the Theatre</u>. Revised edition. New York: Harper and Row, p. 122.
    Brief discussion of Hellman's plays through <u>Toys in the Attic</u>. Comments favorably on <u>Candide</u>.
    Reprinted 1969.48.

1962

1 ANON. "Admirable Film of Hellman Play." <u>The Times</u> [London] (17 August), p. 11a.
    Reviews film adaptation of <u>The Children's Hour</u> (1962), released in England as <u>The Loudest Whisper</u>. Praises the film, especially the performance of Shirley MacLaine as Martha.

1962

2 ANON. "Arts and Letters Institute Names 12." New York Times
     (13 February), p. 40.
         Mentions Hellman's election to a vice-presidency of the
     National Institute of Arts and Letters.

3 ANON. "Cinema: 'That Kind of Love.'" Time, 79 (9 February),
     83.
         Review of The Children's Hour, film director William
     Wyler's "second try at doing right by Lillian Hellman's
     1934 stage melodrama, whose burden was that lesbianism may
     be regrettable, but a nasty, spying child is simply in-
     tolerable." Extraneous scenes after Martha's suicide and
     an implied happy ending hurt the film.

4 ANON. Data on The Children's Hour [film remake]. Film Facts,
     5 (1962), 41.
         Complete credits, etc.

5 ANON. "The Grownups' Hour." New York Sunday News (18 March),
     magazine section, p. 10.
         Photos of the premiere of The Children's Hour (1962 film
     version) and the party that followed.

6 ANON. "A Guide to Current Films." Sight and Sound, 31
     (Autumn), 208.
         Calls William Wyler's second film adaptation of The
     Children's Hour (English title: The Loudest Whisper) "effi-
     cient stage carpentry," but dated.

7 ANON. "Movies: Yesterday's Truth." Newsweek, 59 (12 March),
     101-102.
         Review of The Children's Hour (film). Important things
     are said, at times with skill and dramatic effect, but
     theatrical artificiality periodically "blows reality to
     smithereens." Includes interview with William Wyler about
     his direction of the film. Photo of Wyler with two
     children in the cast.

8 ANON. "Paris Theatres Ready for Seller's Market." The Times
     [London] (22 December), p. 3g.
         Mentions the cool reception of French critics to the
     Paris production of The Little Foxes, adapted by Simone
     Signoret. Says the play was "carefully set and acted
     well."

9 ANON. Review of The Children's Hour [film]. Films in Review,
     13 (April), 236-37.

200

Says this version, which surreptitiously condones lesbianism, "is much inferior to These Three." The script by
John Michael Hayes is confusing.

10 ANON. Review of The Children's Hour [film]. The Sunday Times
[London] (19 August).
Says The Children's Hour, released in England as The
Loudest Whisper, is an "overdone" film.

11 BECKLEY, PAUL V. Review of The Children's Hour [film]. New
York Herald Tribune (15 March), p. 19.
Strongly negative assessment of the screen adaptation
of The Children's Hour.

12 BRANDON, HENRY. "A Conversation with Arthur Miller." World
Theatre, 11 (Autumn), 229-40.
Miller praises Hellman for "a remorseless rising line of
action in beautifully articulated plays." Hellman and
Odets "expressed personality; their works identified them,
but the symbols were often so tuned to the particulars of
the thirties that, when that brief cataclysm passed into
wartime, their world seemed out of date." In English and
French.
Reprinted from The Sunday Times [London] (20 March
1960).

*13 BROCKINGTON, JOHN. "A Critical Analysis of the Plays of
Lillian Hellman." Ph.D. dissertation, Drama, Yale
University.
Listed in American Doctoral Dissertations.

14 BROWN, DEMING. Soviet Attitudes toward American Writing.
Princeton, N.J.: Princeton University Press, pp. 138, 189.
Mentions the appearance of Hellman's plays on the Soviet
stage and the Russian publication in 1959 of a one-volume
collection of her plays.

15 CAMERON, KATE. "A New Children's Hour." New York Sunday News
(4 March), section 2, p. 1.
Feature article on William Wyler and the film remake of
The Children's Hour, about to open in New York. Quotes
Wyler as saying that Hellman was available for conferences
after the adaptation by John Michael Hayes was completed.

16 COREN, HARRY V. "Two Lives Smashed by a Child." New York
Mirror Magazine (11 February).
Photo-essay on the new film version of The Children's
Hour.

1962

17 CROWTHER, BOSLEY. "Not-So-New Films from Old Ones." New
   York Times (18 March), section 2, p. 1.
   Criticizes the new film version of The Children's Hour
   as "unconvincing."

18 _____. "The Screen: New Children's Hour." New York Times (15
   March), p. 28.
   Strongly negative review of the second film adaptation
   of The Children's Hour. Crowther objects to the gulli-
   bility of those who believe Mary Tilford and to the failure
   of the film to show the slander trial on screen. "It is
   incredible that educated people living in an urban American
   community today would react as violently and cruelly to a
   questionable innuendo as they are made to do in this film."

19 DAVIS, BETTE. The Lonely Life: An Autobiography. New York:
   G. P. Putnam's Sons, p. 254.
   Davis discusses her starring role as Regina Giddens in
   the film version of The Little Foxes.

*20 DESCH, KURT, ed. "Lillian Hellman: Zerbrochenes Spielzeug."
   Aus der Romanstrasse, 35 (June), 3.
   Apparently on Toys in the Attic ("Broken Toys"). Cited
   by Manfried Triesch, in The Lillian Hellman Collection at
   the University of Texas, 1966.46. Unlocatable.

21 GAUTIER, JEAN-JACQUES. "Au Théatre Sarah-Bernhardt: Les
   petits renards." Le Figaro (5 December), p. 22.
   Review (in French) of Paris production of The Little
   Foxes, adapted by Simone Signoret. Criticizes the play
   and the production.

22 GILL, BRENDAN. "The Current Cinema." New Yorker, 38 (17
   March), 122-24.
   Blames Hellman's adaptation, John Michael Hayes's
   screenplay, and, particularly, William Wyler's direction
   for a "thoroughly embarrassing" version of The Children's
   Hour.

23 GILLIATT, PENELOPE. "Films." London Observer (19 August),
   p. 19.
   Finds The Loudest Whisper (English title for the 1962
   film adaptation of The Children's Hour) to be "full of the
   gossipy euphemisms that it is supposed to be criticizing."
   Guesses that Hellman would write the play quite differently
   today, "but it is a marvellous theme; if the film had been
   made with a closer sense of the realities of human character and of the way public disapproval can give people a

kind of pride in refusing to save themselves, it could have been a metaphor for witch-hunting, as moving as <u>The Crucible</u>."

24 GUTTMANN, ALLEN. <u>The Wound in the Heart: America and the Spanish Civil War</u>. New York: The Free Press of Glencoe (Division of the Macmillan Company), p. 178.
     Brief references to Hellman.

25 HARTUNG, PHILIP T. "The Screen: 'Grave Alice and Laughing Allegra.'" <u>Commonweal</u>, 75 (2 March), 598-99.
     Calls the screen remake of <u>The Children's Hour</u> "more an exercise in how to handle a delicate subject than a convincing picture of what could happen when a little girl's lie drives a woman to know the truth about herself."

26 HERZBERG, MAX J., ed. <u>The Reader's Encyclopedia of American Literature</u>. New York: Thomas Y. Crowell Company, pp. 174-75, 449, 640, 1200.
     Contains separate entries for Hellman, <u>The Children's Hour</u>, <u>The Little Foxes</u>, and <u>Watch on the Rhine</u>. Notes that Hellman's plays are all marked by intense "psychological conflict and demonic motivations of their characters."

27 HOPPER, HEDDA. "Wyler Discusses <u>Children's Hour</u>." <u>Los Angeles Times</u> (4 September), part 4, p. 6.
     Director of the new version of <u>The Children's Hour</u> discusses the film's progress.

28 KAUFFMANN, STANLEY. "Truth Will Out--Sometimes." <u>New Republic</u>, 146 (16 April), 28.
     Reviews <u>The Children's Hour</u> (film). Hellman's play and its latest film adaptation are structurally flimsy and dramatically illogical.

29 KNIGHT, ARTHUR. Review of <u>The Children's Hour</u> [film]. <u>Saturday Review</u>, 45 (24 February), 37.
     The second film version of <u>The Children's Hour</u> is inventive in William Wyler's use of the camera. But the story is curiously dated and the script fails to provide answers which the audience seeks. Did no one at the trial "suspect the child was lying"?

30 LABADIE, DONALD. "Movies: <u>The Innocents</u> and <u>The Children's Hour</u>." <u>Show</u>, 2 (January), 30-31.
     Discussion of similarities between <u>The Innocents</u>, based on James's <u>Turn of the Screw</u>, and <u>The Children's Hour</u>, both recently filmed. The two works are tied to the

1962

preoccupation in American literature with the nature of
evil, which can be traced to Hawthorne and Melville.
Quotes William Wyler, the director, and Hellman on this
second film version of the play. Wyler: "Actually, in my
mind there's always been a question about whether the elements of Lesbianism existed in the play at all. . . . I
see Miss Dobie as a high-strung girl who comes to believe
a story invented by a malicious child." Hellman: "I think
that there was an element of Lesbianism in Miss Dobie, but
she might never have known it if that child hadn't invented
the story that an actual relationship was going on between
the two women. But for that, Miss Dobie would probably
have remained unconscious of that side of her and turned
into a nice lady who had respectable headaches."

31 LENOIR, JEAN PIERRE. "Miss Signoret Seen in Play She
    Adapted." New York Times (6 December), p. 56.
    Brief report on Simone Signoret's adaptation of The
    Little Foxes, performed in Paris with Signoret as Regina.
    Quotes notices criticizing her for her choice of play and
    for her performance.

32 LEWIS, ALLAN. The Contemporary Theatre: The Significant Play-
    wrights of Our Time. New York: Crown Publishers, Inc., pp.
    38, 68, 121.
    Brief references to Hellman as an Ibsenite realist and
    craftsman; compares Gorky's Yegor Bulitchev to The Little
    Foxes.
    Revised, with identical Hellman material, 1971.19.

33 MEEHAN, THOMAS. "Q: Miss Hellman, What's Wrong with
    Broadway? A: It's a Bore." Esquire, 58 (December), 140-
    42, 235-36.
    Interview with Hellman on the state of the theater. She
    comments on specific playwrights, including Beckett, the
    only man in the theater of the past ten or twelve years
    "who should be taken seriously," and Williams, who was good
    "and will be again." Brecht's The Threepenny Opera and
    Mother Courage "are the great plays of our time." Brief
    comment on Watch on the Rhine.
    Reprinted 1964.8.

34 MEGRET, CHRISTIAN. "Les petits renards de Lillian Hellman, au
    Théâtre Sarah-Bernhardt." Carrefour, no. 951 (5 December),
    27.
    Reviews French production of The Little Foxes, trans-
    lated by Simone Signoret. Says the play is terribly dated,

that it exemplifies the most banal type of realism.
Although The Little Foxes is well constructed, its language lacks "any trace of poetry." In French.

35 MEKAS, JONAS. "Movie Journal." Village Voice, 7 (1 March),
11.
Attacks the new film version of The Children's Hour as
"a muddled-up movie, with no beauty and no knowledge of
things." Mekas condemns filmmakers' reliance on stage
plays as sources for films. "Most of the theatre today is
unbearably bad, and when a play is bad it's worse than a
bad movie."

36 MILNE, TOM. "How Art Is True?" Sight and Sound, 31 (Autumn),
166-71.
Refers briefly to the second film version of The
Children's Hour (released as The Loudest Whisper in
England). This film is "thoroughly competent in all de-
partments but also thoroughly drained of life down to its
last exquisite deep focus drop."

37 MORGENSTERN, JOSEPH. "New Children's Hour--Grim Power of
Gossip." New York Herald Tribune (4 March), section 4,
pp. 1, 4.
Discussion with Hellman about The Children's Hour and
its two film adaptations. Hellman says: "I never meant it
as a Lesbian play. . . . I meant no more than this: that
if the child's lie hadn't driven her to suicide, Martha
would have ended up at fifty, with headaches, a lonely,
irritable, neurotic spinster who had no idea of what had
brought her to where she was."

38 OPPENHEIMER, GEORGE, ed. The Passionate Playgoer. New York:
Viking Press, pp. 227, 250, 294-301, 534, 593-95.
Reprints 1958.13 in a Compass Books edition.

39 PAGET, JEAN. "Les Petits Renards: Du Vieux Théâtre qui n'a
plus d'Age." Combat (5 December), p. 8.
Reviews Simone Signoret's adaptation of The Little
Foxes, produced in Paris. Calls the play a remnant of the
old-fashioned theater that has gained nothing with age.
It is a play for, and about, the "petit-bourgeois"; everything in it is predictable. In French.

40 SCHUMACH, MURRAY. "Hollywood Slant." New York Times (28
October), section 2, p. 7.

Feature article on the casting and making of the film
version of Toys in the Attic. Dicusses changes from the
stage version.

41 SOMERS, FLORENCE. "New Movies." Redbook, 118 (April), 20,
22.
Reviews The Children's Hour, calling the film an "un-
forgettable example of the power of gossip."

42 STRASBERG, LEE. "Introduction" to his Famous Plays of the
1950s. Laurel Drama Series. New York: Dell, pp. 18-19.
Says the flaws of The Autumn Garden resulted from the
production the play received on Broadway and not from
Hellman's writing. "An almost 'Chekhovian' environment
was needed to be created, one that would permit a sense of
continuous action with the characters continuing to live
and behave after their dialogue stopped." This volume
contains the complete text of the play (pp. 23-126).

43 WALSH, MOIRA. "Films: The Children's Hour." America, 107
(2 June), 359-60.
Brief assessment of the screen adaptation of The
Children's Hour. The film is often absorbing and consistently unsensational, but the psychological and social
premises upon which the story rests have become dated.

44 WEALES, GERALD. American Drama Since World War II. New
York: Harcourt, Brace & World, pp. 76, 89-92, 96, 122, 130,
151-52.
Analyzes Another Part of the Forest, The Autumn Garden,
and Toys in the Attic. Forest and Garden are both Chekhovian in that their structures depend upon variations on a
theme: In Forest, that theme is the "corruptive force of
money"; in Garden, it is the "failure of inaction," represented by every character except Sophie. Of the three
plays, only Garden deserves to be taken seriously, although
it suffers by becoming "a kind of psychological vaudeville"
performed by a "collection of Southern types, descendants
of the Hubbards" (pp. 89-92). Weales defends Hellman's
book for Candide, arguing that "it sets up the situations
in which the musical numbers can do their satirical work
and . . . contributes to the satirical effect of the
operetta as a whole. She manages to do what most musical
adaptations never even attempt to do, retain the artistic
intention of the original work in the new form" (p. 152).

45 WHITEHALL, RICHARD. Review of The Children's Hour [film].
Films and Filming, 7 (September), 31-32.

Reviews the remake of The Children's Hour, released in
England as The Loudest Whisper. Criticizes the film for
evading the issues it should have raised.

1963

1 ADLER, JACOB H. "Miss Hellman's Two Sisters." Educational
   Theatre Journal, 15 (May), 112-17.
        Although it is correct to argue that Hellman is a
   disciple of Ibsen from Children's Hour to Another Part of
   the Forest, and that she returns somewhat to Ibsen in Toys
   in the Attic after turning to Chekhov in The Autumn Garden,
   the basic material of Toys finds its source in The Three
   Sisters. The personalities of Olga, Irina, and Masha
   dovetail in Anna and Carrie Berniers, while Julian parallels Andrei. Plot techniques of the two plays differ, but
   "the basic similarity, and the basic difference, between
   characters . . . is that, while in neither play do the
   characters want what they think they want, or ever get it,
   in Toys in the Attic they come to realize the truth and in
   The Three Sisters they do not." However, the plays conclude with precisely the same meaning, for the moments of
   partial insight in Three Sisters and the moments of complete insight in Toys are all finally temporary. The
   characters will proceed as if nothing has happened. As in
   The Autumn Garden and in all of Chekhov's plays, there is
   no villain in Toys; nor do the playwrights urge a particular
   course of action. Hellman has modeled her play on
   "Chekhov's most loosely plotted full-length play in order
   to write a play as tightly constructed as any she ever
   wrote" and the first play in which she combines "all her
   earlier virtues with compassion, truth, detachment, and
   tremendous dramatic power."

*2 ANON. Celebrity Register. New York: Harper and Row, p. 285.
        Cited by Norma Olin Ireland, Index to Women of the
   World, 1970.19, p. 236.

3 ANON. "Cinema: Steel Butterfly." Time, 82 (9 August), 73.
        Review of the screen version of Toys in the Attic. The
   vigor and elegance of Hellman's play remain intact but the
   film is contrived, mechanical. As a playwright, Hellman
   "is like a small, scared Racine. Her lines flip into the
   mind like well-aimed darts. Her scenes stack like well-
   designed dishes. Unhappily, there is seldom much nourish-
   ment in them."

1963

4 ANON. "Family of Gargoyles." Newsweek, 61 (8 April), 85.
   Commendatory review of My Mother, My Father and Me.
   The play, "as fascinating as it is funny," resembles The
   Little Foxes in its depiction of greed but departs significantly from the method of the earlier work. "Acted with
   distinction down to the vivid bit parts, this is an
   imaginative escapade by a woman who could have written a
   merely well-made play with one brain lobe tied behind her."

5 ANON. "From Our Film Critic." The Times [London] (21
   November), p. 17.
   Considers the screen version of Toys in the Attic "a
   first-rate piece of glossy entertainment." Hellman puts
   the mildly unlikely elements "so expertly together that we
   are quite ready not to argue for ninety minutes."

6 ANON. "Most Novel Play of the New York Season." The Times
   [London] (22 April), p. 16a.
   Praises the New York production of My Mother, My Father
   and Me as a desirable antidote to Broadway's ordinarily
   saccharine fare. The play contains dialogue rarely heard
   on Broadway, lines equivalent to the recent attacks on the
   British Establishment.

7 ANON. "Movies: Gains and Losses." Newsweek, 62 (12 August),
   79.
   Review of Toys in the Attic (film). Hellman's original
   characters were sharply etched but were burdened with
   neuroses. The screen version holds to the original theme
   but simplifies the play's complexity and abbreviates the
   subject of miscegenation. Thanks largely to Geraldine
   Page's performance, Carrie has been clarified and deep-
   ened, in contrast to the simplification of other roles.
   Toys in the Attic ends up being more powerful on screen
   than it was on stage.

8 ANON. Review of The Children's Hour [film]. Cinema, 1
   (Number 1), 43.
   Says The Children's Hour is "an actresses' film." Finds
   it disappointing.

9 ANON. "Rutgers Awards Degrees to 2,730." New York Times (6
   June), p. 24.
   Names Hellman as recipient of honorary Doctor of Letters
   degree from Douglass College, the women's division of
   Rutgers University.

10 ANON. "The Theater: Gathering Toadstools." Time, 81 (5
    April), 56.
        Review of My Mother, My Father and Me. Hellman's satire
    is familiar but at times strikingly observant. Yet "she
    lacks the moral suasion of satire that comes from being
    half in love with what one loathes, cherishing the sinner
    while hating the sin." Hellman remains "an arrested child
    of the '30s, and of its idée fixe that the reformation of
    society produces a better crop of humans."

11 ARKADIN. "Film Clips." Sight and Sound, 32 (Winter 1962-63),
    34-35.
        Brief reference to The Loudest Whisper (English title
    of 1962 film version of The Children's Hour) as one of
    several current films involving homosexuality.

12 _____. "Film Clips." Sight and Sound, 32 (Summer), 140-42.
        Brief reference to The Dark Angel.

13 BLUM, DANIEL. Theatre World, Season 1962-1963. Philadelphia:
    Chilton Books, pp. 6, 84.
        Brief references to My Mother, My Father and Me, with
    production credits.

14 BOLTON, WHITNEY. "My Mother, My Father and Me Disappointing
    Play by Hellman." New York Morning Telegraph (26 March).
        Negative review.

15 BRADBURY, JOHN M. Renaissance in the South. Chapel Hill:
    University of North Carolina Press, pp. 15, 37, 189, 190-
    92, 195.
        "For the most part, the history of the Southern Renais-
    sance in drama after its regional period is bound up with
    two names, those of Lillian Hellman and Tennessee Williams."
    Briefly discusses the major plays, comparing them in
    general terms with those of Williams. Suggests that
    Hellman's view of the South appears less harsh in The
    Autumn Garden and Toys in the Attic than in the Hubbard
    plays. She has acquired "a new temperateness and even
    compassion for human frailty."

16 CLURMAN, HAROLD. Review of My Mother, My Father and Me.
    Nation, 196 (20 April), 334.
        Despite "a certain sympathetic savagery and sadness,"
    the play omits very little, while the production lacks the
    necessary sense of abandon and "ferocity of imagination."

1963

17 COLEMAN, ROBERT. "Lillian Hellman Play Is Depressing Farce."
    New York Mirror (1 April).
        Briefly dismisses My Mother, My Father and Me as a far-
    fetched and depressing farce.

18 COMERFORD, ADELAIDE. Review of Toys in the Attic [film].
    Films in Review, 14 (August-September), 439.
        Lillian Hellman "worked off her personal hatred of the
    South more effectively in The Little Foxes than she did in
    Toys in the Attic, and the present cinematization of the
    latter play is not a success."

19 COOKE, RICHARD P. "The Theater." Wall Street Journal (25
    March).
        Says My Mother, My Father and Me begins well but slides
    into "serious satire" that doesn't work.

20 CRIST, JUDITH. "The Self-Defeating Sex Motif: Come-on and
    Come-Uppance." New York Herald Tribune (4 August), section
    4, pp. 1, 3.
        Calls the screen version of Toys in the Attic a far cry
    from the fascinating play. Still, the film "captures some
    of the power of the Hellman play" and is worth seeing for
    the performance of Wendy Hiller and Geraldine Page as the
    Berniers sisters.

21 _____. "Tarnished Toys in Attic." New York Herald Tribune
    (1 August), p. 7.
        Considers Toys in the Attic a run-of-the-mill Hollywood
    film.

22 CROWTHER, BOSLEY. "Old Familiar Faces and Farces." New York
    Times (11 August), section 2, p. 1.
        Severely critical review of the film version of Toys in
    the Attic.

23 _____. "The Screen: Toys in the Attic Opens." New York
    Times (1 August), p. 17.
        Assails the film version of Toys in the Attic as an
    excessive, melodramatic "wreck," based on standard violence
    and a badly confused sex situation.

*24 DESCH, KURT, ed. "Lillian Hellman: Die Kleinen Füchse." Aus
    der Romanstrasse, 46 (September), 1-2.
        On The Little Foxes. Cited by Manfred Triesch, in The
    Lillian Hellman Collection at the University of Texas,
    1966.46. Unlocatable.

25 DYER, PETER JOHN. "Meeting Baby Jane." Sight and Sound, 32
    (Summer), 118-20.
        Interview with Bette Davis, who comments on the film
    version of The Little Foxes.

26 EWEN, DAVID. Encyclopedia of the Opera. New enlarged edi-
    tion. New York: Hill and Wang, pp. 417-18.
        Briefly discusses Regina. See 1971.8.

27 FIDELL, ESTELLE A., and DOROTHY MARGARET PEAKE, eds. Play
    Index, 1953-1960. New York: H. W. Wilson Company, p. 136.
        Lists Hellman plays in anthologies.

28 G., R. Review of Toys in the Attic [film]. Cinema, 1, no. 5
    (August-September), 46.
        Believes the film heightens Hellman's sensationalism of
    the play. Toys in the Attic on screen is brutal and disap-
    pointing.

29 GOTTFRIED, MARTIN. Review of My Mother, My Father and Me.
    Women's Wear Daily (25 March).
        Hellman has "no sense of humor." She was "foolhardly to
    try writing comedy."

30 GOW, GORDON. Review of Toys in the Attic [film]. Films and
    Filming, 10 (December), 38.
        Toys in the Attic contains familiar Lillian Hellman
    topics such as "the crafty financial manoeuvre and the
    deep-seated neurosis," which in the theater seemed reason-
    able but tend to creak a bit on film. The film is well
    acted by the women and Dean Martin "wrestles manfully" with
    the role of Julian Berniers.

31 HEWES, HENRY. "Broadway Postscript." Saturday Review, 46
    (27 April), 27.
        Review of My Mother, My Father and Me. The play, though
    containing some very funny moments, moves hysterically from
    one target to another in its effort to portray the urban,
    middle-class family in all its contradictions.

32 HIMELSTEIN, MORGAN Y. Drama Was a Weapon. Foreword by John
    Gassner. New Brunswick, N.J.: Rutgers University Press,
    pp. 200-201, 205, 208-209, 213-15, 222-23.
        Analyzes "left-wing" theater in New York from 1929 to
    1941. Discusses what appears on the surface to be
    Hellman's Marxist sympathies in Days to Come, The Little
    Foxes, and Watch on the Rhine, but shows how such readings
    ignore her departures from standard Marxist or Communist

1963

doctrine. In Watch on the Rhine, for example, Hellman came
close "to the Communists' revolutionary position, but
failed to identify the Party as the leader of the underground movement. Miss Hellman was so near, and yet so
far."

*33 HINES, JOHN H. "The Intermissions as Essential Dramatic Units
in Well Constructed Realistic Plays, as Illustrated in the
Dramas of Lillian Hellman." Master's thesis, Drama, Tufts
University.
Cited in Emerson and Michael, Southern Literary Culture:
A Bibliography of Masters' and Doctors' Theses, 1979.10.

34 HIPP, EDWARD SOTHERN. "House of Cards." Newark Evening News
(25 March).
Strongly negative review of My Mother, My Father and Me.

35 HODGE, FRANCIS. "German Drama and the American Stage," in
The German Theater Today: A Symposium. Edited by Leroy
Shaw. Austin: University of Texas Press, p. 79.
Quotes Hellman on adapting The Lark. Hodge says that
the ideal adapter should be a playwright himself, not
simply a translator.

36 HODGENS, R. M. "Entertainments." Film Quarterly, 16
(Spring), 58.
Brief, critical remarks about the film remake of The
Children's Hour.

37 KARSCH, WALTHER. "American Drama and the German Stage," in
The German Theater Today: A Symposium. Edited by Leroy
Shaw. Austin: University of Texas Press, pp. 42, 43.
Brief dismissal of Hellman as a dramatist, with a
slightly longer discussion of Watch on the Rhine, produced
in Germany with the title On the Other Side.

38 KAUFFMANN, STANLEY. Review of Toys in the Attic [film]. New
Republic, 149 (17 August), 28.
Toys in the Attic is a dreadful film "that exposes the
inflated reputation" of the original play. Hellman is
"the most overrated American dramatist of the century because she has chosen serious subjects and has plated a
serious-seeming covering over generally hokey melodrama.
Here she has no subject."
Reprinted 1966.32. See also 1975.32.

39 KERR, WALTER. "Miss Hellman," in his The Theater in Spite of
Itself. New York: Simon and Schuster, pp. 235-38.

Slightly revised version of Kerr's review of Toys in the Attic, "Lillian Hellman Whets the Knife of Language," 1960.45.

40 KNIGHT, ARTHUR. Review of Toys in the Attic [film]. Saturday Review, 46 (20 July), 37.
    The screenplay for Toys in the Attic is overly faithful to the dialogue of Hellman's play. "Time may be running out on those stories about sick Southern families whose closeted skeletons begin to rattle whenever a camera draws near."

41 KNOX, SANKA. "Honors Bestowed by Arts Academy." New York Times (23 May), p. 34.
    Reports Hellman's election to the American Academy of Arts and Letters.

42 [LIVINGSTON,] GUY. "Shows Out of Town: My Mother, My Father and Me." Variety (27 February), p. 62.
    Reviews Boston tryout of My Mother, My Father and Me. Calls it a "comedy of ideas, cynicism and wit." The production needs tightening but "the razor sharp Hellman cutting satire should hit hard on Broadway."

*43 LURI, S. "Griaz' na podmostkakh (Khellman, Uil'iams, Elbi)" [Dirt on the stage (Hellman, Williams, Albee)]. Izvestiia (30 May) (Moscow evening edition).
    Cited in Valentina Libman, Russian Studies of American Literature, 1969.31.

44 McCARTEN, JOHN. Review of My Mother, My Father and Me. New Yorker, 39 (30 March), 108.
    Domestic comedy is not Hellman's forte. The play, while amusing at times, suffers from incoherence and vulgarity.

45 McCARTHY, MARY. Mary McCarthy's Theatre Chronicles, 1937-1962. New York: Farrar, Straus and Company, pp. 81, 91.
    Reprint of 1956.32.

46 MADDOCKS, MELVIN. Review of My Mother, My Father and Me. Christian Science Monitor (26 March).
    Says Hellman's anger prevents the play from being a good one.

47 MANNES, MARYA. "The Half-World of American Drama." Reporter, 28 (25 April), 48-50.
    Discusses My Mother, My Father and Me and other recent plays of the Broadway season by major American playwrights.

1963

Hellman takes aim on too many targets at once and the
craftsmanship of her earlier successes is nowhere in evidence. But the play is often funny and, unlike most of the
works considered (including Who's Afraid of Virginia
Woolf?), it does try to deal with large social issues.

48 MILLER, JONATHAN. "The Current Cinema." New Yorker, 39 (10
    August), 60-61.
        Reviews screen adaptation of Toys in the Attic. The
    film suffers from a peculiarly American kind of Freudian-
    ism, which has its roots "in the old egalitarian spirit of
    muckraking and revivalist enthusiasm." The central charac-
    ters are given too little time to display their individual
    complexities; they are somehow subordinated to the plot as
    it hurtles toward its dramatic deadline.

49 [MORRISON,] HOBE. Review of My Mother, My Father and Me.
    Variety (27 March).
        Strongly critical review.

50 NEW YORK THEATRE CRITICS' REVIEWS, 1963. Vol. 24. New York:
    Critics' Theatre Reviews, pp. 302-305.
        Special issue contains reviews of My Mother, My Father
    and Me not published by New York dailies because of a
    newspaper strike. Included here (see below for annota-
    tions) are reviews by Howard Taubman (New York Times),
    Norman Nadel (New York World-Telegram and The Sun), John
    McClain (New York Journal American), Walter Kerr (New York
    Herald Tribune), John Chapman (Daily News). Also included
    are reviews that did appear in the New York Post (Richard
    Watts, Jr.) and the Daily Mirror (Robert Coleman). See
    separate entries for Watts and Coleman.
        HOWARD TAUBMAN: Calls My Mother, My Father and Me a
    "sardonic hymn to hate" in which Hellman is so busy "speak-
    ing some furious truths" that she never gets to be funny,
    engaging, or charming.
        NORMAN NADEL: Considers My Mother, My Father and Me a
    disaster: "distasteful, dismal and dull."
        JOHN McCLAIN: My Mother, My Father and Me reveals that
    Lillian Hellman is "an experienced writer in the field of
    straight comedy." She has devised a "wild and utterly
    outlandish romp which kids the britches off the U.S.
    Establishment."
        WALTER KERR: My Mother, My Father and Me fails to
    "mate the extravagant satirical incoherence of The Theater
    of the Absurd with the homier, milder, and more plausible
    nonsense of You Can't Take It With You." Hellman's tone
    is "indeterminate, vacillating, uncommitted."

JOHN CHAPMAN: Dismisses My Mother, My Father and Me as "flimsy whimsey" that falls completely apart in its second half.

51 OPPENHEIMER, GEORGE. "I Dismember Mama." Newsday (27 March).
    Calls My Mother, My Father and Me an "odd mixture of the abstract and representational."

52 PRYCE-JONES, ALAN. Review of My Mother, My Father and Me. Theatre Arts, 47 (May), 69-70.
    Criticizes the play as a series of revue sketches that fails to portray either a credible family or period. While some of the sequences are funny, Hellman is finally not a writer of comedy "and when a joke fails she is liable to insert a surprising note of commonness in an attempt to bolster it up."

53 QUIGLY, ISABEL. "The Cinema." Spectator, 211 (29 November), 707.
    Writes that Toys in the Attic "has been adapted for the screen with a panache that suggests the director thought it all as much fun as we do, and took it just about as seriously."

54 SCHLESINGER, ARTHUR, JR. "Whatever Became of Lillian and John?" Show, 3 (August), 23.
    Review of screen version of Toys in the Attic (and a film directed by John Huston). Schlesinger condemns the literal-minded attempts to "illustrate" the play's text but finds that the primary problem lies with Hellman's play, which tries "to show Mr. Tennessee Williams that she could beat him at his own game." Toys is "populated by grotesques and spiced by appropriate injections of incest, miscegenation and violence." The direction by George Roy Hill and the performance of Geraldine Page as Carrie at times compel attention but the film "never commands acceptance." Hellman remains a writer of rare theatrical power, "but this mélange is too much even for her."

55 SMITH, MICHAEL. "Theatre Uptown." Village Voice, 8 (28 March), 11, 14.
    Reviews My Mother, My Father and Me. The play does not measure up to what it attempts but is often a nasty, hilarious satire. "As a comedy, which it is not, the play must fail; as what it really is, the impassioned outcry of a Cassandra, it never gets a hearing."

1963

56 SPILLER, ROBERT E., et al., eds. Literary History of the
    United States: Bibliography. Third edition: revised. New
    York: Macmillan; London: Collier-Macmillan Ltd., p. 161.
       Reprint of 1948.18 and 1953.30.
       See 1972.37 and 1974.40.

57 _____. Literary History of the United States: History. Third
    edition: revised. New York: Macmillan; London: Collier-
    Macmillan Ltd., pp. 1314, 1330, 1481.
       Reprint of 1948.17 and 1953.29. Does not update Hellman
    material, which still ends with Another Part of the Forest.
    See 1974.41.

58 TAUBMAN, HOWARD. "Theater: Hellman Satire." New York Times
    (25 March), p. 5.
       Calls My Mother, My Father and Me "a sardonic hymn of
    hate." Some of Hellman's thrusts are inventive and on
    target but this is finally "a series of mordant vignettes
    rather than a tightly made play." Hellman's laughter con-
    tains little mirth.

59 THORP, WILLARD. American Writing in the Twentieth Century.
    Cambridge, Mass.: Harvard University Press, pp. 65, 75,
    96-97.
       Reprint of 1960.60.

60 WATTS, RICHARD, JR. "Two on the Aisle: Angry Comedy by
    Lillian Hellman." New York Post (25 March), p. 36.
       One of the few reviews of My Mother, My Father and Me to
    appear in print during the New York newspaper strike. Con-
    siders the play "relentlessly bitter, angry and sardonic,"
    but in aim of too many targets. "Since Miss Hellman's dis-
    tinguished stature as a dramatist rests on intensely
    serious plays, it is interesting to see her turn her gift
    for angry social criticism to comedy, although a most un-
    genial one. It is also of interest to find her using some
    of the methods of the avant-garde for her own purposes.
    In the process, she sacrifices the hard-driving efficiency
    that drove her earlier work straight to the point, but she
    can write a comic scene that stings, batters and bruises
    without making any bows in the direction of appeal to
    sympathy." The play is not altogether successful but "the
    parts are often brilliantly compounded."

61 WINSTEN, ARCHER. "Reviewing Stand." New York Post (1
    August).
       Calls the film adaptation of Toys in the Attic "too
    contrived on all levels" although it has some excellent

216

aspects. Hellman really "was working the Southern states long before Tennessee [Williams] got there."

1964

1 AGEE, JAMES. Agee on Film: Reviews and Comments. Boston: Beacon Press, pp. 53, 55-58, 65-67, 206, 305.
Reprints 1958.1. Second printing of this Beacon paperback, 1966.1.

2 ANON. "Curtis Publishing Is Named in $3 Million Libel Suit." New York Times (27 February), p. 20.
News item reporting libel suit against Curtis Publishing Company as a result of Hellman's article in Ladies' Home Journal, "Sophronia's Grandson Goes to Washington."

3 ANON. "A Guide to Current Films." Sight and Sound, 33 (Winter 1963-64), 52.
Includes a brief assessment of Toys in the Attic: "Steamy melodrama of Freudian family antics in the Deep South . . . intelligently staged, as a showcase for another dazzling performance by Geraldine Page, but it's a long way from The Little Foxes."

4 ANON. "Miss Hellman and Shahn Honored." New York Times (28 January), p. 28.
Announces Hellman's winning of the National Institute of Arts and Letters gold medal for her achievements in drama.

*5 BARROWS, MARJORIE WESTCOTT, ed. Contemporary American Drama. New York: Macmillan.
See 1968.4.

6 BELLOW, SAUL. "My Man Bummidge." New York Times (27 September), section 2, pp. 1, 5.
Bellow, two days before the New York opening of The Last Analysis, credits Hellman with the suggestion, five years before, that he try his hand at playwriting.

7 BENTLEY, ERIC. The Life of the Drama. New York: Atheneum, pp. 214-15.
Briefly associates Hellman's "melodramatic touch" of the 1930s with that of other American playwrights in their respective decades.
Reprinted 1967.11.

8   CORRIGAN, ROBERT W. The Modern Theatre. New York: Macmillan,
      pp. 1074, 1108-12, 1113-43.
         Reprints Thomas Meehan's interview with Hellman,
      Esquire (December 1962). See 1962.33. Also includes the
      complete text of The Little Foxes and a short excerpt from
      Hellman's introduction to The Selected Letters of Anton
      Chekhov. Contains a 300-word general essay on Hellman:
      "Lillian Hellman is a superb example of the expert play-
      wright whose presence in the theatre ensures its enduring
      vitality. . . . In a realistic style, characteristic of
      Ibsen, she writes of the conflicts of personal morality and
      their public consequences. But she cannot be considered,
      as she so often is, a social writer; rather, she is inter-
      ested in showing damnation as a state of the soul, a con-
      dition that cannot be reformed out of existence or dis-
      solved by sentimentality or easy optimism."

9   GASSNER, JOHN. "The Possibilities and Perils of Modern
      Tragedy," in Theatre and Drama in the Making. Vol. 2.
      Edited by John Gassner and Ralph G. Allen. Boston:
      Houghton Mifflin, pp. 817-29.
         Reprint of 1957.9. Hellman reference appears on p.
      828.

*10 KALAHER, LUCILLE F. "The Theme of Evasive Idealism in the
      Plays of Lillian Hellman." Master's thesis, English,
      University of Wyoming.
         Cited in Emerson and Michael, Southern Literary Culture:
      A Bibliography of Masters' and Doctors' Theses, 1979.10.

11   LAWSON, JOHN HOWARD. Film: The Creative Process. New York:
      Hill and Wang, pp. 129, 135.
         Brief mentions of The Spanish Earth.

12   LEYDA, JAY. Films Beget Films. London: George Allen and
      Unwin Ltd.
         Discusses The Spanish Earth.
         Reprinted 1971.20.

13   MacCANN, RICHARD DYER. "The Problem Film in America," in his
      edition of Film and Society. Scribner Research Antholo-
      gies. New York: Charles Scribner's Sons, pp. 51-59.
         Refers briefly to The North Star (p. 55) as a "pro-
      Russian" wartime film. MacCann's anthology also reprints
      Mervyn LeRoy, "What Makes a Good Screen Story?" See
      1953.22.

14 MELCHINGER, SIEGFRIED. The Concise Encyclopedia of Modern
     Drama. New York: Horizon Press, p. 214.
          Brief comments on Hellman and a list of her plays.
     Calls her "a critic of society and an expert craftsman."

15 MICHAEL, PAUL. The Academy Awards: A Pictorial History.
     Indianapolis, Kansas City, and New York: Bobbs-Merrill,
     pp. 128-29, 134.
          Cites Paul Lukas as Best Actor of 1943 for his film role
     as Kurt Müller in Watch on the Rhine. Photo (p. 134).

16 RABKIN, GERALD. Drama and Commitment: Politics in the
     American Theatre of the Thirties. Bloomington: Indiana
     University Press, pp. 28, 40-41.
          Mentions Hellman briefly. While her three plays of the
     1930s deal with sociopolitical concerns, her work is not
     analyzed at length "because the corpus of her work in the
     thirties is small." Moreover, unlike, say, Odets, "she
     commanded a technique which could survive abrupt changes
     in the winds of doctrine."

*17 ROBERTSON, HELEN E. "Lillian Hellman and the Psychology of
     Evil." Master's thesis, English, University of Texas at
     Austin.
          Cited in Emerson and Michael, Southern Literary
     Culture: A Bibliography of Masters' and Doctors' Theses,
     1979.10.

18 SONTAG, SUSAN. "Going to Theater, Etc." Partisan Review, 31
     (Summer), 389-99.
          Briefly mentions Watch on the Rhine as one of several
     plays that exemplify Broadway liberalism and whose optimism
     and preachiness would embarrass us today.

*19 THOMPSON, ROBERT WAYNE. "A Production and Production Book of
     Lillian Hellman's The Children's Hour." M.F.A. thesis,
     University of Texas.
          Cited by Manfred Triesch, in The Lillian Hellman
     Collection at the University of Texas, p. 99. See 1966.46.

20 TRIESCH, MANFRED. "Lillian Hellman: A Selective Bibliogra-
     phy." American Book Collector, 14 (Summer), 57.
          A brief listing of published plays and film scripts by
     Hellman and twelve discussions on her work appearing in
     books or periodicals. Unannotated.

1964

21 _____. "Lillian Hellman: Eine Analyse und Würdigung ihrer
Dramen." Ph.D. dissertation, English, University of
Frankfurt.
    Traces Hellman's career as social critic in the plays
of the "pink decade" (Days to Come, The Little Foxes,
Another Part of the Forest) through her anti-Fascist position in Watch on the Rhine and The Searching Wind. Triesch
groups The Children's Hour, The Autumn Garden, and Toys in
the Attic as psychological plays and discusses the influence of Freud on the American theater. In German.

22 VILLARD, LEONIE. Panorama du Théatre Americain du Renouveau
1915-1962. Paris: Vent D'Oest, pp. 144-48, 198.
    Summarizes the plot of The Children's Hour, which is
called "a psychological study of an abnormal case--that of
Mary Tilford--as it manifests itself in a love of evil-
doing." Calls the subject matter profound and very new.
Mentions The Little Foxes, Another Part of the Forest, and
Watch on the Rhine. In French.

1965

1 AARON, DANIEL. Writers on the Left. New York: Avon Books, p.
399.
    Reprint of 1961.1. Reprinted 1969.1.

2 BART, PETER. "On a Grim 'Chase' with Sound and Fury." New
York Times (20 June), section 2, p. 11.
    Feature article on the making of The Chase.

3 BENTLEY, ERIC. "The American Drama, 1944-1954," in American
Drama and Its Critics. Edited by Alan S. Downer. Chicago
and London: University of Chicago Press, pp. 188-202.
    Reprint of 1954.1. Hellman references now appear on
pp. 199-200 (The Children's Hour) and p. 196 (The Autumn
Garden).
    Reprinted 1967.10.

4 BESSIE, ALVAH. Inquisition in Eden. New York: Macmillan, p.
68.
    Recollections by one of "The Hollywood Ten," who refused
to testify before the HUAC in 1947 and was later jailed.
Hellman is mentioned only in the most peripheral way but
the book offers an interesting contrast to Scoundrel Time.

5   DIMMITT, RICHARD B. A Title Guide to the Talkies. 2 vols.
    New York and London: Scarecrow Press, passim.
    Lists Hellman films, dates, sources.

6   FUNKE, LEWIS. "Theater: Leonard Bernstein's Songs." New
    York Times (29 June), p. 27.
    Review of program of Leonard Bernstein's songs for the
    theater; mentions the "limited reception" accorded to
    Candide.

7   GARDNER, R. H. The Splintered Stage: The Decline of the
    American Theater. New York: Macmillan; London: Collier-
    Macmillan Ltd., pp. 102-103.
    In a chapter entitled "Sickness on Broadway," Gardner
    discusses Hellman, primarily Toys in the Attic. He says it
    is in many respects an impressive play; its tight structure
    and fully rounded characters "prove that Miss Hellman is
    still one of the most gifted artists writing for the
    American stage." However, its "typically Freudian pre-
    occupation with sex tends to tarnish some of the scenes,
    spoiling their luster with moments of unnecessary sensa-
    tionalism."

8   GASSNER, JOHN. Directions in Modern Theatre and Drama. New
    York: Holt, Rinehart and Winston, pp. 84, 418.
    Expanded edition of Gassner's Form and Idea in Modern
    Theatre (see 1956.19). No change in Hellman references.

9   GOLDSTEIN, MALCOLM. "Body and Soul on Broadway." Modern
    Drama, 7 (February), 411-21.
    Argues that the psychological plays of such dramatists
    as Williams, Inge, and Chayefsky evolve in certain respects
    from the social drama of the thirties, exemplified by the
    works of Hellman and Clifford Odets. The earlier plays,
    generally sociopolitical in nature, gradually become less
    so. While The Children's Hour's "real concern is class
    warfare," with Mrs. Tilford the "class enemy" of Karen and
    Martha, the two Hubbard plays suggest that for Hellman
    "the battle of the classes has dimmed before a widening
    sense of the dramatic possibilities of personal maladjust-
    ment." With Toys in the Attic, American drama of the past
    thirty years appears to have come full circle, "for the
    social dramatists, having given rise to a generation of
    dramatists of another persuasion, have begun to show the
    influence of that second generation."

1965

10 HART, JAMES D. The Oxford Companion to American Literature.
    Fourth edition. New York: Oxford University Press, p. 364.
    Brief survey of Hellman's career to My Mother, My
    Father and Me.

11 KAEL, PAULINE. I Lost It at the Movies. Boston and Toronto:
    Little, Brown and Company, pp. 82, 175-76, 324.
    Reprints "Morality Plays Right and Left," with The
    North Star reference appearing on p. 324. See 1954.6.
    Also refers disparagingly to melodrama out of "Lillian
    Hellmanland" in a review of Hud, reprinted from Film
    Quarterly (1964), p. 82.
    Also includes "A Note on The Children's Hour," pp. 175-
    76, which attacks the 1962 film as "a portentous, lugubri-
    ous dirge." Says Hellman "hates her upper-class stereo-
    types. . . . I've never understood Lillian Hellmanland,
    where rich people are never forgiven for their errors.
    But then, has Miss Hellman ever recognized hers?"
    Reprinted 1966.30.

12 KELLER, ALVIN. "Form and Content in the Plays of Lillian
    Hellman." Ph.D. dissertation, English, Stanford
    University.
    Analyzes Hellman's eight original plays "according to
    the mode of literal scientific criticism." Distinguishes
    among the plays of character, thought and action as method
    of analysis. Relates the structures of the plays to pat-
    terns of tragedy and melodrama. Dissertation Abstracts
    International, 26:6715.

13 LEWIS, ALLAN. American Plays and Playwrights of the Con-
    temporary Theatre. New York: Crown Publishers, Inc., pp.
    42, 59, 99-115, 119, 195, 222.
    Contains numerous brief references and a longer discus-
    sion of the plays in a chapter entitled "The Survivors of
    the Depression" (pp. 99-115). Lewis views Hellman as the
    most "resilient" of American playwrights to come out of the
    1930s, comparing her as well to Ibsen, Chekhov, and
    Williams. Her best plays, "the cycle of New Orleans family
    dramas," echo the "bitter complaint that greed and avarice
    have eroded love, and that the cause is a social system in
    which human relations are a product for sale," as in Toys
    in the Attic and the Hubbard plays.
    Reprinted, with one additional notation on The Little
    Foxes revival of 1967, in a revised edition, 1970.25.

14 LIKENESS, GEORGE C. The Oscar People. Mendota, Ill.: The
    Wayside Press, pp. 77, 92, 95, 139, 141, 146, 156, 185,
    217, 244, 281-82, 296.
        Numerous references to Hellman plays and films, pri-
    marily related to Academy Award nominations for Little
    Foxes and Watch on the Rhine. Photo from Watch.

15 McCALMON, GEORGE, and CHRISTIAN MOE. Creating Historical
    Drama. Carbondale and Edwardsville: Southern Illinois
    University Press, p. 21.
        Quotes Howard Lindsay's remark that unless a writer
    "can write as well as Lillian Hellman" he should not try
    to create a villainous protagonist. See Howard Lindsay,
    "Some Notes on Playwriting," Theatre Arts Anthology, ed.
    Rosamond Gilder et al. New York: Theatre Arts Books,
    1950.9, p. 124.

16 MESERVE, WALTER J. An Outline History of American Drama.
    Totowa, N.J.: Littlefield, Adams and Company, pp. 274,
    278-80, 281, 294, 327, 329, 338, 345, 346.
        Brief comments and passing references to Hellman's
    plays. General survey of the plays between the two world
    wars: pp. 278-80; outline of the plays from 1944 to 1963:
    p. 346.

17 _____, ed. Discussions of Modern American Drama. Boston:
    D. C. Heath and Company, 150 pp.
        Reprints Edith Isaacs, "Lillian Hellman, A Playwright
    on the March" (see 1944.31) and Robert Brustein, "Why
    American Plays Are Not Literature" (see 1959.4.).

18 NOLAN, PAUL T. "Drama in the Lower Mississippi States."
    Mississippi Quarterly, 14 (Winter 1965-66), 20-28.
        Discussion of dramatic activity in Arkansas,
    Mississippi, and Louisiana and plays about these areas.
    Cites Hellman as native playwright.

19 PHILLIPS, JOHN, and ANNE HOLLANDER. "The Art of the Theater:
    Lillian Hellman, an Interview." Paris Review, 33 (Winter-
    Spring), 64-95.
        Revealing, often cited interview on Martha's Vineyard,
    Labor Day weekend, 1964. Subjects include Hellman's
    playwriting method; the germ of The Children's Hour; the
    Hubbards; the "botching" of Days to Come, Candide, and My
    Mother, My Father and Me; her assessment of works by Arthur
    Miller, Tennessee Williams, and Mary McCarthy; the state
    of the modern theater; the influence of Dashiell Hammett
    on her writing; comments on William Faulkner, Nathanael

1965

West, Gertrude Stein, and others; the McCarthy years.
Prints Hellman's letter to the House Committee on Un-
American Activities and a manuscript page from The Little
Foxes; drawing of Hellman by Anne Hollander.
Reprinted in Writers at Work: The Paris Review Inter-
views. Third series. New York: Viking, pp. 115-40. See
1967.45 and 1968.25.

20 SPRINCHORN, EVERT, ed. 20th-Century Plays in Synopsis. New
York: Thomas Y. Crowell, pp. 189-94.
Synopsizes The Children's Hour and The Little Foxes.

21 TAUBMAN, HOWARD. The Making of the American Theatre. New
York: Coward McCann, pp. 224, 236, 250-51, 294, 307, 313,
326-27.
Brief discussions of Hellman's plays. The Children's
Hour, although contrived, established Hellman immediately
as a "tough minded, uncompromising" dramatist. The Little
Foxes is "a horrifying revelation of the nature of human
aggressiveness and greed. No American playwright of our
time has probed more devastatingly under the skin of a
ruthlessly acquisitive society." Watch on the Rhine and
The Searching Wind now seem dated. The Autumn Garden is a
mature work that was misjudged as "Chekhovian," though it
described a genuinely southern and American way of life.
Toys in the Attic is "second-rate stuff." My Mother, My
Father and Me, "even though it contained good stuff,"
failed quickly, one more victim "of wrong-mindedness and
cross-purposes in the course of production."

22 TRIESCH, MANFRED. "Hellman's Another Part of the Forest."
Explicator, 24 (October), item 20.
The title used by Hellman for the sequel to The Little
Foxes is derived from Shakespeare's Titus Andronicus, where
the words "another part of the forest" specify the location
of Act II, scene iv. Marcus and Lavinia are, moreover, the
names of characters in both plays, with striking similari-
ties shared by the Lavinia of Shakespeare and the Lavinia
of Hellman. Another Part of the Forest is thus an effective title in its sense of looking into the background of
the foxes and in its parallel to Shakespeare's concern
with the consequences of inhumanity.

23 _____. "The Lillian Hellman Collection." Library Chronicle
of the University of Texas, 8 (Spring), 16-20.
Describes the Hellman materials (notebooks, letters,
drafts of the plays) acquired by the University of Texas
in 1963. See also Triesch, 1966.46.

24 _____. "Modern Drama Library Collections." Modern Drama, 7
(February), 374.
    Briefly describes Hellman's notebooks and drafts of the
plays held by the Library of the University of Texas. See
1966.46.

1966

1 AGEE, JAMES. Agee on Film: Reviews and Comments. Boston:
Beacon Press, pp. 53, 55-58, 65-67, 206, 305.
    Reprint of 1964.1.

2 ALPERT, HOLLIS. "Peyton Chase." Saturday Review, 49 (19
February), 64.
    Condemns The Chase as "an exaggerated, violent, unin-
tentionally ludicrous" film.

*3 ANON. Article on The Chase. Films in Review, 18 (March),
183-84.
    Cited in Stephen Bowles, Index to Critical Film Reviews
in British and American Film Periodicals. See 1974.9.

4 ANON. "Cinema: Texas Twister." Time, 87 (25 January), 105.
    Calls The Chase "a shockworn message film" that exploits
the violence and intolerance it pretends to condemn. "Miss
Hellman seldom lets a scene end without tacking on her comment: except for a handful of courageous, long-suffering
Negroes and Sheriff Brando, no Texan escapes being singed
by a Statement."

5 ANON. Data on The Chase. Film Facts, 9 (1966), 41.
    Complete credits, etc.

6 ANON. "From Our Film Critic." The Times [London] (8
September), p. 17.
    Says of The Chase that "shortly after the South gave
birth to the blues, it gave birth to the sort of overheated
drama of sex, violence and perversity we associate with the
plays of Tennessee Williams and Lillian Hellman. For this
new Marlon Brando vehicle, Miss Hellman seems to have set
out to win some prize for the Southern drama to end all
Southern dramas."

7 ANON. "Hard-Boiled Suite." Times Literary Supplement (6
October), p. 922.
    Reviews The Dashiell Hammett Story Omnibus (English
edition of The Big Knockover: Selected Stories and Short

1966

Novels of Dashiell Hammett). Calls Hellman's introduction "almost embarrassingly touching and personal."

8 ANON. "Lynch Town." Newsweek, 67 (28 February), 91.
     Strongly criticizes The Chase as a film that "constantly fobs off sensationalism for significance." Hellman's screenplay is "schizoid in purpose--tease the masses and please the eggheads."

9 BROWN, JEFF. "The Making of a Movie." Holiday, 39 (February), 87-88, 92, 94-96, 99.
     Observes filming of The Chase. Questions Horton Foote, who wrote the play on which Hellman's screenplay is based, about changes in her version. ("'The basic concept of this screenplay is really Sam Spiegel's [the producer], not Lillian's.'")

10 BRÜNING, EBERHARD. Das amerikanische Drama der dreissinger Jahre. Berlin: Rütten and Loening, pp. 137-38, 193-95, 253, 316.
     Discusses Days to Come and The Children's Hour as, respectively, examples of American plays on labor and sexual themes. Reference to Watch on the Rhine as an American anti-Fascist play.

11 C.[ALLENBACH], E.[RNEST]. Review of The Chase. Film Quarterly, 20 (Fall), 58-59.
     The Chase is a revisitation of the High Noon theme, with the Decline of the West further along. The script has gaping holes and the film "never manages to go anywhere." The film includes a parody of the murder of Lee Harvey Oswald. "Robert Redford and Jane Fonda swim capably against the vague tide of allegory."

12 CAMERON, IAN. "The Cinema." Spectator, 217 (9 September), 321.
     Argues, in a review of The Chase, that "the conflict between reason and violence is presented in concrete, realistic terms. It is a bleakly pessimistic movie. . . . There has always been a tendency among those who very properly loathe violence to dislike its depiction on the screen. However, it is not possible to make a film against violence without showing it; the beating up of the sheriff is both brutal and repulsive. It is only if the violence is suggested or just glimpsed that it can become titillating in this context."

13   CAMERON, KATE. "The Chase Is Just Run-of-the-Mill Flick."
     New York Daily News (19 February).
         Poor review of The Chase.

14   CHAPIN, LOUIS. Review of The Chase. Christian Science
     Monitor (18 February).
         Inconclusive review of The Chase.

15   CLURMAN, HAROLD. The Naked Image: Observations of the Modern
     Theatre. New York: Macmillan; London: Collier-Macmillan
     Ltd., pp. 202, 209.
         Two brief references to Hellman, one alluding to her
     presence at the 1963 Drama Conference in Edinburgh, the
     other to the 1962 Paris production of The Little Foxes.

16   CRIST, JUDITH. "Cliché, Yes . . . But Successful One." New
     York Herald Tribune (19 February), p. 6.
         The Chase is made up of contrivances, clichés, and
     stereotypes, "balled up with such skill that you roll right
     along with them to a smashing conclusion."

17   _____. "Gourmet Muck for Gluttons." New York Herald Tribune
     Magazine (27 February), p. 29.
         Reviews The Chase. The first half of the film is
     riddled with clichés, but a switch then occurs "from Peyton
     Place to the best of the High Noon and Oxbow Incident kind
     of story and whirling us into a taut lynch-mob thriller
     that builds to a smashing climax."

18   CROWTHER, BOSLEY. "The I.Q. of Hollywood Films." New York
     Times (20 February), section 2, p. 1.
         Ridicules The Chase as a cheap, sensational film. "Even
     though it was written by Lillian Hellman from a stage play
     by Horton Foote, produced by the great Sam Spiegel and
     directed by Arthur Penn, it comes out of an obvious cross-
     breeding of High Noon and Peyton Place, with an intellec-
     tual level no higher than that of the television show of
     the latter name."

19   _____. "The Screen: The Chase." New York Times (19
     February), p. 12.
         Negative review calls The Chase overblown in all
     respects. Hellman's screenplay often obscures the film's
     central character with intrusive material about the
     domestic scandals of the town. The film is in "bad
     taste."

1966

20 DENT, ALAN. "The World of the Cinema." Illustrated London
    News, 249 (4 September), 28.
        Writes of The Chase: "Though the screenplay is by
    Lillian Hellman (whom I usually admire more than any other
    American playwright), it seems to me distinctly to over-
    emphasize the potentialities for violence in a small Texas
    town."

21 DRUTMAN, IRVING. "Hellman: A Stranger in the Theater?"
    New York Times (27 February), section 2, pp. 1, 5.
        Conversation with Hellman about her writing seminar at
    Yale and related matters. She comments on the "peculiar
    form" of playwriting, the "wall" that has always existed
    between her and the theater, and her lack of desire to
    write a new play.

22 [DRUTMAN, IRVING.] "Questioning Miss Hellman on Movies."
    New York Times (27 February), section 2, p. 5.
        Hellman replies to questions on The Chase and the dif-
    ferences between writing film scripts in America and
    Europe. She severely criticizes The Chase, during the
    filming of which others "mauled about and slicked up" her
    work.
        Reprinted in Pauline Kael, Kiss Kiss Bang Bang, 1968.21
    and 1969.26.

23 DURGNAT, RAYMOND. Review of The Chase. Films and Filming,
    13 (October), 6, 8.
        Interesting analysis. Relates The Chase to other
    American films, especially High Noon. The script in-
    geniously observes an "overnight" action time. The town's
    social order capsizes in a chillingly ironic way. The
    Chase creates an intense atmosphere of terror and moral
    courage.

24 FRENCH, PHILIP. "Brando on Lot's Job." London Observer
    (11 September), p. 25.
        Reviews The Chase. Hellman's "coarse-grained script"
    is filled with "crawling stereotypes." Arthur Penn
    directs well, however.

25 GILL, BRENDAN. "The Current Cinema." New Yorker, 42 (26
    February), 106, 108-109.
        Reviews The Chase: "a conventionally opulent melodrama,
    overproduced by Sam Spiegel, overplotted to the point of
    incoherence by the author of the screenplay, Lillian
    Hellman, and overdirected by Arthur Penn."

26 GOUGH-YATES, KEVIN. "The Chase." Screen, 10, no. 4-5 (July-
    October 1969), 88-100.
        Analysis of The Chase, a film complicated by its
    "apparent multiple authorship. Sam Spiegel, the producer,
    Lillian Hellmann [sic], Horton Foote, Ivan Moffat and
    Marlon Brando all appear to have had a hand in the script."
    Further complicating the film are its intricate structure
    and characterizations. The film makes a strong social
    statement about the roles of wealth and violence in con-
    temporary American society. Director Arthur Penn "has
    woven disparate elements into a complete climax. He never
    loses sight of [the film's] central aim, which is to
    explore the nature of inheritance and how the culture
    depicted has become devoid of anything other than lip
    service to its original aim of constructing a society
    which will (a) prove a desirable model for others and (b)
    provide something of moral value to pass on to the young."
    [Note: Article appeared in 1969 but is included with the
    preponderance of 1966 Chase reviews.]

27 GOULD, JEAN. "Lillian Hellman," in Modern American Play-
    wrights. New York: Dodd, Mead and Company, pp. 168-185.
        Chatty overview of the life and career to My Mother, My
    Father and Me. Gould seems heavily dependent upon the
    Paris Review interview (see 1965.19). Full-page photo of
    Hellman teaching a Yale seminar in 1966.

28 HARTUNG, PHILIP T. "The Screen." Commonweal, 84 (1 April),
    55-56.
        Calls The Chase a violent, senseless film. Hellman's
    melodramatic script so exaggerates the story and charac-
    ters "that the whole thing seems more like an anti-southern
    propaganda tract than a movie."

29 HATCH, ROBERT. Review of The Chase. Nation, 202 (7 March),
    p. 280.
        Criticizes The Chase as a bloody film that utilizes
    routine television criteria for high ratings.

30 KAEL, PAULINE. I Lost It at the Movies. New York: Bantam,
    pp. 72-73, 158-59, 292.
        Reprint of 1965.11.

31 _____. "Spring Comes Tottering In." McCall's, 93 (April),
    36, 38, 192-93.
        Reviews several films, including The Chase (pp. 192-93).
    An anti-southern film, The Chase pretends to condemn
    attitudes it simultaneously revels in. "Instead of the

1966

> attraction and moral disapproval we're supposed to feel,
> we're more likely to reject what we see as silly and un-
> convincing."
> Reprinted 1968.21 and 1969.26.

32 KAUFFMANN, STANLEY. A World on Film. New York: Dell
    Publishing Company (Delta Books), pp. 61-62.
    Reprint of 1963.38. See also 1975.32.

33 LAUFE, ABE. Anatomy of a Hit: Long-Run Plays on Broadway from
    1900 to the Present Day. New York: Hawthorn Books, pp. 24,
    39, 134, 138-41, 147-48, 293-98, 335, 337.
        Discusses The Children's Hour and Toys in the Attic with
    brief mentions of the film adaptations of The Children's
    Hour and the film version of Dead End. Defends The
    Children's Hour against the critical claim that the third
    act is anticlimactic. Toys in the Attic treats "unsavory"
    material in an interesting and vigorous manner, although
    Mrs. Prine remains a shadowy figure.

34 MALLET, RICHARD. "Cinema." Punch, 251 (14 September), 411.
        Finds that, "in essentials, The Chase is a Peyton Place
    story: a steamily emotional, melodramatic study of the
    morals of a small town. . . . The tomato ketchup is spat-
    tered with a lavish hand."

*35 MARCHAND, WILLIAM M. "The Changing Role of the Medical Doctor
    in Selected Plays in American Drama." Ph.D. dissertation,
    Theater, University of Minnesota.
        Includes Hellman, according to Emerson and Michael,
    Southern Literary Culture: A Bibliography of Masters' and
    Doctors' Theses, 1979.10.

36 REED, REX. "Penn: And Where Did All The Chase-ing Lead?"
    New York Times (13 February), section 2, p. 3.
        Interview with Arthur Penn, director of The Chase,
    about the film. Quotes Penn as saying that Lillian Hellman
    "is not speaking to me at all," as a result of disagree-
    ments about the production.

37 RICE, ELMER. "Elmer Rice Joins the Disenchanted." New York
    Times (13 March), section 2, pp. 1, 11.
        Letter to the drama editor echoing disenchantment with
    the state of the theater expressed by Hellman in a Times
    interview with Irving Drutman. See 1966.21.

38 RIGDON, WALTER, ed. The Biographical Encyclopaedia and Who's
     Who of the American Theatre. Introduction by George
     Freedley. New York: James H. Heineman, Inc., p. 529.
        Lists biographical information, dates of the plays and
     films, awards through 1964. See 1976.73.

39 RINGGOLD, GENE. The Films of Bette Davis. New York: Citadel
     Press, pp. 8, 110-12, 121-22.
        Lists casts, credits, and synopses of screen versions of
     Little Foxes and Watch on the Rhine; numerous stills from
     the two films.

40 SARRIS, ANDREW. "Films." Village Voice, 11 (7 April), 31.
        Considers The Chase "a fascinating failure." The film
     is worth seeing for its performances but it suffers from
     vagueness and from Arthur Penn's attempt "to manipulate a
     junkyard into a metaphor of America." "High Camp has come
     to High Noon, and Lillian Hellman's vigorous indictment of
     pistol-packing Texas has thereby lost the last shred of
     credibility."

*41 SCHEMERHORN, LEORA H. "Lillian Hellman: Craftsman, Moralist,
     Thinker." Master's thesis, English, Stetson University.
        Cited in Emerson and Michael, Southern Literary Culture:
     A Bibliography of Masters' and Doctors' Theses, 1979.10.

42 SCHICKEL, RICHARD. "Small Flop Grows into a Disaster." Life,
     60 (4 March), 12.
        Review of The Chase. Hellman's screenplay and Arthur
     Penn's direction are desperate and inept. "Miss Hellman
     even presses an elderly couple into service as a Greek
     chorus, as if this were classic tragedy instead of classic
     kitsch."

43 SHEPARD, RICHARD. "Lillian Hellman Teaching at Yale." New
     York Times (1 February), p. 28.
        Reports on a session of Hellman's writing seminar for
     freshmen at Yale.

44 STYRON, WILLIAM. "Lillian Hellman," in Double Exposure, by
     Roddy McDowall. New York: Delacorte Press, pp. 190-93.
        Tongue-in-cheek tribute to Hellman. Photograph by Roddy
     McDowall.

45 TAILLEUR, ROGER. "Elia Kazan and the House Un-American
     Activities Committee." Film Comment, 4 (Fall), 43-58.
        Translation (by Alvah Bessie) of chapter three of
     Tailleur's book Elia Kazan, published in 1966 by Editions

1966

Seghers, Paris, in the series <u>Cinéma d'Aujourd'hui</u>, no. 36. Contains references to Hellman.

46 TRIESCH, MANFRED, comp. <u>The Lillian Hellman Collection at the University of Texas</u>. Austin: Humanities Research Center, University of Texas at Austin, 167 pp.

Describes in detail the collection of Hellman manuscript material at the University of Texas, which includes drafts of the plays and adaptations, film scripts, notebooks on research, letters. Triesch comments on the plays and provides checklists of criticism on the works cited. In his introduction Triesch states: "In some instances the notebooks contribute much to the understanding of Miss Hellman's sources and her method of composition. In addition to the typescripts of the plays there are adaptations and motion picture scripts which Miss Hellman did herself. A descriptive catalogue such as this must be a compromise between mere cataloguing and the attempt to follow the development of each work. The various typescript versions of each play are arranged in a chronological sequence according to internal evidence so the reader can follow the developments of each play." Photos. A useful volume despite occasional inaccuracies in the citing of secondary sources.

46a WALCUTT, CHARLES CHILD. <u>Man's Changing Mask: Modes and Methods of Characterization in Fiction</u>. Minneapolis: University of Minnesota Press, pp. 28-31.

Analyzes, in a chapter entitled "Some Illustrative Versions of Melodrama," the relationship between the action of <u>Toys in the Attic</u> and the development of Carrie's characterization.

47 WALSH, MOIRA. Review of <u>The Chase</u>. <u>America</u>, 114 (5 March), 337-38.

The film tries to deal with serious themes but is so concerned with appealing to a mass audience that it disguises those concerns beneath lurid melodrama and grotesque caricatures. <u>The Chase</u> "is a mess."

48 WHARTON, JOHN F. "An Open Letter to Rice, Hellman." <u>New York Times</u> (27 March), section 2, p. 4.

Defends the state of Broadway theater against criticism leveled by Hellman and Elmer Rice in earlier <u>New York Times</u> pieces (<u>see</u> 1966.21 and 1966.37). Challenges both playwrights to try their hands at new plays.

49 WILSON, DAVID. Review of The Chase. Sight and Sound, 35
(Autumn), 197-98.
The film indicts the violence inherent in American life
and Hellman's screenplay "never shrinks from topical allusion." The Chase has been filmed with "Wagnerian excess,"
and is, therefore, extravagant, hysterical, even preposterous; yet events in American society make fiction pale
before fact so that "within its own exorbitant framework,
the film almost comes off." Photo from the film.

50 WINSTEN, ARCHER. Review of The Chase. New York Post (20
February).
Says Hellman views the South witheringly. The film is
erratic in quality.

1967

1 ADELMAN, IRVING, and RITA DWORKIN. Modern Drama: A Checklist
of Critical Literature on 20th-Century Plays. Metuchen,
N.J.: Scarecrow Press.
Lists thirty-five Hellman items.

2 ANON. "Dorothy Parker Recalled as Wit." New York Times (10
June), p. 33.
Reports on funeral service for Dorothy Parker, at which
Hellman delivered a eulogy.

3 ANON. "Lillian Hellman Files Suit over Little Foxes Telecast." New York Times (21 October), p. 17.
Item reporting Hellman's attempt to prevent telecast of
film version of The Little Foxes.

4 ANON. "The Theater: Greedy Lot." Time, 90 (3 November), 64,
69.
Calls the revival of The Little Foxes "admirable." The
play's "angle of vision is the leftism of the '30s, since
it assumes that the root of all evil is economic." In
1939, the play would have been viewed as "an attack on
predatory capitalist morality." Today, it is more likely
to be relished as "an indictment of greed, hate, and the
lust for power at any time, in any place."

5 ANON. The Vivian Beaumont Theater Program for the Lincoln
Center Revival of The Little Foxes. New York: Saturday
Review, Inc., 48 pp.
Contains interesting selection of extracts on the South
of the play's period, including composite photos of

1967

   newspaper clippings and source items on "the Southern
   woman." Brief biography and photo of Hellman, cast and
   credits of the production, etc.

6 ARNOLD, MARTIN. "Lillian Hellman Says She Found Ferment
   among Soviet Writers." New York Times (31 May), p. 11.
    Report of Hellman's observations on Soviet intellectuals
   upon her return from a two-and-one-half-week stay in the
   Soviet Union. Photo.

7 BANKHEAD, TALLULAH. "Miss Bankhead Objects." New York Times
   (29 October), section 2, p. 5.
    Letter to the drama editor reacting to Hellman's New
   York Times piece (22 October 1967) which commented upon
   her feud with Bankhead.

8 BARNES, CLIVE. "Theater: Return of The Little Foxes." New
   York Times (27 October), p. 53.
    Praises the Lincoln Center production of The Little
   Foxes. The play has not dated, although it is so well
   made "that it might be regarded as its own worst enemy."
   Unlike most plays of the 1930s, The Little Foxes keeps
   tempting us "to accept and analyze it on the highest
   level," although it does not reward that temptation. The
   acting in this production is consistently "magnificent."

9 BAZIN, ANDRÉ. "Theatre and Cinema, Part One," in his What Is
   Cinema? Essays selected and translated by Hugh Gray.
   Berkeley, Los Angeles, and London: University of California
   Press, pp. 76-94.
    Makes several references to The Little Foxes in a dis-
   cussion of screen adaptations of plays. Bazin suggests
   that Wyler's film, based closely on Hellman's play, is one
   of several to give "the problem of filmed theater . . . a
   new lease of aesthetic life."
    Reprinted from Esprit (June 1951).

10 BENTLEY, ERIC. "The American Drama (1944-1954)," in his The
   Theatre of Commitment. New York: Atheneum, pp. 18-46.
    Reprint of 1954.1 and 1965.3. Hellman references appear
   on pp. 39-40 (The Children's Hour) and p. 34 (The Autumn
   Garden).

11 _____. The Life of the Drama. New York: Atheneum, pp. 214-
   15.
    Reprint of 1964.7.

12 BIGSBY, C. W. E. <u>Confrontations and Commitment</u>. Columbia:
University of Missouri Press, pp. xv, 9.
Brief allusions to Hellman as a "middle class" dramatist
whose status "is hardly justifiable by any but the commer-
cial standards which dominate Broadway."

13 BOLTON, WHITNEY. "Revival: Lillian Hellman's <u>The Little
Foxes</u>." New York <u>Morning Telegraph</u> (28 October).
<u>The Little Foxes</u> has been untouched by time. It remains
thrilling theater.

*14 BROWN, KENT R. "Lillian Hellman and Her Critics." Master's
thesis, Dramatic Art, University of California at Santa
Barbara.
Cited in Emerson and Michael, <u>Southern Literary Culture:
A Bibliography of Masters' and Doctors' Theses</u>, 1979.10.

15 BUNCE, ALAN N. "<u>Little Foxes</u> Powerfully Revived." <u>Christian
Science Monitor</u> (3 November).
The Lincoln Center production of <u>The Little Foxes</u> is one
of "control, precision and confident power."

16 BUSH, ALFRED. "Literary Landmarks of Princeton." <u>Princeton
University Library Chronicle</u>, 29 (Autumn), 1-90.
Catalogue of an exhibition at the Princeton University
Library of fiction, drama, and poetry written at Princeton.
Hellman (entry no. 56, pp. 45-46) visited Princeton peri-
odically in the mid-1930s and is included for having writ-
ten part of <u>Days to Come</u> there. She is also cited in the
Hammett entry (no. 55, p. 45).

17 CHAPMAN, JOHN. "Lincoln Center Rep Revival of <u>The Little
Foxes</u> a Humdinger." <u>Daily News</u> (27 October).
Believes <u>The Little Foxes</u> is even more interesting now,
in its Lincoln Center revival, than when it first appeared
in 1939. The production, too, is better than the original.

18 COOK, JOAN. "Furniture Collection That Charts Lillian
Hellman's Career." <u>New York Times</u> (14 November), p. 40.
Interview with Hellman about furniture she kept from
various productions of her plays, her taste in clothes, and
related matters. Photos.

19 COOKE, RICHARD P. "The Theater: A Well-Acted Revival." <u>Wall
Street Journal</u> (30 October).
Considers <u>The Little Foxes</u>, in its Lincoln Center revival, somewhat dated. "Evil today has moved into new
fields for most playwrights. Money-grubbing and its

1967

accompanying family treachery are already a bit old-fashioned as big subjects. But Miss Hellman's knowledge of character is sure, and her play is fortunate in its casting."

20 DOWNER, ALAN. "The Future of the American Theater," in his edition of The American Theater Today. New York: Basic Books, pp. 193-203.
    Refers to Hellman's radical adaptation of The Lark.

21 FREEDMAN, MORRIS. The Moral Impulse. Carbondale: Southern Illinois University Press, pp. 99-114, passim.
    Compares Hellman and other American "social dramatists" to Brecht. The Little Foxes presents what at the outset appears to be a "Brechtian situation, but the picture gets blurred by the details." Regina resembles Hedda Gabler. "She may have been involved, indeed like Hedda, in a process of self-discovery . . . in trying to live, within the limits of her capacity, a richer life than her present one. The emergence of the private, merely whimsical, accidental character of Regina blunts the social point of the play. In Brecht's St. Joan, capitalism rots the souls of all classes; we waste no time ruminating on the private psyches of workers or bosses." Watch on the Rhine, dependent upon stereotypes, obscures its "anti-Nazi message even more strikingly." Brecht would have had the Müller children carrying pistols and knives.

22 GASSNER, JOHN. "Hellman, Lillian," in The Oxford Companion to the Theatre. Third edition. Edited by Phyllis Hartnoll. London: Oxford University Press, p. 438.
    Concise profile of Hellman's career through Toys in the Attic. She has been accused of misanthropy and excessive dependence on the well-made structure, but "her work is, nevertheless, invigorated by sharp characterization and by respect for active idealism." Earlier editions of The Oxford Companion to the Theatre, with less complete Hellman entries: 1951 (first edition; reprinted with minor revisions 1952); 1957 (second edition; reprinted 1962, 1964).

23 _____. "Realism in the Modern American Theatre," in American Theatre. Stratford-upon-Avon Studies 10. Edited by John Russell Brown and Bernard Harris. London: Edward Arnold, pp. 11-28.
    Two brief allusions to Hellman (pp. 19, 25).

236

24 GOLDSTEIN, MALCOLM. "The Playwrights of the 1930's," in The
American Theater Today. Edited by Alan Downer. New York:
Basic Books, pp. 25-37.
Analyzes The Children's Hour and The Little Foxes, along
with plays by Odets and other dramatists of the 1930s.
Praises Hellman as more impressive than Odets because her
plays avoid easy answers. Unlike Odets, whose work is
already dated, Hellman's art has continued to mature.
"Her plays have a life outside the context of the Depres-
sion years."

25 GOTTFRIED, MARTIN. A Theater Divided: The Postwar American
Stage. Boston: Little, Brown and Company, pp. 160, 191.
Brief mentions of the Lincoln Center production of The
Little Foxes and the "heaviness" of Hellman's book for
Candide.

26 _____. "Theatre: The Little Foxes." Women's Wear Daily (27
October).
Reviews Lincoln Center revival of The Little Foxes.
Considers the play dated and overrated. Not even Mike
Nichols's direction can compensate for "this absurdly
naturalistic, heavily built drama about opportunistic
materialism in the Old South."

27 GROSE, PETER. "Soviet's Writers Given Party Line." New York
Times (23 May), p. 12.
Notes Hellman's presence at fourth national congress of
the Union of Writers, in Moscow.

28 HALLER, CHARLES. "The Concept of Moral Failure in the Eight
Original Plays of Lillian Hellman." Ph.D. dissertation,
English, Tulane University.
Analyzes the plays to demonstrate the ways in which
civilized society breaks down and is replaced by a variety
of social and personal evils. Hellman blames the individual, not society, for moral failure, except in Toys in
the Attic. Dissertation Abstracts International, 28:4303A.

29 HANSON, CURTIS LEE. "An Interview with Arthur Penn." Cinema,
3 (Summer), 11-16.
References to The Chase.

30 HARDWICK, ELIZABETH. "The Little Foxes Revived." New York
Review of Books, 9 (21 December), 4-5.
Review-essay on The Little Foxes and its Lincoln Center
revival. The play now appears to be "about a besieged
Agrarianism, a lost Southern agricultural life, in which

virtue and sweetness had a place and, more strikingly,
where social responsibility and justice could, on a personal level at least, be practiced. It is curious what a
catalogue of sentiment about the Old South the play turns
out to be." The inciting action of the play is Regina's
desire to have Horace release his money for the cotton
mill in order for her to have a share. "This is an idea
of great interest, and in Lillian Hellman's failure to do
justice to its complications so much about our theater and
our left-wing popular writers of the Thirties is revealed."
The picture of the South in The Little Foxes "is what many
serious historians believe to be a legend, not to say a
cliché." Also discusses the image of Negroes in Hellman's
plays and other social concerns which Hardwick denigrates.
Says Hellman's plays, contrary to general belief, are awk-
wardly constructed. They "are an unusual mixture of the
conventions of fashionable, light, drawing room comedy and
quite another convention of realism and protest." There is
a serious lack of tragic conflict and intellectual compli-
cation in the character of Horace. Regina and her brothers
go too far but they are alive and interesting characters,
as is the prostitute in Another Part of the Forest. "That
these characters and others should be squeezed to death by
the iron of an American version of Socialist Realism and
the gold of a reigning commercialism is a problem of cultural history." See 1968.13 and 1968.28.

31 HEWES, HENRY. "The Theater: The Crass Menagerie." Saturday
    Review, 50 (11 November), 26.
       Reviews the Lincoln Center production of The Little
    Foxes. The play portrays "the graceless behavior of a
    society in which the more ambitious become scoundrels and
    the more decent stand by and let them get away with ex-
    ploiting the poor." The performances are powerful and at
    times ironic. Anne Bancroft's Regina appears to be "fight-
    ing an inner battle between the compulsion to have her own
    way and her knowledge of right and wrong." When she lets
    Horace die, she thus "seems less the cruel murderess than
    she does the helpless victim."

32 HOUSTON, PENELOPE. "The Nature of the Evidence." Sight and
    Sound, 36 (Spring), 88-92.
       Photo from The Spanish Earth (p. 91).

33 HUNTER, FREDERICK J., comp. A Guide to the Theatre and Drama
    Collections at the University of Texas. Austin: Humanities
    Research Center, University of Texas at Austin, pp. 5, 69.

Briefly describes the Hellman manuscripts at the
University of Texas. See, for a much fuller analysis of
the manuscript holdings, Manfred Triesch, The Lillian
Hellman Collection at the University of Texas, 1966.46.

34 KAPLAN, MORRIS. "Dorothy Parker's Will Leaves Estate of
$10,000 to Dr. King." New York Times (27 June), p. 22.
Names Hellman executrix and trustee of Dorothy Parker's
estate.

35 KERNODLE, GEORGE. Invitation to the Theatre. New York:
Harcourt, Brace and World, pp. 12, 59, 106, 212-13, 572.
Contains several brief mentions and exercises from The
Little Foxes for acting and analysis; comments on film
adaptations of Children's Hour; cites Children's Hour,
Little Foxes, and Toys in the Attic as strong and "realistic" plays which show the damage inflicted by apparently
rational people. Includes photo from the 1934 production
of Children's Hour.

36 KERR, WALTER. "We Could Have Five Little Foxes." New York
Times (5 November), section 2, pp. 1, 3.
The revival of The Little Foxes is "brilliant." While
not a great play, The Little Foxes is "virtually perfect
of its kind, lean and candid, muscular and mettlesome in
the bold black-and-white strokes it makes against a money-
gilded world."
Reprinted 1969.27.

37 KROLL, JACK. "Theater: Chasing the Fox." Newsweek, 70 (6
November), 86.
The Little Foxes seems now to "sum up the liberalism,
the social concern, which was the major force on the
American stage" throughout the 1930s. It is difficult to
stage now, when we have "lost both the self-confidence of
Miss Hellman's classic liberalism and the faith in the
'well-made' play as a carrier of ideas and feelings." The
Lincoln Center revival, directed by Mike Nichols, turns
"an intelligently calculated play" into "an obvious melodrama."

*38 LEDERER, KATHERINE G. "The Critical Reaction to the Dramatic
Works of Lillian Hellman." Ph.D. dissertation, English,
University of Arkansas.
Cited in Emerson and Michael, Southern Literary Culture:
A Bibliography of Masters' and Doctors' Theses, 1979.10.

1967

39 LEWIS, THEOPHILUS. Review of The Little Foxes. America, 117
    (9 December), 723.
         Praises the Lincoln Center production highly. The
    play's vitality, however, derives from Hellman's writing.
    "As distinctively American as the hot dog and as universal
    in its impact as Tartuffe," The Little Foxes merits a place
    in world drama beside Ibsen and Strindberg. It resembles
    The Cherry Orchard in its reflection of a changing society.
    "The play has the factual basis of a documentary and the
    suspense of melodrama."

40 McCARTEN, JOHN. "The Theatre." New Yorker, 64 (4 November),
    162-63.
         Criticizes Lincoln Center production of The Little
    Foxes. The performers, with the exception of Margaret
    Leighton as Birdie, are often unintelligible and have dif-
    ficulty with the southern accent. Hellman's play "is a
    mechanical melodrama."

41 [MORRISON,] HOBE. Review of The Little Foxes. Variety (1
    November).
         The Little Foxes, in its Lincoln Center revival, re-
    mains "a gripping hymn of bitterness."

42 NEW YORK THEATRE CRITICS' REVIEWS, 1967. Vol. 28. New York:
    Critics' Theatre Reviews, pp. 237-40.
         Reprints reviews of the 1967 Lincoln Center revival of
    The Little Foxes from New York newspapers: New York Herald
    Tribune (5 November); New York Times (27 October); Women's
    Wear Daily (27 October); Daily News (27 October); Wall
    Street Journal (30 October); New York Post (27 October).

43 NORTON, ELLIOT. "Broadway after World War II," in The
    American Theater Today. Edited by Alan Downer. New York:
    Basic Books, pp. 41-49.
         Briefly mentions The Lark.

44 PALMER, HELEN, and JANE DYSON, comps. "Lillian Hellman," in
    American Drama Criticism. Hamden, Conn.: The Shoe String
    Press, pp. 74-78.
         Lists reviews of Hellman plays that appeared in maga-
    zines and several collections of drama criticism. Omits
    The Lark and Candide. Cites The Searching Wind and The
    Autumn Garden as Searching the Wind [sic] and Autumn
    Gardens [sic].

45 PHILLIPS, JOHN, and ANNE HOLLANDER. "Lillian Hellman," in
    Writers at Work: The Paris Review Interviews, Third Series.
    Edited by George Plimpton. New York: Viking Press, pp.
    115-40.
        Reprint of 1965.19. Reprinted in Viking Compass edi-
    tion, 1968.25.

46 SHEPARD, RICHARD F. "Little Foxes Gets a Start in Low Key."
    New York Times (20 September), p. 40.
        Reports on rehearsal session for Lincoln Center revival
    of The Little Foxes, with Hellman in attendance. Quotes
    Hellman's remarks to the company: "'This play is really a
    stratification of society,' she said. 'This was the great
    house of the region. They were always a step above the
    poor white trash. Grandpapa probably had a small store.
    They're raw, crude men about to exploit the Negroes and
    whites.'"

47 SIMON, JOHN. Review of The Little Foxes. Commonweal, 87 (1
    December), 304-305.
        Strongly negative assessment of the Lincoln Center re-
    vival of The Little Foxes and of Hellman's work in general.
    Hellman is a "melodramatist," whose reputation as a major
    American playwright is undeserved. Watch on the Rhine is
    "a good piece of melodrama" and The Children's Hour is a
    "sometimes brashly effective broadside," but both plays are
    inferior to The Little Foxes "by almost as much as it is
    inferior to Chekhov, whom, in its best moments, it tries
    to resemble. But, unfortunately, its best moments--I mean
    its attempts at psychology, language, drama--are really its
    weakest. Only when villainy snarls or smiles as it stabs
    does the work come to life--and then only to the second-
    rate life of melodrama."
        Reprinted 1975.46.

48 SMITH, MICHAEL. Review of The Little Foxes. Village Voice,
    12 (9 November).
        Highly positive review of The Little Foxes revival at
    Lincoln Center. "What it says about the American character
    is as important as what many greater plays say about the
    human issue."

49 TAYLOR, JOHN RUSSELL. The Rise and Fall of the Well-Made
    Play. London: Methuen; New York: Hill and Wang, p. 78.
        Brief reference to The Children's Hour. Also published
    as a Hill and Wang Dramabook, 1969, in which edition the
    Hellman reference appears on p. 78.

1967

50 TYNAN, KENNETH. <u>Tynan Right and Left</u>. London: Longmans, pp.
136, 229, 316, 345.
Mentions Julian's inability to make love to Lily in
<u>Toys in the Attic</u> as an example of Broadway's obsession
with impotence. Also notes Hellman's presence at the
Edinburgh Drama Conference and refers briefly to <u>Dead End</u>
and <u>The Little Foxes</u> (film). <u>See</u> 1968.34.

51 WATTS, RICHARD, JR. "Two on the Aisle." <u>New York Post</u> (27
October).
Reviews Lincoln Center revival of <u>The Little Foxes</u>.
Says it remains a fine, powerful play, which uses melo-
drama to become "virtually a clinical study of the preda-
tory ways of the ruthless Hubbards."

52 ZOLOTOW, SAM. "Changes Coming in <u>The Little Foxes</u>." <u>New York
Times</u> (2 November), p. 61.
Announces cast changes in preparation for the shift of
<u>The Little Foxes</u> from Lincoln Center to Broadway. Quotes
Hellman: "'It's a strange feeling to live to be revived.'"

<u>1968</u>

1 ANON. "Miss Hellman Wins Award by College." <u>New York Times</u>
(4 April), p. 58.
Names Hellman as recipient of the first Jackson College
(of Tufts University) award of distinction.

2 ANON. "Seminar Studies U.S. Woes." <u>New York Times</u> (3
December), pp. 491, 61.
Report of Princeton seminar, sponsored by the International Association for Cultural Freedom, in which Hellman
participated. Photo.

3 BARNES, CLIVE. "Theater: <u>The Little Foxes</u> Revisited." <u>New
York Times</u> (6 January), p. 24.
Brief review of the Lincoln Center production of <u>The
Little Foxes</u>, transferred to Broadway with a number of
cast changes. The transfer has made the production somehow
less effective, a feeling which may derive "from seeing
twice in three months a play that should probably only be
seen once in a lifetime."

4 BARROWS, MARJORIE WESTCOTT, ed. <u>The American Experience:
Drama</u>. New York: Macmillan, pp. x, 3-85.
Discusses <u>The Little Foxes</u> (pp. 3-6) as a work in which
Hellman utilizes the nineteenth-century myth of the Old

South. Prints text of the play (pp. 7-81) and questions
for study (pp. 82-85).
Revised edition of Contemporary American Drama. New
York: Macmillan, 1964.5.

5 BROCKETT, OSCAR G. History of the Theatre. Boston: Allyn
and Bacon, pp. 639, 669.
Brief references to Hellman.

6 COWIE, PETER. Seventy Years of Cinema. New York: Barnes and
Company, pp. 124, 139, 272.
Brief reviews of The Little Foxes, The Spanish Earth,
and The Chase, all cited as "important" films of their
respective years.

7 ENSER, A. G. S. Filmed Books and Plays 1928-1967. London:
Andre Deutsch Ltd., passim.
Lists films made from Hellman's plays, with studios and
release dates.
Revised 1971.7.

8 EWEN, DAVID. The Story of America's Musical Theater. Revised
edition. Philadelphia, New York, and London: Chilton Book
Company, p. 236.
Revised edition of 1961.18. Material on Regina and
The Little Foxes is reprinted exactly as it appears in the
original edition.

9 FIDELL, ESTELLE A., ed. Play Index, 1961-1967. New York:
H. W. Wilson Company, p. 156.
Lists Hellman plays in anthologies.

10 FREEDLEY, GEORGE, and JOHN A. REEVES. A History of the
Theatre. Third newly revised edition, with a supplementary
section. New York: Crown Publishers, pp. 598, 631, 806,
881, 892.
Brief survey of Hellman's career through The Little
Foxes, reprinted from the first edition (see 1941.46).
Additional, brief references to Montserrat, The Little
Foxes, Toys in the Attic, and My Mother, My Father and Me
(second edition, 1955).

11 GASSNER, JOHN. Dramatic Soundings. New York: Crown, pp. 71,
298, 364, 387-92, 481-84, 703.
Reprint of 1960.38 (as "Playwrights of the Thirties")
and 1960.36 (review of Toys in the Attic). Other brief
mentions of Hellman include the view that her plays tend to
indict individuals rather than society as a whole (p. 703).

1968

12 GESSNER, ROBERT. The Moving Image. New York: E. P. Dutton
     & Co., pp. 71-72.
        Speaks briefly of The Spanish Earth, attributing "a
     script of a sort" to Hemingway.

13 GILLIATT, PENELOPE, and ELIZABETH HARDWICK. "Letters: Lark
     Pie." New York Review of Books, 10 (1 February), 30.
        Letter to the editor from Gilliatt, objecting to
     Hardwick's "The Little Foxes Revived" (NYRB, 21 December
     1967), and a response from Hardwick. See 1967.30.

14 GOODMAN, WALTER. The Committee. New York: Farrar, Straus
     and Giroux, pp. 181, 213, 305, 392.
        Examines "the extraordinary career of the House
     Committee on Un-American Activities." Goodman refers to
     Hellman's position before the committee and includes
     excerpts from her 1952 letter. Arthur Miller's refusal
     in 1956 to cite names of Communists for the committee was
     expressed "in words similar to those Lillian Hellman wrote
     in 1952."

15 HEILMAN, ROBERT. Tragedy and Melodrama. Seattle: University
     of Washington Press, pp. 76-78, 80, 81, 85.
        Watch on the Rhine contains the simple structure and
     popular emotional appeal found in melodrama but alters the
     stereotypes of the genre, "thus forcing the audience into
     responses less easy than the conventional ones." Kurt's
     murder of Teck complicates the pleasure of siding with the
     hero. We are still "with" him but "we have to pay a higher
     price for being on his side." If the action of the play
     "were to include Kurt's conflict with his own guilt, his
     split between political and moral imperatives, the play
     would be moving toward tragedy." Although Kurt explicitly
     condemns his own action, Hellman does not wish to treat
     the dilemma in tragic terms. The character permits the
     audience to enjoy that "wholeness of a practical competence
     that leads to a swift and sure action," experienced through
     melodrama, not tragedy.

16 HIGHAM, CHARLES, and JOEL GREENBERG. Hollywood in the
     Forties. International Film Guide Series. Edited by Peter
     Cowie. London: A. Zwemmer Limited; New York: A. S. Barnes
     & Co., pp. 74-75, 96, 99, 116.
        Praises the film adaptation of The Searching Wind as "a
     rarity, a film of ideas that presented a valid point of
     view in terms of believable action and conflict and
     character." Also commends the acting, direction, and
     "probing acerbity of Miss Hellman's lines" (pp. 74-75).

Comments briefly on The North Star (p. 96). Criticizes the
screen version of Watch on the Rhine (in which Bette Davis
gave "one of the worst performances of her screen career"),
the "theatrical direction" of Herman Shumlin, and "the
simpleminded symbolism of a script" which called one of the
villains "Herr Brecher ('destroyer') and the chief German
anti-Fascist Max Freidank ('free-thought')" (p. 99). Also
dislikes film adaptations of The Little Foxes and Another
Part of the Forest. "Cold and mechanical, though technically expert," Foxes offered "a kind of frigid profi-
ciency, acceptable enough as a rendering of the author's
lines but emotionally uninvolving." Davis's performance
as Regina lacked "clear focus." Only in the final scenes
did the film become powerful (p. 116).

17 ISAAC, DAN. "Can We Still 'Awake and Sing'?" New York Times
    (18 August), section 2, pp. 1, 3.
        Includes The Little Foxes in a discussion of revivals of
    American plays. Objects to the recent Lincoln Center re-
    vival of the play: "There is something very suspect about
    the way 'liberal' New York audiences have lapped up all
    that sin and corruption that seem to have grown out of the
    soil of the decadent South. In much the same way that the
    Elizabethans set the action of their most savagely sexual
    plays in Italy, The Little Foxes represents the strategy of
    displacement." The real thematic center of the play re-
    volves around the unwillingness or inability of women to
    conform to the passive role expected of them. "But in our
    time, when the image of the woman--filtered through Albee's
    prism of the absurd--has been further masculinized, The
    Little Foxes has the feel of the comfortably old-fash-
    ioned."

18 JACOBS, LEWIS. "World War II and the American Film." Cinema
    Journal, 7 (Winter 1967-68), 1-21.
        Mentions Watch on the Rhine and The North Star. Says
    the central conflict of Watch on the Rhine is "the strategy
    of ideologies."
        Reprinted in The Movies: An American Idiom, ed. Michael
    McClure (see 1971.22).

19 KAEL, PAULINE. "The Comedy of Depravity," in Film 67/68.
    Edited by Richard Schickel and John Simon. New York:
    Simon and Schuster, pp. 97-102.
        Review of Accident, containing brief references to
    Hellman; reprinted from Kael's Kiss Kiss Bang Bang. See
    1968.21.

1968

20 _____. "The Current Cinema: Making Lawrence More Lawrentian."
    New Yorker, 43 (10 February), 100, 103-105.
         Briefly compares the triangle of the film adaptation of
    The Fox to that of The Children's Hour.
         Reprinted in Kael's Going Steady. See 1970.20.

21 _____. Kiss Kiss Bang Bang. Boston and Toronto: Little,
    Brown and Company, pp. 21, 60, 107, 151-53, 251, 252.
         Reprint of 1966.22 and 1966.31. Other scattered, brief,
    but interesting references to Hellman, The Chase, and The
    Little Foxes. "In the theatre and movies, truly dedicated
    selfishness is amusing; and it is somehow liberating to
    laugh at a family of monsters. Isn't that the secret of
    the success of plays like Tobacco Road and The Little
    Foxes . . .? The monsters of a melodramatist like Lillian
    Hellman are rich and decadent white Southerners or Nazis,
    and these people who lust are contrasted with the good,
    straight, affirmative people who are for civil rights and
    Life and who have healthy, decent impulses." (From Kael's
    review of Accident, entitled "The Comedy of Depravity.")
         Reprinted 1969.26. See also 1968.19.

22 KEMPER, ROBERT GRAHAM. "Drama: Evil Revisited." Christian
    Century, 85 (13 March), 332.
         The Little Foxes must be played "in the grand manner,"
    and the Lincoln Center revival, now moved to Broadway, is
    so enacted. The play is an exercise in nostalgia. Orig-
    inally an indictment against capitalist excesses, The
    Little Foxes no longer moves its affluent audience to pro-
    test against the system. "We are now--as man and as
    society--occupied with other manifestations of evil."

23 MILLER, J. WILLIAM. Modern Playwrights at Work. Vol. 1.
    New York: Samuel French, Inc., pp. 38, 389, 393-94, 403,
    405, 412, 431, 437, 444, 456, 472, 480.
         Cursory references to Hellman.

24 NOVICK, JULIUS. Beyond Broadway: The Quest for Permanent
    Theatres. New York: Hill and Wang, pp. 76, 205, 208.
         Discusses the decision to open the all-star revival of
    The Little Foxes at Lincoln Center.
         Reprinted 1969.37.

25 PHILLIPS, JOHN, and ANNE HOLLANDER. "Lillian Hellman," in
    Writers at Work: The Paris Review Interviews, Third Series.
    Edited by George Plimpton. New York: Viking Press, pp.
    115-40.

Viking Compass edition of 1967.45.
Reprint of 1965.19.

26 PIETZSCH, INGEBORG. "Dresden: Kleines Haus, Herbstgarten von
    Lillian Hellman." Theater der Zeit: Blätter für Bühne,
    Film und Musik, 23 (1968), 30.
        Favorably reviews Dresden production of The Autumn
    Garden. Says the play's message points to the responsi-
    bility of man with regard to his own existence. In German.

27 POGGI, JACK. Theater in America: The Impact of Economic
    Forces 1870-1967. Ithaca, N.Y.: Cornell University Press,
    pp. 222, 274.
        Two brief references to Hellman and the Lincoln Center
    revival of The Little Foxes.

28 POIRIER, RICHARD, FELICIA MONTEALEGRE, and ELIZABETH HARDWICK.
    "Letters: Raising Hellman." New York Review of Books, 10
    (18 January), 32.
        Letters to the editor criticizing Elizabeth Hardwick's
    review (NYRB, 21 December 1967) of the Lincoln Center pro-
    duction of The Little Foxes, with a response from Hardwick.
    Poirier asserts that Hardwick misreads the play in order
    to interpret it politically and that her notion of melo-
    drama ignores the legitimate dramatic possibilities within
    the play. Montealegre accuses Hardwick of lacking
    knowledge about the transference of drama from page to
    stage. Hardwick maintains that Birdie represents a "sen-
    timental, plantation idea of Culture" and that Horace "is
    a dull puppet of righteousness." See 1967.30.

29 SARRIS, ANDREW. The American Cinema: Directors and Directions
    1929-1968. New York: E. P. Dutton and Company, pp. 135,
    167.
        Says the film adaptation of The Little Foxes owes more
    to Gregg Toland's camera than to William Wyler's direction.
    Also lists The Chase in a discussion of the directing tech-
    niques of Arthur Penn. Index includes titles of Hellman
    films with names of directors.

30 SHENKER, ISRAEL. "A Hit and Myth Gathering of Intellectuals."
    New York Times (8 December), section 4, p. 2.
        "News of the Week in Review" report on Princeton con-
    ference, in which Hellman participated, held to discuss
    America's problems, image, and impact. Photo.

1968

31 _____. "Intellectuals Look at the World, the U.S. and Them-
selves and Find All 3 in Trouble." New York Times (7
December), p. 52.
Briefly quotes Hellman's wry comments at Princeton
seminar on "The United States, Its Problems, Impact and
Image in the World."

32 _____. "Kennan Analysis Coolly Received." New York Times (4
December), p. 93.
Quotes Hellman's response to lecture by George Kennan
at Princeton seminar on problems of American society.

33 TANNER, LOUISE. All the Things We Were. Garden City, N.Y.:
Doubleday and Company.
Mentions film adaptations of Dead End and The Children's
Hour (as These Three, 1936). Partially reprinted in The
Movies: An American Idiom, ed. Michael McClure. See
1971.22.

34 TYNAN, KENNETH. Tynan Right and Left. New York: Atheneum,
pp. 136, 229, 316, 345.
American edition of 1967.50; identical pagination.

35 WEALES, GERALD. "What Kind of Fool Am I?" Reporter, 38 (11
January), 36-37.
Dismisses the Lincoln Center revival of The Little Foxes
as inept and "ridiculously overpraised."

36 WEINTRAUB, STANLEY. The Last Great Cause: The Intellectuals
and the Spanish Civil War. New York: Weybright and Talley,
pp. 189, 288-89.
Refers to Hellman's involvement with The Spanish Earth.
Also quotes from her article "A Day in Spain" (New
Republic, 94 [13 April 1938]).

37 WHITESIDES, GLENN. "Lillian Hellman: A Biographical and
Critical Study." Ph.D. dissertation, English, Florida
State University.
Studies Hellman's life and work and the relationship
between the two. Dissertation Abstracts International,
29:2287A.

38 WHITMAN, ALDEN. "Lillian Hellman Gives Her Harvard Seminar
Lesson in Writing for Screen." New York Times (10 May),
p. 54.
Records interchange among Hellman and her seminar
students at Harvard, where she taught in the spring 1968
semester; includes Hellman's advice on ways to adapt other

248

sources for the screen, citing as an illustration Graham
Greene's story, "The End of the Party."
Other New York Times edition for this date lists title
as "Lillian Hellman a Harvard Don."

39 WILLIS, JOHN. Theatre World, 1967-68 Season. Vol. 24. New
York: Crown, pp. 6, 79.
Mentions the revival of The Little Foxes; includes pro-
duction credits.

40 WILSON, EDMUND. "An Open Letter to Mike Nichols." New York
Review of Books, 9 (4 January), pp. 5-6, 8.
Makes suggestions, prompted by the Lincoln Center revival of The Little Foxes which Nichols directed, for
American plays that should be considered for similar revivals. Says Hellman seems in certain respects to derive
from the Belasco period but that she does not deserve
critical complaints that her plays are too well constructed
and melodramatic. "I do not regard these as valid re-
proaches; and the very important respect in which The
Little Foxes is not old-fashioned is that Miss Hellman does
not only not feel under any obligation to write 'a tragedy
with a happy ending' but is not even aware of any necessity for calling her play either a tragedy or a comedy.
(I am not sure, however, that the old impedimenta of
realistic staging did not to some extent interfere with
the success of her more recent and for her quite novel
piece My Mother, My Father and Me, which I saw in its first
stages in Boston and which seemed to me then badly
hampered by the machinery of too many changes.)"

41 WOODRESS, JAMES. Dissertations in American Literature 1891-
1966. Durham, N.C.: Duke University Press, items 1258-62.
Lists five doctoral theses on Hellman.

1969

1 AARON, DANIEL. Writers on the Left. New York: Avon Books, p.
399.
Discus edition.
Reprint of 1961.1 and 1965.1.

2 ACKLEY, MEREDITH. "The Plays of Lillian Hellman." Ph.D.
dissertation, English, University of Pennsylvania.
Argues that all but one of Hellman's plays depend upon
a similar dramatic pattern. Dissertation Abstracts International, 30:4441A.

1969

3 ADLER, JACOB. <u>Lillian Hellman</u>. Southern Writers Series, no.
  4. Austin, Texas: Steck-Vaughn Company, 44 pp.
    Incisive monograph on Hellman's plays and her kinship
  with other dramatists. Analyzes the nature of melodrama in
  order to demonstrate that Hellman uses it primarily for
  legitimate ends, as in <u>The Children's Hour</u>: melodrama—
  intense interest in what happens—here "directs us toward
  character and toward meaning." <u>The Children's Hour</u>, contrary to Hellman's assertion, concludes as it should and
  must. Hellman "is the single most important American
  Ibsenian outside of Arthur Miller." The total depravity
  of the Hubbards, comparable to that of Faulkner's Flem
  Snopes, probably prevents "us from seeing them as typical
  of a class of exploiters, whether Southern, American, or
  universal. And so a part of Miss Hellman's purpose fails."
  Alexandra's departure ends <u>The Little Foxes</u> on a note of
  optimism. <u>Another Part of the Forest</u> depends upon "the
  technique of the end-play," which Hellman has rarely employed. "The play opens near the end of a very long story;
  and it is the revelation of earlier events in that story
  to someone who had been unaware of them which motivates
  events bringing the story to a conclusion." Of all
  Hellman's well-made plays, "this is the most complex,
  constant, and clever in its shifts of power from one
  constant to another." In <u>The Autumn Garden</u>, she achieves
  something which Chekhov strived for but never managed until
  his last play: "the omission of violence." Carrie
  Berniers, in <u>Toys in the Attic</u>, resembles Blanche DuBois.
  The play is impressive as fable and as a theatrical piece.
  "But it is artificial, and one is left with the choice of
  either rejecting it because it is not believable on
  realistic premises or accepting it because it makes its
  point with strength, fascination, and total credibility if
  the standards of realism are forgotten." Few American
  playwrights can surpass Hellman's list of deserved successes. Her craftsmanship is not the whole story. "What
  sustains her, too, is a concentrated presentation of sheer,
  almost supernatural evil, to be matched in almost no other
  modern playwright anywhere." She also shows goodness, as
  in <u>Watch on the Rhine</u> and <u>The Little Foxes</u>, "as unmistak-
  able and convincing." She writes with wit and humor, a
  fact often ignored by critics. "There is hope in Miss
  Hellman's world—hope, indeed, in the very act of presenting it."

1969

4 _____. "Lillian Hellman," in A Bibliographical Guide to the
Study of Southern Literature. Edited by Louis D. Rubin,
Jr. Baton Rouge: Louisiana State University Press, pp.
219-220.
Cites fifteen Hellman items.

5 ANON. "An Interview with Lillian Hellman." Audio Cassette.
New York: Jeffrey Norton Publishers.
"Lillian Hellman discusses her plays and other writings
and reminisces. 46 min." Available: Jeffrey Norton
Publishers, Inc.; Audio Division; 145 East 49th Street;
New York, N.Y. 10017.

6 ANON. "A New Lillian Hellman Looks at Yesterday and Today."
New York Times (1 July), p. 33.
Interview with Hellman in which she comments on Freud,
college students, parents and children, death and dying.

7 ANON. Review of An Unfinished Woman. Kirkus Reviews, 37 (15
April), 484.
Judges An Unfinished Woman as "an intimate and eloquent
reminiscence."

8 ANON. Review of An Unfinished Woman. Publishers Weekly,
195 (14 April), 94.
Considers An Unfinished Woman a compelling autobiography
by a "brilliantly gifted woman."

9 BAILEY, PAUL. "Beyond the Veil." Listener, 82 (23 October),
567-68.
Criticizes Hellman's reticence in An Unfinished Woman
but praises the tribute to Dashiell Hammett and the section
devoted to the servants, Helen and Sophronia. The book
seems "inferior in every way to the autobiographies of its
author's two most distinguished interpreters, Tallulah
Bankhead and Bette Davis."

10 BARKHAM, JOHN. "The Literary Scene." New York Post (30
June).
Review of An Unfinished Woman.

11 BEAUFORT, JOHN. Review of An Unfinished Woman. Christian
Science Monitor, 61 (24 July), 7.
"For those who know Miss Hellman mainly as a dramatist
. . . An Unfinished Woman may prove an incomplete book."

12 BOARDMAN, KATHERYN G. "Hemingway, Hammett, Etc." St. Paul
    [Minnesota] Sunday Pioneer Press, n.d.
        Reviews An Unfinished Woman. Considers the book one of
    the year's treats.

13 BRIDGES, KATHERINE. "Some Representative Louisiana Writers."
    Catholic Library World, 40 (February), 352-55.
        Mentions the setting of The Autumn Garden as "vaguely
    Louisiana." Hellman, whose New Orleans setting of Toys in
    the Attic has much in common with "the nightmare city of
    Tennessee Williams' Streetcar Named Desire," also resembles
    him in her use of mad or vicious characters and the sub-
    jects of incest and miscegenation.

14 BROWN, JOHN MASON. Broadway in Review. Freeport, N.Y.:
    Books for Libraries Press.
        Reprint of 1940.8.

15 CAMERON, KENNETH, and THEODORE HOFFMAN. The Theatrical
    Response. New York: Macmillan, pp. 170, 365.
        Two brief citations on The Little Foxes, "probably the
    best example of well-made serious drama in the Ibsen
    tradition to come from the United States."

16 CURLEY, DOROTHY NYREN, MAURICE KRAMER, and ELAINE FIALKA
    KRAMER, comps. and eds. A Library of Literary Criticism:
    Modern American Literature. Vol. 2. Fourth edition. New
    York: Ungar, pp. 61-65.
        Brief extracts from thirteen articles and books on
    Hellman. Updates earlier editions (1960, 1961, 1964),
    edited by Dorothy Nyren. See also 1976.86.

17 EPSTEIN, JOSEPH. "No Punches Pulled." New Republic, 161
    (26 July), 27-29.
        Praises An Unfinished Woman highly. An impressive per-
    formance by an impressive woman, it has "something of the
    quality of a very superior American movie of the thirties."
    Those who object to Hellman's omission of her life in the
    theater fail to see that it was never in the realm of pos-
    sibility that she "would come on as Great Lady of the
    Theater. Whatever else she is, Lillian Hellman is not
    Helen Hayes." Honesty of motive, for Hellman, is "second
    only to the noble act." An Unfinished Woman shows that
    "Hellman's distinction is that, knowing what the noble act
    is, and yearning after it as she has, she is quite incap-
    able of faking it, and there is nobility in that." She
    reminds us of a "female and super-literate Humphrey
    Bogart."

18 EZERGAILIS, A. Letter to the Editor. New York Times (30
    August), p. 20.
        Objects to Hellman's references to Anatoly Kuznetsov in
    a recent New York Times piece.

19 FRENCH, PHILIP. "A Difficult Woman." New Statesman, 78 (24
    October), 580.
        Discusses An Unfinished Woman, in which Hellman "has
    taken modesty a little too far." Her book is often vague
    and elliptical, though the final three chapters are strong.
    The piece on Dashiell Hammett is "remarkable" and the essay
    on Dorothy Parker is as good as anything ever written about
    her. The chapter on Helen "is a subtle study in race rela-
    tions and the liberal conscience."

20 GASSNER, JOHN, and EDWARD QUINN, eds. The Reader's Encyclo-
    pedia of World Drama. New York: Thomas Y. Crowell Company,
    pp. 419, 595, 888.
        Biographical sketch and review of Hellman's Broadway
    career by Milton Levin, who calls Little Foxes and Another
    Part of the Forest her "most fascinating plays." Also men-
    tions Hellman's collaboration on Candide, in an essay on
    musical comedy by Glenn Loney (p. 595), and her role in
    the American drama, in an analysis of its development since
    1914 by Leonard R. N. Ashley (p. 888).

21 GOLDMAN, WILLIAM. The Season: A Candid Look at Broadway.
    New York: Harcourt, Brace and World, pp. 148, 262-65, 272,
    413.
        Criticizes Mike Nichols's direction of the 1967 produc-
    tion of The Little Foxes, citing specific examples of stage
    business which "have the characters behave as if their sub-
    conscious were common knowledge."

21a GOUGH-YATES, KEVIN. "The Chase." Screen, 10, no. 4-5 (July-
    October), 88-100.
        See 1966.26.

22 GRANT, ANNETTE. "Lively Lady." Newsweek, 73 (30 June), 89-
    90.
        Considers An Unfinished Woman "an admirable mirror and
    a provocative image" of two generations "of leading
    American personalities."

23 GRUMBACH, DORIS. "Extraordinary Autobiography: Taking Pride
    in Falling." National Catholic Reporter, n.d.
        Strongly positive review of An Unfinished Woman.
    Hellman is a woman of extraordinary honesty and humility

1969

"who sees the people she admires and loves as the center
of her existence, not herself."

24 HABER, JOYCE. "Lillian Hellman: Theater's Very Bad." New
York Post (1 November).
Interview with Hellman in Hollywood.

25 HERRON, IMA HONAKER. The Small Town in American Drama.
Dallas: Southern Methodist University Press, pp. 237, 238,
264-67, 342-44, 398, 442-44.
Discusses locale in the Hubbard plays, The Children's
Hour, and The Autumn Garden. At the end of The Little
Foxes, Hellman, "as a defender of the underdog, leaves
unfavorable impressions of a man-made environment--an
Alabama cotton-mill town where labor is cheap and no
strikes are permitted, at its worst a symbol of the vices
and inhumanity of American capitalism." The title for
Another Part of the Forest, Herron claims, is taken from
Act III, scene 5 of As You Like It. The conservative town
of Lancet is central to the role of slander in The
Children's Hour. The Autumn Garden portrays a "microcosm
of resort town society." Also mentions the New Orleans
setting of Toys in the Attic, which is "similar in theme
to various small-town themes which hinge upon the exposure
of carefully hidden family skeletons."

26 KAEL, PAULINE. Kiss Kiss Bang Bang. New York: Bantam Books,
pp. 26, 75, 132, 185-88, 311, 312.
Reprint of 1968.21.

27 KERR, WALTER. Thirty Plays Hath November. New York: Simon
and Schuster, pp. 30-31, 129-32, 221.
Reprints Kerr's review of The Little Foxes revival, pp.
129-32 (see 1967.36). Other brief references to Hellman
and The Little Foxes.

28 KOTLOWITZ, ROBERT. "The Rebel as Writer." Harper's, 238
(June), 87-88, 90-92.
Review-essay on Hellman and An Unfinished Woman. The
sense of "rue, of misguided effort and misplaced hopes--
all of it faced in the famous unflinching Hellman style--
permeates the book," as it permeates The Autumn Garden,
Toys in the Attic, and Days to Come. Hellman tends to
remain "perhaps too vain about her own integrity," but the
memoir is "lucid, flinty, vulnerable," with hard, occasionally brilliant prose and dialogue "like one pithy
speech after another out of a Hellman play."

29 LEHMANN-HAUPT, CHRISTOPHER. "Books of The Times: The Incom-
    pleat Lillian Hellman." New York Times (30 June), p. 37.
        Review of An Unfinished Woman. Objects to Hellman's
    reticence, especially about her own writing and the Ameri-
    can theater. The reader eventually comes to understand
    her method, however. "By juxtaposing odd pieces of her
    life, she has given us a detailed portrait of a person who
    doesn't want to be portrayed."

30 LEWIS, EMORY. Stages, The Fifty Year Childhood of American
    Theatre. Englewood Cliffs, N.J.: Prentice-Hall, pp. 25,
    36, 61, 65, 69, 77-78, 79, 81, 104, 105, 119, 168-69, 170-
    72, 173.
        Frequent references to Hellman. The Children's Hour is
    a good but contrived work; The Little Foxes, her master-
    piece, offers "an uncompromising attack on acquisitive
    society, without sentimentality or illusion." The play
    deserves a position near Volpone. Praises Hellman for her
    dignity before the House Committee on Un-American Activi-
    ties. Calls The Autumn Garden and Toys in the Attic her
    best and poorest plays, respectively. In the latter play,
    she seems to have joined "the tattered Williams band of
    Southern revivalists, with their showy violence, intima-
    tions of sexual aberrations, and the other baggage of
    magnolia-scented melodrama." My Mother, My Father and Me
    "is a high point of theatre in the 60's. Sardonic,
    Voltairean, Lillian Hellman recognizes the rot in the
    social fabric and she is magnificently angry." Quotes
    laudatory remarks on the play by Robert Lowell and Edmund
    Wilson.

31 LIBMAN, VALENTINA, comp. Russian Studies of American Litera-
    ture. Translated by Robert V. Allen. Edited by Clarence
    Gohdes. Chapel Hill: University of North Carolina Press,
    pp. 39, 95.
        Lists ten articles on Hellman published in Russia.

32 LITTO, FREDERIC M. American Dissertations on the Drama and
    the Theatre: A Bibliography. Kent, Ohio: Kent State
    University Press.
        Lists two Ph.D. dissertations on Hellman.

*33 LOEFFLER, DONALD L. "An Analysis of the Treatment of the
    Homosexual Character in Dramas Produced in the New York
    Theatre from 1950 to 1968." Ph.D. dissertation, Speech,
    Bowling Green State University.

1969

Includes Hellman, according to Emerson and Michael,
Southern Literary Culture: A Bibliography of Masters' and
Doctors' Theses, 1979.10.

34 MABRY, ROBERT. "How Well She Knows the Forest!" Minneapolis
Tribune (31 August), section E, p. 5.
Praises An Unfinished Woman as one of the best books of
1969. Says Hellman is one of America's three best playwrights.

35 McNAMEE, LAWRENCE F. Dissertations in American Literature.
Supplement One. Theses Accepted by American, British and
German Universities. New York and London: R. R. Bowker,
p. 349.
Cites three dissertations on Hellman.

36 MILLER, JORDAN Y. "Drama: The War Play Comes of Age," in The
Forties: Fiction, Poetry, Drama. Edited by Warren French.
DeLand, Florida: Everett/Edwards, Inc., pp. 63-82.
Analyzes Watch on the Rhine as one of many war plays of
the 1940s. Also briefly cites The Searching Wind as "a
play more about national morality and individual responsibility" than about war itself.

37 NOVICK, JULIUS. Beyond Broadway: The Quest for Permanent
Theatres. New York: Hill and Wang, pp. 76, 205, 208.
Reprint of 1968.24. Includes an updated preface.

38 PRITCHETT, V. S. "Stern Self-Portrait of a Lady." Life, 66
(27 June), 12.
Praises An Unfinished Woman highly, citing the theater's
influence on the book's "short, strong scenes" and on
Hellman's "remarkable directness."

39 RABINOWITZ, DOROTHY. "Experience as Drama." Commentary, 48
(December), 95-98.
In An Unfinished Woman, history and personal material
combine to form a "compelling" memoir. Hellman's style is
graphic, yet often enigmatic. She "nails her dramatic
scenes so often with . . . silence that it becomes a leit-
motif, a reassuring thud that persuades the reader that no
more ever happened, which means everything."

40 ROGERS, W. G. "Personal History." Saturday Review, 52 (5
July), 30-31.
Applauds An Unfinished Woman for its "vivid, thrilling
theater; the littlest incident is whipped up into a dramatic scene. There will be curtain calls galore."

Hellman's treatment of sexual matters is as honest and un-
affected as all the other subjects of the book.

41 RUBIN, LOUIS D., JR., ed. A Bibliographical Guide to the
    Study of Southern Literature. Baton Rouge: University of
    Louisiana Press, pp. 219-20.
        Lists fifteen items relating to Hellman, compiled by
    Jacob Adler.

42 SALEM, JAMES M. Drury's Guide to Best Plays. Second edition.
    Metuchen, N.J.: Scarecrow Press, pp. 22, 231.
        Lists The Lark and Montserrat, with brief synopses and
    royalty fees.

43 STINNETT, CASKIE. "The Confessions of a Holy Terror." New
    York, 2 (25 August), 58-59.
        Praises the candor and style of An Unfinished Woman.
    "It is highly civilized, and it is written in a prose
    style so sparkling that every sentence is a delight."

44 VAN DEN BERGH, LILY. "Alice's Restaurant." Sight and Sound,
    38 (Spring), 67-69.
        Contains references by Arthur Penn, in an interview with
    him, to The Chase and its relationship to other films he
    directed.

45 WARDLE, IRVING. "On Not Falling Sadly Apart." The Times
    Saturday Review [London] (18 October), p. IVd.
        Reviews An Unfinished Woman. "Like her life, her book
    rarely settles down." Hellman's oblique approach does not
    prevent the reader from piecing together the major phases
    of her career. She emerges as a courageous woman who gives
    no sign of having made peace with herself and her environ-
    ment.

46 WEALES, GERALD. The Jumping-Off Place: American Drama in the
    1960's. New York: Macmillan; London: Collier Macmillan
    Ltd., pp. 1-2, 195.
        Begins with a discussion of the 1967 Lincoln Center re-
    vival of The Little Foxes, which Weales considers "gim-
    micky." The play seems "old-fashioned" in the light of the
    drama of the 1960s.

47 WEEKS, EDWARD. Review of An Unfinished Woman. Atlantic
    Monthly, 224 (July), 106.
        Seeing life through Hellman's gaze, "which is often in-
    dignant and rarely tender, is an uninhibited adventure,"

1969

although it is a shortcoming of the memoir that so little
is said of the theater--especially of her failures there.

48 WHITING, FRANK M. An Introduction to the Theatre. Third
    edition. New York: Harper and Row, pp. 117-18.
    Reprint of 1961.29.

49 YOUNG, STANLEY. Review of An Unfinished Woman. New York
    Times Book Review (29 June), p. 8.
    An Unfinished Woman is a "short and modest memoir" which
    often appears evasive about Hellman's life in the theater.
    She is also reluctant to discuss "her dramatic associations
    with liberal political causes, from the Spanish Civil War,
    through McCarthyism and her own appearance before the
    House Un-American Activities Committee, to the Hollywood
    blacklist and Vietnam." Most readers will respond to the
    "rare imagination and literary skill" revealed in the
    book, especially when its subject is Dashiell Hammett.
    Photo.

50 ZIEROLD, NORMAN. The Moguls. New York: Coward-McCann, pp.
    124, 136, 140, 143-44, 154.
    Discusses Hellman's work for Samuel Goldwyn's films and
    her relationship with him.

1970

1 ANGERMEIER, BROTHER CARROL. "Moral and Social Protest in the
   Plays of Lillian Hellman." Ph.D. dissertation, University
   of Texas at Austin.
   Analyzes the eight original plays as topical dramas
   which attack moral and social delinquency. Dissertation
   Abstracts International, 32:3986A.

2 ANON. "Miss Hellman Loses Little Foxes Plea." New York Times
   (27 February), p. 26.
   Item noting Hellman's loss of suit against the Columbia
   Broadcast System for its telecast of the film version of
   The Little Foxes.

3 ANON. "Paperbacks: An Unfinished Woman." Publishers Weekly,
   197 (11 May), 42.
   Notes the impending publication of An Unfinished Woman
   in a paperback edition. Considers it a "candid and understated story of an important life."

4   ANON. "Probing without Pattern." Times Literary Supplement
        (22 January), p. 75.
            Praises An Unfinished Woman highly. The force of this
        memoir lies in Hellman's remarkable gift for dialogue and
        in "the deep probes which she sends into certain moments
        of the past, coming up with words, images and emotions that
        seem still fresh and authentic." What finally seems, per-
        haps, to carry the most weight "is the obstinate decency of
        the woman's basic attitudes, as seen in her opinions about
        friendship and malice, or her contempt for the easy cor-
        ruptibility of intellectuals."

5   ANON. Review of An Unfinished Woman. Choice, 7 (April), 246.
            Although An Unfinished Woman contains several notable
        portraits, it is a disappointing book. "Allusion annoy-
        ingly replaces definition, the tone is often that of gos-
        sip, and the organization is essentially personal and
        chaotic."

6   ATKINSON, BROOKS. Broadway. New York: Macmillan, pp. 258,
        262, 295, 298-300, 357, 392, 446.
            Considers Hellman "the most clearheaded and the best
        organized" of writers opposed to the status quo in American
        society. Briefly discusses the two Hubbard plays, The
        Children's Hour and Watch on the Rhine. Calls Candide "a
        distinguished work." Photo from Watch on the Rhine.

7   _____. Broadway Scrapbook. Westport, Conn.: Greenwood Press,
        pp. 107-10, 192-95, 222, 255-57.
            Reprint of 1947.2.

8   CAREY, GARY. "The Lady and the Director: Bette Davis and
        William Wyler." Film Comment, 6 (Fall), 18-24.
            Includes discussion of the film version of The Little
        Foxes.

9   CHICOREL, MARIETTA, ed. Chicorel Theater Index to Plays in
        Anthologies, Periodicals, Discs and Tapes. Vol. 1.
        Veronica Hall, assistant editor. New York: Chicorel
        Library Publishing Company, pp. 196-97.
            Lists anthologies containing plays by Hellman.

10 CLINES, FRANCIS X. "F.B.I. Head Scored by Ramsey Clark."
        New York Times (18 November), p. 48.
            Mentions Hellman as a member of the executive council of
        a newly formed Committee for Public Justice, "an organiza-
        tion of private citizens concerned that the nation has en-
        tered what was called a 'period of political repression.'"

1970

11 DRIVER, TOM F. Romantic Quest and Modern Query: A History of
   the Modern Theatre. New York: Delacorte Press, pp. 299,
   302, 318, 370.
        Passing references to Hellman.
        Reprinted 1971.6.

12 EVANS, JOHN W. "An Unfinished Woman," in Masterplots 1970
   Annual, Magill's Literary Annual, Books of 1969. Edited
   by Frank Magill. New York: Salem Press, pp. 322-25.
        Analyzes An Unfinished Woman. Praises Hellman's direct,
   informal style and her honest self-examination. She "has
   viewed herself with a severity that is not altogether war-
   ranted."

13 EWEN, DAVID. New Complete Book of the American Musical
   Theater. New York: Holt, Rinehart and Winston, pp. 73-74,
   449.
        Updated edition of 1958.7 and 1959.6. Candide material
   is essentially the same, with slight additions; Regina
   material is identical.

14 FILM CULTURE, no. 50-51 (Fall-Winter), pp. 30, 77; insert, p.
   47.
        Special double issue on Hollywood blacklisting.
   Hellman is mentioned briefly in pieces by Dalton Trumbo and
   Gordon Hitchens. Special insert reprints 1952 Annual
   Report of the Committee on Un-American Activities, which
   cites Hellman's appearance before the committee, at which
   she "refused to affirm or deny membership in the Communist
   Party."

15 GRAHAM, SHEILAH. The Garden of Allah. New York: Crown
   Publishers, pp. 13, 48, 60-61, 123, 176, 184, 217-18.
        Gossipy account of The Garden of Allah, the Hollywood
   bungalow hotel. Contains references to Hellman and her
   circle of friends in the Hollywood days.

16 GRIFFITH, RICHARD, and ARTHUR MAYER. The Movies. Revised
   edition. New York: Simon and Schuster, pp. 343, 364, 370.
        Cites film version of The Little Foxes and The North
   Star. Also includes brief comments on Dead End, with
   still. First published, 1957.

17 HEILMAN, ROBERT B. "Dramas of Money." Shenandoah, 21
   (Summer), 20-33.
        Analyzes a number of plays, including The Little Foxes,
   that depend upon the acquisition of wealth and its connection to moral issues. "The one line of continuity from

Jonson's 'The Fox' to Hellman's <u>The Little Foxes</u> is the
ironic theme of dishonor among thieves." Hellman seems to
see a natural law "that men's rapacity is bounded by the
rapacity of their pals. In this there is some irony, and
indeed a touch of black comedy." But Hellman also seems to
be reassuring us that the bad guys will some day receive
their due, "if only at the hands of each other."

18 HIGHAM, CHARLES. <u>Hollywood Cameramen</u>. Bloomington, Ind. and
London: Indiana University Press, pp. 14, 48.
Brief references to the screen version of <u>The Searching
Wind</u>. Quotes its cameraman, Lee Garmes: The film "wasn't
very good. It had a poor cast."

19 IRELAND, NORMA OLIN. <u>Index to Women of the World</u>. Westwood,
Mass.: F. W. Faxon, Inc., p. 236.
Lists eight items related to Hellman.

20 KAEL, PAULINE. <u>Going Steady</u>. Boston and Toronto: Little,
Brown and Company, pp. 29-35, 174.
Reprint of 1968.20. Contains other brief reference to
<u>The Little Foxes</u>.

21 KEATS, JOHN. <u>You Might as Well Live: The Life and Times of
Dorothy Parker</u>. New York: Simon and Schuster, 319 pp.,
passim.
Quotes from <u>An Unfinished Woman</u> on Hellman's friendship
with Dorothy Parker. Notes (p. 8) that Hellman chose "not
to be involved with this biography in any way. Her stated
reason has been Mrs. Parker's desire that she should never
be the subject of biography."

22 KIENZLE, SIGFRIED. <u>Modern World Theater</u>. Trans. Alexander
and Elizabeth Henderson. New York: Ungar.
Brief synopsis of <u>Toys in the Attic</u>.

23 LARIMER, CYNTHIA. "A Study of Female Characters in the Eight
Plays of Lillian Hellman." Ph.D. dissertation, Purdue
University.
Examines female characters in Hellman's plays for autobiographical references and dramatic artistry. Determines
that Hellman uses five basic types of female characters in
<u>The Children's Hour</u>, which she reemploys in her subsequent
plays. <u>Dissertation Abstracts International</u>, 31:5410A.

24 LEARY, LEWIS, comp. <u>Articles on American Literature 1950-
1967</u>. Durham, N.C.: Duke University Press, p. 262.

1970

> Lists six Hellman items. Incorrectly cites the 1965
> Paris Review interview as 1962.

25 LEWIS, ALLAN. American Plays and Playwrights of the Con-
    temporary Theatre. Revised edition. New York: Crown
    Publishers, Inc., pp. 42, 59, 99-115, 119, 195, 222, 249.
       Revised edition of 1965.13. Hellman material is identi-
    cal, except for one added reference to The Little Foxes
    revival of 1967.

26 LONG, E. HUDSON, comp. American Drama from Its Beginnings to
    the Present. New York: Appleton-Century-Crofts, p. 32.
       Bibliographical listing of fifteen items by and about
    Hellman.

27 MARTIN, JAY. Nathanael West: The Art of His Life. New York:
    Farrar, Straus and Giroux, pp. 27, 68, 75, 93, 137, 159,
    166, 175, 271, 347, 351, 376.
       Records Hellman's observations of West.

28 NELSON, ELIZABETH. Review of An Unfinished Woman, in The
    Library Journal Book Review 1969. Edited by Judith
    Serebnick. New York: R. R. Bowker, p. 132.
       Brief comments on An Unfinished Woman. The book is at
    times intensely personal and, at others, sketchily anec-
    dotal.

29 OLFSON, LEWY, ed. 50 Great Scenes for Student Actors. New
    York: Bantam, 315 pp.
       Includes scene from The Autumn Garden.

30 PALMER, HELEN, and JANE DYSON, comps. American Drama Criti-
    cism, Supplement I. Hamden, Conn.: The Shoe String Press,
    pp. 27-28.
       Lists fourteen items related to The Children's Hour,
    The Little Foxes, and Toys in the Attic.

31 PATTERSON, CHARLOTTE A., comp. Plays in Periodicals: An
    Index to English Language Scripts in Twentieth-Century
    Journals. Boston: G. K. Hall and Company, entries 183,
    535, 1867, 3710, 3947.
       Cites issues of Theatre Arts containing scripts of The
    Autumn Garden, The Children's Hour, The Lark, and Toys in
    the Attic. Also cites an excerpt from Watch on the Rhine
    in Scholastic.

32 RAYMONT, HENRY. "Winners of 1969 Book Awards Named." New
    York Times (3 March), p. 34.

Cites Hellman as winner of National Book Award for <u>An Unfinished Woman</u>.

33 SAAL, ROLLENE. "Pick of the Paperbacks." <u>Saturday Review</u>, 53 (28 November), 38-39.
Refers to <u>An Unfinished Woman</u> as a book that "cuts less close to the core" of Hellman's own being than to the center of her "uncommonly lively circle."

34 SARRIS, ANDREW. <u>Confessions of a Cultist: On the Cinema, 1955-1969</u>. New York: Simon and Schuster, pp. 199, 276.
Fleeting references to Hellman.

35 _____. "Notes on the Auteur Theory in 1970." <u>Film Comment</u>, 6 (Fall), 6-9.
Brief, disparaging references to <u>Watch on the Rhine</u> (play and film) and to "Lillian Hellman's Marxist mayonnaise."
Reprinted in <u>The Primal Screen</u>. See 1973.52.

*36 SCANLAN, THOMAS MICHAEL. "The American Family and Family Dilemmas in American Drama." Ph.D. dissertation, University of Minnesota.
Cited in Scanlan's <u>Family, Drama, and American Dreams</u>. <u>See</u> 1978.61.

<u>1971</u>

1 ANDERSON, MICHAEL, JACQUES GUICHARNAUD, KRISTIN MORRISON, JACK D. ZIPES, and others. <u>Crowell's Handbook of Contemporary Drama</u>. New York: Thomas Y. Crowell Company, pp. 227-28.
Entry on Hellman briefly surveys her career through <u>An Unfinished Woman</u>. "She is essentially a successful playwright of the 30's and early 40's."

2 ANON. <u>The New York Times Directory of the Film</u>. Introduction by Arthur Knight. New York: Arno Press.
Lists Hellman's work for the screen. Abridged edition, 1974.

3 BENTLEY, ERIC, ed. <u>Thirty Years of Treason</u>. New York: The Viking Press, pp. 531-43.
A compilation of testimony from numerous House Un-American Activities Committee hearings held between 1938 and 1968, with emphasis on the alleged Communist infiltration of Hollywood in the late 1940s and early 1950s.

1971

Included is an edited transcript of Hellman's widely publicized appearance before an HUAC Subcommittee on May 21,
1952. Bentley also includes brief, relevant excerpts from
An Unfinished Woman. See 1972.7.

4 CHICOREL, MARIETTA, ed. Chicorel Theater Index to Plays in
Anthologies, Periodicals, Discs and Tapes. Vol. 2.
Richard Samuelson, associate editor. New York: Chicorel
Library Publishing Company, pp. 178-79.
Lists anthologies containing Hellman plays but not in-
cluded in volume 1, 1970.9.

5 COHN, RUBY. Dialogue in American Drama. Bloomington, Ind.
and London: Indiana University Press, p. 5.
A study of the dialogue of several major dramatists that
excludes Hellman from close analysis on the grounds that
her language (along with that of Maxwell Anderson, Barry,
Behrman, Howard, Kingsley, Odets, Rice, and Sherwood) does
not deserve it. Cohn cites The Little Foxes as one of a
few "atypical" twentieth-century American plays, however,
that does not depend upon "genteel, anonymous English."

6 DRIVER, TOM F. Romantic Quest and Modern Query: A History of
the Modern Theatre. New York: Dell Publishing Company, pp.
299, 302, 318, 370.
Delta reprint of 1970.11.

7 ENSER, A. G. S. Filmed Books and Plays 1928-1969. London:
Andre Deutsch Limited, 509 pp., passim.
Updates 1968.7 through 1969. Hellman listings are un-
affected.

8 EWEN, DAVID. The New Encyclopedia of the Opera. New York:
Hill and Wang, p. 571.
Briefly discusses Regina, citing its production history,
musical highlights, and the Hellman source. Revised and
substantially updated edition of the original Encyclopedia
of the Opera, published in 1955 and revised in 1963.

9 FERGUSON, OTIS. The Film Criticism of Otis Ferguson. Edited
by Robert Wilson. Philadelphia: Temple University Press,
pp. 13-17, 190-93, 362, 383-85, 394.
Reprint of 1941.42, 1937.26, and 1941.43. Other brief
references.

10 FURHAMMER, LEIF, and FOLKE ISAKSSON. Politics and Film.
Translated by Kersti French. New York and Washington:
Praeger Publishers, pp. 72, 74, 111-15.

Mentions the blacklisting of Hellman (p. 72) and The
North Star (p. 74). Analyzes The Spanish Earth for its
political impact.

11 GEISINGER, MARION. Plays, Players and Playwrights. New York:
Hart Publishing Company.
Illustrated history of the theater. Discusses Hellman.
Photos.
Revised 1975.19.

12 GOULD, JACK. "TV: Of War and Hostages but Lacking Persua-
sion." New York Times (2 March), p. 71.
Criticizes television production of Montserrat. The
producer's citation of Hellman's remark that the play has
"relevancy for all foreign occupations" suggests that audiences search for a parallel to the Vietnam war. But the
effort fails.

13 GRAY, HUGH. "Translator's Introduction," in his edition of
What Is Cinema? Volume II, by André Bazin. Berkeley, Los
Angeles, and London: University of California Press, pp.
9-10.
Refers to discussion by Bazin of deep focus photography
in the film version of The Little Foxes. See 1951.6a.

14 HILL, PHILIP G. The Living Art: An Introduction to Theatre
and Drama. San Francisco: Rinehart Press, pp. 9-75.
Anthology contains the complete text of The Little
Foxes, with a close exegesis of the script's well-made
structure (pp. 49-64) and an analysis of the ways in which
principles of acting might be applied to its performance
(pp. 65-75). Hill demonstrates that, while the characterizations, theme, and language of the play contribute to its
success, The Little Foxes, like most Scribean plays,
depends primarily upon plot for its energy. Introductory
account of Hellman's career, photos from the 1939 and 1967
New York productions, and graphs of the well-made structure.

15 HOUGHTON, NORRIS. The Exploding Stage. New York: Weybright
and Talley, pp. 54, 82, 241, 243.
Brief references to Hellman.
Reprinted 1973.34.

16 HUNTER, FREDERICK J., comp. Drama Bibliography: A Short-
Title Guide to Extended Reading in Dramatic Art for the
English-Speaking Audience and Students in the Theatre.
Boston: G. K. Hall and Company, pp. 33, 102.

1971

> Lists four plays by Hellman and cites An Unfinished
> Woman. More important, the volume contains lists of
> titles, bibliographies, encyclopedias, names of magazines,
> etc., useful to the student of theater and film, passim.

17 JOHNSON, ANNETTE. "A Study of Recurrent Character Types in
    the Plays of Lillian Hellman." Ph.D. dissertation,
    University of Massachusetts.
>   Describes four categories of character types in
> Hellman's plays. Says there is nothing really positive in
> Hellman's man and his society. Dissertation Abstracts
> International, 31:6614A.

18 KELLER, DEAN H. Index to Plays in Periodicals. Metuchen,
    N.J.: Scarecrow Press, pp. 24, 187.
>   Lists issues of Theatre Arts containing scripts of,
> respectively, The Autumn Garden, The Children's Hour,
> Toys in the Attic, and The Lark.

19 LEWIS, ALLAN. The Contemporary Theatre: The Significant
    Playwrights of Our Time. Revised edition. New York:
    Crown Publishers, Inc., pp. 38, 68, 121.
>   See 1962.32.

20 LEYDA, JAY. Films Beget Films. New York: Hill and Wang, pp.
    40-42.
>   Paperback reprint of 1964.12.

21 McCARTY, CLIFFORD. Published Screenplays: A Checklist.
    Kent, Ohio: Kent State University Press, pp. 71, 102.
>   Items 256 and 368 cite, respectively, editions of The
> North Star (New York: Viking, 1943) and Watch on the Rhine
> (in Best Film Plays of 1943-44, ed. John Gassner and
> Dudley Nichols [New York: Crown, 1945]).

22 McCLURE, MICHAEL, ed. The Movies: An American Idiom.
    Rutherford, Madison, and Teaneck, N.J.: Fairleigh
    Dickinson University Press.
>   Reprints: excerpts from Louise Tanner, All the Things
> We Were, as "The Celluloid Safety Valve" (1968.33); Lewis
> Jacobs, "World War II and the American Film" (1968.18);
> and Siegfried Kracauer, "National Types as Hollywood
> Presents Them" (1949.51).

23 PICKARD, R. A. E. Dictionary of 1,000 Best Films. New York:
    Association Press, pp. 99, 259.
>   Cites The Little Foxes and Dead End.

24 REED, REX. <u>Big Screen, Little Screen</u>. New York: Macmillan,
pp. 355-58.
Attacks all aspects of <u>The Chase</u>, especially Hellman's
screenplay. "I tremble to think what this picture cost.
I shudder even more to think about the disintegration of
playwright Lillian Hellman. In joining the vogue for turning bad trash into artful mass entertainment she has failed
even in the first step. She has not been able to write
even one trash scene that bites or stings or even makes
coherent sense."

25 SALEM, JAMES M. <u>A Guide to Critical Reviews, Part IV: The
Screenplay from the Jazz Singer to Dr. Strangelove</u>. 2
vols. Metuchen, N.J.: Scarecrow Press, 617 pp., passim.
Lists reviews of the following films: <u>The Dark Angel</u>,
<u>Dead End</u>, <u>The North Star</u>, <u>These Three</u>, <u>The Little Foxes</u>,
<u>Another Part of the Forest</u>, <u>Watch on the Rhine</u>, <u>The
Searching Wind</u>, <u>Toys in the Attic</u>, <u>The Spanish Earth</u>, <u>The
Children's Hour</u>.

26 SCHULTHEISS, JOHN. "The Eastern Writer in Hollywood."
<u>Cinema Journal</u>, 11 (Fall), 13-47.
Interesting analysis of Hollywood's effects on the work
of "Eastern" writers who were recruited to write for films.
Includes brief discussion of Hellman, arguing that "rather
than being stunted by Hollywood, [she] turned her excellent
plays into superior motion pictures." Also mentions
Dorothy Parker as a contributor to the screenplay of <u>The
Little Foxes</u>.

27 SCOTT, NATHAN, JR. <u>Nathanael West: A Critical Essay</u>. Grand
Rapids, Mich.: William B. Eerdmans, p. 11.
Brief reference to Hellman.

28 SENNETT, TED. <u>Warner Brothers Presents</u>. Secaucus, N.J.:
Castle Books, Inc., pp. 36, 254, 260-62, 325-26, 400.
Discusses the Warner Brothers adaptation of <u>Watch on
the Rhine</u>. Includes a still from the film and lists its
credits, awards, and review excerpts.

29 TRUMBO, DALTON. "The Blacklist Was a Time of Evil." <u>Film
Culture</u>, 50-51 (Fall-Winter 1970-71), 29-30.
Briefly mentions Hellman.

30 VON SZELISKI, JOHN. <u>Tragedy and Fear: Why Modern Tragic Drama
Fails</u>. Chapel Hill: University of North Carolina Press,
pp. 36, 41, 45, 224, 227, 232, 238.

1971

> Brief references to Hellman, all claiming that <u>The Children's Hour</u> is a modern American tragedy based on "erring libido." The play's theme argues that "life is a psychological and sexual hell."

31 WEALES, GERALD. <u>Clifford Odets, Playwright</u>. New York: Pegasus, Bobbs-Merrill, Inc., p. 152.
Brief, deprecatory reference to <u>The North Star</u>.

1972

1 ADLER, RENATA. "A Review Reviewed." <u>New York Times Book Review</u> (9 July), p. 39.
Criticizes Charles Thomas Samuels for his review of Hellman's <u>Collected Plays</u> and <u>Lillian Hellman</u> by Richard Moody (<u>New York Times Book Review</u>, 18 June). Says Samuels misreads Martha's speech before her suicide in <u>The Children's Hour</u> and that "most of his insights raise terrible problems with the history of the theater." Argues that Samuels ignores Hellman's exploration of physical and moral suffering throughout her plays. <u>See</u> 1972.32.

2 ANON. "From Show Biz to Groves of Academe." <u>Variety</u> (4 October), p. 2.
Reports on Hellman's appointment to a professorship at Hunter College.

3 ANON. Review of <u>The Collected Plays</u> by Lillian Hellman. <u>Choice</u>, 9 (September), 830.
Says publication of Hellman's <u>Collected Plays</u> will be a boon to students and professors of American drama. What is already available in editions of selected plays "will suffice for the general public."

*4 BARBER, JOHN. "One Woman and Her Fears." London <u>Daily Telegraph</u> (2 October), p. 9.
Cited in the <u>British Humanities Index</u>, 1972, p. 201. Article accompanied by photo.

5 BEHLMER, RUDY, ed. <u>Memo from David O. Selznick</u>. New York: Viking, 1972, pp. 255, 457, 489.
Selznick memos reveal that Hellman was considered as screen writer for <u>Rebecca</u> and that she was consulted about dialogue for the screen adaptation of <u>Tender Is the Night</u>.

6 BENTLEY, ERIC. <u>Are You Now Or Have You Ever Been</u>. Harper Colophon Books. New York: Harper and Row, pp. 111-13.

The investigation of show business by the HUAC, 1947-1958, edited and arranged for presentation in dramatic form. Includes Hellman's letter to the Committee and a photo (p. 111).

7 _____. "The Greatest Show on Earth," in his Theatre of War. New York: The Viking Press, pp. 283-305.
An analysis of the activities of the House Un-American Activities Committee. Hellman is viewed as one who unwittingly performed "legal gymnastics" when she tried to use the Fifth Amendment in 1952, although her politics and ethics are seen, in retrospect, as "exemplary." Bentley's introduction to this essay contains slightly revised excerpts from his foreword to Thirty Years of Treason. See 1971.3.

8 BLITGEN, SISTER CAROL, B.V.M. "The Overlooked Hellman." Ph.D. dissertation, University of California, Santa Barbara.
Explores various aspects of Hellman's plays, including the concept of women, her artistic maturation, her view of economics. Says the last two plays show a mellowing. Dissertation Abstracts International, 346:6166A.

9 BREED, PAUL F., and FLORENCE M. SNIDERMAN, comps. and eds. Dramatic Criticism Index: A Bibliography of Commentaries on Playwrights from Ibsen to the Avant-Garde. Detroit: Gale Research Company, pp. 296-98.
Lists thirty-seven items on Hellman and her plays. Some duplication of items.

10 CLURMAN, HAROLD. "Introduction" to Lillian Hellman, Playwright, by Richard Moody. New York: Pegasus, Bobbs-Merrill, Inc., pp. xi-xv.
Says Hellman's "inner self" is present in her plays, although she rarely uses direct autobiographical material. Clurman considers The Autumn Garden, which he directed, her finest play. He speaks also of her "toughness" and "difficulty" in relation to the stage and to her stage colleagues. Unlike most moralists, she is not inclined to retreat from the consequences of her positions.
Reprinted in Contemporary Dramatists, edited by James Vinson, 1973.65. See also 1972.26.

11 _____. On Directing. New York: Macmillan, pp. 47, 49-50, 83, 197-205.
Includes Clurman's notes for his direction of the Broadway production of The Autumn Garden (pp. 197-205) and

1972

other references to Hellman. Quotes a conversation with
Hellman during Autumn Garden rehearsals in which Clurman
suggested that the play's "Chekhovian" characters did not
appear as "forgivable" as Chekhov's. Hellman responded,
according to Clurman: "'True, but I'm not as good as
Chekhov'" (pp. 49-50).
Reprinted 1974.12.

12 COGLEY, JOHN. Report on Blacklisting: Part I, The Movies.
New York: Arno Press, pp. 96, 100-101, 170, 274.
Reprint in the Arno Press Cinema Program of the study
sponsored by the Fund for the Republic. See 1956.14.

13 DUKORE, BERNARD, et al. "Lillian Hellman," in Encyclopedia of
World Drama. Vol. 2. New York: McGraw-Hill, pp. 324-30.
Profile of Hellman and brief analysis of her playwriting
method, along with plot synopses of the major plays. Lists
dates of Broadway openings and selected anthologies in
which the plays appear. Says Hellman is a "moral" writer
who frequently "resorts to melodrama and rhetorical curtain
speeches." Photos from the productions.

14 ECKMAN, FERM MARJA. "Lillian Hellman--Plenty of Class." New
York Post (14 October), pp. 3, 5.
Observes Hellman's seminar at Hunter College.

15 GIANNETTI, LOUIS D. Understanding Movies. Englewood Cliffs,
N.J.: Prentice-Hall, p. 93.
Mentions William Wyler's effective use of deep-focus
photography in his film versions of The Little Foxes and
The Children's Hour.
Expanded edition 1976.36.

16 GREENE, GRAHAM. The Pleasure Dome: The Collected Film Criti-
cism 1935-40. Edited by John Russell Taylor. London:
Secker and Warburg, pp. 25, 28, 69, 72, 180-81.
Reprints reviews of The Dark Angel (1935.39), These
Three (1936.47), and Dead End (1937.30).

17 HANDLER, M. S. "Lillian Hellman Is Among Nine Named to City
University Chairs." New York Times (26 September), p. 38.
Reports on Hellman's appointment to a distinguished
professorship at Hunter College.

18 HOFFMAN, NANCY. "Women All Our Lives: Reading and Writing
Women's Autobiographies," in Female Studies VI. Closer to
the Ground. Women's Classes, Criticism, Programs--1972.

Second edition. Edited by Nancy Hoffman, Cynthia Secor, and Adrian Tinsley. Old Westbury, N.Y.: The Feminist Press, pp. 178-91.

Passing references (pp. 183, 191) to *An Unfinished Woman* as an appropriate autobiography for a women's literature class.

19 ISRAEL, LEE. *Miss Tallulah Bankhead*. New York: G. P. Putnam's Sons, 384 pp., passim.

Discusses *The Little Foxes*, Bankhead's stormy relationship with Hellman, and the Finnish relief benefit controversy.

20 KILKER, MARIE. "The Theatre of Emmanuel Roblès: An American Introduction with a Checklist on Criticism and Production." Ph.D. dissertation, Southern Illinois University.

Claims Hellman's adaptation of *Montserrat* distorts the original Roblès version, thereby harming his American reputation. *Dissertation Abstracts International*, 33:5339A.

21 KUHNS, WILLIAM. *Movies in America*. Dayton, Ohio: Pflaum, pp. 230-31.

Brief remarks on *The Chase*.

22 LUMLEY, FREDERICK. *New Trends in 20th Century Drama*. Fourth edition. New York: Oxford University Press, pp. 116, 348.

Two brief references to Hellman.

23 MARKER, LISE-LONE. Review of *Lillian Hellman, Playwright* by Richard Moody. *Modern Drama*, 15 (December), 344-46.

Considers Moody's book "a readable and useful introduction" to Hellman's achievement as a playwright.

24 MATLAW, MYRON. *Modern World Drama: An Encyclopedia*. New York: E. P. Dutton and Co., pp. 30-31, 48, 140-41, 350-51, 447, 468-70, 770.

Contains separate entries for Hellman, *The Little Foxes*, *The Children's Hour*, *The Autumn Garden*, *Another Part of the Forest*, *Toys in the Attic*, and *The Lark*. The Hellman entry (pp. 350-51) provides a useful, succinct overview of the life and theater career, with brief mention of *An Unfinished Woman*. Matlaw sees *The Children's Hour*, *The Little Foxes*, *The Autumn Garden*, and *The Lark* as her most successful works and argues that her other plays have suffered from moral excesses and contrived endings. He admires her concern for social justice and her plots, which often create "first-rate theatre." Most entries for

1972

specific plays include plot synopses. Photo of original
production of The Little Foxes (p. 469).

25 MOERS, ELLEN. "Family Theater." Commentary, 54 (September),
     96-99.
          Reviews The Collected Plays of Lillian Hellman and
     Lillian Hellman, Playwright by Richard Moody. Moody's
     book is "blandly appreciative but also occasionally illumi-
     nating." The world of Hellman's plays is "built around
     two consuming obsessions: family and capital." While the
     plays at times deal with large and public themes, Hellman's
     characters display an "arrogant assumption that the great
     battles of the outside world are secondary to, but dis-
     tantly dependent on, their family squabbles." Their
     crackling meanness and dialogue account for continuing
     audience interest in them. "And one comes away from the
     plays convinced that, for all their excesses and limita-
     tions, the Hellman people are members of a real family."

26 MOODY, RICHARD. Lillian Hellman, Playwright. New York:
     Pegasus, Bobbs-Merrill, Inc., 372 pp.
          One of the few book-length studies of Hellman's plays.
     Analyzes manuscript versions of the plays and provides
     considerable information on their Broadway productions.
     The biographical information and quotations from Hellman
     are heavily derivative, however, especially from An
     Unfinished Woman. The book suffers from an excessively
     adulatory tone and prose that seems to put thoughts into
     the heads of Hellman and others, without substantiation.
     ("For several weeks [in 1942] she struggled with a
     scenario centering on the Versailles Peace Conference
     [later to become The Searching Wind]. When that failed to
     take form, she may have thought of Joshua Farrelly, whose
     portrait had hung in full view throughout Watch on the
     Rhine. In his days in the American foreign service he must
     have known what was happening in the world. Perhaps now,
     if he stepped down, he could tell us where and when we
     failed to see the danger ahead," p. 137.) Includes plot
     synopses of the plays and much useful information, though
     far from a scholarly analysis of the life and work.

27 MURRAY, EDWARD. The Cinematic Imagination: Writers and the
     Motion Pictures. New York: Frederick Ungar Publishing
     Co., p. 101.
          Slightly distorts Hellman's contention, originally made
     in the New York Times (May 10, 1968), that "mediocre
     stories . . . written with technical skill" often make the

best screenplays. Murray quotes the statement, claiming it is mediocre "plays," not "stories," to which Hellman refers. <u>See</u> 1968.38.

28 NICOLL, ALLARDYCE. <u>Film and Theatre</u>. New York: Arno Press and the <u>New York Times</u>, 255 pp.
    Reprint, in the Literature of Cinema series, of 1936.60.

29 O'CONNOR, JOHN. "TV Review." <u>New York Times</u> (3 October), p. 91.
    Reviews Hollywood Television Theater production of <u>Another Part of the Forest</u>. Calls the play and the television adaptation "serviceable." Hellman drops hints that she is interested in a socioeconomic interpretation of the Old South but she is, finally, a dramatist, not a social historian. She is able "to disguise the fact that the centers of her drama may be hollow."

30 PHILLIPS, ELIZABETH C. "Command of Destiny as Exemplified in Two Plays: Lillian Hellman's <u>The Little Foxes</u> and Lorraine Hansberry's <u>A Raisin in the Sun</u>." <u>Interpretations</u>, 4, no. 1 (1972), 29-39.
    Article published in the journal of the Department of English, Memphis State University, Memphis, Tennessee. Identifies links between <u>The Little Foxes</u> and <u>A Raisin in the Sun</u>. Argues that both plays "affirm the belief that man may command his own destiny."

31 REINHOLD, ROBERT. "Academy Split over Plan to Honour Ezra Pound." <u>The Times</u> [London] (6 July), p. 6g.
    Mentions Hellman as a member of the American Academy of Arts and Sciences committee which nominated Ezra Pound for the annual Emerson-Thoreau medal.

32 SAMUELS, CHARLES THOMAS. Review of <u>Lillian Hellman</u> by Richard Moody and <u>The Collected Plays</u> by Lillian Hellman. <u>New York Times Book Review</u> (18 June), pp. 2-3, 16, 18.
    Finds Moody's study of Hellman "deplorable as well as inept," almost entirely dependent upon <u>An Unfinished Woman</u> for its biographical data and unstinting in its praise of Hellman's work. The bulk of this essay analyzes Hellman's plays, which Samuels largely dismisses as dated, basically unserious, and aimed primarily at comforting middle-class Broadway audiences. Samuels criticizes Hellman's failure to disturb "her audience with intimations of the inscrutable," even in <u>The Autumn Garden</u>, which is as dependent upon contrivance as the other "well-made" plays in the canon. Only <u>The Little Foxes</u>, "for all its faults . . .

1972

remains stageworthy." Like Neil Simon, in whose league
Hellman's plays belong, she is "a thorough professional.
Like him, she concocts plays that maintain interest, quick-
en the pulse, provide--as one says--'an evening in the
theater.'" Photos.

33 _____. "The Reviewer Replies." New York Times Book Review
(23 July), p. 27.
Samuels defends his critical review (NYTBR, 18 June
1972) of Hellman's Collected Plays against an attack by
Renata Adler (NYTBR, 9 July 1972), claiming that he judged
Hellman "as a playwright, not as a person." He contends
that Adler misread him, that he continues to deplore
Hellman's dependence on overheard conversations. "What I
argued was that Miss Hellman's plays don't create any suffering that the audience must witness and identify itself
with and that, when the plays appear to do so, Miss
Hellman contrives equivalent mitigation." See 1972.1 and
1972.32.

34 SELDES, GILBERT. Review of Dead End, in American Film Criti-
cism. Edited by Stanley Kauffmann with Bruce Henstell.
New York: Liveright, pp. 357-58.
Reprints, with minor excisions, 1937.47.

35 SMILEY, SAM. The Drama of Attack. Columbia: University of
Missouri Press, pp. 30, 32, 63, 79, 91-114, passim.
Analyzes The Little Foxes as a uniquely didactic play
which "contains a beginning and middle, but no end." Com-
pares the play to Odets's Golden Boy; briefly discusses
Days to Come and The Children's Hour as "didactic" works.

36 SPACKS, PATRICIA MEYER. "Free Women." Hudson Review, 24
(Winter 1971-72), 559-73.
An Unfinished Woman reveals the "degree to which
feminine freedom may depend on ignorance, derive from
fantasy, and produce paradoxical limitation. Miss Hellman
dreams of living successfully by masculine standards:
honor, courage, aggression." The "image" of the memoir--
substantiated by Hellman's life--suggests that "her central
effort has been to create, for her own benefit as well as
for others, a character to meet masculine standards."
Spacks also contrasts Hellman with Anaïs Nin and relates
their self-portraits to the depiction of "emancipated"
heroines in the fiction of Doris Lessing and others. "To
arrive at freedom, these women indicate, through direct
self-presentation or fictional creation, is to triumph
over actuality. The qualified triumphs they adumbrate

depend at least partly on denial or avoidance: Hellman
denying significant difference between the sexes, Nin
avoiding self-confrontation by self-display, Lessing's
heroines retreating from intolerable experience into the
wider expanses of conscious or sub-conscious reshaping of
it."
Revised 1975.48.

37 SPILLER, ROBERT E., et al., eds. Literary History of the
United States. Bibliography Supplement II. New York:
Macmillan; London: Collier-Macmillan, Ltd., pp. 312-13.
Lists Hellman's works through An Unfinished Woman and
selected criticism on her career. See 1974.40.

38 SZOGYI, ALEX. "The Collected Plays by Lillian Hellman."
Saturday Review, 55 (12 August), 51-52.
Penetrating review-essay on The Collected Plays and
Hellman's influence on the American theater. The
Children's Hour, like Ibsen's A Doll's House, "represents
a moment in stage candor." The two Hubbard plays and Toys
in the Attic, "her triad of southern works, are Lillian
Hellman at her best." Toys in the Attic is the best written and the only Hellman play "in which poetry pre-empts
prose at every turn, with the most provocative characters
best illustrating Lillian Hellman's foremost theme: the
desire for flight and the inevitability of inertia." The
adaptations further emphasize the themes of the earlier
plays. "Finally, Miss Hellman's purpose in the theater
seems to have been to ferret out truth in lives frittered
away by aberrant lying obsesions: Her characters play
dangerous games in dangerous situations until something
occurs that makes it all clear." When the final list of
the most important American plays of our time is drawn,
"several Hellman creations will be among them." Photo.

39 TEICHMANN, HOWARD. George S. Kaufman: An Intimate Portrait.
New York: Atheneum, pp. 50, 284-85, 333.
Recounts amusing anecdotes involving Hellman, Dorothy
Parker, and Kaufman.

40 TYLER, PARKER. Screening the Sexes. New York: Holt,
Rinehart and Winston, pp. 250-51, 274.
Discusses The Children's Hour and its two screen adaptations. The play is "a labored essay" whose true purpose
is "sensation mongering for regular patrons of the Broadway
drama." Hellman is concerned with the fatal harm caused by

the "constriction of natural sexual curiosity through im-
posed school discipline."
Reprinted 1973.62.

1973

1 ADLER, JACOB. "Professor Moody's Miss Hellman." Southern
   Literary Journal, 5 (Spring), 131-40.
       Review-essay on Lillian Hellman, Playwright, by Richard
   Moody. Adler calls the book "a useful contribution to the
   Hellman revival," beneficial mostly for its detailed
   analysis of the manuscripts of the plays, thus offering a
   good account of their development from early to final versions. Adler doubts whether conclusions concerning the
   relationship between Hellman's life and characters or in-
   cidents in the plays are adequately supported. The book
   will disappoint readers who would like to see Hellman's
   dramatic lineage--Ibsen, Strindberg, Chekhov--explored
   beyond brief references; and it will also disappoint "the
   literary critic of drama." Moody excessively attributes
   to Freudian influence any treatment of sex in Hellman's
   plays. Plot summaries are "sometimes just slightly askew."
   Lillian Hellman, Playwright is "a reasonably good book,
   then, but by no means a great one. Time will tell whether
   the great one on Miss Hellman is needed, and whether it
   will appear."

2 ANON. "15 from Stage in Hall of Fame." New York Times (20
   November), p. 30.
       Announces Hellman's election to the Theatre Hall of
   Fame.

3 ANON. "Paperbacks: An Unfinished Woman." The Times [London]
   (22 February), p. 11a.
       Calls An Unfinished Woman "a painful, honest book."

4 ANON. Review of Pentimento. Kirkus Reviews, 41 (15 June),
   792.
       Laudatory review of Pentimento.

5 ANON. Review of Pentimento. Publishers Weekly, 204 (16
   July), 106.
       Praises Pentimento as an absorbing and probing series
   of portraits.

6 ARMATO, PHILIP. "'Good and Evil' in Lillian Hellman's The
   Children's Hour." Educational Theatre Journal, 25
   (December), 443–47.
      Patterned after The Merchant of Venice, The Children's
   Hour revolves around the ways in which human relationships
   are often devoid of mercy and compassion. The play is not
   merely a melodramatic struggle between the "good" teachers
   and the "evil" Mary Tilford, but a forceful moral study of
   what happens when adults too often behave like "children."
   Those who criticize the third act as recapitulation, tedious without Mary's presence, miss the central point of the
   play: In the last moments, Karen "accepts Amelia's atonement and thereby extends compassion—the ultimate good in
   the world of the play."

7 ATKINSON, BROOKS, and HARRY HIRSCHFELD. The Lively Years,
   1920–1973. New York: Association Press, pp. 163–66.
      Atkinson text analyzes Watch on the Rhine. The members
   of the Müller family are the most "ingratiating" characters
   Hellman ever created but the play is not as tightly constructed as The Children's Hour and The Little Foxes, resulting in a contrived rather than organic work. Kurt's
   farewell to his children, inspiring in 1941, is "hackneyed
   rhetoric" today. Drawing from the play by Hirschfeld.

8 BELFRAGE, CEDRIC. The American Inquisition 1945–1960.
   Indianapolis and New York: Bobbs-Merrill, pp. 79, 89, 98,
   170, 215.
      Year-by-year analysis of the McCarthy period and its
   aftermath. Mentions Hellman's role in the Wallace campaign
   and the Arts, Sciences and Professions Committee; also includes comments she made at the 1949 ASP world peace conference and her position before the HUAC.

9 BLAKE, GARY. "Herman Shumlin: The Development of a Director."
   Ph.D. dissertation, City University of New York.
      Includes discussion of Shumlin's involvement with
   Hellman productions. Dissertation Abstracts International,
   34:898A.

10 BLUM, DANIEL. A New Pictorial History of the Talkies. Revised and enlarged by John Kobal. New York: G. P. Putnam's
   Sons, pp. 91, 95, 132, 133, 138, 147, 148, 152, 187, 285,
   298, 325.
      Numerous stills from Hellman films, including Dead End,
   The Little Foxes, The Children's Hour (1962), Another Part
   of the Forest, The Chase, and Watch on the Rhine. Earlier
   editions, 1958 and 1968.

1973

11 BONIN, JANE F. Prize-Winning American Drama. Metuchen, N.J.:
    Scarecrow Press, pp. x, 52, 75, 77-79, 153, 155-56.
        References to The Children's Hour as a play that should
    have won the Pulitzer Prize for 1934-35. Synopses of Watch
    on the Rhine and Toys in the Attic (Drama Critics' Circle
    award winners for 1940-41 and 1959-60, respectively).

12 BROCKETT, OSCAR, and ROBERT FINDLAY. Century of Innovation:
    A History of European and American Theatre and Drama Since
    1870. Englewood Cliffs, N.J.: Prentice-Hall, pp. 459, 524,
    525-26, 567.
        Several brief citations. Hellman is a moralist, pri-
    marily concerned with the evil within man or his society.
    Her plays are melodramas but they lack the traditional
    ending in which poetic justice is dispensed. Evil tends
    to dominate finally because "the morally upright have
    failed to assert themselves."

13 CARROLL, CARROLL. "Lil [sic] Hellman Unlocks Cupboards of
    Past." Variety (17 October).
        Calls Pentimento "absorbing reading on several levels."

14 CASTY, ALAN. "The Gangster and the American Social Drama of
    the Thirties: A Study of the Interaction of an Icon of
    Popular Culture and the Conventions of Drama." Ph.D.
    dissertation, University of California, Los Angeles.
        Devotes a chapter to Hellman. Dissertation Abstracts
    International, 34:7224A.

15 CHICOREL, MARIETTA, ed. Chicorel Index to the Spoken Arts on
    Discs, Tapes and Cassettes. Chicorel Index Series, Vol. 7.
    New York: Chicorel Library Publishing Company, pp. 142-43.
        Lists recording ofa scene from The Little Foxes, with
    Tallulah Bankhead. Also cited in Volume 7B, 1974, pp.
    133-34.

16 _____, ed. Chicorel Theater Index to Plays in Periodicals.
    Chicorel Index Series, Vol. 8. New York: Chicorel Library
    Publishing Company, p. 180.
        Lists issues of Theatre Arts containing scripts of,
    respectively, The Autumn Garden, The Children's Hour, Toys
    in the Attic, and The Lark.

17 CRYER, GRETCHEN, ROSALYN DREXLER, LILLIAN HELLMAN, et al.
    "Where Are the Women Playwrights?" New York Times (20
    May), section 2, pp. 1, 3.
        Symposium in which eight women playwrights, including
    Hellman, respond to the question, "Why don't more women

write for the theater?" Hellman comments on her own disen-
chantment with the theater and her current preference for
writing books. Photo.

18 DOWDY, ANDREW. Movies Are Better Than Ever. New York:
    William Morrow and Company, pp. 18, 26, 32.
        Analyzes American films of the 1950s. Includes refer-
    ences to Hellman's stand before the House Un-American
    Activities Committee and to The North Star. Also published
    by Morrow in paperback edition as The Films of the Fifties:
    The American State of Mind, 1973. Hellman material and
    pagination are identical.

19 DUFFY, MARTHA. "Half-Told Tales." Time, 102 (1 October),
    114-16.
        Review of Pentimento. Criticizes Hellman for the evas-
    ive style. "Singular and moving memories flicker every-
    where, but few emerge clearly." The writing, recalling the
    prose of Gertrude Stein, is "obdurate, flat and mannered."
    Its elliptical quality may have served Hellman well in her
    plays but in Pentimento she "seems to take pride in leaving
    out connectives."

20 EATMAN, JAMES. "The Image of American Destiny: The Little
    Foxes." Players, 48 (1973), 70-73.
        Examines the semidocumentary tone of authenticity, com-
    bined with the critical detachment of historiography, in
    The Little Foxes. The play reflects traditional accounts
    of the Deep South at the turn of the century; "its central
    action is a microcosmic version of a society in transition
    from agrarianism to industrialization. The play simul-
    taneously adheres to the dramaturgy of social realism, in
    which human responses are dominated by economic reorganiza-
    tion." In ignoring the potentially positive contribution
    of the Hubbards to the southern economic recovery and
    focusing instead on their predatory nature, Hellman belongs
    to the tradition of Ibsenite social realism, exemplified
    by The Pillars of Society and An Enemy of the People. She
    is also responding to the skepticism toward free enter-
    prise evidenced in the 1930s. "By examining an age of
    progress according to views from an age of skepticism, Miss
    Hellman reconstructs a crucial dilemma for American liberal
    democracy then and now: how to uphold both private freedom
    and public concerns when the two are at odds."

21 EMERSON, GLORIA. "Lillian Hellman: Still Writing, Still Rest-
    less." New York Times (7 September), p. 24.
        Interview with Hellman at Martha's Vineyard. Photo.

1973

22 EPHRON, NORA. "Lillian Hellman Walking, Cooking, Writing,
    Talking." New York Times Book Review (23 September), pp.
    2, 51.
        Interview with Hellman at Martha's Vineyard upon publi-
    cation of Pentimento. Matters discussed include the
    Hammett and Dorothy Parker estates, the writing of the
    memoirs, the McCarthy years, the decision of Hellman and
    Hammett not to marry, the women's movement. Ephron briefly
    quotes Hellman from this interview in "A Star Is Born," in
    Crazy Salad: Some Things About Women. New York: Alfred A.
    Knopf, p. 141. See 1975.14.

23 ____. "Women." Esquire, 80 (October), 58, 86.
        In a discussion of Dorothy Parker, Ephron calls An
    Unfinished Woman a "marvelous memoir" which portrays
    Parker affectionately and movingly. "Still, the Hellman
    portrait is of a sad lady [Parker] who misspent her life
    and her talent."
        Reprinted as "Dorothy Parker," in Ephron's Crazy Salad:
    Some Things About Women. See 1975.14.

24 FALB, LEWIS. American Drama in Paris, 1945-1970. Chapel
    Hill: University of North Carolina Press, pp. 1, 2, 54-55,
    158, 166.
        Reviews the vehemently negative critical reaction to
    Simone Signoret's adaptation of The Little Foxes, produced
    in Paris in 1962.

25 FIDELL, ESTELLE A., ed. Play Index, 1968-72. New York: H. W.
    Wilson Company, p. 130.
        Lists Hellman plays in anthologies.

26 FREMONT-SMITH, ELIOT. "Lillian Hellman: Portrait of a Lady."
    New York, 6 (17 September), 82-83.
        Pentimento is a book of "extraordinary richness and
    candor and self-perception." An Unfinished Woman was the
    more hesitant tryout for this book, which explores and
    resolves what in the earlier memoir seemed "unfinished or
    ungenerous." Photo.

*27 HASBANY, RICHARD. "Rituals of Reassurance: Studies in World
    War II American Drama." Ph.D. dissertation, Michigan
    State University.
        Includes Hellman. Dissertation Abstracts International
    34:3398A. Cited in 1973 MLA International Bibliography.
    Vol. 1, item 9326.

28 HASSAN, IHAB. <u>Contemporary American Literature 1945-1972</u>.
New York: Frederick Ungar Publishing Company, pp. 108,
138.
Brief references to Hellman as coauthor of <u>Candide</u> and
as a "notable" playwright of the 1930s and 1940s.

29 HEILMAN, ROBERT B. <u>The Iceman, the Arsonist, and the Troubled
Agent: Tragedy and Melodrama on the Modern Stage</u>. Seattle:
University of Washington Press, pp. 47, 298, 300, 301-302,
305, 308, 321, 328.
Brief references and a longer discussion (pp. 301-302)
of <u>The Little Foxes</u>. As melodrama, <u>The Little Foxes</u> combines slick theatrical manipulation with a substantial
sense of reality. "What is substantial is Miss Hellman's
sense of the intensity of monetary self-seeking, of love
of power, of how it works and what it leads to." She
alters the "basic monopathic character of melodrama" in
her ending: She "sees the successful worldlings in a final
uneasy stasis in which their own rivalries render triumph
ambiguous."

30 HIGHAM, CHARLES. <u>The Art of the American Film</u>. Garden City,
N.Y.: Anchor Press/Doubleday, pp. 170, 174, 176, 299-300.
References to Hellman films: <u>Dead End</u> (noted as having
too sophisticated a script "by William [sic] Hellman"),
<u>The Little Foxes</u>, <u>These Three</u>, <u>The Children's Hour</u>, <u>The
Chase</u>. Says the screen adaptation of <u>The Little Foxes</u>
"failed to make up for the coldness" of Hellman's dialogue.
Commends William Wyler's use of off-screen sound effects in
<u>These Three</u>.
Reprinted 1974.23.

31 HIRSCH, FOSTER. Review of <u>Pentimento</u>. <u>America</u>, 129 (29
December), 508, 510.
Only in the chapter on the theater, "surely the most
direct statement we will ever have from the playwright herself about her own work," does Hellman disappoint. Here,
as elsewhere in the book, however, she is disarmingly candid. Occasionally too melodramatic in her plays, Hellman
in her memoirs "is neither obvious nor melodramatic."
<u>Pentimento</u> and <u>An Unfinished Woman</u> "represent the finest
work of her career."

32 HOLMIN, LORENA ROSS. <u>The Dramatic Works of Lillian Hellman</u>.
Acta Universitatis Upsaliensis, Studia Anglistica
Upsaliensia, 10. Uppsala, Sweden: Almqvist and Wiksell,
178 pp.

1973

Ph.D. dissertation, printed in Uppsala University's English Studies series. Examines Hellman's original plays (excluding Days to Come, which is limited to a long footnote). Maintains that her work belongs in a category of its own and should not be ranked with that of other American playwrights. "She did not bring to bear the genius of a Eugene O'Neill or of a Tennessee Williams." Still, she deserves a place among the handful of best American playwrights. Excessively dependent on plot summaries. In English.

33 HOMER, FRANK X. J. "Books to Hoard, Books to Give: Pentimento." America, 129 (17 November), 379.
      Recommends Pentimento as a "bittersweet" series of autobiographical sketches. "The same dramatic prose and attention to detail which distinguished Miss Hellman's plays are evident throughout the book."

34 HOUGHTON, NORRIS. The Exploding Stage. New York: Dell, pp. 54, 82, 241, 243.
      Reprints 1971.15.

35 KAEL, PAULINE. "The Current Cinema: Humanoids and Androgynes." New Yorker, 49 (26 November), 183-87.
      Compares the character portrayed by Glenda Jackson in the film entitled Triple Echo to "the young Lillian Hellman of Pentimento."
      Reprinted in Kael's Reeling, 1976.53.

36 KANFER, STEFAN. A Journal of the Plague Years. New York: Atheneum, pp. ix, 33, 35, 50, 57, 82-83, 94, 108-109, 139, 172-73, 196-97, 237, 288.
      A study of the blacklist of the 1950s, with numerous references to Hellman, who "with characteristic candor, recalled some crucial moments of personal history" for Kanfer. Includes excerpts from editorial written by Hellman, called "The Judas Goats," for the Screen Writers' Guild magazine, in opposition to the House Un-American Activities Committee (pp. 82-83).

37 KELLER, DEAN H. Index to Plays in Periodicals: Supplement. Metuchen, N.J.: Scarecrow Press, p. 101.
      Cites publication of The Little Foxes in Il Dramma, n.s., 73 (15 November 1948), 9-35. Trans. Ada Salvatore.

38 KREBS, ALBIN. "Notes on People." New York Times (4 December), p. 55.

Mentions Hellman's admission into the Theater Hall of Fame.

39 LEHMANN-HAUPT, CHRISTOPHER. "Seeing Others to See Oneself."
    New York Times (17 September), p. 31.
        Reviews Pentimento. The portraits of other people in
    the book "add up to nothing less than a self-portrait of
    Miss Hellman, an autobiography of her soul." The chapter
    called "Turtle" is rich and complex in its symbolism; "in
    fact it is in some respects a veritable Freudian dream."
    Hellman seems to have discovered from writing the final
    chapters of An Unfinished Woman that writing about others
    allows her to see and reveal her own soul.

40 LEONARD, JOHN. "1973: An Apology and 38 Consolations." New
    York Times Book Review (2 December), p. 2.
        Round-up of the year's recommended books. While the
    sketches in Pentimento are not quite up to the portraits of
    Dorothy Parker and Dashiell Hammett in An Unfinished Woman,
    "the whole shines with a moral intelligence, a toughness of
    character, that inspires even as it entertains, and the
    prose is as precise as an electron microscope."

41 LEVINE, JOANN. "Author Lillian Hellman--A Portrait in Words."
    Christian Science Monitor (21 December), p. B2.
        Interview; large photo.

42 MARKOWITZ, NORMAN. The Rise and Fall of the People's Century:
    Henry A. Wallace and American Liberalism, 1941-1948. New
    York: Free Press, p. 310.
        Brief reference to Hellman.

43 MAY, ROBIN. A Companion to the Theatre. New York: Hippocrene
    Books, Inc., p. 43.
        Brief biographical entry.

44 MELLEN, JOAN. "Lesbianism in the Movies," in Women and Their
    Sexuality in the New Film. New York: Horizon Press, pp.
    74-105.
        Analyzes the 1962 screen adaptation of Children's Hour
    in terms of its attitude toward lesbianism. Mellen criti-
    cizes Hellman and William Wyler, the director, for failing
    to pursue Martha's story by having her commit suicide in-
    stead of "allowing her to search for a place in the world
    as a lesbian despite societal dismay." Mellen praises the
    treatment of Karen, particularly her rejection of her
    fiancé, which thus allows her to remain "true to the
    decency of the relationship she had with Dobie." The film

1973

        is most interesting "from a sociological point of view, in
showing the intolerance of a puritanical, self-righteous
community which would drive a woman to death for her sexual
preferences."
        Reprinted 1975.30.

45 NAVASKY, VICTOR. "To Name or Not to Name." New York Times
     Magazine (25 March), pp. 34-35, 110-12, 118-21.
        Discussion of the "Hollywood Ten" cites Hellman's stand
before the House Un-American Activities Committee and a
remark attributed to her by Dalton Trumbo: "'Forgiveness
is God's job, not mine.'"

46 NORDELL, RODERICK. Review of Pentimento. Christian Science
     Monitor, 65 (14 November), 17.
        The "wryly, elegiacally evoked memories, with their
spats, slights, appreciations, and intrusive bits of vul-
garity have less interest than the underlying portrait of
the artist as a young girl and maturing woman." Hellman
may be testing her own thesis of The Autumn Garden: "'At
any given moment you're only the sum of your life up to
then. There are no big moments you can reach unless you've
a pile of smaller moments to stand on.'"

47 POIRIER, RICHARD. Reivew of Pentimento. Book World
     [Washington Post] (16 September), pp. 1, 4-5.
        Pentimento is one of those rare works in which "the
moral value of a book is wholly inextricable from its
immense literary worth, where the excitations, the pacing
and the intensifications offered by the style manage to
create in us perceptions about human character that have
all but disappeared from contemporary writing." The emotional and narrative momentum of "Julia," the most accom-
plished segment of the book, "derives from a Tolstoyan
centrality and largeness of feeling." Despite Hellman's
great past achievements--including the authorship of
several plays with a claim to major distinction--she is
able to write Pentimento "as if divested of the renown, the
honors, the public heroism that has marked her life." Her
decision to focus mostly on obscure people "simply means
that they and not Tallulah Bankhead or FDR, of whom we are
given relishing glimpses, have meant most to her. It is a
choice so free of self-congratulation or pastoral con-
descensions that one comes away feeling that these people
. . . are all important not because they knew Hellman but,
as she would have it, because they allowed her to know
them."

48 PRESCOTT, PETER. "Leftover Life." <u>Newsweek</u>, 82 (1 October),
    95-96.
        Reviews <u>Pentimento</u>, calling it a "well-made memoir."
    Hellman was a remarkably strong storyteller in her plays.
    "She sustains that difficult art throughout this transla-
    tion into a different, perhaps equally demanding genre."
    Photo.

48a RABINOWITZ, DOROTHY. "Books in Brief." <u>World</u>, 2 (28 August),
    39.
        Highly favorable review of <u>Pentimento</u>.

49 ROSEN, MARJORIE. <u>Popcorn Venus: Women, Movies and the</u>
    <u>American Dream</u>. New York: Coward, McCann & Geoghegan, pp.
    168, 192-93, 334.
        Comments on <u>Watch on the Rhine</u> (one of Hollywood's "war-
    widow films") and the two screen versions of <u>Children's</u>
    <u>Hour</u> ("circumventive, but sympathetic to the definitive
    latency of their schoolteacher protagonists").
    Reprinted 1974.35.

50 SALEM, JAMES M. <u>A Guide to Critical Reviews Part I: American</u>
    <u>Drama, 1909-1969</u>. Metuchen, N.J.: Scarecrow Press, pp.
    200-206.
        Checklist of reviews and other items relating to
    Hellman's plays and adaptations. Omits <u>Candide</u>.

51 SARRIS, ANDREW. "Films in Focus: <u>Stage of Siege</u> (Part II)."
    <u>Village Voice</u>, 18 (26 April), 75-78.
        Criticizes <u>Stage of Siege</u> as a film resembling "those
    old Warners historical allegories like <u>The Life of Émile</u>
    <u>Zola</u> and <u>Juarez</u> with a touch of <u>Watch on the Rhine</u>." That
    Hellman work dramatizes "how some murders were less evil
    than others, and how the end sometimes justified the
    means, especially when Mother Russia was being menaced by
    fascist Finland."
        Reprinted in Sarris's <u>Politics and Cinema</u>, 1978.60.

52 _____. "Notes on the Auteur Theory in 1970," in his <u>The</u>
    <u>Primal Screen</u>. New York: Simon and Schuster, pp. 54-61.
        Reprint of 1970.35.

53 SCHORER, MARK. Review of <u>Pentimento</u>. <u>New York Times Book</u>
    <u>Review</u> (23 September), pp. 1-2.
        Praises Hellman highly for the "dramatic quality" of
    the book and the "poised power over the units of scene
    that few writers of fiction possess." Her prose is "as
    brilliantly finished as any that we have these years."

1973

Schorer especially admires a structure that permits the
reader to view the "major outlines" of Hellman's life and
the "pervasive presence . . . of her person," although the
book is not intended to be an autobiography. Photo.

*54 SCHULTHEISS, JOHN. "A Study of the 'Eastern' Writer in
Hollywood in the 1930's." Ph.D. dissertation, University
of Southern California.
Dissertation Abstracts International, 34:4473A.

55 SIGGINS, CLARA M. Review of Pentimento. Best Sellers (1
October), 303.
Suggests that Hellman is reaching for self-understanding
in Pentimento but she never achieves her "Chekhovian moment
of truth" because she is too careful an editor.

56 SPACKS, PATRICIA MEYER. "Reflecting Women." Yale Review, 63
(October), 26-42.
In a discussion of women's autobiography, Spacks alludes
to Hellman as a writer who "can describe a life apparently
dominated by a mythic self-image with no obvious understanding that such an image is itself an artistic creation"
(p. 30).

57 STEELE, MIKE. "Hellman's Superb 'Book of Portraits.'"
Minneapolis Tribune (30 September), p. 7D.
Considers Pentimento "a baring and courageous" series of
reminiscences.

58 SULLIVAN, VICTORIA, and JAMES HATCH, eds. Plays By and About
Women. New York: Random House, pp. vii-xv, 19-96, 423.
Anthology includes text of The Children's Hour and com-
mentary on the play's "uniquely female vision." "Perhaps
Lillian Hellman is suggesting that if a woman can learn to
love herself, she will not be afraid to love another."
Reprinted 1974.43.

59 TALLMER, JERRY. "Woman in the News: Lillian Hellman." New
York Post (13 October), p. 21.
Interview, with photos.

60 THOMAS, ROBERT C., ed. Book Review Index 1972. Vol. 8.
Detroit: Gale Research Company, p. 212.
Cites reviews of The Collected Plays.

61 THOMPSON, HOWARD. "TV Favorites," in Favorite Movies:
Critics' Choice. Edited by Philip Nobile. New York:
Macmillan Publishing Co., pp. 246-53.

Prefers <u>These Three</u> to the second film version of <u>The Children's Hour</u> (p. 251). Also briefly mentions the film adaptation of <u>Dead End</u> (p. 252).

62 TYLER, PARKER. <u>Screening the Sexes</u>. Garden City, N.Y.: Anchor Books, pp. 247-48, 271-72.
Reprints 1972.40.

63 VAN GELDER, LAWRENCE. "Notes on People." <u>New York Times</u> (7 December), p. 30.
Item noting Hellman's being named recipient of the Woman of the Year Award of the New York University Alumnae Club.

64 VERMILYE, JERRY. <u>Bette Davis</u>. A Pyramid Illustrated History of the Movies. Ted Sennett, general editor. New York: Pyramid Publications, pp. 66, 78-80, 84, 87-88, 107, 131.
References to Davis's roles as Regina Giddens and Sara Müller in film adaptations of <u>Little Foxes</u> and <u>Watch on the Rhine</u>. Photos.

65 VINSON, JAMES, ed. <u>Contemporary Dramatists</u>. With a preface by Ruby Cohn. London: St. James Press; New York: St. Martin's Press, pp. 363-67.
Hellman entry contains biographical information and bibliography of the major works. Also reprints Harold Clurman's Introduction to <u>Lillian Hellman, Playwright</u>, by Richard Moody. <u>See</u> 1972.10.

66 WALT, JAMES. "An Honest Memoir." <u>New Republic</u>, 169 (20 October), 27-28.
Calls <u>Pentimento</u> highly readable and valuable as a portrait "of a woman and writer in the making." "Julia" is a chapter reminiscent of Graham Greene.

67 WATTERS, PAT, and STEPHEN GILLERS, eds. <u>Investigating the FBI</u>. Garden City, N.Y.: Doubleday and Company, p. viii.
Book based on a conference held at Princeton in 1971, sponsored by the Committee for Public Justice and others. Acknowledges Hellman's assistance to the conference and to the committee, of which she is a member.

68 WILSON, GARFF B. <u>Three Hundred Years of American Drama and Theatre</u>. Englewood Cliffs, N.J.: Prentice-Hall, pp. 418-20, 452, 459, 464, 483.
Brief survey of Hellman's playwriting career (pp. 418-20) with additional passing references.

<u>1974</u>

1 ANNAN, GABRIELE. "Professional Portraits." <u>Listener</u>, 91 (25 April), 535-36.
    Reviews <u>Pentimento</u>, in which Hellman strikes an "authoritative and slightly portentous" tone. Six of the seven sections are carefully done and self-contained. The chapter called "Theatre" is, however, "a collection of mostly ill-natured show-biz and literary gossip." Hellman knows how to build suspense and to create varied dialogue. "She writes it in all sorts of dialects: Southern folksy, Hammett tough talk, Hemingway laconic, Algonquin wisecrack." Hellman finally resembles "Maugham: her very professionalism and craftsmanship injure her credibility. But, like Maugham, she keeps everyone turning the pages."

2 ANON. "Flashback." <u>Economist</u>, 251 (25 May), 143-44.
    Considers <u>Pentimento</u> a remarkable form of autobiography. Experience has been pared down to the merest detail. Hellman "is funny, a merciless gossip, a good reporter and an acerbic self-critic." Moral courage may be "the essential quality of good writing."

3 ANON. Item. <u>Yale Alumni Magazine</u> (June), 18-20.
    Photo of Hellman and notation of her receiving a Doctor of Letters degree from Yale University.

4 ANON. "New in Paperback: <u>Pentimento</u>." <u>New York Times Book Review</u> (13 October), p. 46.
    Brief comments on <u>Pentimento</u>, newly published in paperback (New American Library); cites Mark Schorer's original review praising the book's "brilliantly finished" prose. <u>See</u> 1973.53.

5 ANON. "N.Y.U. Graduates 2,300 in Garden." <u>New York Times</u> (7 June), p. 20.
    Mentions Hellman as a recipient of an honorary doctorate from New York University.

6 ANON. "Painted Over." <u>Times Literary Supplement</u> (26 April), p. 440.
    Reviews <u>Pentimento</u>. The essays resemble short stories--the "modern, allusive, back-to-front kind." The "Julia" segment "reads like a film scenario." <u>Pentimento</u> is a "strange, fascinating book, which attempts to impose the clear structures of fiction upon the real world, yet gains in artistry whenever the untidiness of reality breaks in to confuse the pattern."

7 ANON. Review of Pentimento. Choice, 10 (January), 1718.
      Comments on Pentimento, praising it as "a brilliant
      series of sketches, reminiscences, portraits."

8 BARAKA, IMAMU AMIRI, DICK CAVETT, et al. "Some Notables Name
      Their Bests." New York Times (6 January), section 2, p. 9.
      Hellman, Tennessee Williams, and other writers, artists,
      and celebrities name their favorite films of 1973. Hellman
      cites The Sorrow and the Pity, Cries and Whispers, and
      State of Siege.

9 BOWLES, STEPHEN E. Index to Critical Film Reviews in British
      and American Film Periodicals. Three vols. in two. New
      York: Burt Franklin and Company, pp. 81, 82, 444, 525.
      Lists reviews in film journals of The Chase (1966), The
      Children's Hour (1962), The Searching Wind (1946), and Toys
      in the Attic (1963).

10 CHICOREL, MARIETTA, ed. Chicorel Theater Index to Plays for
      Young People in Periodicals, Anthologies and Collections.
      Chicorel Index Series, Vol. 9. New York: Chicorel Library
      Publishing Company, p. 141.
      Two listings for Watch on the Rhine: Literary Cavalcade,
      13 (February 1961); Scholastic, 43 (September 1943).

11 CLURMAN, HAROLD. All People Are Famous. New York and London:
      Harcourt Brace Jovanovich, pp. 247, 261.
      Clurman's memoirs, written "instead of an autobiography,"
      include brief comments on Hellman, whom he admires for her
      probity and honesty. He especially applauds her admission
      that a speech he had requested for The Autumn Garden (which
      he directed) was finally written by Dashiell Hammett.

12 _____. On Directing. New York: Collier Books, pp. 47, 49-50,
      83, 197-205.
      Reprint of 1972.11.

13 COLEMAN, JOHN. "Exits and Entrances." London Observer (28
      April).
      Reviews Pentimento. The book has "a double function:
      therapeutic for the author, entertainment for us." Hellman
      appears to be somewhat elliptical about the larger issues--
      Spain, Russia, the McCarthy era: "she curtly, quizzically,
      withholds herself." The chapter called "Willy" contains
      the probable seeds of Toys in the Attic. "Julia" is a
      "sad, brilliant episode."

1974

14 DURBIN, JAMES H., JR. "The Collected Plays," in Masterplots
    1973 Annual, Magill's Literary Annual. Edited by Frank
    Magill. Englewood Cliffs, N.J.: Salem Press, pp. 83-88.
        Provocative analysis of The Collected Plays. Says The
    Children's Hour, like a number of later Hellman plays, con-
    tains an Ibsenite moment of truth for Martha Dobie, who
    resembles Skipper in Tennessee Williams's Cat on a Hot Tin
    Roof. Days to Come, a caricature, is interesting as a pre-
    cursor of The Little Foxes. Regina Giddens, along with
    Hedda Gabler and the wife in Strindberg's Dance of Death,
    is one of the "great bitches of modern drama." Watch on
    the Rhine and The Searching Wind are "more propaganda than
    art." Hellman's book for Candide has been underpraised;
    this musical comedy is one of America's finest. The Autumn
    Garden is her best play. She is less sure of herself as a
    dramatist in her other adaptations and in Toys in the
    Attic, where "all the leading characters are failures, from
    the heroic ones like Joan of Arc and Montserrat to the
    comic ones like Candide and Bernie Halpern," and where
    there seems to be "little place in the world for honesty,
    decency, or happiness."

15 FRENCH, PHILIP. "Cops." Sight and Sound, 43 (Spring), 113-
    15.
        Refers to The Chase as one of "the two outstanding
    police pictures of 1966" and as an "impeccably liberal"
    film.

16 _____. "A Difficult Woman." The Times [London] (25 April),
    p. 12e.
        Reviews Pentimento. Hellman's plays had already assured
    her a permanent position in the American theater and her
    exemplary conduct as a victim of McCarthyism will guarantee
    her place in American social history. Pentimento, along
    with the earlier memoir, shows that she is also "a masterly
    writer of prose and a major witness to our times, particu-
    larly as they impinged upon America's hard-drinking, radi-
    cal writers of the inter-war years."

17 GERLACH, JOHN C. and LANA. The Critical Index: A Bibliography
    of Articles on Film in English, 1946-1973, Arranged by Names
    and Topics. New York and London: Teachers College Press, 720
    pp.
        Cites occasional articles which include Hellman. Format
    requires ferreting.

18 GOLD, ARTHUR, and ROBERT FIZDALE. "Lillian Hellman's Creole
    Cooking." Vogue, 163 (June), 98-99, 150-51.

Small talk with Hellman (including an amusing anecdote about Samuel Goldwyn and The Little Foxes), while she prepares "Rich Man's Gumbo" [sic]. Recipes.

19 GOLDSTEIN, MALCOLM. The Political Stage: American Drama and Theater of the Great Depression. New York: Oxford University Press, 482 pp., passim.

Contains many brief references to Hellman with longer discussions of The Children's Hour (pp. 148-50), Days to Come and The Little Foxes (pp. 401-403). Goldstein is especially helpful in setting Hellman's early work and attitudes within the social and political context of the 1930s. He suggests that Hellman's plays of the period side with the young against the obstructionism of the old, thus reflecting New Deal legislation sympathetic to young people. "Hellman's inability to encourage the young without chastizing the old revealed an unbecomingly vindictive spirit, but undoubtedly contributed to the appeal of her writing." In The Little Foxes, "Hellman attempts to demonstrate that in the process of amassing wealth the individual goes through the parallel process of deciviliz- ing himself--of losing ground as a human being and falling into the way of the jungle. Moreover, the promise of con- tentment is not fulfilled, for at the close Regina is entirely alone, having alienated her daughter Alexandra, the one remaining person from whom, had she been less ego- centric, she might have derived some comfort. Like Amelia Tilford and Andrew Rodman, Regina at the close, speaking with her daughter, tries to make up for her offenses of the past, only to be rebuffed." Photos of the original production of The Children's Hour and of Hellman, Tallulah Bankhead, and Herman Shumlin at a rehearsal of The Little Foxes.

20 GROSSMAN, EDWARD. "The Past Refinished." Commentary, 57 (February), 88-90.

Review of Pentimento. Finds the book portentous, pre- tentious, baffling. Compares the memoir to An Unfinished Woman: "Both books--the earlier not hopelessly--labor under the requirements of adhering to a code that might once have been fine, but has since become archaic with age, abuse, and custom, but which forever insists on being ex- pressed first and last in language." The Hemingway- Hammett style no longer works.

20a GUERNSEY, OTIS L., JR., ed. Playwrights, Lyricists, Composers on Theater. New York: Dodd, Mead, pp. 250-57.

1974

        Contains "Miss Hellman Reflects on Her Own Reflection," a transcript of Hellman's question and answer session with members of the Dramatists Guild.

21 HASKELL, MOLLY. From Reverence to Rape: The Treatment of Women in the Movies. New York: Holt, Rinehart and Winston, pp. 218, 219, 326.
        Refers to the "invisible competition" between Tallulah Bankhead and Bette Davis in their respective stage and screen portrayals of Regina, in The Little Foxes. Also cites briefly the 1962 version of The Children's Hour.

22 HAYNES, MURIEL. "More on the Unfinished Woman." Ms., 2 (January), 31-33.
        Finds Pentimento a triumph, in which Hellman has found "her richest subject--the study of herself." Such "self-scrutiny has replaced moral fervor, to the benefit of art."

23 HIGHAM, CHARLES. The Art of the American Film. Garden City, N.Y.: Anchor Press, Doubleday, pp. 170, 174, 176, 299-300.
        Reprint of 1973.30.

24 HOHENBERG, JOHN. The Pulitzer Prizes: A History of the Awards in Books, Drama, Music and Journalism Based on the Private Files of Six Decades. New York: Columbia University Press, pp. 149-50, 155, 208, 263-66.
        Details the failures of Pulitzer Prize juries ever to honor a Hellman play, although The Children's Hour and Toys in the Attic both had influential support.

25 HORWITZ, CAREY. Review of Pentimento. The Library Journal Book Review 1973. Edited by Janet Fletcher. New York: R. R. Bowker, p. 107.
        "Rarely do we get the opportunity to look so deeply into another's life; nor do we often have the chance to see that the pentimento reveals to us our own image."

26 JAMES, CLIVE. "Stars and Stripes." New Review (May), 88-90.
        Criticizes Hellman's writing style in Pentimento and An Unfinished Woman.

27 KAGAN, NORMAN. The War Film. A Pyramid Illustrated History of the Movies. Ted Sennett, general editor. New York: Pyramid Publications, pp. 51-52.
        Briefly cites North Star as one of numerous films about the resistance to the German occupation of Europe. Photo, p. 52.

28 KAUFFMANN, STANLEY. "On Theater: Candide." New Republic,
     170 (30 March), 16, 33-34.
          Review of the Candide revival mentions that Hellman's
     book for the original production "has been replaced by Hugh
     Wheeler's shorter, lighter one."
          Reprinted in Persons of the Drama, 1976.54.

29 MAGILL, FRANK, ed. "Lillian Hellman," in Cyclopedia of World
     Authors. Vol. 2. Englewood Cliffs, N.J.: Salem Press, p.
     826.
          Sketch of the life and works to Candide, with brief
     bibliographical listing.

30 MORLEY, SHERIDAN. "Memoirs of 'an Unfinished Woman.'" The
     Times [London] (1 May), p. 11.
          Interview with Hellman. "Lillian Hellman is, and must
     always have been, the kind of lady played by Katharine
     Hepburn in films of the 1930s: more than that, her contri-
     bution to the American theatre has been considerable even
     if over here, as she says, her plays always look 'like
     they're being done in translation.' Yet she doesn't think
     of herself as a playwright or ('God forbid') as the first
     of the liberated women."

31 MOYERS, BILL. Interview with Lillian Hellman. Telecast on
     National Educational Television (April).
          Probing interview with Hellman; included is Hellman's
     moving reading of sections of "Julia." Interview available
     under the title "Lillian Hellman: The Great Playwright
     Candidly Reflects on a Long, Rich Life." The Center for
     Cassette Studies.

32 NEMY, ENID. "A Rocky Road to Romance, and a Home on Park
     Ave." New York Times (12 May), p. 52.
          Brief reference to Hellman.

33 NICOLL, ALLARDYCE. "Film Reality: The Cinema and the Theatre,"
     in Focus on Film and Theatre. Edited by James Hurt.
     Englewood Cliffs, N.J.: Prentice-Hall, pp. 29-50.
          Reprints chapter five of Nicoll's Film and Theatre (see
     1936.60 and 1972.28). Contains reference to The Children's
     Hour.

34 RILEY, CAROLYN, and BARBARA HARTE. Contemporary Literary
     Criticism. Vol. 2. Detroit: Gale Research Company, pp.
     187-88.
          Excerpts reviews of The Collected Plays. See 1972.25,
     32, and 38.

1974

35 ROSEN, MARJORIE. Popcorn Venus: Women, Movies and the
   American Dream. New York: Avon Books, pp. 179, 205, 354.
      Reprint of 1973.49.

36 SAMPLES, GORDON. The Drama Scholars' Index to Plays and Film-
   Scripts: A Guide to Plays and Filmscripts in Selected
   Anthologies, Series and Periodicals. Metuchen, N.J.:
   Scarecrow Press, pp. 163, 171-72.
      Lists Hellman scripts and Dashiell Hammett's screenplay
   of Watch on the Rhine.

37 SCHUBERT, KARL. "Lillian Hellman: The Autumn Garden," in Das
   Americanische Drama. Edited by Paul Goetsch. Düsseldorf:
   August Bagel, pp. 252-75.
      The Autumn Garden is about people who in one way or
   another lie to themselves; in this respect, the play
   achieves a thematic unity which makes it more intellectually vital than critics who view the play as merely Chekhovian would admit. In retrospect, The Autumn Garden is a
   unique drama, merging private and public truths. In
   German, with citations from the play in English.

38 SHENKER, ISRAEL. "Perelman Shaken by Florida's Charms." New
   York Times (27 April), p. 25.
      S. J. Perelman's droll reflections on Florida with
   occasional references to Hellman.

39 _____. "Those in the New Privileged Class, the Carless, Don't
   Miss their Droshkys." New York Times (18 January), p. 35.
      Tongue-in-cheek article quotes well-known New Yorkers,
   including Hellman, who refuse to own cars.

39a SIMON, JOHN. "Pentimental Journey." Hudson Review, 26
   (Winter 1973-74), 743-52.
      Acerbic review of Pentimento. Concludes with Simon's
   personalized criticism of Hellman.

40 SPILLER, ROBERT E., et al., eds. Literary History of the
   United States: Bibliography. Vol. 2. Fourth edition:
   revised. New York: Macmillan; London: Collier-Macmillan,
   Ltd., pp. 161, 1371.
      Merely mentions the three plays listed in the 1948 LHUS
   Bibliography (The Children's Hour, The Little Foxes, Watch
   on the Rhine). Adds brief mention (p. 1371) of Candide.

41 _____. Literary History of the United States: History. Vol.
   1. Fourth edition: revised. New York: Macmillan; London:
   Collier-Macmillan, Ltd., pp. 1402, 1520.

Devotes only four lines to Hellman's plays; ignores the
memoirs. Says she proceeded effectively but uncertainly
from The Children's Hour "to chart a mid-course between
tragedy and social message with The Little Foxes (1939),
Watch on the Rhine (1941), and Toys in the Attic (1961)."

42 STINE, WHITNEY. Mother Goddam: The Story of the Career of
Bette Davis. New York: Hawthorn Books, Inc., pp. 4, 7, 57,
105, 148-53, 165, 170-72, 270, 313, 314, 352, 353.
Detailed account of Davis's film career, with numerous
references to her roles as Regina Giddens (The Little
Foxes, 1941) and Sara Müller (Watch on the Rhine, 1943).
Contains specific information on changes made in the
screenplay of The Little Foxes by Hellman, Arthur Kober,
Dorothy Parker, and Alan Campbell (pp. 148-53) and on
additional material by Hellman and Hammett for Watch on
the Rhine (pp. 170-72). Photos from the two films (pp.
155, 174).

43 SULLIVAN, VICTORIA, and JAMES HATCH, eds. Plays By and About
Women. New York: Vintage Books, pp. vii-xv, 19-96, 423.
Reprint of 1973.58.

44 SYMONS, JULIAN. "Drunk, But Not Disorderly." London
Magazine, 14 (August-September), 137-39.
Although Pentimento is a charming and candid book, it
is not the masterpiece American reviewers have said it is.
"It is, rather, a collection of sketches of a fairly
familiar kind, which blend real people known to history
and Lillian Hellman."

45 THEROUX, PAUL. "Dowager Empress." New Statesman, 87 (26
April), 587-88.
Reviews Pentimento; contrasts it to An Unfinished Woman.
In Pentimento, there is sadness but "little regret and no
self-pity. Miss Hellman survived an age that killed her
friends, ruined her financially and scattered her family;
she writes calmly, as a survivor, with her elegance intact,
like a dowager empress surveying a lost kingdom from the
last throne in the land."

46 THOMAS, ROBERT C., ed. Book Review Index 1973. Vol. 9.
Detroit: Gale Research Company, p. 218.
Lists reviews of The Collected Plays, An Unfinished
Woman, and Pentimento.

1974

*47   YEE, CAROLE ZONIS. "Lillian Hellman, Her Attitude About Self
       and Identity." Paper presented at the Convention of the
       Modern Language Association in New York (December).
            Cited in Carol Fairbanks Myers, Women in Literature:
       Criticism of the Seventies. See 1976.84.

                              1975

1   AARON, JULES. "Theatre in Review: The Little Foxes."
       Educational Theatre Journal, 27 (December), 553-54.
            Reviews production of The Little Foxes at the University
       of California, Santa Barbara, with Barbara Rush as Regina.

2   ANON. "8 'Women of the Year' Honored by Magazine." New York
       Times (20 April), p. 16.
            Names Hellman as one of the Ladies' Home Journal's
       "women of the year."

3   ANON. "Sweetest Smelling Baby in New Orleans." Audiotape,
       Pacifica Tape Library.
            "Collage-type [sic] interview" on audiotape, in which
       Hellman discusses her life and career. Includes readings
       from the memoirs and excerpts from recordings of her plays,
       interviews and speeches. Available from Pacifica Tape
       Library, 5316 Venice Blvd., Los Angeles, California 90019.

4   BATTY, LINDA. Retrospective Index to Film Periodicals 1930-
       1971. New York and London: R. R. Bowker Company, 425 pp.
            Useful bibliography. Lists articles and reviews in
       film journals that concern Hellman films (The Children's
       Hour [1962]; Toys in the Attic; The Chase). Categorizes
       articles by general subject and specific film title.

5   BELL, ARTHUR. "Bell Tells." Village Voice, 20 (17 November),
       126.
            Report on the tribute to Hellman at the Circle in the
       Square.

6   BRADY, KATHLEEN. "Lillian Hellman's Hour." Village Voice, 20
       (13 January), 35-36.
            General interview with Hellman on subjects including
       equality of the sexes ("There's no sense arguing about who
       takes out the garbage can if you don't have the money to
       leave"), her writing, her present distaste for theater-
       going, Dashiell Hammett, the House Un-American Activities
       Committee.

7 CARLSON, EUGENE. "Lillian Hellman's Plays as a Reflection of
   the Southern Mind." Ph.D. dissertation, University of
   Southern California.
   Traces the southern environment through four Hellman
   plays. Maintains that Hellman's picture of the Southerner
   is more accurate than has been acknowledged. Dissertation
   Abstracts International, 36:7054A.

8 CARR, VIRGINIA SPENCER. The Lonely Hunter: A Biography of
   Carson McCullers. Garden City, N.Y.: Doubleday, pp. 372-
   75, 405, 412, 463.
   Describes Hellman's acquaintance with Carson McCullers
   and her husband, as recorded by Carr from telephone interviews with Hellman.

9 CHADBOURNE, LARRY. "Lillian Hellman: Provocation on Film."
   Providence, R.I., FRESH FRUIT/Brown Daily Herald, 3 (5
   December), 11.
   Discusses film adaptations of Hellman's plays in anticipation of the Hellman film retrospective at Trinity Square
   Repertory Theatre. Compares the two cinematic treatments
   of The Children's Hour; suggests that Watch on the Rhine
   has dated as a film "in a likable way." Considers The
   Little Foxes the best Hellman film. Notes that she "believed in 'opening up'" The Little Foxes for the screen
   and that "during the forties, when her friend Eisenstein
   was teaching film, he used to show it as a model."

10 COALE, SAMUEL. "The Little Foxes: The Saga of the Hubbard
   Family Continues." Providence, R.I., East Side (18
   December), p. 11.
   Reviews Trinity Square Repertory Company production of
   The Little Foxes. Analyzes the play in relation to Another
   Part of the Forest, performed earlier in the season.

11 COCKS, JAY, DAVID DENBY, et al. "Film Maudit Dossier:
   Memories of 'Justice.'" Film Comment, 11 (July-August),
   16-17.
   Strong defense of Marcel Ophuls's The Memory of Justice,
   by film critics and other writers, including Hellman, who
   calls the film "as brilliant and important a picture as
   one would expect from . . . one of the great filmmakers of
   the world."

12 CUMMING, RICHARD. "A Tribute to Lillian Hellman and a Love
   Letter to the American Actor." Trinity Square Repertory
   Company Program [Providence, R.I.] (November-December), pp.
   23-24, 26.

1975

Impressions of Hellman's plays in the context of Trinity
Square's productions of Another Part of the Forest
(November) and The Little Foxes (December).

13 DEES, ROBERT. "Pentimento," in Masterplots 1974 Annual,
Magill's Literary Annual. Edited by Frank Magill.
Englewood Cliffs, N.J.: Salem Press, pp. 303-306.
Anzlyes Pentimento. Considers "Theatre" the weakest
section of the book but finds the work complex, subtle and
highly readable overall. "Pentimento is a love story, but
it is a good deal more than that, too. That we are given
few, if any, real details about her life with Hammett or
that we are never told explicitly of her true feelings for
him, is inconsequential."

14 EPHRON, NORA. "Dorothy Parker," in her Crazy Salad: Some
Things About Women. New York: Alfred A. Knopf, pp. 133-36.
Reprint of 1973.23. Also quotes from 1973.22 (p. 141).

15 ESTRIN, MARK W. "An Evil World Well-Made." Trinity Square
Repertory Company Program [Providence, R.I.] (November-
December), pp. 9-11.
Program notes for Trinity Square productions of Another
Part of the Forest (November) and The Little Foxes
(December). Connects the two plays and discusses their
satirical and structural elements.

16 GALE, WILLIAM K. "Cain Returns to Trinity." Providence
[Rhode Island] Sunday Journal (2 November), p. H15.
Interview with William Cain on his impending roles as
Marcus and Horace in, respectively, Another Part of the
Forest and The Little Foxes, at Trinity Square Repertory
Company. "Everybody will come and hate the Hubbards. . . .
Even though 98 per cent of the business of the country is
done this way, people will say, 'Aren't they awful?'"

17 _____. "Taking Off 20 Years Can Be Embarrassing." Providence
[Rhode Island] Sunday Journal (16 November), p. H15.
Interview with Zina Jasper, who portrays Regina in the
Trinity Square Repertory productions of the Hubbard plays.
Photos from the productions.

18 GALLAGHER, TAG. "Arthur Penn's Night Moves." Sight and
Sound, 44 (Spring), 86-89.
Brief comments by Penn on The Chase, which he directed.

19 GEISINGER, MARION. Plays, Players and Playwrights. Revised
     edition. Updated by Peggy Marks. New York: Hart
     Publishing Company, pp. 548-53.
     Revised edition of 1971.11.

20 GEORGAKAS, DAN, and LENNY RUBENSTEIN. "I Prefer Films That
     Strengthen People." Cinéaste, 4, no. 4 (1975).
     Interview with Jane Fonda in which she discusses the
     film version of Julia.
     Reprinted in abridged form 1977.51.

21 GOING, WILLIAM T. "The Prestons of Talladega and the
     Hubbards of Bowden: A Dramatic Note," in his Essays on
     Alabama Literature. Studies in the Humanities no. 4.
     University, Ala.: University of Alabama Press, pp. 142-55.
        Compares The Little Foxes and Another Part of the
     Forest to Augustus Thomas's play, Alabama (1891), and
     other works that use Alabama settings. The horrors per-
     petrated by the Hubbards are reminiscent of the tradition
     of such Elizabethan dramatists as Ford and Webster.
     Addie's speech--"Well, there are people who eat the
     earth . . ."--in The Little Foxes is spoken by the wrong
     person. "If Miss Hellman's rage for order drives her
     toward a new ethical rationale for modern drama, she
     should not weaken it by putting important speeches in the
     mouth of a house maid, where they seem too casual in a
     too glamorous garden of evil." Additional brief mention
     of Hellman, "Introduction," p. 8.

22 GUSSOW, MEL. "For Lillian Hellman, More Honors and a New
     Book." New York Times (7 November), p. 28.
        Interview with Hellman on art and politics, in antici-
     pation of benefit in her honor at Circle in the Square
     Theatre. Discusses the forthcoming Scoundrel Time.

23 _____. "Stage: Lillian Hellman's Sad, Comic Autumn Garden
     Revived." New York Times (23 April), p. 30.
        Reviews production of The Autumn Garden by the Joseph
     Jefferson Theatre Company. Says the revival stresses the
     comic aspects of the play, whose characters "are easily
     separated into the weak and silly, the bitter and will-
     less."

24 JOSEPHSON, MATTHEW. "Leane Zugsmith: The Social Novel of the
     Thirties." Southern Review, 11 (Summer), 530-52.
        Mentions Hellman several times as a girlhood friend of
     Zugsmith.

1975

25 KINSMAN, CLARE D., ed. Contemporary Authors. Vols. 13-14.
   Detroit: Gale Research Company, pp. 376-78.
   Lists Hellman's works, awards, personal statistics.
   Briefly quotes assessments of her writing by several
   critics. Updates 1965 edition.

26 KLION, STANLEY R. Letter to the Editor. New York Times (21
   June), p. 26.
   Response to Hellman's Barnard College Commencement
   address, printed in the New York Times (4 June).

27 LOPATIN, LAURA, STU DICKERMAN, and LARRY CHADBOURNE.
   "Hellman's Art." Providence, R.I., FRESH FRUIT/Brown Daily
   Herald, 3 (12 December), 10.
   Excerpts from an interview given by Hellman to students
   during her lectureship at the Massachusetts Institute of
   Technology. Focuses on the difficulty of writing about the
   McCarthy days and Hellman's attitudes toward the current
   generation of college students. Hellman registers her dis-
   like for Eric Bentley's play Are You Now or Have You Ever
   Been, which dramatizes the House Un-American Activities
   Committee hearings and features a reading of her famous
   letter to the committee.

28 MacCANN, RICHARD DYER, and EDWARD S. PERRY. The New Film
   Index: A Bibliography of Magazine Articles in English,
   1930-1970. New York: E. P. Dutton and Company, 522 pp.
   Lists occasional articles which touch upon Hellman
   films. Organization of the bibliography makes them difficult to locate. Hellman is not listed in the index.

29 MARX, SAMUEL. Mayer and Thalberg. New York: Random House,
   pp. 215-16.
   Anecdote.

30 MELLEN, JOAN. "Lesbianism in the Movies," in Women and Their
   Sexuality in the New Film. New York: Dell Publishing
   Company, pp. 71-96.
   Reprint of 1973.44.

31 MERSAND, JOSEPH, ed. Guide to Play Selection: Third Edition.
   New York: R. R. Bowker, 292 pp.
   Lists The Lark and The Children's Hour, with brief
   descriptions, acting editions, and fees.

32 MURRAY, EDWARD. Nine American Film Critics: A Study of Theory
   and Practice. New York: Frederick Ungar, pp. 156-57.

Comments on Stanley Kauffmann's analysis of acting methods in the film version of Toys in the Attic. See also 1963.38 and 1966.32.

33 NACHMAN, GERALD. "A Tribute in Her Own Time." New York Daily News (11 November), p. 39.
Reports on the Hellman tribute at Circle in the Square.

34 PHILLIPS, GENE, S.J. "The Boys on the Bandwagon: Homosexuality in the Movies," in Sexuality in the Movies. Edited by Thomas R. Atkins. Bloomington: University of Indiana Press, pp. 157-71.
Briefly cites the two film adaptations of The Children's Hour (pp. 158-59). Suggests that the revelation of homosexuality in The Children's Hour is typical of "third-act" sensationalism, especially in the obligatory suicide which follows.

35 PINKERTON, ANN. "Hellman's Angels." Women's Wear Daily (11 November), pp. 1, 18.
Photos and report on the tribute to Hellman at the Circle in the Square and the dinner that followed.

36 REED, REX. "Lillian Hellman Remembers." New York Sunday News (9 November).
Interesting interview, with photo. Discusses Hellman's career in connection with the tribute to be held in her honor at the Circle in the Square (9 November). "It's the constant rediscovery in herself that charges her work with distinction. . . . Tallulah Bankhead used to nastily say Lillian Hellman looked like George Washington. Tallulah was wrong. She only lives like him--with humility, courage, truthfulness, and, after tonight, the honor that is justly hers whether she wants it or not."
Reprinted in Reed's Valentines and Vitriol, 1977.100.

37 RILEY, CAROLYN, ed. Contemporary Literary Criticism. Vol. 4. Detroit: Gale Research Company, pp. 220-22.
Excerpts review of Toys in the Attic (see 1968.11) and reviews of Pentimento (see 1973.19, 26, 47, 48, 53, 55; 1974.22 and 44).

38 RIPLEY, ANTHONY. "Appeals Court Will Move Quickly on Nixon Records." New York Times (2 February), p. 44.
Discusses legal tangle surrounding the ruling on ownership of Nixon tapes and documents, following suits by Hellman and others.

1975

39 _____. "U.S. Judge Rules Nixon Documents Belong to Nation."
New York Times (1 February), pp. 1, 10.
Report on ruling involving suits by Hellman and others
for access to tapes and documents assembled during Richard
Nixon's White House years.

40 RISSO, RICHARD. "About the Playwright." Trinity Square
Repertory Company Program [Providence, R.I.] (November-
December), pp. 3-4.
Briefly summarizes Hellman's life and career for Trinity
Square's productions of Another Part of the Forest
(November) and The Little Foxes (December).

41 RODRIGUES, ANN. "The Autumn Garden by Lillian Hellman."
Unpublished Master's seminar paper, English Department,
Rhode Island College, 12 pp.
Original and incisive analysis of the structure, themes,
and characterizations of The Autumn Garden. Argues that
the play resembles The Iceman Cometh in several respects,
especially in the dramatic functions of Larry Slade
(Iceman) and Ned Crossman (Garden), as cynical observers
of other people's lives, and of Hickey (Iceman) and Nick
(Garden), who catalyze the action of their respective
plays.

42 SAFFORD, EDWIN. "The Hubbards After 20 Hard Years."
Providence [Rhode Island] Journal-Bulletin (6 December),
Weekend section, p. 5.
Reviews Trinity Square Repertory Theatre production of
The Little Foxes. Compares it to the company's production
of Another Part of the Forest. Considers The Little Foxes
the better play because "it does not explain everything
outright" and because the writing is tighter.

43 SALE, ROGER. "The Hammett Case." New York Review of Books,
22 (6 February), 20-22.
Brief mention, in a review of Dashiell Hammett's The
Continental Op, of his "undetailed beautiful relationship
with Lillian Hellman."

*44 SCHELLER, BERNHARD. "Der paradoxe bürgerliche Held." Wemarer
Beiträge, 21, no. 9 (1975), 116-37.
Includes Hellman. Cited in Southern Literature 1968-
1975: A Checklist of Scholarship, ed. Jerry T. Williams.
See 1978.72.

45 SIMON, JOHN. Singularities: Essays on the Theater 1964-1974.
New York: Random House, p. 76.

302

Alludes briefly to The Little Foxes as "period melodrama." Mike Nichols, in directing the Lincoln Center revival, "managed to turn the play, despite all his angling
for effects, into a water out of fish [sic]."

46 _____. Uneasy Stages: A Chronicle of the New York Theater,
1963-1973. New York: Random House, pp. 116, 117-18, 194.
Reprint of 1967.47.

47 SMITH, SHARON. Women Who Make Movies. New York: Hopkinson
and Blake, p. 27.
Cites Hellman as one of several women writers who
"brought a new luminescence to the screen" in the forties.
Their scripts were "marked by a sensitivity to female
characterization."

48 SPACKS, PATRICIA MEYER. The Female Imagination. New York:
Alfred A. Knopf, pp. 3, 297-314, 318, 320.
Includes revised version of 1972.36 (pp. 297-314).
Additional Hellman material includes comparison to Isak
Dinesen and further analysis of the Hellman persona.
"Self-absorption is the foundation of Miss Hellman's free-
dom."
Reprinted 1976.97.

49 STARK, JUDY. "Greed and Dislike All in the Family in Hellman
Play." Providence, R.I., Evening Bulletin (18 July), p.
A9.
Reviews Harvard Summer School Repertory Theater revival
of Another Part of the Forest.

50 STEWART, DONALD OGDEN. By A Stroke of Luck! London and New
York: Paddington Press Ltd., p. 267.
Autobiography of the playwright, screenwriter and
socialite; contains brief reference to Hellman.

51 SWAN, BRADFORD F. "Little Foxes Playing on Trinity Stage."
Providence, R.I., Evening Bulletin (3 December), p. B6.
Reviews Trinity Square Repertory Company production of
The Little Foxes. Praises Adrian Hall's direction, which
"fits Miss Hellman's material perfectly," and Robert
Soule's sets.

52 _____. "Trinity Square Offers Hellman Drama." Providence
[Rhode Island] Journal (5 November).
Reviews Trinity Square Repertory production of Another
Part of the Forest. Strongly praises the play and the
production.

1975

53 TARBERT, GARY, ed. Book Review Index 1969. Vol. 5. Detroit:
   Gale Research Company, p. 260.
   Lists reviews of An Unfinished Woman.

54 _____. Book Review Index 1970. Vol. 6. Detroit: Gale
   Research Company, p. 229.
   Lists reviews of An Unfinished Woman.

55 _____. Book Review Index 1974. Vol. 10. Detroit: Gale
   Research Company, p. 225.
   Lists reviews of Pentimento and one review of The Big
   Knockover.

56 THOMPSON, LAWRENCE S. Nineteenth- and Twentieth-Century
   Drama: A Selective Bibliography of English Language Works.
   Boston: G. K. Hall and Company, 456 pp.
   Includes Hellman.

57 VESPA, MARY. "It's Hellman's Hour, as Scores of Her Pals
   Salute a Distinguished Writer." People Weekly, 4 (24
   November), 18-20.
   Reports on a tribute to Hellman at Circle in the Square
   Theatre and a dinner in her honor to raise funds for the
   Committee for Public Justice. Photos of Hellman and
   attending celebrities by Henry Grossman.

58 WALTERS, MARY ANN. "Anton Chekhov and American Theater in the
   Fifties: A Study in Influence." Ph.D. dissertation,
   Michigan State University.
   Discusses The Autumn Garden. Argues that Hellman shares
   Chekhov's sobering vision of life and that the structure of
   The Autumn Garden resembles that of Uncle Vanya. Disserta-
   tion Abstracts International, 36:3705A.

59 WINNINGTON, RICHARD. Film Criticism and Caricatures, 1943-53.
   Selected with an introduction by Paul Rotha. New York:
   Barnes and Noble Books, p. 37.
   Caricature by Winnington of Bette Davis and Paul Lukas
   in a scene from the film adaptation of Watch on the Rhine.
   The film is not, however, reviewed here.

60 ZASTROW, SYLVIA. "The Structure of Selected Plays by American
   Women Playwrights: 1920-1970." Ph.D. dissertation,
   Northwestern University.
   Includes discussion of Hellman. Dissertation Abstracts
   International, 36:4117A.

<u>1976</u>

1 AMERICAN FILM INSTITUTE. Telecast: A Tribute to William
   Wyler. Columbia Broadcasting System (14 March).
   Presentation of the American Film Institute Life
   Achievement Award to William Wyler, director of several
   Hellman films. Appearance and laudatory comments by
   Hellman.

2 ANON. Advertisement. <u>New Yorker</u>, 52 (25 October), 7.
   Full-page photo of Hellman in an advertisement for
   Blackglama mink coats. This ad, one of a series featuring
   well-known women, is headed "What becomes a Legend most?"
   and also appears in other magazines, including the <u>New
   York Times Magazine</u>, during this period.

3 ANON. "Being Too Comfortable." <u>Economist</u>, 261 (20 November),
   140.
   Says parts of <u>Scoundrel Time</u> are "offensively patrician
   in tone." Hellman's period of trial "was no more testing
   than that for many others and her sense of betrayal no more
   shocking than that suffered by several who have documented
   their experiences more fully and with greater political
   insight."

4 ANON. "Dialogue on Film: William Wyler." <u>American Film</u>, 1,
   no. 6 (April), 37-52.
   Transcript of an interview with Wyler and Fellows of
   the American Film Institute's Center for Advanced Film
   Studies. Brief mention of Wyler's direction of <u>Dead End</u>
   and <u>The Little Foxes</u>, with stills from both films.

5 ANON. "Ideas and Trends: McCarthy Era Revisited." <u>New York
   Times</u> (3 October), section 4, p. 8.
   "News of the Week in Review" analysis of the Lillian
   Hellman-Diana Trilling disagreement, prompted by Little,
   Brown's cancellation of its plans to publish Trilling's
   book. Suggests that "the affair may be symptomatic of the
   enduring effects of the political climate of the late
   forties and early fifties on an entire generation, particularly intellectuals."

6 ANON. Review of <u>Scoundrel Time</u>. <u>Choice</u>, 13 (July-August),
   663.
   Considers <u>Scoundrel Time</u> "literature of a high order."

1976

7   ANON. Review of Scoundrel Time. Critic, 35 (Winter), 87.
        Scoundrel Time is "a brilliant recall of a disgraceful
    time in American history."

8   ANON. Review of Scoundrel Time. Kirkus Reviews, 44 (15
        February), 232.
        Characterizes Scoundrel Time as "eloquent, the more so
    for what remains unsaid."

9   ANON. Review of Scoundrel Time. Library Journal, 101 (1
        May), 1110.
        Expresses reservations.

10 ANON. Review of Scoundrel Time. New Yorker, 52 (26 April),
        147.
        Briefly praises Scoundrel Time for its humor and absence
    of self-pity and self-righteousness.

11 ANON. Review of Scoundrel Time. Publishers Weekly, 209 (1
        March), 90.
        Calls Scoundrel Time a vibrant, important document about
    a disturbing period in American political history.

12 ANON. Review of Scoundrel Time. The Sunday Times [London]
        (7 November), p. 40.
        Review, with photo.

13 APPLEBAUM, STANLEY, ed. The New York Stage: Famous Produc-
        tions in Photographs. New York: Dover Publications, Inc.,
        pp. 120, 144.
        Photos from the original Broadway productions of The
    Children's Hour and The Little Foxes.

14 BAKER, JOHN. "PW Interviews: Lillian Hellman." Publishers
        Weekly, 209 (26 April), 6-7.
        Hellman speaks of the newly published Scoundrel Time,
    current projects, her fondness for the writing of Christina
    Stead, Thomas Pynchon, and Jean Rhys, her early reviewing
    days, her doubts about her own writing.

15 BALFOUR, KATHERINE. "Talking to Lillian Hellman." Family
        Circle, 87 (April), pp. 24, 27.
        Interview with Hellman in her New York home. Discusses
    the women's movement, her 1944 trip to Russia, her adher-
    ence to principles. Photo.

16 BALIO, TINO, ed. The American Film Industry. Madison:
    University of Wisconsin Press, pp. 234, 410-31.
       Excerpts John Cogley, Report on Blacklisting, Part I:
    The Movies, pp. 410-31 (see 1956.14). Also includes a
    photograph taken on the set of Dead End in an article by
    Mae D. Huettig, "The Motion Picture Industry Today," p.
    234.

17 BAWDEN, LIZ-ANNE. The Oxford Companion to Film. New York
    and London: Oxford University Press, pp. 127, 181, 326-27,
    421.
       Contains separate entries on Hellman and the film
    versions of The Little Foxes, The Chase, Dead End, and The
    Spanish Earth.

18 BAXTER, JOHN. The Hollywood Exiles. London: Macdonald and
    Jane's Publishers, Ltd., pp. 100, 109.
       Records brief anecdotes involving Hellman.

19 BEICHMAN, ARNOLD. "Playwright Lillian Hellman's Memoir:
    Scoundrel Time." Christian Science Monitor, 68 (17 May),
    23.
       Criticizes Hellman for failing to see the Stalin menace.
    Nor does Scoundrel Time explain why it took her so long to
    see what was going on in the Soviet Union.

20 BROCKETT, OSCAR G. The Essential Theatre. New York: Holt,
    Rinehart and Winston, 398 pp.
       Condensed edition of Brockett's The Theatre: An Intro-
    duction. Hellman references.

21 CAMERON, JAMES. "Introduction." Scoundrel Time by Lillian
    Hellman. London: Macmillan, pp. 13-21.
       Introduction for the English edition of Scoundrel Time,
    which also reprints the American introduction by Garry
    Wills (1976.108). Cameron questions why Great Britain
    never suffered the McCarthy trauma and suggests that the
    more recent Watergate events reveal to the English for the
    first time "the true hallucinatory quality of American
    politics, of which the persecution of Lillian Hellman and
    others even more vulnerable had been an almost-forgotten
    part." In Scoundrel Time Hellman defines the characters,
    "as she has done a dozen times in some of the best drama
    of our generation." She says that she can no longer accept
    liberalism. "It sounds like the epitaph of a fine dream,
    and it is, I would guess, a little wearily unfair. A
    nation cannot blame an entire creative community for indif-
    ference, for giving no leadership and no rallying-cries,

1976

however stifled, when that community produced the likes of
Lincoln Steffens and I. F. Stone and Lillian Hellman."

22 CARMODY, DEIRDRE. "Trilling Case Sparks Publisher-Loyalty
Debate." New York Times (30 September), p. C34.
Reactions to Little, Brown's refusal to publish Diana
Trilling's book because it contained passages critical of
Hellman, one of the company's leading authors.

23 CLEMONS, WALTER. "The Way It Was." Newsweek, 87 (26 April),
96.
Reviews Scoundrel Time. Considers the book Hellman's
"most sustained piece of narrative," in spite of its
brevity.

24 COOK, BRUCE. "Notes on a Shameful Era." Saturday Review, 3
(17 April), 28-29.
Reviews Scoundrel Time. This book, like the two earlier
memoirs, is "a triumph of tone."

25 CUMMINGS, JUDITH. "Columbia Grants Degrees to 6,700." New
York Times (13 May), p. 19.
Names Hellman as recipient of an honorary degree from
Columbia University.

26 DYMENT, ALAN R. The Literature of the Film: A Bibliographical
Guide to the Film as Art and Entertainment, 1936-1970.
Detroit, Mich.: Gale Research Company.
Refers to Hellman films.

27 EASTON, CAROL. The Search for Sam Goldwyn. New York: William
Morrow and Company, pp. 29, 129-31, 153, 158, 202-204, 218-
22.
Discusses the "stormy" Hellman-Goldwyn relationship and
the Goldwyn films written by Hellman.

28 EDDLEMAN, FLOYD E., comp. American Drama Criticism, Supplement II. Hamden, Conn.: The Shoe String Press, pp. 70-72.
Lists twenty-seven Hellman items.

29 EDWARDS, VERNE, JR. Review of Scoundrel Time. Journalism
Quarterly, 53 (Winter), 751-52.
Calls Scoundrel Time a "beautifully emotional volume."

30 ENGEL, LEHMAN. The Critics. New York: Macmillan, pp. 23-31,
61, 62, 75, 99.
Brief references to Hellman.

31 FORSBURGH, LACEY. "Why More Top Novelists Don't Go Holly-
      wood." New York Times (21 November), section 2, pp. 1, 13-
      14.
        Discussion with major writers, including Hellman, on
      their concerns about film adaptations of their work.
      Quotes Hellman on reasons for her rejection of an offer to
      film sections of her memoirs, in contrast to her acceptance
      of the Julia offer. Photo.

32 FREMONT-SMITH, ELIOT. "Second Sights: Scoundrel Time."
      Village Voice, 21 (29 March), 42.
        Brief comments on Scoundrel Time, "a brief, intense
      memoir."

33 FRENCH, PHILIP. "I Puritani." New Statesman, 92 (5
      November), 635-36.
        Review-essay on Hellman and Scoundrel Time. Hellman's
      continuing anger and lack of charity, "however strong a
      barrier against sentimentality," present a liability.
      "Somehow Miss Hellman wants us to excuse her naïveté and
      misjudgment while at the same time respecting her fore-
      sight and political sagacity. What one does respect is
      her insight as a dramatist, her courage and her eloquence."
      The three books of Hellman memoirs recreate Hellman and
      Hammett as figures in history--"as Lilly and Dash, the
      exemplary heroic couple of committed Thirties seriousness
      to match the now unfashionable Zelda and Scott, the repre-
      sentatives of disengaged Twenties frivolousness." The
      couples in fact resemble each other in several respects.
      "There is even an odd correspondence between the names they
      chose for their autobiographical characters--Nick and Nora
      Charles, Dick and Nicole Driver."

34 FRIEDMAN, LEON, et al. "Blacklisting--the Debate Continues."
      New York Times (7 November), section 2, p. 24.
        Six letters to the editor concerning Hilton Kramer's
      "The Blacklist and the Cold War." New York Times (3
      October). Numerous references to Hellman and Scoundrel
      Time. See 1976.62.

35 FUSSELL, PAUL. "Treason of the Clerks." Spectator, 237 (13
      November), 20-21.
        Reviews Scoundrel Time and the controversy that fol-
      lowed its publication in the United States. Fussell criti-
      cizes the excessive anger of the book, which "all but
      destroys" Hellman's style. She is angriest at the failure
      of American intellectuals to assist her in the McCarthy
      days. "What she really cannot forgive is their being

1976

Trotskyists who naturally declined to rescue a person they
conceived to be a Stalinist. What she cannot understand
yet is that politics is politics and full of tough cookies,
and that writers who meddle in it solicit destruction by
it." The book is too short and its introductions by Garry
Wills and James Cameron (the latter added for the British
edition) are, respectively, self-righteous and absurd.
Hellman confuses literature and action; Scoundrel Time is
an "odd and interesting" book, "engaging and repellent by
turns."

36 GIANNETTI, LOUIS D. Understanding Movies. Second edition.
Englewood Cliffs, N.J.: Prentice-Hall, pp. 174-75, 231.
Expanded edition of 1972.15. Includes slightly amended
material on William Wyler's use of deep focus photography
in his Hellman films and adds a brief discussion, with
still, of The Spanish Earth.

37 GLAZER, NATHAN. "An Answer to Lillian Hellman." Commentary,
61 (19 June), 36-39.
Denies charges made against Commentary and Partisan
Review by Hellman in Scoundrel Time. Glazer accuses her of
simplifying history and belittles her stand before the
House Un-American Activities Committee. "And what does
Lillian Hellman make of the introduction [by Garry Wills]
that disgraces her memoir? Perhaps it was hard to tell in
1952 just who were the principal enemies of freedom then.
Is it so hard to tell in 1976?"

38 GOODMAN, WALTER. "Fair Game." New Leader, 59 (24 May), 10-
11.
Discusses Scoundrel Time and the McCarthy background.
Finds it "a self-celebrating piece of work, by a skilled
writer who knows that the best way to persuade readers of
one's honesty and right-thinkingness is to concede that
one has made passing 'mistakes,' and the best way to sell
one's courage is to make much of one's weaknesses." Also
attacks Garry Wills's Introduction as heated and hurried
revisionism. "By this account, the precursors of Joe
McCarthy were those liberals who turned against the Russians the ideology and the emotions that had spurred their
fight against Fascism."

39 GORNICK, VIVIAN. "Neither Forgotten Nor Forgiven." Ms., 5
(August), 46-47.
Calls Scoundrel Time a moving, intense memoir, told in
the distinctive voice of "a writer who seeks to describe in

measured sentences as precisely as possible the imprecise
flow of life as it has moved through her and all around
her."

40 GRAY, PAUL. "An Unfinished Woman." Time, 107 (10 May), 83.
       Review of Scoundrel Time. The book is a memorable por-
    trait of "a polished stylist and an invaluable American."
    Its understated anger is unforgettable but its absolutism
    and "inference that Hellman alone had a monopoly on con-
    science" are not entirely attractive.

41 GREEN, STANLEY. Encyclopedia of the Musical Theatre. New
       York: Dodd, Mead and Company, pp. 58-60, 479, 485.
       Gives production history and outline of Candide. Also
    cites recordings of Candide and Regina in the Discography.

42 GUSSOW, MEL. "Dour Autumn Garden at Long Wharf." New York
       Times (16 November), p. 52.
       Reviews production of The Autumn Garden at the Long
    Wharf Theater, New Haven, Connecticut. The play's atmo-
    sphere "is too acerbic to be Chekhovian"; Hellman's fun-
    niest, sharpest dialogue is present here. But "cleverness
    abounds, much of it arising from character, some of it
    superimposed as if the author wanted to distribute the
    verbal wealth evenly." Hellman should have trusted her
    characters more and been less concerned with traditions of
    dramaturgy. "Can such sad, useless people have so many in-
    sights into their own behavior?" But The Autumn Garden
    still reminds one of Hellman's urbanity and incisiveness
    and it is receiving a "faultless revival."

43 HARTNETT, ROBERT C. Review of Scoundrel Time. America, 135
       (4 September), 102-104.
       Compares Scoundrel Time to another book under review,
    Men against McCarthy, by Richard M. Fried. Finds Hellman
    somewhat one-sided and insufficiently specific in her
    criticism of liberal intellectuals. "Her purpose is self-
    revelation."

44 HERSEY, JOHN. "Lillian Hellman." New Republic, 175 (18
       September), 25-27.
       Witty homage to Hellman, written on the occasion of her
    receiving the MacDowell prize. Drawing of Hellman by Jack
    Coughlin.
       Reprinted in The Conscious Reader, ed. Caroline Shrodes,
    Harry Finestone, and Michael Shugrue. Second edition. New
    York: Macmillan, 1978, pp. 501-505. Also excerpted in the

1976

> Boston Sunday Globe, with introductory remarks about
> Hellman, 5 September 1976.

45 HIGGINS, AIDAN. "Blacklist." Hibernia (3 December), p. 19.
   Reviews Scoundrel Time upon its publication in England
   by Macmillan. Higgins severely criticizes the book as a
   "brief, heavily-laden diatribe" written in "sometimes
   turbulent syntax" by Hellman, a "disenchanted radical."
   Lillian Hellman "strikes me as being an egoarch, like
   Arthur Miller, another inferior playwright of leftish per-
   suasion."

46 HOGENKAMP, BERT. "Film and the Workers' Movement in Britain,
   1929-39." Sight and Sound, 45 (Spring), 68-76.
   Brief reference to The Spanish Earth.

47 HOMER, FRANK X. J. Review of Scoundrel Time. America, 135
   (13 November), 336.
   Brief comments on Scoundrel Time, in a round-up of new
   biographies. Says Hellman's feeling of betrayal by friends
   and associates gives the book a "compelling personal quality."

48 HOWARD, MAUREEN. Review of Literary Women by Ellen Moers.
   New York Times Books Review (7 March), p. 6.
   Criticizes the enlistment of Hellman and other female
   writers in Moers's argument that women writers are more
   concerned with money than men.

49 _____. Review of Scoundrel Time. New York Times Book Review
   (25 April), pp. 1-2.
   Considers Scoundrel Time a compelling and "beautiful
   work of self-definition," told with the rhetorical directness of Thoreau at the beginning of Walden, yet finally
   comparable to the tradition of a fine moral essay, exemplified by Emerson's "The American Scholar." Hellman "has
   forged a remarkable autobiographical style which relates
   the emotionally charged moment to a wide cultural reference.
   The precedent for Scoundrel Time is 'Julia,' the resonant
   story in Pentimento of a girlhood friendship, which seems
   to extend itself almost effortlessly as we read it." The
   past--"then"--is skillfully told, "but the 'now,' the
   alert, tough mind of Lillian Hellman watching herself, is
   what gives life to her story."

50 HOWE, IRVING. "Lillian Hellman and the McCarthy Years."
   Dissent, 23 (Fall), 378-82.

Alleges that Hellman distorts and misrepresents facts in Scoundrel Time. Howe accuses Hellman of pro-Russian bias, of assuming "the existence of a unified body of intellectuals, all holding the same views about Communism" and McCarthyism, and of clinging to "fragments of old dogmas that, at other and more lucid moments, she knows she should have given up long ago." Hellman's charge that positions taken by the anti-Stalinist intellectuals were later perverted into the Vietnam War and the Nixon presidency is "preposterous"; yet nothing in Scoundrel Time "is as false and . . . vulgar as the Introduction Garry Wills has written for it."
Reprinted 1979.18.

*51 HUGHES, CATHERINE. American Playwrights, 1945-75. London: Pitman, 114 pp.
Cited in Charles A. Carpenter, "Modern Drama Studies: An Annual Bibliography." Modern Drama, 20 (June 1977), 174.

52 HUNT, DAVID. "Clean Conscience." The Listener, 96 (18 November), 656.
Reviews Scoundrel Time. Although Hellman assumes too much knowledge on the part of her readers, it is a moving story. "The abiding impression that remains is of the warmth and endurance of Lillian Hellman in her ordeal."

53 KAEL, PAULINE. "Humanoids and Androgynes," in her Reeling. Boston and Toronto: Little, Brown and Company, pp. 216-22.
Reprint of 1973.35.

54 KAUFFMANN, STANLEY. Persons of the Drama. New York: Harper and Row, pp. 263-66.
Reprint of 1974.28.

55 KELLOGG, MARY ALICE. "Newsmakers." Newsweek, 88 (11 October), 52-53.
Brief report on the Hellman-Diana Trilling contretemps over the publication of Trilling's We Must March My Darlings.

56 KEMPTON, MURRAY. "Witnesses." New York Review of Books, 23 (10 June), 22-25.
Review of Scoundrel Time. Kempton praises Hellman for "her summit," her stand before the House Un-American Activities Committee as reported in this memoir, but faults her rancor toward those who did not share her opinions. He suggests that her recollections are not always "true," for all her "honesty" as a witness in 1952, and criticizes the

1976

inadequacy of her treatment of such matters as the 1949
Cultural and Scientific Conference for World Peace at the
Waldorf-Astoria and the Wallace campaign. Includes a
caricature of Hellman by David Levine.

57 KERR, WALTER. "This 'Garden' Is Nearly Perfect." New York
    Times (28 November), section 2, pp. 3, 42.
        The Autumn Garden, in an "exquisite revival by the Long
    Wharf Theatre in New Haven," emerges as one of Hellman's
    best plays. A study of middle life, this production mutes
    the melodramatic third act device that marred the other-
    wise engaging 1951 performance. See 1979.21.

58 KING, KIMBALL. "The Works of Lillian Hellman." Cassette
    Curriculum. DeLand, Florida: Everett/Edwards, Inc.
        Audio cassette lecture surveys Hellman's plays and first
    two memoirs. Suggests that blackmail operates as a meta-
    phor for power in the plays. Available from Everett/
    Edwards, P.O. Box 1060, DeLand, Florida 32720.

59 KISSEL, HOWARD. "Lillian Hellman: Survival and the McCarthy
    Era." Women's Wear Daily (5 November), p. 28.
        Interview with photos.

60 KLEMESRUD, JUDY. "Lillian Hellman Denies Role in Book Rejec-
    tion." New York Times (29 September), p. C28.
        Hellman denies playing any role in the decision by
    Little, Brown not to publish Diana Trilling's book con-
    taining "several passages critical of Miss Hellman."

61 KOWALSKI, ROSEMARY R. Women and Film: A Bibliography.
    Metuchen, N.J.: Scarecrow Press, pp. 91-92, 130.
        Lists Enser, Filmed Books and Plays (1968.7) and the
    script of The North Star (New York: Viking, 1943).

62 KRAMER, HILTON. "The Blacklist and the Cold War." New York
    Times (3 October), section 2, pp. 1, 16-17.
        Criticizes Hellman's version of the McCarthy years ex-
    pressed in Scoundrel Time. Alleges that Hellman ignored
    the sins of the Stalinist regime. "Sitting through The
    Front and Hollywood on Trial [films] and turning the pages
    of Scoundrel Time and reading the endless reviews that
    lavished it with so much praise, one is haunted by the
    question once posed, albeit in another context, by William
    Hazlitt: 'Were we fools then, or are we dishonest now?'"

63 KREBS, ALBIN. "Notes on People." New York Times (30 June), p. 34.
   Reports the naming of Hellman as recipient of the Edward MacDowell Medal for outstanding contributions to literature.

64 ____. "Notes on People." New York Times (6 October), p. 40.
   Reports the naming of Hellman as recipient of the Actors' Equity Association's third annual Paul Robeson award.

65 ____. "Notes on People." New York Times (9 October), p. 25.
   Includes announcement that Harcourt Brace Jovanovich will publish Diana Trilling's We Must March My Darlings (incorrectly cited as We Must Watch My Darlings), after Little, Brown, objecting to passages critical of Hellman, refused to publish the book.

66 LEHMANN-HAUPT, CHRISTOPHER. "Books of the Times." New York Times (30 July), p. C19.
   Brief recommendation of Scoundrel Time as "a clear-eyed, pithily written account."

67 ____. "Going One's Own Way." New York Times (15 April), p. 31.
   Praises Scoundrel Time as a "meditation on Miss Hellman's self--wry, ironic, not quite apologetic but close to it, suffused with that curious combination of diffidence and determination we have come to know from her earlier autobiographical writings." Garry Wills's revisionist introduction throws the book somewhat off-kilter.

68 LEONARD, JOHN. "Critic's Notebook: An Evening with 2 Walking Anachronisms." New York Times (26 May), p. 24.
   Discusses Hellman, Scoundrel Time, and other matters. Says "her sense of the nature of guilt is Augustinian." Compares Hellman to Ross MacDonald, who, in his novels, also "has set up literary housekeeping in the discrepancy between what 'ought to be' and the 'not doing' of it."

69 LEWIS, JEREMY. "Memoirs: All the Better to Know You With." The Times [London] (18 November), p. 11.
   Reviews Scoundrel Time along with the memoirs of Tennessee Williams and others. Considers it an impressive, though brief, account.

70 McCABE, CAROL. "Hellman Before HUAC: There Was a Catch in It." Providence [Rhode Island] Sunday Journal (9 May), p. H38.

1976

> Reviews <u>Scoundrel Time</u>. Its primary virtue is its "im-
> mediacy, its personal point of view." The book is "all
> readable, if a bit annoying for its elite tone."

71 McCARTHY, MARY. "Mary McCarthy Goes to the Movies." <u>Film
Comment</u>, 12 (January-February), 32-34.
> Discusses Hollywood propaganda films of World War II,
> including <u>The North Star</u>.
> Reprinted from <u>Town and Country</u>, 1944.

72 McFADDEN, ROBERT D. "Diana Trilling Book is Canceled; Reply
to Lillian Hellman Is Cited." <u>New York Times</u> (28
September), pp. 1, 46.
> Report of Little, Brown's refusal to publish a book by
> Diana Trilling, allegedly critical of Hellman in its
> response to charges made in <u>Scoundrel Time</u>. Photo.

73 McGILL, RAYMOND, ed. <u>Notable Names in the American Theatre</u>.
Foreword by Paul Myers. Clifton, N.J.: James T. White and
Co., p. 815.
> "New and revised edition" of <u>The Biographical Encyclo-
> paedia and Who's Who of the American Theatre</u>, ed. Walter
> Rigdon, 1966. Biographical information, TV appearances,
> teaching activity, awards: through 1973.

74 McPHERSON, MICHAEL. "Lillian Hellman and Her Critics."
Ph.D. dissertation, University of Denver.
> Analyzes critics' reactions to Hellman's eight original
> plays. Contains a thorough list of reviews of Hellman
> productions but the text relies somewhat heavily on quota-
> tions from the critics. <u>Dissertation Abstracts Interna-
> tional</u>, 37:3989A.

75 McWILLIAMS, CAREY. "Time Is the Scoundrel." <u>Nation</u>, 222 (19
June), 741-42.
> Chides Hellman for not mentioning in <u>Scoundrel Time</u> the
> anti-McCarthy position of the <u>Nation</u>.

76 MALOFF, SAUL. "Jewel without Price." <u>Commonweal</u>, 103 (1
July), 438-42.
> Analyzes <u>Scoundrel Time</u> and the McCarthy era. This book
> and the two preceding Hellman memoirs comprise "the finest
> work of a distinguished career and a notable work of auto-
> biography by the most exacting standards; and though one
> hopes she goes on writing her memoirs, to the end of the
> century and beyond, this volume has the feel of an ending,
> not because she has exhausted her life as material for art
> or memoir . . . but because the climactic event is the one

for which the others have been clearing a space all along--
the obligatory scene in the drama of her life: the moral
test and proving-ground."

77 MARCUS, GREIL. "Remembering the Witch Hunts." Rolling Stone
    (20 May), 97.
        Scoundrel Time review. Recommends the book but resents
    Hellman's "condescension to the rest of the world" and
    Garry Wills's introduction.

78 MARX, ARTHUR. Goldwyn. New York: Norton, 376 pp., passim.
        Contains numerous references to Hellman's relationship
    with Goldwyn and the films she wrote for his studio.

79 MAYNE, RICHARD. "Ishmael and the Inquisitors." Times
    Literary Supplement (12 November), p. 1413.
        Review of Scoundrel Time. The book "is a tainted sand-
    wich--one slice of inner life between two layers of bad
    history [introduction by Garry Wills and one added for the
    English edition, by James Cameron]." Hellman gives the
    false impression that only she and a few others stood up
    against McCarthyism. The form of Scoundrel Time "reflects
    its uneasy nature. Musing, ruminating, it ranges to and
    fro with no very obvious time-scale, interspersing its
    reflections with extracts from Miss Hellman's diary. In
    this way it manages to be more than either a gloss or a
    narrative, although the drama of the story is gripping
    enough."

80 _____. Letter to the Editor. Times Literary Supplement (10
    December), p. 1560.
        Reply to criticisms (TLS, 3 December) of Mayne's review
    of Scoundrel Time (TLS, 12 November). See 1976.79 and
    1976.103.

81 MEE, CHARLES L., JR. "A Woman of Courage." Horizon, 18
    (Summer), 104-105.
        An appreciation of Scoundrel Time and, especially, of
    Hellman for her stand against McCarthyism.

82 MOERS, ELLEN. Literary Women. New York: Doubleday and
    Company, pp. xvi, 77-78, 293.
        Suggests that Hellman's persistent concern with money
    in her plays is characteristic of certain women writers.
    "The presence of money contributes a crackling realism to
    her family melodramas." Includes a list of the plays and
    memoirs to 1973, with the curious omission of The Autumn
    Garden.

1976

83 MOOREHEAD, CAROLINE. "A Witch-Hunt Survivor with Unfashion-
    able Conscience Still Intact." The Times [London] (3
    December), p. 18.
        Interview with Hellman in London. Emphasizes Scoundrel
    Time and its background. Moorehead considers it a "politi-
    cally fuzzy" account, but probably the most evocative por-
    trayal of the McCarthy era, from which Hellman emerges as a
    "discreet and dignified heroine." Hellman discusses
    student movements and her inability to adjust quickly to
    new patterns in her life.

84 MYERS, CAROL FAIRBANKS. Women in Literature: Criticism of the
    Seventies. Metuchen, N.J.: Scarecrow Press, pp. 88-89.
        Lists thirteen items related to Hellman (dissertations,
    articles, etc.).

85 NICOLL, ALLARDYCE. World Drama: From Aeschylus to Anouilh.
    Revised edition. New York: Harper and Row, pp. 704-705.
        Revised edition of 1949.61. No change in Hellman
    material.

86 NYREN, DOROTHY, MAURICE KRAMER, and ELAINE FIALKA KRAMER,
    comps. and eds. A Library of Literary Criticism: Modern
    American Literature. Vol. 4. Supplement to the fourth
    edition. New York: Ungar, pp. 221-22.
        Includes brief extracts from three articles on An
    Unfinished Woman and Pentimento: Spacks, 1972.36; Schorer,
    1973.53; and Walt, 1973.66. See also Dorothy Nyren Curley,
    1969.16.

*87 OLAUSSON, JUDITH L. B. "Representative American Women Play-
    wrights, 1930-1970; and a Study of Their Characters."
    Ph.D. dissertation, University of Utah.
        Dissertation Abstracts International, 37:3989-90A.

88 P.[HILLIPS], W.[ILLIAM]. "What Happened in the Fifties."
    Partisan Review, 43 (Number 3), 337-40.
        Answers Hellman's charges in Scoundrel Time that
    Partisan Review failed to take an editorial stand against
    Joseph McCarthy and to defend Americans defamed or jailed
    as a result of his attacks. Phillips claims that some of
    these people were, in fact, Communists "and what one was
    asked to defend was their right to lie about it." He
    accuses Hellman of not defending "those who had been killed
    or defamed by the Communists." She has also remained
    silent, he says, about "the persecution of writers in
    Russia" and Russian anti-Semitism. "Perhaps . . . she does
    not distinguish sufficiently between the anti-Communism of

the Right and the anti-Communism of the Left." Phillips
concludes his essay by criticizing Garry Wills's Introduction to Scoundrel Time as "pop revisionist history."

89 ROEDER, BILL. "Newsmakers." Newsweek, 88 (1 November), 60-
    61.
        Mentions Hellman's advertisement for Blackglama minks.
    Photo. See 1976.2.

90 SALEM, JAMES M. A Guide to Critical Reviews: Part II: The
    Musical, 1909-1974. Second edition. Metuchen, N.J.:
    Scarecrow Press, pp. 69, 266, 408-409.
        Lists reviews of Candide and Regina.

91 SAMPLES, GORDON. How to Locate Reviews of Plays and Films: A
    Bibliography of Criticism from the Beginnings to the
    Present. Metuchen, N.J.: Scarecrow Press, 124 pp.
        Useful volume for identifying likely locations of
    Hellman reviews.

92 SARRIS, ANDREW. "Revivals." Village Voice, 21 (2 February),
    117.
        Comments on The North Star on the occasion of its New
    York showing in the original, blacklisted version. Says
    there's actually more Marxist propaganda in The Little
    Foxes than in The North Star.

93 SCHLESINGER, ARTHUR, JR., ALFRED KAZIN, ARLENE CROCE, BRUCE
    COOK, HILTON KRAMER, et al. Letters to the Editor. New
    York Times (17 October), section 2, pp. 12, 28.
        Varying responses to Hilton Kramer's criticism of
    Hellman and others in "The Blacklist and the Cold War,"
    New York Times (3 October). Reply to the letters by
    Kramer, who states: "Like the authors of The Front,
    Hollywood on Trial and Scoundrel Time the revisionists
    still cannot bring themselves to face a simple fact:
    without Stalinism there would have been no McCarthyism and
    no black list." See 1976.62.

94 SCHULTHEISS, JOHN. "George Jean Nathan and the Dramatist in
    Hollywood." Literature/Film Quarterly, 4 (Winter), 13-27.
        Considers Hellman one of several major dramatists who
    "produced work of significance in both theatre and film."
    Such dramatists of superior stature were not devoured by
    Hollywood.

95 SHENKER, ISRAEL. "Rhetoric of Democrats in 1976 Leans Heavily
    on Unity and God." New York Times (16 July), p. 15.

Quotes Hellman on the political rhetoric of the Democratic National Convention.

96 SHERRILL, ROBERT. "Books and the Arts: Wisdom and Its Price." Nation, 222 (19 June), 757-58.
    Praises Hellman for her behavior during and following the McCarthy years and for her "sense of humor and a miraculous sense of perspective," displayed in Scoundrel Time. The book contains very little bitterness. Supports Hellman's criticism of Commentary magazine which, says Sherrill, "tacitly endorsed the McCarthy efforts at the time." Scoundrel Time does well at reminding us "that people we assume to be allies can turn out to be treacherous indeed."

97 SPACKS, PATRICIA MEYER. The Female Imagination. New York: Avon Books, pp. 1, 380-402, 409, 411.
    Reprint of 1975.48.

98 STEVENS, GEORGE, JR. "The Test of Time: William Wyler." American Film, 1, no. 6 (April), 4.
    Introduction to special issue, honoring Wyler. Brief mention of Wyler's association with Hellman.

99 SWINDELL, LARRY. "William Wyler: A Life in Film." American Film, 1, no. 6 (April), 7-27.
    Comprehensive appreciation of film director William Wyler's career, in honor of his Life Achievement Award from the American Film Institute. Discusses the screen adaptations of Dead End and The Little Foxes and the two versions of The Children's Hour, all directed by Wyler. Includes a tribute to Wyler by Hellman, in which she credits him with having taught her what she knows about movies. Stills from Dead End and The Little Foxes.

100 SYMONS, JULIAN. Letter to the Editor. Times Literary Supplement (17 December), p. 1586.
    Objects to Richard Mayne's review of Scoundrel Time, TLS, 12 November. See 1976.79.

101 TARBERT, GARY, ed. Book Review Index 1975. Vol. 11. Detroit: Gale Research Company, p. 223.
    Lists one review each of Pentimento and An Unfinished Woman.

102 TRAVERS, MARY. Review of Scoundrel Time. San Francisco, 18 (July), 92-93.
    Positive reaction with reservations.

103 TRILLING, DIANA, A. D. MACLEAN, and OTTO NATHAN. Letters to
     the Editor. Times Literary Supplement (3 December), p.
     1516.
         Responses to Richard Mayne's review of Scoundrel Time,
     TLS, 12 November. See 1976.79.

104 WEBER, OLGA S., ed. Literary and Library Prizes. Ninth
     edition. New York: R. R. Bowker Company, pp. 49, 159, 163,
     325, 326.
         Lists awards won by Hellman.

105 WEINRAUB, JUDITH. "Two Feisty Feminists Filming Hellman's
     Pentimento." New York Times (31 October), section 2, p.
     17.
         Feature story on the filming of Julia. Quotes Jane
     Fonda and Vanessa Redgrave, who play Hellman and Julia,
     and Fred Zinnemann, the director, on the screenplay, the
     original story, and Hellman.

*106 WIESNER, JEROME. "In Celebration of Lillian Hellman: Origins
     of the CPJ." CPJ Newsletter (Spring), p. 4.
         An appreciation of Hellman's role in founding the
     Committee for Public Justice. Cited by Doris Falk in
     Lillian Hellman (New York: Ungar, 1978), pp. 24, 159. See
     1978.27.

107 WILLS, GARRY. "At the Waldorf." New York Review of Books,
     23 (24 June), 41.
         Letter to the editor in response to the Murray Kempton
     review of Scoundrel Time (10 June). See 1976.56.

108 _____. "Introduction," Scoundrel Time by Lillian Hellman.
     Boston and Toronto: Little, Brown and Company, pp. 3-34.
         A frequently ironic discussion of the social and politi-
     cal forces which paved the way for McCarthyism. Wills is
     particularly critical of leading American liberals and
     "ideologues" of all persuasions. He praises Hellman, who
     "was as little qualified to understand the Committee as it
     was to grasp her code of honor. . . . The ideologue's
     mentality is so foreign to her that she must explain
     fanaticism to herself as mere opportunism. In fact, the
     Red-hunters were so dangerous precisely because they con-
     sidered themselves saviors of the country from a diabolical
     plot." Although she has spent most of her life creating
     vivid stage characterizations, "the thought of a McCarthy
     intent on destroying whole classes and types of people is
     almost too horrible for her to contemplate."

1976

109 WOLFF, GEOFFREY. "The Find-Out Kick." New Times, 6 (30
       April), 64-65.
          Discusses the Hellman persona of the three memoirs.

110 WRATHER, BONITA GRANVILLE. Untitled Tribute to William
       Wyler. American Film, 1, no. 6 (April), 13.
          One of a number of tributes in a special section honor-
       ing Wyler; recalls the casting of Wrather by Wyler and
       Hellman as Mary Tilford in These Three, the 1934 film
       version of Children's Hour.

1977

1 ABRAHAMS, WILLIAM. Letter to the Editor. Times Literary
      Supplement (7 January), p. 13.
         Criticizes Richard Mayne's review of Scoundrel Time,
      his subsequent defense of that review, and Diana Trilling's
      letter on the review. (TLS: 12 November 1976; 10 December
      1976; 3 December 1976.) See 1976.79, 80, and 103.

2 ANON. "Fonda on Film." Films Incorporated's Chairman's
      Choice, 2, issue 1 (Fall), 7.
         Interview with Jane Fonda, emphasizing her role as
      Hellman in Julia. "It's the first time in my 30 films
      that I've ever had the opportunity to play a very intelli-
      gent woman, to be in a movie that is about the friendship
      between women: not neurotic, not homosexual, or anything
      like that, but just a deep, profound, abiding friendship."
      Full-page still of Fonda and Vanessa Redgrave from the
      film (p. 1). Films Incorporated, 1144 Wilmette Avenue,
      Wilmette, Illinois 60091.

3 ANON. Item. Time, 109 (11 April), 90.
         Brief mention of Hellman as a presenter at the 49th
      Academy Awards telecast.

4 ANON. "Lillian Hellman Gets Store's Award." New York Times
      (10 November), p. B16.
         Reports on formal dinner-dance in honor of Hellman's
      winning the Lord and Taylor Rose Award, given annually to
      "an outstanding individual whose creative mind has brought
      new beauty and deeper understanding into our lives."
      Photo.

5 ANON. "Michigan Opera to Revive Regina." New York Times (22
      September), p. 21.

Notes impending revival of Regina, infrequently performed, by the Michigan Opera Theater in Detroit. Gives
Regina's production history.

6 ANON. "New Musical among Six Shows Set for McCarter." New
York Times (7 September), p. C15.
Notes scheduled revival (March 1978) of Toys in the
Attic by the McCarter Theater Company, Princeton, New
Jersey.

7 ANON. "Non Fiction Reprints." Publishers Weekly, 211 (7
February), 94.
Announces paperback publication of Scoundrel Time.
Quotes PW's original assertion that the book is "an im-
portant document."

8 ANON. "Notes on Current Books: Scoundrel Time." Virginia
Quarterly Review, 53 (Winter), 28.
Brief comments on Scoundrel Time. Calls Hellman "a
brilliant playwright and courageous friend. . . . Her
bitterness toward those who knuckled still rankles."

9 ANON. "Noting the 'r' in October, Lillian Hellman Hosts a
Bash at the Oyster Bar." People Weekly, 8 (17 October),
44.
Society item. Photos.

*10 ANON. "Pentimento: Was Character Political or Imaginary?"
The Sunday Times [London] (6 November), 35.
Cited in The Times Index (November 1977), p. 68.

11 ANON. "People Picks and Pans." People Weekly, 8 (10
October), 22.
Brief review of Julia. Considers the film haunting but
uneven. Julia is "a breakthrough film, for once pitting
two strong women against each other in the leads instead
of a macho Newman-Redford bonding. It already has the
smell of Oscars."

12 ANON. Photo from Julia. Sight and Sound, 46 (Winter 1976/
77), p. 25.
Photo of Fred Zinnemann directing a scene from Julia.

*13 ANON. Review of Julia. Macleans, 90 (17 October), 76.
Cited in The Magazine Index, which says the review rates
Julia as an "A" film.

1977

*14   ANON. Review of Julia. Texas Monthly, 5 (November), 156-58.
      Cited in Access, The Supplementary Index to Periodicals,
      1977.

15   ANON. "Show Business: Growing Fonda of Jane." Time, 110 (3
      October), 90-91.
           Interview with Jane Fonda prior to the release of Julia.
      Included are her comments on Hellman and the film. Photo
      of Fonda as Hellman.

16   ANON. "Writers' Writers." New York Times Book Review (4
      December), pp. 3, 58, 62, 66, 70, 74.
           Compendium of opinions by well-known writers who identi-
      fy their own favorite writers. Hellman cites Thomas
      Pynchon as potentially "our best novelist since Faulkner"
      and Christina Stead as deserving of the Nobel Prize for
      literature (pp. 3, 58).

*17   BARBOUR, JOHN. Review of Julia. Los Angeles, 22 (November),
      242+.
           Cited in Access, The Supplementary Index to Periodicals.

18   BLAKE, PATRICIA. "Self-Destruct History." Time, 109 (13
      June), 98-99.
           Reviews We Must March My Darlings by Diana Trilling.
      Discusses Trilling's objections to some of Hellman's
      assertions in Scoundrel Time.

19   BLAKE, RICHARD. "Women: Friends to Each Other." America, 137
      (22 October), 268-69.
           Considers Julia a disappointment. The Lilly of the film
      is perhaps a "reflection of the current Hellman cult." Too
      much attention is paid to Hellman and not enough to Julia.

20   BLAU, ELEANOR. "Blitzstein's Regina Revived in Church." New
      York Times (25 February), p. 19.
           Discusses Regina, newly revived by the Bel Canto Opera,
      in relation to The Little Foxes.

21   BOGARD, TRAVIS, RICHARD MOODY, and WALTER MESERVE. The Revels
      History of Drama in English. Volume VIII. American Drama.
      London: Methuen; New York: Barnes and Noble, pp. 51, 55,
      56, 58, 61, 63, 131, 251-52, 275, 276.
           Generally brief but often interesting references to
      Hellman's plays. Refers to Regina Giddens as one of many
      "destroying mothers" in American drama. Compares Arthur
      Miller's dialogue to Hellman's. Considers Hellman "a tra-
      ditionalist in form" who was part of the "New American

Drama" that began with Sydney Howard in 1924--"that main-
stream of Ibsen-inspired, realistic social drama which
provided the bulk of theatre fare between the World Wars."
In Toys in the Attic, Hellman is again the "moralist and
melodramatist," concerned with social evils and "the
destruction which may result from the unfulfilled dreams
of the desperately lonely and from the innocent who fall
in love with truth."

22 BRÜNING, EBERHARD, KLAUS KÖHLER, and BERNHARD SCHELLER.
    Studien zum amerikanischen Drama nach dem zweiten Welt-
    krieg. Berlin: Rütten and Loening, pp. 42, 230, 243, 266,
    268, 296.
        Hellman references, particularly to The Autumn Garden.

23 BUCKLEY, WILLIAM F., JR. "Night of the Cuckoo." National
    Review, 29 (29 April), 513.
        Attacks Hellman and Scoundrel Time. "The difference
    between Lillian Hellman and Albert Speer is that Albert
    Speer repented his professional service in behalf of
    totalitarianism in two considerable books, while Lillian
    Hellman's apology for her generation-long unpaid defense
    of Stalinism is discharged in a formalistic sentence in her
    book, otherwise devoted to vilifying every American,
    liberal or conservative, who attempted to tell the truth
    about the hideousness of the Soviet regime. Would Albert
    Speer have got a standing ovation in Hollywood [at the
    1977 Oscar Awards ceremony]?"

24 _____. "Scoundrel Time: & Who Is the Ugliest of Them All?"
    National Review, 29 (21 January), 101-106.
        Condemns Scoundrel Time, Hellman, and Garry Wills's
    introduction. Buckley denounces Scoundrel Time as unreli-
    able history, an "awful book" of which Hellman should be
    ashamed. "What does one go on to say about a book so dis-
    orderly, so tasteless, guileful, self-enraptured? The
    disposition to adore her, feel sorry for her, glow in the
    vicarious thrill of her courage and decency . . . runs into
    hurdle after hurdle in the obstacle course of this little
    book." Buckley also criticizes Hellman for failing to
    sever relations with Little, Brown after its refusal to
    publish Diana Trilling's book because she refused "to alter
    an essay on Miss Hellman in her manuscript."

25 CANBY, VINCENT. "Julia Tries to Define Friendship." New
    York Times (3 October), p. 40.
        Review of the film adaptation of the "Julia" segment of
    Pentimento criticizes the dependence upon continual

flashback interruption of present action. The story has
been amplified to create a film that is finally "well-
meaning and on the side of the angels but with the exception of a half-dozen scenes, lifeless." Included are
several good, tough scenes between Hellman (Jane Fonda)
and Hammett (Jason Robards) that make one wish the film
had stressed that relationship instead of the one between
Hellman and Julia.

26 _____. "The New Hollywood Is Old Hat." New York Times (23
October), section 2, pp. 13, 16.
A Sunday survey of new films, including Julia, which
Canby calls "an eight-by-10 glossy enlargement of Lillian
Hellman's short story." Although the acting is outstand-
ing, the movie "embalms Miss Hellman's anger and self-
searching in the righteous attitudes of important, expen-
sive filmmaking." Photo of Jane Fonda as Hellman.

27 CERF, BENNETT. At Random. New York: Random House, pp. 31,
36, 110.
Reminiscences. Brief references to Hellman.

28 CHICOREL, MARIETTA, ed. Chicorel Theater Index to Plays in
Anthologies and Collections, 1970-1976. New York:
Chicorel Library Publishing Corporation, pp. 157-58.
Lists Hellman plays in anthologies.

29 COE, RICHARD L. "The Importance of Being Lillian: A Hellman
Mini-Festival." Washington Post (20 February), p. K3.
Discusses Hellman's plays, especially The Autumn Garden
and Toys in the Attic, in connection with their respective
productions by the Arena Stage and the Baltimore Stage.
Says both plays are linked by Hellman's concept of love
and by her girlhood memories of her Louisiana family. She
is "the cautious dramatist who veils her heart with her
mind."

30 CORLISS, RICHARD. "Movies: In Fall a Filmmaker's Fancy Turns
to Love." New Times, 9 (14 October), 82-83.
Reviews several films, including Julia. Says the film
is "botched," with too much of its time taken up "with
Lillian the budding playwright. . . . You shouldn't come
out of a story about a death-defying platonic love thinking, 'My, wasn't it pretty!' Lillian and Julia--and Fonda
and Redgrave--deserved better."

31 CRIPPS, THOMAS. Slow Fade to Black: The Negro in American
      Film, 1900-1942. New York: Oxford University Press, pp.
      304, 368-70, 373.
          Calls The Little Foxes a "self-consciously liberal"
      vehicle which relegates blacks to the function of "mere
      atmosphere and chorus." References to characters in the
      film appear somewhat confused. Photo from the film (p.
      369).
          Also issued in 1977 in a paperback edition (London,
      Oxford, and New York: Oxford University Press, same page
      references).

32 CRIST, JUDITH. Review of Julia. New York Post (3 October).
          Applauds Julia as a triumph on every level. A compari-
      son with the film's source in Pentimento reveals "how a
      film can indeed translate the heart of a literary matter
      into cinematic terms. This one does honor to both media."

33 DOUDNA, CHRISTINE. "A Still Unfinished Woman: A Conversation
      with Lillian Hellman." Rolling Stone, no. 233 (24
      February), pp. 52-57.
          Interview during July 4th weekend, 1976, on Martha's
      Vineyard. Hellman discusses her writing methods, her
      family's role in The Little Foxes, the filming of Julia,
      her relationships with Dashiell Hammett and Dorothy Parker,
      the feminist movement and its literature and language.
      Photos.

34 DRABBLE, MARGARET. "Jane Fonda: Her Own Woman at Last?"
      Ms., 6 (October), 51-53, 88-89.
          Interview with Jane Fonda on location for the filming
      of Julia; contains numerous references to the film and to
      Fonda's role as Hellman.

35 DREW, BERNARD. "Woody Allen Is Feeling Better." American
      Film, 2, no. 7 (May), 10-15.
          Brief mention of Hellman is made by Allen during an
      interview which analyzes his humor.

36 DUNNING, JENNIFER. "Valentino and Julia Bring Stars Out in
      the Rain." New York Times (3 October), p. 26.
          Describes a screening party of Julia to benefit the
      Committee for Public Justice, a group founded by Hellman
      "to act as a citizens' early-warning system against threats
      to constitutional rights." Photo.

1977

37   EDWARDS, THOMAS R.   Review of We Must March My Darlings by
      Diana Trilling.   New York Times Book Review (29 May), pp.
      1, 17.
           Discusses the controversy between Hellman and Diana
      Trilling, sparked by Hellman's comments in Scoundrel Time
      and Trilling's response in We Must March My Darlings.
      Edwards says that Trilling "is very severe with Hellman,"
      whose own "response to persecution [was] so humanely ad-
      mirable."   Hellman's words about the Trillings in Scoundrel
      Time were "mild enough."   Drawing of Hellman.

*38 ENGLE, GARY.   Review of Julia.   Cleveland, 6 (December), 219+.
           Cited in Access, The Supplementary Index to Periodicals,
      1978.

39   ESSLIN, MARTIN, general ed.   Encyclopedia of World Theatre.
      New York: Scribner's, pp. 138-39.
           Brief entry on Hellman (p. 138) surveys her career to
      An Unfinished Woman.   Photo of Tallulah Bankhead as Regina
      Giddens in The Little Foxes (p. 139).   Also cites titles
      of Hellman's plays, passim.

40   EVANS, GARETH LLOYD.   The Language of Modern Drama.   London,
      Melbourne, and Toronto: J. M. Dent and Sons; Totowa, N.J.:
      Rowman and Littlefield, p. 17.
           Fleeting reference to Hellman as a practitioner of the
      well-made play.

41   FALB, LEWIS W.   Jean Anouilh.   New York: Frederick Ungar,
      p. 113.
           Brief comments on Hellman's adaptation of The Lark.

42   FALK, RICHARD A.   "Comment: Scoundrel Time: Mobilizing the
      American Intelligentsia for the Cold War."   Performing
      Arts Journal, 1 (Winter), 97-102.
           Discusses the denunciations of Scoundrel Time by "the
      anti-Communist wing of the New York intellectual establish-
      ment."   Falk sides with Hellman in the controversy and
      shares her view, expressed in Scoundrel Time, that "the
      ambivalent response to McCarthyism on the part of anti-
      Communist liberals" led to "the full excesses of cold war
      diplomacy" and, eventually, American involvement in
      Vietnam.   Scoundrel Time is a book to be read carefully:
      Hellman, like Solzhenitsyn, "is warning us that we risk
      everything by risking too little."

43 FARBER, STEPHEN. Review of <u>Julia</u>. <u>New West</u>, 2 (10 October),
      81-82.
        Generally critical review.

44 FELDMAN, SYLVIA. Review of <u>Julia</u>. <u>Human Behavior</u>, 6
      (December), 81.
        Very favorable review.

45 FERRIS, SUSAN. "The Making of <u>Julia</u>." <u>Horizon</u>, 20 (October),
      86, 88-90.
        Discussion of <u>Julia</u>'s evolution from memoir to film
      (changes in script, process of casting and shooting). The
      film tends to soften the Hellman personality, partly be-
      cause it is always difficult to portray a writer on film.
      The "sensitive Lillian Hellman who wrote <u>The Children's
      Hour</u> . . . never comes through. Nor does the Lillian
      Hellman of <u>The Little Foxes</u>, with its scorn for the
      hypocrisy and pretense of a southern landed family." But
      the script is always literate and probable and the beauti-
      fully portrayed relationships between Hellman and Julia
      and Hellman and Hammett "add up to a haunting film."

46 FRENCH, PHILIP. Review of <u>Julia</u>. <u>Sight and Sound</u>, 47
      (Winter 1977-78), 53-54.
        Criticizes Hellman and <u>Julia</u>, a film which "sets the
      capstone on the process by which Lillian Hellman has been
      transformed from a minor radical author into a major
      cultural monument." What this film provides "is not an
      image of reality, but sentimentalised mythology, that for
      all its hardboiled posturing is a cosy apology for Lillian
      Hellman's life. The movie seeks to set aside forty years
      of agonising social and political history and replace it
      with nostalgic romantic melodrama." Everyone but Hellman
      and Hammett, who "is there to validate her art," is made
      to appear "irredeemably corrupt." What we know of Dashiell
      Hammett is largely what Hellman has created for us. "In
      the morality play that is her autobiographical trilogy he
      exists in the same imaginative dimension as Julia, who
      could quite easily be a projection of Miss Hellman's fan-
      tasies. In this reading Julia would be the beautiful
      playmate that every lonely child creates, who became the
      sacrificial victim of death and intolerance and insensi-
      tivity, her death indicting with equal vehemence America
      and Europe, and thus justifying Miss Hellman's otherwise
      unmotivated isolation and unfocused anger."

47 FRIEDMAN, SHARON P. "Feminist Concerns in the Works of Four
      Twentieth-Century American Women Dramatists: Susan

Glaspell, Rachel Crothers, Lillian Hellman and Lorraine
Hansberry." Ph.D. dissertation, New York University.
Applies feminist theory and traditional textual analysis
to the works of Hellman and others. Says she "demonstrates
the ways in which the social and economic powerlessness of
women may give rise to the most demonic behavior." But her
women are not stereotypes; "they are firmly rooted in their
circumstances as women." Dissertation Abstracts International, 39:858A.

48 FULLER, RICHARD. "Films: A Time for Heroines." Philadelphia
Magazine, 68 (December), 67-76.
Includes review of Julia. The film depends on self-
conscious photography and art work and the "overcalculated"
direction of Fred Zinnemann. "In Julia one is rarely
allowed to forget the craft. . . . And for me, the real
Hellman and real Hammett are too much with me to believe
in Fonda and Robards, good as they are." Fuller also reviewed Julia, according to Access, The Supplementary Index
to Periodicals, for Gold Coast Pictorial, 14 (December
1977), 18-22, and for St. Louis, 9 (December 1977), 35-42.

49 GASSNER, JOHN, and DUDLEY NICHOLS, eds. Best Film Plays 1943-
44. New York and London: Garland Publishing, Inc., pp. ix-
xx, 299-356.
Reprint of 1945.6 in the Garland Classics of Film
Literature series.

50 GELMIS, JOSEPH. "He Not Only Gets Older, but Better."
Minneapolis, Minn., Star Journal (7 October).
Syndicated column by Gelmis, of Newsday, on Fred
Zinnemann and his direction of Julia. Zinnemann is quoted
as saying that Hellman suggested Vanessa Redgrave for the
title role and that, on a scale of one to ten, she rates
the film a nine.

51 GEORGAKAS, DAN, and LENNY RUBENSTEIN. "Interview with Jane
Fonda," in Women and the Cinema: A Critical Anthology.
Edited by Karyn Kay and Gerald Peary. New York: E. P.
Dutton, pp. 292-99.
Abridged reprint of 1975.20.

52 GILLAM, RICHARD. "Intellectuals and Power." Center Magazine,
10 (May-June), 15-29.
Includes discussion of the Scoundrel Time controversy
(pp. 27-28). Gillam criticizes Nathan Glazer's "dolorous
tirade" against Hellman and Garry Wills in Commentary. See
1976.37.

53 GRAY, RICHARD. The Literature of Memory. Baltimore: Johns
      Hopkins University Press, p. 354.
        Lists three Hellman plays (Another Part of the Forest,
      The Little Foxes, and Toys in the Attic) in a bibliography
      of works about the South.

54 GREEN, MARC. "Lillian Hellman, Embellished for the Screen."
      Chronicle of Higher Education, 15 (7 November), 19.
        Suggests that cool critical response to Julia results
      from the inevitable reaction against "Hellman's growing
      legend" and from dismissal of Fred Zinnemann's style of
      direction as "middlebrow" and "passé." In fact, the film
      is commendable in its objective portrait of the Hellman
      persona, especially in its use of that persona as a foil
      to be contrasted with the nearly mythic Julia.

55 GUSSOW, MEL. Review of The New Women's Theatre by Honor
      Moore. New York Times (10 June), p. C25.
        Brief reference to Hellman.

56 HALIWELL, LESLIE. The Filmgoer's Companion. Sixth edition.
      New York: Hill and Wang, pp. 335, 439, 707.
        Brief entries for Hellman (incomplete list of her
      films), The Little Foxes ("admirable" screen adaptation),
      and These Three. Earlier editions: 1965, 1967, 1970, 1974,
      1976. Fourth edition, revised and enlarged, also published
      in paperback (New York: Avon, 1975).

57 _____. Halliwell's Film Guide. London: Granada Publishing,
      897 pp., passim.
        Surveys 8,000 English-language films, including several
      involving Hellman. Lists credits, with brief summaries
      and evaluative comments.

58 HARRIS, ROBERT R. "The Hollywood Connection." Book Views,
      1, no. 1 (September), 28-29.
        Roundup of books on which current television shows and
      movies are based. Mentions Julia and Pentimento. Photo
      of Jane Fonda as Hellman and Jason Robards as Hammett.

59 HASKELL, MOLLY. "On Not Seeing the Trees for the Forest."
      New York, 10 (10 October), 61-62.
        Reviews Julia. The film disappoints because we want to
      know everything about the Hellman-Julia relationship that
      the story left out but the emotional and political terrain
      remains unexplored. Julia, who "exercises a kind of moral
      blackmail," is ideal "as a Hellman heroine in a story that,
      like many of Hellman's own works, reveals its own

1977

> 'pentimento'--after a period of time, an ulterior or an-
> terior meaning suggests itself." The scenes depicting
> Hellman as writer are cliché-ridden. "Everyone in the
> film was no doubt transfixed by the presence of Hellman
> herself, fierce watchdog of her own memorial, but in
> treating the story as holy writ, they have come up with a
> film that has the virtues of neither fiction nor biography,
> that means nothing if we don't know who the characters are,
> and little more if we do."

60 HATCH, ROBERT. "Films." Nation, 225 (5 November), 475-76.
    Criticizes Julia as a film "gone sudsy." It attempts to
    tell three stories simultaneously, none with particular
    depth. Pentimento is a "highly personal" book that is a
    "solo flight--not to be attempted by a company, however
    competent and resourceful."

61 HERBERT, IAN, ed. Who's Who in the Theatre. Sixteenth edi-
    tion. Detroit: Gale Research Company, pp. 718-19.
    Concise biography of Hellman through 1976. Earlier edi-
    tions including Hellman are the eighth (1936) through
    fifteenth (1972).

62 HIGHAM, CHARLES. "Jane Fonda at 40." Us, 1, no. 14 (1
    November), 28-31.
    Review of Fonda's career, emphasizing her portrayal of
    Hellman in Julia. Includes comments by Fonda about Hellman
    and a photograph of the two of them.

63 HOOK, SIDNEY. "Lillian Hellman's Scoundrel Time." Encounter,
    48 (February), 82-91.
    Detailed attack on Scoundrel Time. Hook alleges that
    the book is a self-serving polemic which portrays a myth
    about Hellman's past "at the expense of truth, honour and
    common sense." He accuses Hellman of having conformed to
    "almost every twist and turn of the [Communist] Party
    line." Despite her claim that she knew little of politics,
    the internal evidence of Scoundrel Time and her explicit
    statement about her political education in an earlier book
    "make it extremely difficult to swallow her artful picture
    of herself as a rebel and a Bohemian not seriously
    interested in politics." Her attempt "to impugn the
    integrity of liberal anti-Communists like Lionel Trilling
    and others of his circle is an act of political obscenity."

64 HOWE, IRVING. Review of We Must March My Darlings by Diana
    Trilling. New Republic, 177, nos. 8 and 9 (20 and 27
    August), 31-33.
    In the Hellman-Trilling battle involving personal

histories and moral and political issues, "Mrs. Trilling is
largely right."

*65 JAHR, CLIFF. Review of Julia. Viva, 5 (December), 37.
     Cited in The Magazine Index, which states that the re-
     view approximates an "A-" rating.

 66 KAEL, PAULINE. "The Current Cinema: A Woman for All Seasons?"
     New Yorker, 53 (10 October), 94, 99-102.
     Review of Julia analyzes the Hellman persona at length,
     comparing the film's version to the one presented in the
     memoirs. Whatever we think or feel about the Hellman
     played by Jane Fonda "seems an intrusion on a life, yet an
     intrusion that has been contracted for by Lillian Hellman
     herself--perhaps unwittingly." The memoirs are more excit-
     ing than the plays, for they create "tension between what
     she's giving you and what she's withholding." Hellman's
     "Hemingway-Hammett stripped-down, hard-boiled writing"
     brings "thrift and plain American speech to a form of self-
     denial." The friendship between Hellman and Julia "is
     obviously the emotional basis--the original material--for
     The Children's Hour." The film has excellent performances,
     cinematography, and musical score but suffers from its own
     reserve; it is "romantic in such a studied way that it
     turns romanticism into a moral lesson." Its major faults
     result from "the decision to treat the story as literary
     history, as a drama of conscience . . . with Lillian
     Hellman herself as a legendary figure, and the relation-
     ships she has written about . . . assumed to be common
     knowledge. Pity the screenwriter impaled on the life of a
     living person."

 67 KAUFFMANN, STANLEY. "On Films: Julia." New Republic, 177 (15
     October), 32-33.
     Finds that the film adaptation of the Pentimento chapter
     never approaches the material's potentially tragic texture.
     Compares Julia with its source in some detail, noting the
     problem inherent in translating the Hellman "I" of the
     memoir into the Hellman (Jane Fonda) of the film. Finally
     views Julia as an undemanding, "lush filmic package" that
     contains some good elements, most notably the acting of
     Vanessa Redgrave as Julia and Jason Robards as Hammett.

 68 KAYE, PHYLLIS JOHNSON, ed. National Playwrights Directory.
     New York: Drama Book Specialists, pp. 135-36.
     Published under the auspices of the O'Neill Theatre
     Center, Waterford, Connecticut. Lists Hellman's work,
     awards, acting editions of her plays. Photo. Hellman's
     year of birth is cited erroneously as 1907, instead of
     1905.

1977

69 KAZIN, ALFRED. "The Legend of Lillian Hellman." Esquire, 88
       (August), 28, 30, 34.
           Discusses the Diana Trilling-Lillian Hellman controversy
       over Trilling's We Must March My Darlings. Says there is
       little to which Hellman could object in Trilling's book.
       Most of Kazin's essay analyzes Scoundrel Time and criti-
       cizes Hellman for her simplifications therein. That book
       appeals to a generation that has been led to believe that
       Hellman alone stood up against McCarthyism. In Scoundrel
       Time, "historically a fraud," she is easy on Hammett and
       she is easy on herself, but "exquisitely nasty" to those
       who disagree with her. "Her book has pleased all those who
       think that Stalin lived in the time of Ivan the Terrible
       and that her taking the Fifth Amendment in 1952 gives
       political sanction and importance in the 1970's to her
       self-approval and her every dogged resentment."

70 KERR, WALTER. "Is It Wrong to Be 'Untrue to Life'?" New
       York Times (6 April), p. 23.
           Discussion of contrived situations which function posi-
       tively in three recent New York productions (The New York
       Idea, Gemini, and Romeo and Juliet). Kerr bemoans the
       scarcity of such moments in contemporary drama, citing
       Regina's refusal to give Horace his medicine in The Little
       Foxes as a famous and vital "situation" in earlier drama.

*71 KETNER, KEN. Review of Julia. San Diego Magazine, 30
       (December), 48-54.
           Cited in Access, The Supplementary Index to Periodicals,
       1978.

72 KNELMAN, MARTIN. "Starring . . . The Writer." Atlantic
       Monthly, 240 (November), 96-98.
           Discusses Julia, whose arrival on screen completes "the
       transformation of Lillian Hellman into a popular phenome-
       non." The film works best as a political thriller but is
       not simply a slick, commercial adaptation of the Pentimento
       excerpt. "Even giving Regina [Giddens] her due, the most
       unforgettable character Lillian Hellman has ever created is
       Lillian Hellman." She can be terribly wrongheaded, as she
       is in Scoundrel Time, still failing to see, after all
       these years, that the evils of McCarthyism do not vindicate
       the follies of the Hollywood Left," but one must admire her
       code of honor and her dignity. Writing about her own life,
       Hellman "has become a literary version of the ideal talk-
       show guest. Like the turtle that rose from the dead [in
       Pentimento], she has become an icon of survival with honor.

It is this emergence of the writer as star personality that the movie celebrates." Caricature of Hellman.

73 KNIGHT, ARTHUR. "Writing the Screenplay for Julia: An Interview with Screenwriter Alvin Sargent." Films Incorporated's Chairman's Choice, 2, issue 1 (Fall), 6.
   Knight interviews Sargent on his adaptation of "Julia" for the screen. "The big decision was how much of Julia should I put into the film. In the end I think the balance was correct. She was a memory, even an idea. Lillian loved her, wished she could be as brave and as dedicated and I suppose as beautiful as Julia was. I knew I had to be careful that Julia didn't take over the movie, I mean physically." Films Incorporated, 1144 Wilmette Avenue, Wilmette, Illinois 60091.

74 KOPELEV, LEV. To Be Preserved Forever. Translated and edited by Anthony Austin. Philadelphia and New York: J. B. Lippincott Company, 268 pp.
   Contains foreword by Hellman, who describes her friendship with Kopelev and his wife, Raya.

75 KROLL, JACK, MARTIN KASINDORF, and KATRINE AMES. "Hollywood's New Heroines." Newsweek, 90 (10 October), 78-82, 87.
   Cover story incorporating review of Julia with feature article on Jane Fonda and new films depicting women in a mature fashion. Hellman's original memoir is a "small gem of sophisticated writing," which uses time and memory in a Proustian manner. The film suffers from some "legacies from Hellman's seductively graceful but sometimes ambiguous original." The young Hellman as portrayed in the film is much more innocent politically than we can believe of "someone with her ideological toughness." But Julia on screen is stunningly acted and "moving in its glowing commitment to the power of friendship." Includes comments by Fonda about Hellman (p. 82) and photos from the film (cover and pp. 78-79).

76 LACY, ALLEN. "Custodians of the Mind." Chronicle of Higher Education, 15 (12 September), p. 14.
   Review of We Must March My Darlings by Diana Trilling. Says Trilling's remarks about Hellman are "moderate and brief."

77 LATOUR, MARTINE. "Interview: Meryl Streep on Julia." Mademoiselle, 83 (March), 76.
   Interview with actress Meryl Streep about Julia, in which she appears.

1977

78 LAUFE, ABE. Broadway's Greatest Musicals. Revised edition.
    New York: Funk and Wagnalls, pp. 121, 394.
        Brief references to The Children's Hour and Candide.

79 LEONARD, JOHN. "Books of the Times." New York Times (19
    May), p. 31.
        Reviews We Must March My Darlings by Diana Trilling.
    Discusses the Hellman-Trilling controversy. Leonard finds
    much of Trilling's section on "Liberal Anti-Communism Re-
    visited" unsatisfactory.

80 _____. "Books of the Times: The End of a Joy Ride." New York
    Times (28 February), p. C25.
        Reviews Haywire by Brooke Hayward. Leonard alludes
    briefly to Hellman as one of numerous celebrities whose
    career was managed by Leland Hayward, Brooke's father.

81 LIMBACHER, JAMES L. Feature Films on 8mm and 16mm, Fifth
    Edition. New York: R. R. Bowker, passim.
        Lists availability of Hellman film titles for rental,
    with names and addresses of distribution companies.

82 LUNDEGAARD, BOB. "Reverent Abstractions Detract from Good
    Qualities of Julia." Sunday Minneapolis [Minnesota]
    Tribune (13 November).
        Julia withholds too much information from its audience.
    The Hellman-Hammett relationship, for example, lacks de-
    tail. Julia is worth seeing but Hellman and director Fred
    Zinnemann have constructed "reverent abstractions."

83 LUTZE, PETER. Review of Julia. Christian Century, 94 (21
    December), 1198-99.
        Rave review.

84 LYONS, HARRIET, and SUSAN BRAUDY. "Julia & Lillian & Jane &
    Vanessa: Such Good Friends?" Ms., 6 (October), 53-55.
        Review of Julia cites the film as the most interesting
    screen study of women to come along in recent years, but
    faults Zinnemann, the director, for not finding cinematic
    parallels for the emotional subtleties of Hellman's friend-
    ship with Julia, as analyzed in Pentimento. Full-page
    still of Fonda.

85 McCABE, BRUCE. "Goodbar, Julia & Feminism." Boston Globe (30
    October), pp. E12, E16.
        Says Julia is excessively caught up in the women's move-
    ment and that the film is self-conscious. "Jane Fonda
    seems paralyzed with reverence for Hellman."

86 MAILER, NORMAN. "Of a Small and Modest Malignancy, Wicked
    and Bristling with Dots." Esquire, 88 (November), 125-148.
        Account of Mailer's television appearances and related
    matters; includes brief mention of a conversation with
    Hellman about Dorothy Parker.

87 MARILL, ALVIN H. Samuel Goldwyn Presents. Cranbury, N.J.:
    A. S. Barnes; London: Thomas Yoseloff, 320 pp.
        Includes credits, summaries, and other material related
    to Hellman films.

88 MELLEN, JOAN. Big Bad Wolves: Masculinity in the American
    Film. New York: Pantheon Books, p. 142.
        Mentions Hellman as one associated with the Hollywood
    Ten in the context of the following assertion: "Many of
    the male images of the late 1930's and early 1940's were
    shaped by Communist screenwriters and sympathizers of the
    party. The Hollywood Ten alone were responsible for 159
    films from 1935 to 1949, while others associated with them
    were almost as prolific or influential." Cites The North
    Star as one of those films.

89 MITFORD, JESSICA. A Fine Old Conflict. New York: Alfred A.
    Knopf, pp. 199-200.
        Brief mention of Hellman's stand before the House
    Committee on Un-American Activities.

90 MOORE, HONOR. "Introduction," in The New Women's Theatre: Ten
    Plays by Contemporary American Women. Edited by Honor
    Moore. New York: Vintage Books, pp. xi-xxxvii.
        Discusses women playwrights who achieved success in
    various periods and countries. Defends Hellman against the
    charges that she is obsessed with evil and too dependent on
    the well-made form. Moore suggests that the relationship
    between Karen and Martha in The Children's Hour
    "acknowledges a kind of friendship between women--trusting,
    conscious and intimate--that is rarely dramatized." The
    Little Foxes, usually treated as a battle between Regina
    and her brothers, is also the story of a women embittered
    by provincial life and the "identity drama of the young
    daughter Alexandra, who must choose among the different
    ways of being a woman that she sees." Moore also believes
    that while the well-made play worked successfully for
    Hellman's theatrical vision, "the form her sensibility
    created was the form of the speculative memoir."

1977

91 MORRISON, DON. "Entertainment: Julia Tells a Grim Tale Re-
    markably." Minneapolis [Minnesota] Star (31 October), p. 14A.
    Praises Julia as "an altogether remarkable film."

92 MURF. Review of Julia. Variety, 288 (21 September), 16.
    Praises Julia highly. The film will be mistakenly
    characterized as a "woman's picture." The impact of the
    story "derives not from the sex of the principals: instead,
    it arises from the outrage one experiences when a longtime
    true friend becomes victimized by injustice."

93 OCCHIOGROSSO, FRANK. "Murder in the Dark: Dashiell Hammett."
    New Republic, 177 (30 July), 28-30.
    Analysis of Hammett's writing, with emphasis on the
    Continental Op as "the essential Hammett hero." Several
    references to Hellman.

94 O'CONNOR, JOHN. "TV: A Sex Comedy by Innuendo." New York
    Times (31 March), p. 49.
    Alludes to Hellman's appearance at the Academy Awards
    telecast. She "brought an unusual element of wit, dignity
    and warmth to her appearance. Miss Hellman got the only
    standing ovation of the evening, which, for a change, was
    deserved."

95 O'CONNOR, THOMAS. "Lillian Hellman: 'A Chance to Try All
    One's Capacities.'" Arena Stage Program Book (Washington,
    D.C.), pp. 14-17.
    Program notes for Arena Stage production of The Autumn
    Garden. O'Connor reviews Hellman's career, emphasizing the
    Chekhovian strains of The Autumn Garden. "She is, at once,
    an enigma and one of our most public lives; a writer whose
    works transcend nationalism and are quintessentially
    American; critically acclaimed and commercially successful,
    yet often overlooked in assessments of leading literary
    lights."

96 OWEN, GUY. "Scoundrel Time," in Magill's Literary Annual,
    1977. Edited by Frank Magill. Englewood Cliffs, N.J.:
    Salem Press, pp. 702-705.
    Finds Scoundrel Time distinctly inferior to the earlier
    Hellman memoirs. Although sections are poignant and the
    paying off of old debts reminds one of Hemingway's A Move-
    able Feast, the book is "self-serving and opportunistic."
    Any importance it may have "is as a curious piece of minor
    history."

97 PATRAKA, VIVIAN MARY. "Lillian Hellman, Dramatist of the
      Second Sex." Ph.D. dissertation, University of Michigan.
         Focuses on Hellman's use of female characters; concludes
      that in her artistically successful plays these characters
      are autonomous and complex. In the memoirs, she is freer
      to explore female perceptions without the imposition of
      dramatic realism. Dissertation Abstracts International,
      38:3502A.

*98 PEERY, BEVERLY HAMER. Lillian Hellman, the Woman and the
      Playwright. In progress.
         Cited in Educational Theatre Journal, 29 (March 1977).

99 RATHER, DAN. Interview with Lillian Hellman. "Who's Who,"
      CBS network telecast (8 March).
         Interview with Hellman forms one segment of this tele-
      cast. Topics include her career, politics, and college
      lectures.

100 REED, REX. "Lillian Hellman," in his Valentines and Vitriol.
      New York: Delacorte Press, pp. 103-108.
         Reprint of 1975.36.

101 _____. Review of Julia. Vogue, 167 (November), 54.
         Generally positive review, with some reservations.

102 RICH, FRANK. "Cinema: A Convoluted Memoir of the '30s."
      Time, 110 (10 October), p. 83.
         Review of Julia pronounces the film a failure. Instead
      of adapting Hellman's story cinematically, the intricate
      narrative structure is mistakenly reproduced. The result
      is a "glossy bio flick that superficially charts the rise
      of Lillian Hellman, Young Leftist Playwright."

103 RONAN, MARGARET. Review of Julia. Senior Scholastic, 110 (15
      December), 21-22.
         Highly favorable review. Names Julia winner of the
      magazine's "Bell Ringer Award." Photo from the film.

*104 ROURKE, MARY. Review of Julia. W., 6 (30 September), 10.
         Cited in Access, The Supplementary Index to Periodicals,
      1977.

105 RYAN, DESMOND. "Julia: A Deeply Affecting Film."
      Philadelphia Inquirer (13 October), p. 6B.
         Considers Julia "a superlative film about memory."
      Photos.

1977

106 SARRIS, ANDREW. "Oscar Postscript: To Err Is Human." Village
     Voice, 22 (11 April), 45.
         Reflections on the 1977 Oscar telecast, including brief
     comments on Hellman's appearance. Her remarks to an audi-
     ence which had just given her a standing ovation reflected
     her inability, "as always . . . to rise above her rancor."

107 _____. Review of Julia. Village Voice, 22 (10 October), 47.
         Criticizes Julia for its fragmented style and evasive-
     ness. It would have been impossible for anyone connected
     with the film to have made Dorothy Parker and Alan Campbell
     "more substantial when the whole raison d'etre of Julia
     herself, poor pathetic victim that she was, consisted of
     making everyone but Lillian Hellman seem trivial and
     frivolous by comparison." The film is adapted as if "from
     sacred text." "I have never considered it a particular
     privilege to worship at the shrine of Lillian Hellman."

108 SCHENKER, SUSAN, comp. "Pundits' Page." Take One (November).
         Excerpts five film critics' comments on Julia.

109 SCHIER, ERNEST. "Julia a Hushed and Passive Movie."
     Philadelphia Evening Bulletin (13 October), p. A33.
         Evaluates Julia as "a passive film, so determinedly
     highclass that it lacks the theatrical qualities necessary
     to an interesting film." The best scenes of the film
     occur when Hellman is together with Hammett at her beach
     house.

110 SCHIFF, STEPHEN. "Two Women: In Defense of Julia." Boston
     Phoenix, 6 (18 October), section 3, pp. 5, 8, 10.
         Argues that the anti-Hellman backlash evident in some
     critical reactions to Julia is the inevitable and thinly
     veiled response to the gradual "canonization of Saint
     Lillian." The film, for all its "Major Motion Picture
     stodginess," takes numerous risks which it brings off suc-
     cessfully, and has the "pictorial feel of David Lean's
     Dickens adaptations." Schiff's review details the Hellman-
     Julia relationship of story and film, responds to specific
     criticisms made by Pauline Kael, Andrew Sarris, and Molly
     Haskell, and includes segments of a telephone interview
     with Fred Zinnemann, the director.

111 SCHLESINGER, ARTHUR M., JR. "The Duplicitous Art." Saturday
     Review, 5 (29 October), 46-48.
         Mostly negative review of Julia. "Illumination dwindles
     into anecdote," although the film succeeds as melodrama and
     is quite tolerably entertaining." Photo from the film.

112 SEYMOUR-SMITH, MARTIN. Who's Who in Twentieth Century Literature. New York: Holt, Rinehart and Winston, pp. 155-56.
   Brief remarks on Hellman's career. Considers The Children's Hour, Another Part of the Forest, and The Autumn Garden her best plays.
   Reprinted as paperback, New York: McGraw Hill, 1977.

113 SHALIT, GENE. Review of Julia. Ladies' Home Journal, 94 (December), 10.
   Glowing review.

114 SIMON, JOHN. "Berlin on $50,000 a Day." National Review, 29 (25 November), 1375-77.
   Negative review of Julia. The film should more honestly have been entitled Lillian. It functions for the more cultivated viewer "as a comic-strip version of what it is like to be a famous writer or a dedicated anti-Nazi fighter like Julia."

115 SMITH, LIZ. Review of Julia. Cosmopolitan, 183 (November), 22.
   Excellent review.

116 SPRING, MICHAEL. "Talking Cinemately [sic] re. Films: Julia." Twentieth-Century-Fox Discussion Guide, unpaged.
   Guide for discussion of Julia, issued by Twentieth-Century-Fox. Relates the film to other Hellman works and to the "Julia" segment of Pentimento; lists cast and production credits, biographical information on Hellman, Hammett, and Fred Zinnemann, the director. Questions for discussion. Available from Twentieth-Century-Fox, 1345 Avenue of the Americas, New York, N.Y. 10019.

*117 STABINER, KAREN. Review of Julia. Mother Jones, 2 (September-October), 61-63.
   Cited in Access, The Supplementary Index to Periodicals, 1977.

118 STEPHENS, JAN. "One Happy, Two Not." The Times [London] (6 August), p. 7.
   Reviews An Unfinished Woman, upon its English paperback publication. Hellman "is like nobody one has ever met, so that there is a touch of the secret, black and midnight about the whole book. She even laughs with a straight face."

119 STINNETT, CASKIE. Grand and Private Pleasures. Boston and Toronto: Little, Brown and Company, 203 pp.

1977

A collection of travel essays dedicated to Hellman.
Preface alludes to Hellman's distaste for travel, which she
approaches "with dread and foreboding" (p. x).

120 STOOP, NORMA McLAIN. "Equus and Julia." After Dark, 10
(November), 32-38.
Praises Julia highly. Hellman's memoir "has been made
into a paragon of a movie that illuminates loyalty, love,
self-doubt, and self-sacrifice with the electricity of its
passionate commitment to excellence." Stills.

121 TARBERT, GARY, ed. Book Review Index 1976. Vol. 12.
Detroit: Gale Research Company, p. 194.
Lists reviews of Scoundrel Time.

122 THOMSON, DAVID. America in the Dark: Hollywood and the Gift
of Unreality. New York: William Morrow and Company, pp.
118-19.
In a discussion of popular versus highbrow appeal in
film, Thomson cites Mervyn LeRoy's acid dismissal of
"critics' pictures." LeRoy notes that Another Part of
the Forest "was a critic's picture. It was beautifully
done, but it was not a picture most people wanted to see.
. . . They needed a talking mule in Another Part of the
Forest."

123 TRILLING, DIANA. "Liberal Anti-Communism Re-Visited," in her
We Must March My Darlings. New York and London: Harcourt
Brace Jovanovich, pp. 41-66.
Responds to Hellman's statements in Scoundrel Time con-
cerning the politics of Diana and Lionel Trilling during
the days of the McCarthy hearings. Criticizes Garry
Wills's introduction to Scoundrel Time and the "almost
universally uncritical reception" the book has received as
historical statement. Lengthy footnotes describe
Trilling's view of the publicity that developed from the
refusal of Little, Brown, Hellman's publisher, to publish
We Must March My Darlings without deletions of certain
passages concerning Hellman.
Reprinted 1978 (A Harvest/HBJ Book; New York and London,
pp. 41-66).

124 _____, and THOMAS R. EDWARDS. Letters to the Editor. New
York Times Book Review (31 July), pp. 33-34.
Letter from Diana Trilling, objecting to Thomas R.
Edwards's defense of Hellman in his review of We Must March
My Darlings, and a reply from Edwards. See 1977.37.

125 TURNER, ALICE K. "Reading for an Air-Conditioned Bower." New York, 10 (11 July), 55.
 Alludes briefly to Pentimento as a book that belongs "on the shelf of personal revisionist histories by our First Ladies of Letters."

126 WILL, GEORGE. "There Is a Limit." Providence [Rhode Island] Journal (3 November), p. All.
 Syndicated column critical of Jane Fonda. "Her previous enthusiasm was North Vietnam, and her current enthusiasm is Lillian Hellman, a sort of former Jane Fonda, a figure in the entertainment world whose enthusiasm was the Soviet Union."

127 WILLIAMSON, BRUCE. Review of Julia. Playboy, 24 (December), 28.
 Praises Julia highly. The film is "less concerned with Hellman's public triumphs or private affairs than with other qualities she values--courage, loyalty, friendship and stubborn integrity."

128 WILSON, JANE. "Hollywood Flirts with the New Woman." New York Times (29 May), section 2, pp. 1, 11, 24.
 Brief mention of Julia in a survey that distinguishes between films and television programs which present a credible and serious view of female experience and those which "simply use women to flesh out the imaginings of men." Photo of Jane Fonda as Hellman and Vanessa Redgrave as Julia (p. 1).

129 WOOD, ROBIN. "American Cinema in the '70s: Dog Day Afternoon." Movie, no. 23 (Winter 1976-77), 33-36.
 Contains several references to The Chase. Suggests that Dog Day Afternoon, the film analyzed here, reflects a movement "central to the American cinema since The Chase: a rapidly escalating progress from a precarious, already troubled order into breakdown and chaos--a progress expressed through the shift of tone from comedy to desperation and underlined by the movement from light to darkness in the film's strict time-scheme."

1978

1 ANON. "Back Talk." Film Comment, 14 (January-February), 78.
 Speculates briefly on Oscar chances for Jane Fonda and Vanessa Redgrave in Julia.

1978

2 ANON. "Bellow Gets Arts-Club Medal of Honor." New York Times (24 February), p. C28.
    Concluding paragraph notes that Hellman had been slated to receive a National Arts Club medal in 1977 but that the award "had been called off by mutual agreement."

3 ANON. "Frances Sternhagen Joins Hellman Letter Readers." New York Times (8 November), p. C24.
    Reports that Frances Sternhagen is the third actress to take the stage in Eric Bentley's play, Are You Now or Have You Ever Been, to read Hellman's 1952 letter to the House Un-American Activities Committee. She follows Rosemary Murphy and Colleen Dewhurst, and will be succeeded by Tammy Grimes and Barbara Baxley. "The reading is apparently a labor of love on the part of actresses, who have been fitting it into their schedules at no pay or for minimum rates."

4 ANON. "Lillian Hellman Fails to Bar Her 'Toys' from Opening." New York Times (12 May), p. C13.
    Registers Hellman's complaints about impending WPA Theater production of Toys in the Attic.

*5 ANON. Review of Julia. New Guard, 18 (March-April), 28.
    Cited in the Popular Periodicals Index for January-June 1978. No author listed.

6 ARDITO, MARY. "What Lillian Hellman and the Wizard of Oz Can Tell You About Managing People." Bell Telephone Magazine, 57, no. 4 (Midsummer), 31-33.
    Bizarre piece written for the Bell System's in-house publication. Uses examples from The Little Foxes, Toys in the Attic, Another Part of the Forest, and the memoirs to show that Hellman's work, in its varied depiction of human relationships, "is applicable to the art of [corporate] management."

7 BARNES, CLIVE. "Children's Hour Belongs to Woodward and Knight." New York Post (8 August), p. 40.
    Praises revival of The Children's Hour at Stockbridge, Massachusetts. Says the play is impressive in a melo-dramatic way.

8 BENNETTS, LESLIE. "Creative Women of the 20's Who Helped to Pave the Way." New York Times (10 April), p. A20.
    Report on conference at Rutgers University on "Women and the Arts in the 1920's in Paris and New York," in which Hellman participated. Photo.

9 BIGSBY, C. W. E. "Drama as Cultural Sign: American Dramatic
   Criticism, 1945-1978." American Quarterly, 30 (Autumn),
   331-57.
      Cites three items of Hellman criticism written in the
   past decade (Adler, 1969.3; Moody, 1972.26; and Holmin,
   1973.32). Considers her accomplishments as a dramatist to
   be "of a minor kind, the clash between simple humanity and
   the drive for power which she projects against a fast-
   changing South lacking the metaphysical engagement of a
   Faulkner or the occasional symbolic depth of a Williams"
   (p. 340).

*10 BLUEMIE, ROBERT L. Review of Julia. Phoenix, 13 (January),
   43-44.
      Cited in Access, The Supplementary Index to Periodicals,
   1978.

11 BOSWORTH, PATRICIA. Montgomery Clift. New York and London:
   Harcourt Brace Jovanovich, pp. 83, 98-100, 103, 160, 421-
   22.
      References to Clift's Broadway role in The Searching
   Wind. Quotes briefly from Pentimento. Mentions that Clift
   was considering a film based on Norman Mailer's The Naked
   and the Dead, with a script by Hellman. Gives full production credits of The Searching Wind.
      Paperback reprint: New York: Bantam Books, 1979.

12 BRAUN, DEVRA. "Lillian Hellman's Continuing Moral Battle."
   Massachusetts Studies in English, 5, no. 4 (1978), 1-6.
      Argues that the moral issues of Hellman's plays pre-
   figure those concerning the McCarthy era, depicted in
   Scoundrel Time.

13 BRYER, JACKSON R., and RUTH M. ALVAREZ. "American Drama 1918-
   1940: A Survey of Research and Criticism." American
   Quarterly, 30 (Autumn), 298-330.
      Brief discussion of Hellman criticism (pp. 318-19).
   Aptly notes the surprising fact that "considering the controversies aroused by Hellman's plays and extra-dramatic
   activities, her work has prompted relatively little serious
   examination." Deplores the scarcity of in-depth criticism
   of Hellman as dramatist.

14 BRYFONSKI, DEDRIA, and PHYLLIS MENDELSON, eds. Contemporary
   Literary Criticism. Vol. 8. Detroit: Gale Research
   Company, pp. 280-82.
      Five excerpts from articles on Pentimento (Clive James,
   1974.26), Scoundrel Time (Bruce Cook, 1976.24; Maureen

1978

Howard, 1976.49; Vivian Gornick, 1976.39), and The Little
Foxes (John Simon, 1975.46).

15 BYRON, STUART. "Back Talk." Film Comment, 14 (March-April),
    78-79.
        Speculates on Oscar prospects of actors in Julia.

16 CANBY, VINCENT. "In the Afterglow of the Oscars." New York
    Times (16 April), section 2, pp. 15, 20.
        Discusses the controversy at the Academy Awards presen-
    tations concerning Vanessa Redgrave's remarks, after she
    was named best supporting actress for her role in Julia.

17 _____. "Who Keeps House in Those Women's Films?" New York
    Times (12 March), section 2, p. 15.
        Discusses Julia and other films about career women.
    "Though we never see them washing a dish, Lillian and Dash
    don't appear to live in filth. We're not told but it seems
    likely that they have a local girl who comes in twice a
    week to sweep up and empty the ashtrays."

18 CLURMAN, HAROLD. Review of Are You Now Or Have You Ever Been
    by Eric Bently. Nation, 227 (4 November), 484-85.
        Mentions Hellman's fine letter to the House Un-American
    Activities Committee, read by Colleen Dewhurst.

19 _____. Review of Days to Come. Nation, 227 (25 November),
    587-88.
        Reviews WPA Theatre revival of Days to Come. Hellman
    "has certainly written better plays than Days to Come, yet
    I found it interesting for a variety of reasons, even for
    its faults. For a start, it is about something real, some-
    thing that matters."

20 COLEMAN, JOHN. Review of Julia. New Statesman, 95 (27
    January), 126.
        Generally favorable review, with reservations.

21 COLLINS, WILLIAM B. "Hingle Is a Success in Debut as Direc-
    tor." Philadelphia Inquirer (23 March), p. 4-B.
        Reviews production of Toys in the Attic by the McCarter
    Theater Company, which turns the play into "fairly absorb-
    ing drama." In contrast to her earlier realism, Hellman
    here "moves her people to a plane just outside the norm."

22 CORRY, JOHN. "Broadway." New York Times (12 May), p. C2.
        Notes impending production of The Children's Hour,

starring Joanne Woodward and Shirley Knight, at the
Berkshire Festival, Stockbridge, Massachusetts.

23 DAVIES, RUSSELL. "Cinema: Repentance." London Observer (29
    January), p. 27.
        Reviews Julia. The film is finally "Ms. Hellman's elegy
    for the things she left undone that she ought to have done
    . . . a sort of honourable self-indulgence." She has "made
    as much a profession of being a writer as she has of writ-
    ing; and what's more, she has tended to see other people as
    functioning parts of her conscience. Or to put it more
    badly, as actors in the play of her life. This is how
    Julia works, too, with its shimmering flashbacks and rumi-
    nations. There is too much attitude to experience in it,
    and not enough experience."

24 DAVIS, PETER G. "Blitzstein's Regina Revived." New York
    Times (18 November), p. 11.
        Discusses Encompass Theater's revival of Regina.

25 DURBIN, KAREN. "Such Good Friends." Village Voice, 23 (23
    January), 33-35.
        Discusses the female friendship theme in Julia and other
    recent films. Julia is more successful than The Turning
    Point and One Sings, the Other Doesn't because it is more
    elegantly written. Its treatment of the women's experience
    overrides the tendency toward slickness and simplification
    displayed elsewhere in the film.

26 EDER, RICHARD. "Children's Hour Staged at the Berkshire
    Festival." New York Times (29 July), p. 12.
        Reviews production of The Children's Hour at Stockbridge,
    Massachusetts, starring Joanne Woodward and Shirley Knight.
    "Time has eaten away at the underpinnings" of the play;
    although it still contains emotional power, there is "not
    enough to still the squeak of restless improbabilities."
    The performances of the stars compensate but the parts of
    the children suffer from the "doubtful writing."

27 FALK, DORIS V. Lillian Hellman. New York: Frederick Ungar
    Publishing Company, 180 pp.
        Discusses Hellman's eight original plays, three memoirs,
    and their respective dramatic and narrative methods.
    Falk's book, published as part of Ungar's series of modern
    literature monographs, is useful but uneven. It glibly
    divides the plays into two categories: those concern-
    ing "despoilers," who exploit or destroy other characters
    for selfish purposes (The Little Foxes, Another Part of the

Forest, Watch on the Rhine); and those about "bystanders,"
lower-keyed, more discursive dramas in which the characters
"are unable to act positively or with conviction" and thus
become the "passive victims of the despoilers and themselves." Falk makes interesting but at times forced connections between the plays and memoirs and virtually ignores Hellman's film career except in the biographical
introduction and in passing references. The analyses of
the individual works include gallant attempts
to compare Hellman to other writers. Falk compares the
young runaway Hellman, in one section of An Unfinished
Woman, to Hawthorne's Robin in "My Kinsman, Major
Molineux." Melville's Queequeg, she maintains, is equivalent to Hellman's black characters, "the servants who are
really the masters and mistresses because they can with-
stand hardship, and because they see the truth under appear-
ances." Comments on the plays and memoirs rely heavily on
plot, but Falk's study does convey a good sense of
Hellman's moral concerns and of the persona which emerges
especially from her later work. The book provides a succinct introduction to Hellman which will primarily benefit
the nonacademic reader. The brief final chapter ably sorts
out the central controversies which followed publication of
Scoundrel Time.

28 FIDELL, ESTELLE A., ed. Play Index, 1973-1977. New York: H.
    W. Wilson Company, p. 146.
        Lists Hellman plays in anthologies.

29 FOX, TERRY CURTIS. "Early Work." Village Voice, 23 (6
    November), 127, 129.
        Interesting review of Days to Come revival at WPA
    theater, in New York City. Notes that it is the first re-
    vival of the play permitted by Hellman. Considers Days to
    Come a "warm-up" for The Little Foxes and "one of those
    crucial transitional works." The writing "is far more
    compelling and less explanatory than in" The Children's
    Hour.

30 _____. Review of The Children's Hour. Village Voice, 23 (21
    August), p. 117.
        Analyzes production of The Children's Hour at Berkshire
    Playhouse, Stockbridge, Massachusetts, starring Joanne
    Woodward and Shirley Knight. Compares the play to Fritz
    Lang's film Fury in theme. The now-dated text is not as
    good as the performances of this production.

31 FRASER, C. GERALD. "33 Playwrights Protest 'Censure' of
      'Robeson.'" New York Times (18 May), p. C20.
          Cites Hellman as one of the signers of a Dramatists
      Guild statement protesting attempts "to influence critics
      and audiences against" the one-man play Paul Robeson.

32 FRENCH, PHILIP. "The Year of the Feminist." London Observer
      (31 December).
          Refers briefly to Julia as one of a welcome group of
      films on feminist themes: "slick and trendy, old-fashioned
      women's pictures given a new twist."

33 FRIDAY, NANCY. My Mother/My Self. New York: Dell Publishing
      Company, p. 214.
          Quotes briefly from p. 119 of Pentimento on a woman's
      tendency to repress anger: "Anna [sic]-Marie was an in-
      telligent girl, flirtatious, good mannered with that kind
      of outward early-learned passive quality that in women so
      often hides anger."
          Paperback reprint of Delacorte Press edition, 1977.

34 GREGER, DEBORA. "Pentimento." New Yorker, 54 (22 May), 36.
          Poem drawing on and prefaced by Hellman's definition of
      "pentimento."

35 GROSS, EDITH LOEW, JILL SPAULDING, and ALEXANDRA ANDERSON.
      "Smash-hit Women: in Three Hit Movies--Network, Annie Hall,
      Julia--the Best Hollywood Designers Look at the American
      Woman--and It's You." Vogue, 168 (August), 176-81.
          Costumes designed for Julia.

36 GUSSOW, MEL. "Lillian Hellman's Toys in the Attic Revived."
      New York Times (4 March), p. 12.
          Reviews McCarter Theater Company (Princeton, New Jersey)
      revival of Toys in the Attic. The production "wistfully
      evokes dominant Hellman themes and characters." The play's
      core is the "incipiently incestuous" current between Julian
      and Carrie.

37 HABERMAN, CLYDE, and ALBIN KREBS. "Notes on People." New
      York Times (21 November), p. C8.
          Notes that Peggy Cass will play the role of Lillian
      Hellman in the New York revival of Eric Bentley's play Are
      You Now Or Have You Ever Been. "She follows Colleen
      Dewhurst, Tammy Grimes, and Rosemary Murphy in the role."

38 HARMETZ, ALJEAN. "Annie Hall Wins 4 Academy Awards." New
      York Times (4 April), p. 24.

1978

        Reports on Vanessa Redgrave's controversial remarks at the Oscar ceremonies after being named best supporting actress for her role in Julia.

39 HEILMAN, ROBERT BECHTOLD. The Ways of the World: Comedy and Society. Seattle and London: University of Washington Press, p. 66.
      Alludes to Watch on the Rhine.

40 HUGHES, CATHERINE. Review of Are You Now Or Have You Ever Been by Eric Bentley. America, 139 (2 December), 411.
      Mentions Hellman as one who, like Arthur Miller, "held out" against naming names to the House Un-American Activities Committee.

41 KAZIN, ALFRED. New York Jew. New York: Alfred A. Knopf, pp. 64, 185, 224, 269, 273.
      Hellman references, generally critical. Calls The North Star a "meretricious propaganda film"; alludes to Hellman's "self-dramatizing gifts."
      Reprinted 1979.20.

42 KERNODLE, GEORGE and PORTIA. Invitation to the Theatre. Brief second edition. New York: Harcourt Brace Jovanovich, Inc., p. 137.
      Photo from Indiana University production of Toys in the Attic, included to demonstrate "simplified realism" of the set design.

43 KERR, WALTER. Review of Are You Now Or Have You Ever Been by Eric Bentley. Supplementary material from the New York Times News Service and the Associated Press (20 October), pp. 71-72.
      Reviews Bentley's documentary drama about the House Un-American Activities Committee hearings. Says Hellman's "celebrated letter is read with quiet dignity by Colleen Dewhurst (will be succeeded by other actresses after two weeks)."
      Note: Regular editions of the New York Times were not published because of a strike.

44 KINNEY, ARTHUR F. Dorothy Parker. Twayne's United States Authors Series. Boston: Twayne Publishers/G. K. Hall and Company, pp. 37, 44, 54, 60, 61-62, 64, 67, 71, 74, 140, 181.
      Quotes Hellman (especially from Pentimento and An Unfinished Woman) on Dorothy Parker. Notes that Parker invested $500 in The Spanish Earth. Briefly alludes to

Parker's having written additional scenes for the film version of The Little Foxes. Notes that Parker dedicated one of her books to Hellman and Hellman dedicated The Searching Wind to Parker. Mentions Parker's contributions to Candide. Quotes from Hellman's eulogy for Parker. Also quotes Parker's introduction to the special, limited edition of Watch on the Rhine. See 1942.30.

45 KNIGHT, ARTHUR. The Liveliest Art. Revised edition. New York: Macmillan, pp. 224, 228, 250.
    Brief mention of Hellman in the context of the McCarthy years. Also refers to The North Star and The Spanish Earth. First edition (Macmillan, 1957; paperback reprint New American Library, 1959) includes only the latter two references.

46 LACAYO, RICHARD. Review of Julia. National Catholic Reporter, 14 (13 January), 13.
    Critical review.

*47 LAUFE, ABE. The Wicked Stage: A History of Theater Censorship and Harassment in the United States. New York: Ungar.
    Cited by Charles A. Carpenter, "Modern Drama Studies: An Annual Bibliography." Modern Drama, 22 (June 1979), 143.

48 LINDSEY, ROBERT. "Oscars Stir Redgrave Dispute Anew." New York Times (1 February), p. C15.
    Report on controversy surrounding Vanessa Redgrave's potential Oscar nomination for her title role in Julia.

49 McCOURT, JAMES. "Davis." Film Comment, 14 (March–April), 46-48.
    Discusses the film performances of Bette Davis, including her struggle with director William Wyler over her role of Regina Giddens in The Little Foxes.

50 MELLEN, JOAN. "Hollywood Rediscovers the American Woman." New York Times (23 April), section 2, pp. 1, 15.
    Briefly discusses Julia as an example of a film that portrays women realistically. "Jane Fonda as a successful playwright is aided in her creative work by a man, instead of the other way around. The title character, Julia, is an intellectual who reads Darwin, Hegel, Engels and Einstein and plans to study with Freud."

51 MILLER, HENRY S., JR. "Lillian Hellman: 'No Simple Answers.'" Harvard Magazine, 80 (January–February), 84.

1978

Reports on a question and answer session between Hellman
and an audience of 200 people during her appointment as
Frederic W. Atherton lecturer at Harvard.

52 MITGANG, HERBERT. "Sampling of New Nonfiction Shows That Many
Lives Are an Open Book." New York Times (3 December),
section 1, p. 100.
Notes scheduled publication in 1979 of Three, a new edition of Hellman's three memoirs with new commentaries.

53 MORRISON, FRANCES ROWENA. "Seeing, And Seeing Again: Self-
Discovery in the Plays of Lillian Hellman." Ph.D. dissertation, University of North Carolina at Chapel Hill.
Asserts that critics have failed to reach consensus on
Hellman's plays and that attempts to categorize them as
well-made melodramas have obscured the unifying principle
of her work: "the moral necessity of self-awareness and
purposive action in life." The theme of self-discovery
appears in Hellman's plays in varying contexts, including
troubled marriage and other family crises. Refers to
Hellman's memoirs, "where relevant, for interpretive detail." Dissertation Abstracts International, 40:251-52A.

54 MUNK, ERIKA. "Bearing Witness." Village Voice, 23 (23
October), 127-28.
Reviews Are You Now Or Have You Ever Been, Eric
Bentley's "exemplary documentary" based on House Un-
American Activities Committee transcripts. Mentions that
rotating "'leading ladies' are going to be brought in" to
play Hellman, including Colleen Dewhurst.

55 O'CONNOR, JOHN J. "TV: Oscar Awards Back in Old Form." New
York Times (5 April), p. C28.
Discusses Vanessa Redgrave's controversial remarks at
the Oscar presentations after being named best supporting
actress for her title role in Julia.

56 PARKER, DAVID L., and BURTON J. SHAPIRO. "William Wyler," in
Close-Up: The Hollywood Director. Edited by Jon Tuska,
Vicki Piekarski, and David Wilson. Metuchen, N.J., and
London: Scarecrow Press, pp. 136-201.
Analyzes films directed by William Wyler, including The
Little Foxes. Discusses the film in some detail, espe-
cially use of the camera.

57 RICH, FRANK. "Cinema: Warren Beatty Strikes Again." Time,
112 (3 July), 70-74.
Briefly quotes Hellman on her friendship with Beatty.

58 SACHAROFF, MARK. "Lillian Hellman: Studies in Evil." Program
     for Annenberg Center, University of Pennsylvania (21-26
     March), p. 9.
          Program notes for McCarter Theater Company performances
     of Toys in the Attic, at the Zellerbach Theater of the
     Annenberg Center. Argues for Hellman's "abiding stature."
     Even the best critics have misread her method of charac-
     terization and have been guilty of the "naïve and insati-
     able craving" in America for "even-handed, warm-hearted,
     forgiving attitudes in writers, even when the avowed pur-
     pose of these writers is scathing denunciation."

59 SARRIS, ANDREW. "Notes on the Fascination of Fascism."
     Village Voice, 23 (30 January), 1, 33, 36.
          Critical allusions to Hellman and her work. "To this
     day Lillian Hellman reflects thirties leftist attitudes on
     the Jewish Question when she quotes the martyred Julia on
     wanting to help not just the Jews, but all sorts of politi-
     cal prisoners." Hellman's confessions are "nothing if not
     self-righteous." Jane Fonda's "Miz Lillian [in Julia]
     knock[s] an F. Scott Fitzgerald gossip out of his chair for
     imputing a lesbian relationship between Lillian and Julia.
     Again, Marx and Freud never mixed for the Old Left, and
     there is no nonsense in Watch on the Rhine about a fascist
     lurking even in an anti-fascist."
          Reprinted in Sarris's Politics and Cinema, 1978.60.

60 _____. Politics and Cinema. New York: Columbia University
     Press, 215 pp.
          Reprints 1973.51 (pp. 72-77) and 1978.59 (pp. 107-115).
     Also contains references to Hellman in "Politics and
     Cinema" (pp. 9-15): Lillian Hellman "has transformed the
     art of self-deprecation into a form of self-glorification
     as she tries to make history itself conform to the pompous
     polemics of The Children's Hour, The Little Foxes, Watch
     on the Rhine, and North Star. She has now become the sum
     total of all her incredibly virtuous heroes and heroines in
     an incredibly villainous world. . . . When I look at
     Watch on the Rhine and The North Star, in which good left-
     ists solemnly teach themselves the historical necessity of
     killing fascists and even obstacle-creating opportunists in
     cold blood, I conclude that the left has little to teach
     us about liberty or justice."
          "Politics and Cinema" is incorrectly cited as having
     first appeared in American Film (February 1978). Sarris's
     article in that issue--"My Criticism, My Politics"--is re-
     printed in this collection as the Introduction, not as the
     title essay.

1978

61 SCANLAN, TOM. <u>Family, Drama, and American Dreams</u>. Contributions in American Studies, no. 35. Westport, Conn., and
London: Greenwood Press, pp. 5, 181-84, 187-89, 194, 198,
215.
Discusses Hellman's plays which center on families. She
resembles Miller in that "her strength as a social writer
seems directly related to the subject of the self against
the family, although the Hubbard family, her most vivid
creation, is otherwise nothing like the Lomans." Also like
Miller, she works in the well-made tradition. The "corrosive effect of enclosed family is the central situation
of her dramatic world. She is at her best when presenting
a well-made family war." Also compares Hellman to Odets.
Regina Giddens is one of the most repellent and commanding
women in the American drama.

62 SCHIER, ERNEST. "A Review: Effort Is Serious in <u>Toys</u>."
Philadelphia <u>Evening Bulletin</u> (23 March), p. 37.
Reviews McCarter Theater Company production of <u>Toys in
the Attic</u>, directed by Pat Hingle, performed at the
University of Pennsylvania's Annenberg Center. Considers
the play more despairing and realistic than any of her
previous works, but "oddly shrill and melodramatic, without
the structural smoothness of this fine writer."

63 SCHILLACI, PETER. "Where Have All the Heroes Gone?" <u>Media
and Methods</u>, 15 (December), 12-14, 16-24.
Brief discussion of <u>Julia</u> as an example of a film
featuring female relationships. Certain ambiguities in
the Hellman-Julia friendship, "which provided the subject
of Hellman's play, <u>The Children's Hour</u>, were left un-
examined by the film."

64 SCHUTH, H. WAYNE. <u>Mike Nichols</u>. Boston: Twayne Publishers/
G. K. Hall and Company, p. 45.
Brief reference to Nichols's direction of the 1967
Lincoln Center revival of <u>The Little Foxes</u>.

65 SHALIT, GENE. "What's Happening." <u>Ladies' Home Journal</u>, 95
(January), 8, 12.
Interview with Jane Fonda about her role as Hellman in
<u>Julia</u> and other matters.

66 SHRODES, CAROLINE, HARRY FINESTONE, and MICHAEL SHUGRUE. <u>The
Conscious Reader</u>. Second edition. New York: Macmillan,
pp. 225-38, 501-505.
Reprints Hellman's "Dashiell Hammett," from <u>An Unfinished Woman</u>. Also reprints John Hersey's tribute,

"Lillian Hellman," New Republic, 175 (18 September 1976), 25-27. See 1976.44.

67 SOBILOFF, ELLEN. "Friends Indeed." Providence, R.I., East Side (2 February), p. 12.
Considers Julia a moving, stunning film which focuses on two main themes: "aggression at its most brutal with the impending Holocaust, and love in the deepest nonphysical sense between two members of the same sex."

68 SUTHERLAND, CYNTHIA. "American Women Playwrights as Mediators of the 'Woman Problem.'" Modern Drama, 21 (September), 319-36.
Brief references to Hellman and The Children's Hour (pp. 330, 336).

*69 TALLEY, GIDNEY. Review of Julia. S.A. (the magazine of San Antonio), 1 (January), 59-62.
Cited in Access, The Supplementary Index to Periodicals, 1978.

70 TARBERT, GARY, ed. Book Review Index 1977. Vol. 13. Detroit: Gale Research Company, p. 195.
Lists reviews of Scoundrel Time and one review each of An Unfinished Woman and Pentimento.

71 VOWLES, RICHARD B. Review of Kjeld Abell by Frederick J. Marker. Modern Drama, 21 (September), 342-43.
Brief comparison of Abell's stature in Denmark to Hellman's in the United States.

72 WILLIAMS, JERRY T., ed. Southern Literature 1968-1975: A Checklist of Scholarship. Boston: G. K. Hall and Company, pp. 152-53.
Cites fourteen items on Hellman.

73 YOUNG, TRACY. "Fonda Jane." Film Comment, 14 (March-April), 54-57.
Includes references to Fonda's Hellman role in Julia.

1979

1 ANDEREGG, MICHAEL A. William Wyler. Boston: Twayne Publishers/G. K. Hall and Company.
Study of Wyler in Twayne's Theatrical Arts Series. Includes discussions of Hellman films which he directed.

1979

2   ANON. "Arts: Who Is 'Paparazzo' Pigozzi's Favorite Subject?
    It's Not Dolly, Faye or Belushi But Himself." People
    Weekly, 12 (9 July), 73-75.
        Includes photo of Hellman taken by Jean Christophe
    Pigozzi, the subject of this piece. "Pigozzi followed an
    American group to Egypt and snapped Lillian Hellman dealing
    a hand of poker while barging down the Nile on a tourist
    boat" (p. 74).

3   ANON. "Julia, Fonda and Dreyfuss top U.K. Film Academy
    Prizes." Variety, 294 (28 March), 6.
        Notes British film citations for Julia.

4   ANON. "Long Wharf to Give Watch on the Rhine." New York
    Times (27 September), p. C18.
        Announces impending production of Watch on the Rhine at
    the Long Wharf Theatre, New Haven, Connecticut.

5   ANON. Review of Three. Library Journal, 104 (15 May), 1142.
    Mixed reaction.

6   ANON. Review of Three. Publishers Weekly, 215 (2 April), 61.
    Highly favorable assessment.

7   BOBKER, LEE R. Elements of Film. Third edition. New York:
    Harcourt Brace Jovanovich, Inc., p. 141.
        Briefly discusses a sequence from Julia, in which
    Hellman and Julia walk through Oxford University, as a
    superb example of film montage. Photo from the film in the
    unpaged section of stills following p. 80.

8   BUCKLEY, TOM. "Is It About Headlines or People?" New York
    Times (27 December), p. C13.
        Discusses the impending Broadway revival of Watch on the
    Rhine, based on the Long Wharf Theatre production in New
    Haven, Connecticut. Discusses the political aspects of the
    play and Hellman's approval of the production, directed by
    Arvin Brown. Brown maintains that the play has not dated
    and that Kurt Müller is one of the "authentic heroes of the
    American drama."

9   CUSHMAN, ROBERT. "Theatre: Disturbed by Goldoni." London
    Observer (15 April).
        Reviews several productions, including the British
    premiere of The Autumn Garden, in Watford. "A shapeless
    and interminable round of domestic fidgets in a residential
    rooming-house on the Gulf of Mexico is given . . . a lacka-
    daisical production almost in excess of its demerits."

10 EMERSON, O. B., and MARION C. MICHAEL, comps. and eds.
Southern Literary Culture: A Bibliography of Masters' and
Doctors' Theses. Revised and enlarged edition. University,
Ala.: University of Alabama Press, 400 pp., passim.
Updates 1955 edition, compiled and edited by Clyde H.
Cantrell and Walton R. Patrick. Lists masters' theses and
dissertations to 1970 which include Hellman. This volume,
though incomplete, is especially useful for locating theses
and dissertations which include but are not limited to
Hellman.

11 EVANS, NANCY. Review of Three. Glamour, 77 (June), 68.
Strongly positive reaction.

12 GUSSOW, MEL. "Drama: Watch on the Rhine Revived." New York
Times (16 October), p. C20.
Reviews Long Wharf Theatre (New Haven, Connecticut) production of Watch on the Rhine. The play in its own time
was politically "prescient." Its message now appears somewhat simplistic, but Watch on the Rhine is more durable
than most antiwar dramas. Sara is "a fictional representa-
tion of the author's friend, Julia."

13 HABERMAN, CLYDE, and ALBIN KREBS. "Notes on People." New
York Times (18 January), p. C14.
Mentions the appearance of Liza Minelli, reading
Hellman's 1952 letter to the Committee on Un-American
Activities, in performances of Eric Bentley's play Are You
Now Or Have You Ever Been.

14 _____. "Notes on People." New York Times (29 January), p.
C12.
Notes Hellman's objections to Eric Bentley's use of her
1952 letter to the House Un-American Activities Committee
in his play, Are You Now Or Have You Ever Been.

15 HANDMAN, WYNN, ed. Modern American Scenes for Student Actors.
New York: Bantam.
Includes sequences from Hellman plays.

16 HERMAN, ROBIN. "Celebrities Sought as Graduation Speakers."
New York Times (27 May), p. 34.
Mentions Hellman as a favored choice of college students
for commencement speaker.

17 HOFFMAN, DANIEL, ed. Harvard Guide to Contemporary Writing.
Cambridge, Mass., and London: The Belknap Press of Harvard
University Press, pp. 345, 391, 398, 399, 437.

1979

In an essay on "Women's Literature," Elizabeth Janeway excludes Hellman's plays (and Mary McCarthy's fiction) from that category because "these writers base their interpretations of women's needs and desires on standards that are essentially masculine even if they are not conventionally so." Janeway applauds Patricia Meyer Spacks, in The Female Imagination (1975.48), for her sensitivity to the shared outlook of Hellman and McCarthy "that sets them somewhat apart from ordinary female experience and legitimizes for them the use of masculine standards." Surprisingly, Janeway never herself specifically examines or even cites Hellman's memoirs.

Gerald Weales, in an essay entitled "Drama," praises The Autumn Garden as "a perceptive treatment of the consequences of inaction," though he faults the play for overstating its points, "a familiar Hellman shortcoming." He considers Hellman's book for Candide the wrongly maligned, properly "spare and sardonic" vehicle for so clever and uncompromising a work. Weales also refers positively to Regina.

18 HOWE, IRVING. "Lillian Hellman and the McCarthy Years," in his Celebrations and Attacks: Thirty Years of Literary and Cultural Commentary. New York: Horizon Press, pp. 206-12.
Reprint of 1976.50.

19 JACOBS, LEWIS, ed. The Documentary Tradition. Second edition. New York: W. W. Norton and Company, passim.
A collection of articles by various writers, containing two brief mentions of Hellman (pp. 141, 165) and more detailed discussions of The Spanish Earth and its director, Joris Ivens. Includes piece on The Spanish Earth by Basil Wright, reprinted from World Film News [London] (December 1937).

20 KAZIN, ALFRED. New York Jew. New York: Vintage Books, pp. 97, 284, 343, 411, 417.
Paperback reprint of 1978.41.

21 KERR, WALTER. Journey to the Center of the Theater. New York: Alfred A. Knopf, pp. 95, 175-79, 218, 222.
"How Does Your Garden Grow?" (pp. 175-79). Reprint, with minor revisions, of Kerr's review of the Long Wharf Theatre's production of The Autumn Garden (see 1976.57). Other passing references to Hellman's plays.

22 LASK, THOMAS. "Publishing: A Director Takes Author's Role." New York Times (30 March), p. C26.

Passing reference to Hellman by Robert Lewis, the director, who is interviewed about his books in progress.

23 LEDERER, KATHERINE. <u>Lillian Hellman</u>. Boston: Twayne
    Publishers/G. K. Hall and Company, 159 pp.
    Study of Hellman in Twayne's United States Authors
    Series. Argues forcibly and intelligently for a reassessment of Hellman's plays, through which "automatic genre
    labeling" might be abandoned. Lederer maintains that in
    her best plays Hellman is at her most ironic and novelistic
    and that <u>Pentimento</u>, in which she "most completely employs
    fictional techniques and a controlling ironic voice," is
    her best memoir. Analyzes the eight original plays, the
    shorter newspaper and magazine pieces (especially as they
    point to the persona developed in the memoirs), and the
    three memoirs. Plot synopses of the plays are commendably
    brief and the individual discussions contain interesting
    observations on Hellman's dramatic devices and themes, both
    often misunderstood by critics. Lederer seems less sure in
    her reading of the memoirs, particularly when she
    skirts the complexities surrounding the <u>Scoundrel Time</u> controversy. She tacitly accepts Hellman's version and lumps
    together politically disparate critics of <u>Scoundrel Time</u>
    as "the political Right." Surprisingly, she omits any
    critical analysis of Hellman's Broadway adaptations which,
    in fact, would have buttressed her arguments about the
    original plays; she mentions the screenplays only in
    passing. Still, Lederer's book provides a knowledgeable
    overview of Hellman's work with generally reliable correctives to the usual critical misreadings of the plays.

24 McCARTHY, KEVIN. "In Her Own Words." <u>People Weekly</u>, 12 (12
    November), 92, 95-96, 99.
    Interview with Mary McCarthy, conducted by her brother,
    Kevin, in which she expresses dislike for Hellman's writing
    and attacks Hellman for allegedly having defamed John Dos
    Passos in an episode at Sarah Lawrence College in 1948.

25 MAGILL, FRANK N. <u>Magill's Bibliography of World Literature</u>.
    Vol. 2. Englewood Cliffs, N.J.: Salem Press, pp. 903-905.
    Lists selected items on Hellman's plays and memoirs.

26 PACE, ERIC. "Herman Shumlin, 80, Dies; Leading Producer-
    Director." <u>New York Times</u> (15 June), p. A18.
    Obituary of Herman Shumlin. Describes his association
    with Hellman as producer and director of her plays. Quotes
    from <u>Pentimento</u>.

1979

27 POIRIER, RICHARD. "Introduction" to Three by Lillian Hellman.
    Boston and Toronto: Little, Brown and Company, pp. vii-xxv.
        Incisive analysis of Hellman's style and method in the
    three memoirs. Poirier describes her sense of place and of
    people as "strongly Southern . . . because she intuitively
    responded to the intense familial and communal relation-
    ships she encountered there." In both her plays and her
    prose, Hellman as a writer "works against her own tenden-
    cies to be assertive, stabilized, moralistic, and knowing.
    Her paragraphs are supported not by dogma but by qualifica-
    tions, by words like 'perhaps,' 'however,' by admissions of
    what she could not remember and of what she is not prepared
    to say." The eccentricity of Arthur Cowan, in Pentimento,
    is "of a Dickensian variety, like that of Ginger Nut and
    Turkey" in Melville's Bartleby the Scrivener. Hellman's
    successful redirection from one literary form to another
    is "unprecedented in our literature."

28 STEELE, MIKE. "Nolte Takes a Second-rate Play, Converts It
    into First-rate Theater." Minneapolis Tribune (25 April).
        Reviews production of Another Part of the Forest,
    directed by Charles Nolte in Minneapolis, Minnesota. He
    has dealt amazingly well with the play, "as though it were
    Chekhov rather than Hellman." We see sides of the charac-
    ters that "I'm not sure even Hellman saw."

29 THOMPSON, HOWARD. "Going Out Guide: Front and Center." New
    York Times (17 April), p. C10.
        Notes the inclusion of a painting of Hellman in a
    display saluting prominent women of the 1970s at the
    Parsons School of Design.

30 VAUGHAN, PETER. "TRP Excellent with Hellman's Forest."
    Minneapolis Star (23 April), pp. 1C, 4C.
        Considers Theatre in the Round production of Another
    Part of the Forest, in Minneapolis, Minnesota, a gripping
    study of recognizable people.

Index